ABERRANT DEVELOPMENT IN INFANCY
Human and Animal Studies

ABERRANT DEVELOPMENT IN INFANCY

Human and Animal Studies

Edited by
NORMAN R. ELLIS

University of Alabama

LAWRENCE ERLBAUM ASSOCIATES, PUBLISHERS

1975   Hillsdale, New Jersey

DISTRIBUTED BY THE HALSTED PRESS DIVISION OF

JOHN WILEY & SONS
New York Toronto London Sydney

Lawrence Erlbaum Associates, Inc., Publishers
62 Maria Drive
Hillsdale, New Jersey 07642

Distributed solely by Halsted Press Division
John Wiley & Sons, Inc., New York

Library of Congress Cataloging in Publication Data

Gatlinburg (Tennessee) Conference on Research and Theory
    In Mental Retardation, 7th, 1974.
    Aberrant development in infancy.

    1. Child development deviations—Congresses.
I. Ellis, Norman R. II. Title.
RJ135.G37 1974   618.9'28'5884   75-9657
0 470-23859-3

Printed in the United States of America

CONTENTS

PREFACE

On their face, these papers deal with animals and human infants. The titles reflect a mosaic of issues and problems ranging from the significance of sucking responses in the newborn, the development of memory, effects of rearing conditions in monkeys, and brain damage in animals, to processes underlying abnormal development of language. While the investigators may appear to be concerned with diverse issues, actually there is a common theme. One question is posed: How and why does normal development fail to occur in some human infants? The papers show that there are many causes of aberrations: physical or psychological trauma, disease, inheritance, and drugs. Although one may be primary, "multiple causation" would still appear to be a sound principle in developmental pathology. It is also clear that pathogenic agents may have different effects at different ages in the developing infant. These effects may be profound, resulting in vegetative organisms, some nonviable and others living for 50 years or more. Still other infants may show mild disorders that go undetected until school age or later.

Aberrant development is an ubiquitous problem of immense dimensions. Some six to seven million people in the United States are labeled mentally retarded; those referred to as brain damaged or minimal brain dysfunction, learning disordered, psychotic or autistic, epileptic, cerebral palsied, and those with sensory and motor disorders add additional millions. Obviously, prevention is the most desirable goal, and many of the papers presented describe research committed to this end. At the same time society has a firm resolve to care for, treat, educate, and habilitate the vast numbers among us with these handicaps. Some of the papers address these issues. Still other investigators are concerned with detecting disorders at an early age and in measures that will reinstate normal development. There is much creativity and ingenuity reflected in these papers.

And in the conference from which they derived there was an intensive interchange of ideas as well as an expressed appreciation for the work of others. This is reflected most clearly in the several "overviews" presented toward the end of the book, which were prepared by senior investigators. Some of the investigators are young and just beginning their careers; others are well-established scientists with international reputations. All are dedicated and creative. One could not read these papers without feeling some optimism. New ways of preventing disorders will be found. Effective remediation methods will be devised.

These papers were prepared for and presented at the seventh annual "Gatlinburg (Tennessee) Conference on Research and Theory in Mental Retardation." This conference began, rather spontaneously, in 1968. It was prompted mainly by the need for a scientific forum on behavioral aspects of mental retardation. The large national organization meetings and conventions seemed concerned with professional and other nonscientific issues. Those of us initiating the meeting, and those invited, were interested in a conference that concerned itself exclusively with the main subject matter of our field. All those attending were themselves active researchers in mental retardation and/or developmental disorders. The meeting was well received and has continued on an annual basis. The success of the conference is due to a concerted effort on the part of a number of investigators — A. A. Baumeister, David Zeaman, Richard E. Butcher, Gershon Berkson, M. Ray Denny, Keith G. Scott, Rathe Karrer, George Kella, Douglas Detterman, Earl Butterfield, John Belmont, Robert Sprague, Herman Spitz, Frank Berry, and a host of others.

We are especially appreciative of the work of Theodore D. Tjossem in planning the seventh annual conference from which these papers derived. Finally we acknowledge the support of the National Institute of Child Health and Human Development, National Institutes of Health. All of the conference concerned with aberrant development in infancy was financially supported by this agency.

NORMAN R. ELLIS
University of Alabama

1

THE MYTH OF RECOVERY
FROM EARLY BRAIN DAMAGE [1,2]

Robert L. Isaacson
University of Florida

A myth is a story, not necessarily false, whose origins have been forgotten in history. A current myth is that brain damage occurring early in life is less debilitating than comparable damage later in life. A related myth is that when damage occurs early in life other portions of the brain are able to "take over" the functions of the damaged area and, as a result, the behavioral consequences of the damage will be minimal or perhaps even nonexistent.

As a generalization, such a view must be incorrect. If the developing brain were completely "plastic" (a most unfortunate word) and any part capable of doing the work of any other, how are we to explain the tragedies of mental retardation resulting from biological problems occurring before birth?

In fact, determination rather than plasticity seems to be the governing rule of natural development. Undifferentiated nerve cells follow tortuous pathways to predetermined destinations. Budding neural processes seek synaptic destinations far from their cells of origination, forsaking invitations extended by other cells they pass. The neural transmitters to be used by a cell are produced in it essentially from its moment of formation. Yet, in face of extensive experimental evidence for early specification of a cell and its connections, there remains the view that the brain, or parts of it, are flexible, changeable in regard to behavior.

The effects of brain damage can only be understood in the context of the many changes that follow any trauma or insult to the brain. Understanding these changes, and the differences found in them when the damage occurs at various ages, may provide a different perspective from which the behavioral effects of brain damage may be viewed.

[1]The studies performed in my laboratory on the effects of early brain damage have been supported by grant NSF-GB-17354.

[2]I would like to thank the following people for their helpful comments on a preliminary version of this manuscript: Dr. P. S. Goldman, Ms. Linda Lanier, Dr. F. A. King, Dr. S. J. Jourard, Dr. Karl H. Pribram, Dr. Carol Van Hartesveldt, and Dr. D. G. Stein. In addition, I would like to thank Dr. Kenneth Heilman for information about language disorders in adults and children.

PHYSIOLOGICAL AND ANATOMICAL CONSEQUENCES OF BRAIN DAMAGE

Any insult to the brain causes a variety of reactions that go far beyond the actual destruction of a collection of nerve cells. The nature of these reactions depends upon the way in which the lesion is made, the age of the animals at the time of the insult, and other constitutional and experimental factors. The reactions include:

1. The action destruction or death of tissue at location of the insult;
2. The disruption of neural activity in nearby regions due to the physical or metabolic distortions produced by the lesions;
3. Astrocytic reactions at the border of the lesion (and sometimes well beyond);
4. Phagocytosis and invasion by microglia;
5. Proliferation of blood vessels in a wide area around the lesion;
6. The development of ''irritative'' reactions at edge of the lesion;
7. Edema;
8. The disruption of activity in nearby tissues due to the pressure exerted by enclosed areas of bleeding (hematomas);
9. Changes in the cerebrospinal fluid, including pressure, composition, and pollution with blood or infectious agents;
10. The creation of neural areas that exhibit a relatively permanent form of denervation supersensitivity due to decreased input from the brain region actually destroyed;
11. The creation of neural areas that exhibit a transient form of denervation supersensitivity due to decreased input from brain regions whose own activity has been temporarily suppressed due to pressure, blood vessel interruption, or other factors;
12. Retrograde changes in areas in which cells are located whose axons were destroyed by the lesion. Reactions include gliosis, phagocytosis, and possibly, in rare instances, a transsynaptic degneration of cells.
13. Anterograde changes produced upon neurons normally reached by the damaged cells which may be altered by the loss of neural input or the loss of other trophic effects. These anterograde changes may be transsynaptic;
14. The proliferation of newly formed axons (sprouts) into cellular regions that had been supplied by fibers from the damaged regions;
15. The formation of aberrant fiber tracts (if the damage occurred in infancy);
16. Widespread changes that affect the size and composition of the brain. These are found most often after early brain damage.

Many of the effects of brain damage are of transient nature. As new blood supplies become established, as hematomas are absorbed, as edema lessens, areas that had been temporarily reduced in their activities may return to near-normal status. As a result, the functions in which these regions participate will be restored and a corresponding behavioral recovery may be observed. This restoration of activity in temporarily suppressed regions and systems is a natural consequence of changes occurring after brain damage. Therefore, progressive changes in behavior do not imply that other tissues have come to take over the usual functions of the damaged area.

The restoration of certain behavioral capacities that were lost immediately after damage is a natural and anticipated occurrence. The number and degree of severity of original symptoms should decrease over time. The reduction of the damage-produced effects should continue until the transient changes have returned to their before-lesion status or stabilized in a new mode of activity. Secondary changes occurring after brain damage may lead either to temporary or permanent functional changes in the brain. Sometimes these progressive changes have been taken to mean that an individual can recover from brain damage.

Progressive changes in behavior can arise from the reduction of hypertrophied astrocytes, the spinning off of astrocytic fibers and the encapsulation of the wounded area, the reduction of edema, the formation of new blood vessels, the restoration of normal cerebrospinal fluid pressure and composition, and the reduction of denervation supersensitivity. All of these physical changes may produce alterations in the mental and behavioral activities of the individual.

PERMANENT CHANGES OF A SECONDARY NATURE

Some of the changes produced by brain damage result in permanent alterations in brain structure. These include some portions of the astrocytic response, proliferation of blood vessels, the development of irritative reactions, death of nerve cells in other regions due to losses in blood supplies or pressure, supersensitivity, retrograde or anterograde neural effects, sprouting, the formation of new fiber tracts, and more general changes in brain composition. Some of these secondary permanent alterations, of special concern to my own research, will be considered in some detail.

Sprouting. This term refers to the proliferation of axon collaterals into areas that have had their normal synaptic input decreased to some degree (Goodman & Horel, 1966; Liu & Chambers, 1958; McCough, Austin, Liu, & Liu, 1958; Raisman, 1969). Newly formed axon collaterals of intact neurons may make physiologically effective contacts on neurons whose synaptic input has been reduced by damage to other areas (Lynch, Deadwyler, & Cotman, 1973). However, despite the fact that physiologically effective contacts are made by the sprouting collaterals, it is not known whether the effects on behavior that are produced by these contacts are of benefit or harm to the individual.

The results of sprouting could lead to quite an abnormal set of conditions in a particular system. For example, if the cells of a target region normally receive one-third of their input from each of three different sources (call them A, B, C) then immediately after the lesion of region A there will be a 33% reduction of total input.

In addition, the cells in the target area will be entirely controlled by the remaining sources, that is, B and C. At this time, each source would contribute equally (one-half) to the activation of target area cells. Now suppose axons from source B begin to sprout (while those from C do not) and occupy all of the former synaptic sites of source A. This would mean that source B has its original 33% of the synapses and, in addition, has captured the 33% originally belonging to source A. B will then control 66% of the synapses in the target area.

Therefore, after the lesion there will be a time in which B and C exert equally effective regulatory influences on the target area, but, at some future time, B will come to exert a preponderant influence due to sprouting. At this time the neural systems of the lesioned animal will be abnormal not only because of the loss of input from source A but becuase of the greater than normal influence of source B on the target region. This means that as many of the transient effects of the brain damage are decreasing, new effects of a permanent nature are developing.

Several empirical questions need to be asked about the effects of sprouting of nerve fibers in response to brain damage. The simplest and most important pertains to whether it is "good" or "bad" for the brain damaged animal. Does the occurrence of sprouting help to reduce the functional consequences of the brain damage or does it aggravate them? It could help by adding new functional synapses to replace those that have been lost. Perhaps these additional synapses could help reduce denervation supersensitivity or provide some general trophic influences. It could hinder the individual by the creation of abnormal regulatory influences upon the remaining systems. It is possible, of course, that sprouting would be useful after certain kinds of damage but harmful after others. At the present time there is insufficient evidence available to resolve these matters. An answer to this question could be of significance to brain damaged people of all ages, because it is not a phenomenon restricted to young animals.

In a dissertation recently completed in my laboratory, Baisden (1973) undertook an initial attempt to determine whether sprouting is beneficial or not. Just before surgical destruction of the hippocampus, he injected a drug into the septal area of the brain which destroys catecholaminergic terminals. This was an attempt to inhibit the sprouting of adrenergic fibers in that area, which normally occurs after destruction of the fibers to the septal area from the hippocampus (Moore, Björklund, & Stenevi, 1971). He then measured the behavior of animals treated in this fashion against animals with hippocampal damage where no effort was made to prevent sprouting in the septal area. His results suggest that the injection of the drug that prevents sprouting into the septal area reduced some, but not all, of the usual consequences of hippocampal destruction. One of the great unresolved questions concerning sprouting pertains to whether sprouting occurs in the same way or to the same degree after damage in infants as it does in adults. Differences in sprouting after damage at different ages could help explain differences in behavior resulting from the lesions.

Abnormal Major Structural Changes
after Lesions Early in Life

Major structural changes that occur after brain damage seem to be confined to animals damaged at early ages. This includes the formation of abnormal, sometimes peculiar, fiber connections of the brain. Some of these malformations of neocortical and limbic fiber pathways were shown in Isaacson, Nonneman, and Schmaltz (1968) and Isaacson and Nonneman (1972). In some cases fiber pathways of limbic system origin come to be diverted into neocortical white matter. These aberrant tracts suggest that it may be possible for nerve fibers in the infant brain to accept unusual sites of termination, although the synaptic contacts made by these aberrant tracts are not known. This greater flexibility in the infant brain is another source of abnormal connections, in addition to the phenomenon of sprouting. It differs from sprouting in that its effects are more massive (e.g., large fiber systems can be diverted) and the locations of the new associations may be far removed from those at which normal connections of the system are established (e.g., neocortical white matter versus limbic regions as places of termination of fibers in the fimbria). Other examples of aberrant tract formation (Hicks & D'Amato, 1970; Lund, Cunningham, & Lund, 1974) will be discussed below.

It may be that some of the aberrant fiber tracts that develop as a consequence of early damage are useful to the animal but others are not. There are suggestions that abnormal motor and sensory tracts may be of value, but the matter is not proven. On the other hand, it is hard to imagine how the unusual fiber tracts of limbic system origin could improve the behavioral capabilities of the individual.

Widespread changes of the brain. Another major change in structure, which is only found after brain damage in the neonatal period, is a generalized reduction in brain size. This occurs even with relatively small amounts of brain damage restricted to the neocortex. We first noticed this general hemispheric reduction in cats receiving neocortical or hippocampal damage as neonates (Isaacson *et al.*, 1968), and Nonneman (1970) made careful measurement of it in rabbits in his thesis.

The general reduction in tissue extends throughout the entire neocortex above the rhinal fissure and there are related reductions in neural tissue in the thalamus and brain stem. The reduction amounts to about 20% of the volume of the neocortex. In the rabbit it only occurs if the surgical damage is produced in the first ten days of life. After that only a small volume reduction occurs near the site of damage.

As far as we can tell, the reduction of the hemisphere is restricted to the side of the damage. The reductions of thalamus and brain stem also are only found ipsilateral to the lesion.

Since the general reduction of brain size is found only after infant brain damage, and since it is often accompanied by the formation of abnormal tracts and abnormal configurations of neural cells, it seems that from a structural point of view early brain damage must be considered to be *more* disatrous than later brain damage. In the adult, or even the juvenile, results of surgical damage are more localized, aberrant tracts are not formed, and the overall brain volume is not reduced. The permanent functional consequences of brain damage and the residual behavioral alterations must be considered to be the result of all of the permanent changes produced by the lesion. These include the direct effects produced by the destruction of cells at the site of damage *and also* all of the permanent secondary changes. The final set of permanent changes can only be approximated by allowing long recovery periods, although for some lesion-induced changes, an infinite amount of time might be needed. This means that it is almost impossible to determine the isolated effect of destruction of one region of the brain; behavior after brain damage represents both the direct damage and indirect changes in many areas.

Another example of the more pervasive effects of brain damage occurring early, rather than later, in life is the observation that unilateral destruction of the hippocampus in the infant produces behavioral effects only found after bilateral destruction of the structure in the adult (Douglas, 1975).

ESTIMATING THE EFFECTS OF BRAIN DAMAGE

The importance of an accurate and consistent estimate of the deficits produced by adult brain damage is easily demonstrated. Without such an estimate it is impossible to determine if any "recovery" or "sparing" occurs. If the notion of "recovery of function" after early brain damage has any meaning beyond those behavioral alterations related to transient secondary changes, it must refer to the permanent consequences of a specific type of lesion. It must also be considered independently of the rate at which postoperative changes occur. If there are procedures or treatments that produce "recovery," such procedures or treatments must be evaluated against the most consistent, long-term consequences of the lesion, and not against transitory effects.

The question of "recovery" must be posed so that the answer is made in terms of behavioral capacities compared with the expected long-term results of a specific form of brain damage. At this time, therefore, it may be useful to review briefly some of the experimental literature often considered to demonstrate "recovery."

RECOVERY AFTER DAMAGE MADE EARLY IN LIFE

About 35 years ago Kennard (1936, 1938) reported that motor cortical lesions made early in life produced less impairment of motor ability and deportment than lesions sustained at seven months of age. This report preceded a flurry of other studies that, in general, tended to support the view that a lesion made very early in an animal's life was less debilitating than comparable damage later on. Frankly, I am still somewhat unsettled by the Kennard studies. There is no doubt that animals who were brain damaged at the later developmental times were severely affected, and those damaged early were less affected. The problem is that the lesions made later in life produced a far greater degree of debilitation than would be expected after destruction of the motor neocortical regions (see Bucy, 1966; Lawrence & Kuypers, 1968).[3] It is difficult for me to believe that the extreme debilitation produced by the neocortical damage at seven months of age adequately represents the usual long-term consequences of the neocortical destruction involved. If it doesn't, the "beneficial" effects of the early lesions only represent the usual consequences of neocortical destruction made in the mature animal. Even with the "recovery" found by Kennard, there were certain abnormalities from which the animal did not recover after early damage. These included deviations of the head and eyes, as well as rigidity and spasticity that developed slowly after the lesions (Kennard, 1940, 1942).

The effect of disruption of the medullary pyramids in infancy produces the same impairment in finger dexterity as found after similar damage in adult monkeys (Lawrence & Hopkins, 1970). Using a more extensive procedure, Hicks and D'Amato (1970) studied the effect of hemispherectomy in infant and mature animals. They found relatively few observable effects of this radical procedure in either the infant- or adult-lesioned animals. One of the few motor effects found after this great amount of damage was a loss of the tactile placing response on the side opposite to the lesion. This loss occurred, regardless of the age of the animal at the time of damage. In the infant-lesion subjects the placing response was not lost immediately, however. It disappeared about the 17th postnatal day. All lesioned animals could perform visual discriminations and to gauge jumping distances effectively. About the only change that occurred after adult lesions but did not follow lesions in infancy, was a difference in the stride of the animals. A correlated observation was that of a structural difference in the brains of the animals lesioned at the two ages. In the infant-lesioned animals there was an uncrossed cortico-spinal system, usually not found in the rat.

Studying the visual system, Lund et al. (1974) found a similar result. Removal of an eye in newborn rats produced an increased number of fibers from the remaining eye to ipsilateral subcortical structures, in particular the lateral geniculate nucleus and the superior colliculus. The development of these abnormal fibers only occurs in the new-born and is not found in animals with eyes removed at 10 days of age or older.

These studies show that the possibility of neuronal growth in the infant is remarkable. They suggest, but do not establish, that the growth of "aberrant" tracts are the basis of some behavioral benefits produced by lesions early in life. More important, however, is the demonstration that substantial residual motor and sensory capacities exist following hemispherectomy both after early and late lesions. This conclusion is supported by Glassman (1973). He investigated the effects of early (2–14 days) and late (5 month) destruction of sensorimotor cortex in

[3]In a personal communication, Dr. Karl Pribram indicated in reviewing the histological material from these studies that the animals receiving damage as juveniles had more extensive lesions, involving deeper fiber systems and the more medial structures.

cats. The effects of these lesions on placing and hopping reactions were independent of the animals' ages at the time of damage.

Until recently, it was thought that there was some sparing of visual functions in cats after early lesions of the visual system which did not occur after adult lesions (e.g., Doty, 1961). However, according to a more recent report Doty (1971) now believes that his original results were due to the fact that certain portions of visual neocortical areas 18 and 19 were not destroyed in animals with neonatal lesions. He believes these areas can subserve visual pattern discriminations in the absence of area 17 even with substantial degeneration of the dorsal lateral geniculate nucleus. Relative to "recovery," Doty (1971) now states, ". . . comparison of the effects of removing striate cortex in adult versus neonatal cats does not now encourage the belief that any extensive neural reorganization accrues to the advantage of the neonatal subject [p. 353].

Recently, Murphy and Stewart (1974) failed to find any beneficial effects of making striate lesions in infancy (relative to adulthood) on learning a brightness or a pattern discrimination task. This result stands in contrast to the results reported by Stewart and Riesen (1972). These latter authors reported that infant-lesioned animals were able to perform well upon a visual cliff, in visual placing, and in avoiding obstacles relative to adult-lesioned control animals. It is perhaps most important to note that Stewart and Riesen believe that their adult-lesioned animals could have done these tasks, too. The difference between the infant- and adult-lesioned animals could be only that the former require no training to do so. This also suggests that the adult-lesioned animals might have been able to perform the task if longer recovery times were allowed, even without specific training.

In a series of experiments Cornwell and his associates (Cornwell, Cornwell, & Overman, 1972; Cornwell & Overman, 1972; Cornwell, Overman, & Nonneman, 1972; Cornwell, Overman, & Ross, 1972; Cornwell, Ross, Overman, & Levitsky, 1972) have shown that neonatal damage to the visual neocortex always produced some deficit in visual discrimination performance. Being raised in an enriched environment postoperatively did not improve the performance of the subjects. It is of special interest that "visual cliff performance" was impaired by the early lesions in some, but not all, animals. The lesioned animals either at chance levels or at levels fully comparable with those of intact animals. This "all-or-none" effect of brain damage will be discussed below.

In a recent study with monkeys, no favorable effect was observed to follow infant damage to the caudate nucleus relative to lesions made in juvenile monkeys when tested on a delayed response task (Goldman & Rosvold, 1972). Damage to the dorsomedial nuclei of the thalamus in infant monkeys produces a clear deficit on the delayed alternation problem that is at least as great as found after similar damage in adulthood (Goldman, 1974). Kurtz, Rozin, and Teitelbaum (1972) reported that lesions of the ventromedial nuclei of the hypothalamus led to the expected hyperphagia, even though the onset of the exaggerated eating did not occur until several weeks after the lesion was made. This delayed onset of symptoms is reminiscent of the delayed loss of the placing response found by Hicks and D'Amato (1970) and the delayed onset of other neurological signs after early brain damage. Kurtz *et al.* believe that the delayed onset of hyperphagia is due to transient inactivation of the ventromedial nucleus by growth hormones in the young rat. Lesions in the dorsomedial nucleus of the hypothalamus in the weanling does not protect these animals from the usual hypophagia and hypodipsia that normally follow the lesions in adult animals (Bernardis, 1972).

Behavioral effects resulting from damage to the septal area fail to be reduced by the earliness of the lesion. For example, septal lesions made at seven days of age produced enhanced avoidance responding, fixed-ratio responding, and social behavior, just as adult lesions did (Johnson, 1972). A potential indicator of a benefit derived from the earliness of the lesion, i.e., a greater resistance to extinction after avoidance conditioning, turned out to be related to handling effects (Johnson, Poplawsky, Bielauskas, & Liebert, 1972). Johnson (personal communication) has found a similar failure of recovery after early septal lesions on a DRL operant task.

My own work with lesions of the limbic system made in cats of different ages has revealed "recovery" to be task-dependent, and I will discuss these studies separately in a subsequent section. In general, however, many animals with lesions made in infancy are just as impaired as animals receiving similar damage in adulthood.

The vast majority of reports of sparing or recovery of functions after early lesions have come from studies of the effect of neocortical destruction. The conclusions of Tsang (1934, 1936, 1937a, b) to the effect that the earliness of the lesions protects the animals in brightness discrimination tasks and maze learning have been accepted, rather uncritically, for many years. However, it now seems that the production of posterior neocortical lesions early in the life of the rat only produces decreased deficits, relative to lesions made in adulthood, on the acquisition of an 8-cul maze but not upon pattern discrimination learning in a Thompson–Bryant box (Thompson, 1970). Bland and Cooper (1969) were unable to find any sparing of function in a pattern discrimination task after posterior neocortical lesions made on the first day after birth.

Most of the research on the effects of neocortical destruction in primates has involved the prefrontal lobes, and until recently the story has been quite complicated and confusing. The primary observation, now well-established in the literature, is that destruction of the dorsolateral prefrontal cortex early in life fails to produce the classic delayed response deficit when the animals are tested at about one year of age (Akert, Orth, Harlow, & Schiltz, 1960; Goldman, 1971; Harlow, Blomquist, Thompson, Schiltz, & Harlow, 1968; Kling & Tucker, 1967; Tucker & Kling, 1969).

However, Goldman (1971) has shown that an interpretation based on a permanent sparing of function related to this task can not be correct. Monkeys given either dorsolateral or orbitofrontal lesions between postnatal days 48 and 85 were tested at 12–18 months of age on problems known to be sensitive to prefrontal lesions made in adulthood. They were retested again at 24 months of age. At the first testing, the animals with lateral prefrontal lesions were less impaired than animals receiving lesions in young adulthood, while the animals with orbitofrontal lesions were just as deficient as those with lesions made later in life. When tested again at 24 months of age, the situation was reversed: The animals with dorsolateral lesions were impaired; those with orbitofrontal lesions were not.

This line of research was extended by Goldman (1974) who now reports additional evidence that animals with dorsolateral prefrontal damage develop a severe impairment in the delayed response problem. With advancing age, a progressive inability to perform the delayed response problem becomes manifest.

In contrast, the animals with orbitofrontal lesions early in life seem to be impaired when tested about a year after surgery but not at later periods. However, if the testing of animals with orbitofrontal damage is done shortly after surgery, there is no difference between them and age-matched controls (Goldman, 1974). Even though the animals were tested on only one problem (object discrimination reversal), this would indicate that the effects of orbitofrontal and lateral frontal lesions may be qualitatively similar: immediately after damage there is a period in which no behavioral deficits are found but the animals come to "grow into" behavioral deficits over time. The difference between the effects of orbitofrontal and dorsolateral lesions lies in the time required for the behavioral disruptions to appear.

In 1973, Miller, Goldman, and Rosvold reported data from animals receiving orbitofrontal lesions at one week, four weeks, and eight weeks of life. (Four of seven animals in the eight-week group were previously reported by Goldman in 1971.) The animals were tested on a delayed response problem, an object reversal problem, and a delayed alternation problem at one year of life and retested again on the delayed alternation problem at two years of life. At age one year, the lesion groups were impaired on all problems regardless of the age at which the lesion was made. However, by two years of age the orbitofrontal animals were much improved on the delayed alternation task. Miller and co-workers conclude that this improvement in delayed alternation performance was due to the functional maturation of "another cortical region," probably the lateral prefrontal area, between the first and second years of life.

Recently, the effects of dorsolateral prefrontal lesions in animals that had "recovered" from orbitofrontal lesions were evaluated. The effects obtained were similar to the effects produced by dorsolateral lesion in adulthood: a permanent disruption of the capacity to perform the delayed alternation problem (Goldman, 1974). This suggests that the functional capacity to perform the delayed alternation task develops in systems related to the dorsolateral prefrontal cortex along a time-based maturational sequence regardless of whether or not the orbitofrontal damage is intact. This is also consistent with the view that the integrity of the orbitofrontal cortex is not essential to performance on this task. The deficits in delayed alternation tasks found after orbitofrontal lesions in adult monkeys may be the consequence of an interference with dorsolateral functions, perhaps by producing abnormal degeneration or activity in regions, like certain portions of the caudate nucleus, upon which dorsolateral and orbitofrontal influences converge. Damage to the orbitofrontal cortex early in life may not produce such interference because of differences in transneuronal degeneration in young animals (Goldman, 1974).

This approach to the deficits produced by damage to the prefrontal region is exciting and most valuable. It offers an explanation of the behavioral effects that is not based upon the ''taking over'' of the functions of one area by another, but rather upon principles of neural maturation and neural degeneration.

It would be a mistake, however, to think that any anatomical region of the brain is involved in only one system regulating behavioral activity or capacity. It is likely that all regions participate in many behavior-oriented systems which can mature at different rates. Support for differences in the times of development of behavior systems comes from the work of Thompson, Harlow, Blomquist, and Schiltz (1971) who found that lesions of the dorsolateral prefrontal neocortex of 5-month-old monkeys, (a time when such lesions fail to influence delayed response performance), produce just as great an effect on the learning of an oddity problem as lesions made later in life. This would indicate that ''recovery'' found after early prefrontal lesions is not general but dependent upon the specific behaviors being evaluated.

As I interpret the studies that have attempted to find a sparing of behavioral deficits after lesions early in life, there are few positive results. Most often, the behavioral deficits after early damage may be at least as great as those found after similar damage in adulthood. The studies often considered to show ''sparing of function'' seem to be explained on the basis of differences in the brain damage or on the basis of having tested the animals at times during development when the damaged areas were not essential to performance. In light of these considerations, it would appear that there is less plasticity in the brain than previously supposed. Therefore, it will be useful to examine the data from another experimental paradigm often thought to demonstrate the plasticity of the brain: the production of damage by a series of small lesions.

SEQUENTIAL LESIONS

Another frequently used technique to show ''recovery of function'' is that of making seriatim lesions of a brain region. The behavioral effects of destruction of bilaterally represented structures, such as the visual cortex, can be evaluated in animals in which the cortex of both hemispheres is destroyed in one operation (one-stage) or in two operations separated by some interval of time (two-stage). It is also possible to destroy a target more slowly, that is, in three, four, or more operations. In general, the view held by some researchers is that this sequential destruction of a target area leads to less debilitation than an all-at-once lesion because the brain has a chance to ''reorganize'' its functions between each lesion stage. By the time the last shred of the target structure is gone, reorganization has proceeded so completely in other areas that only a small behavioral deficit, if any, remains.

An extensive review of many of the experimental reports concerning the effects of serial brain damage has recently been published (Finger, Walbran, & Stein, 1973). This review described the scientific situation in regard to serial lesions, although I believe that it fails to give sufficient attention to some procedural issues that may make the beneficial effects of serial damage less certain. Many of the benefits of the serial destruction procedure relate to reducing the stress of surgery, including allowing animals to live. Sometimes the serial lesions are so large or placed in such biologically crucial areas that death results if a one-stage procedure is used. The use of a multiple-stage procedure reduces the secondary reactions to brain damage (mentioned earlier in this paper) to levels that can be tolerated. Probably the reduction of these secondary reactions also accounts for faster "recovery" after multiple-stage procedures. For example. Tanaka (1974) found that monkeys receiving a one-stage lesion of the prefrontal regions were more impaired on an escape from shock response than were two-stage operates. However, the one-stage animals did recover after surgery; it just took longer (12 weeks). In this case and in others (e.g., Greene, Stauff, & Walters, 1972) serial destruction hastens recovery but does not alter the final behavioral outcome.

Because recovery is slower after single-stage procedures than after multiple-stage procedures, the amount of time allowed the animals for recovery is a crucial variable in such experiments. Dawson, Conrad, and Lynch (1973) have pointed this out most effectively in regard to the beneficial effects produced by serial destruction of the hippocampus previously reported by Stein, Rosen, Graziadei, Mishkin, and Brink (1969).

A fundamental issue arising from the serial-lesion experiments is whether or not this procedure results in any substantial difference in the long-term consequences of the brain damage, and to determine this, the effects of the serial procedure must be evaluated against the anticipated or usual permanent effects of single-stage damage. As noted by Finger *et al.* (1973) "Nevertheless, the results of a rapidly growing number of behavioral studies are demonstrating that lesions in supposedly 'critical' areas may be less deleterious to the functioning of the organism than previously has been believed [p. 15]."

This quotation reflects the fact that damage to the visual neocortical area does not destroy all vision and that damage to the auditory neocortex does not eliminate audition. With modern methods of testing, many more residual capacities are being found after single-stage lesions than had been discovered 10 or 20 years ago. This highlights the point made earlier that recovery can only be assessed against absolutely definite long-term consequences of restricted brain damage in the adult. Many of the earlier studies evaluated the benefits of serial destruction against baseline performances that were not accurate estimates of residual capacities after single-stage damage.

RECOVERY OF LANGUAGE CAPABILITIES

The most frequently cited indicator of greater recovery after early versus late brain damage is that of speech. Two types of evidence are involved. The first is that incidence of "full recovery" from aphasic disturbances after brain damage is much greater in children than in adults. The second is that, with age, there is an increasing localization of language functions to the left side of the brain.

Brain damage can produce aphasic symptoms in both children and adults. In about one-half of the adult patients, recovery takes place with few residual disturbances. The processes underlying recovery take place rather quickly and, if it is to occur, it is often fairly complete about five months after the damage. Children with brain damage almost always recover speech abilities and there are few, if any, long-lasting, residual symptoms. However, these data do not show a greater tendency for recovery of a behavioral capacity after early brain damage than after brain damage in maturity, since there is no evidence that the damage leading to aphasia in childhood and adult are similar. In adults, aphasia most frequently results from occlusion of cerebral blood vessels (stroke), whereas childhood aphasia most frequently follows traumatic damage or seizures. The anatomical areas involved and the secondary processes initiated by these two types of events are probably quite different. In early childhood, damage to either side of the brain can produce temporary disturbances in language. Over the course of development, the situation changes so that damage to the left side of the brain becomes more likely to produce aphasic symptoms and damage to the right side less likely to do so. Where damage to the left side of the brain has occurred early in life, mechanisms of the right side seem to be able to subserve language functions. These observations are compatible with the view that both sides of the brain can subserve language functions early in life. Indeed, in some few people language does not seem to be localized within the brain's left side but remains bilaterally represented. In most people, however, language becomes localized over time to mechanisms of the left hemisphere and this may be due to a supressive effect of activity in the left hemisphere upon the right (Sperry, 1967). According to this view, the activity in fibers crossing through the corpus callosum prevents the symmetrical representation of memories and of language functions in the two hemispheres. This asymmetric storage of information seems to be a characteristic found uniquely in higher primates and man.

The supression of language activities in the right hemisphere seems to be a gradual process. The frequency of language-related problems after damage to the left hemisphere slowly increases with age. Therefore, if damage occurs to the left hemisphere in childhood before the intercortical supression is complete, the right hemisphere can exert its own capability to subserve language. Since it has the constitutional capacity to subserve language, this result would not be surprising or require an area of the brain to change its predetermined functional characteristics. Furthermore, the differences in symptoms of adult and childhood aphasia are marked. In children, the most pronounced language disturbance resulting from trauma or fever is an inability to speak. In adults, language disturbances are numerous and varied, but most often they are much more than an inability to speak.

It must also be emphasized that when childhood brain damage is severe enough to produce observable intellectual or developmental impairments, language is almost always affected. The point that severe biological disturbances early in life are always associated with language and vocabulary deficiencies in later life led Hebb (1942) to conclude that brain damage in early life was more generally debilitating than brain damage in adulthood.

TASK-DEPENDENT RECOVERY

In my own work of the past ten years, some animals seemed to show recovery after early brain damage (Isaacson & Nonneman, 1972; Nonneman & Isaacson, 1973). In essence we found that the earliness of the lesion reduced the number of animals evidencing impaired performance on some tasks.

The notion of task-dependent effects of early brain damage is not new. Indeed, Teuber and Rudel (1962) pointed out that early brain damage can produce less disabling, equally disablilng, or more disabling effects than later brain damage on different tests of mental function. This could be called a test-dependency of early brain damage in humans, comparable to the conclusion that Nonneman and I have reached at the animal level.

When evaluating all of the studies that have been considered to demonstrate "sparing" or "recovery" of behavioral abilities after early brain damage or after serial lesions, it would seem that the lessened debility always is found in relation to some particular aspect of behavior, i.e., the behavioral changes are task specific. Goldstein (1940) has noted a similar phenomenon in brain damaged patients, namely, that they often failed with some types of tasks under certain conditions but, under other conditions, they behaved in a normal fashion. Furthermore, not all patients with "similar" brain damage were affected the same way. The question is how to explain these results. To do so requires a change in our view of the effects of brain damage to one that can account for the variability of expression of brain damage among individuals.

BRAIN DAMAGE CONSIDERED AS A GENOTYPIC CHANGE

The consequences of brain damage produced by experimental surgery are not always the same even when comparable damage is inflicted upon similar animals, by means of identical techniques, in the same laboratory. Often the behavioral differences among lesioned animals cannot be explained on the basis of accidental differences in the size or location of the lesions (e.g., Thomas, 1971). The explanation of these different responses to brain damage has to be based upon presurgical differences in the animals. In a gross way this has been demonstrated by Nash (1971) who found that differences in the effects of neonatal irradiation on postnatal growth of a number of organs were dependent upon the genotype of the mouse. This study also demonstrated a greater overall effect of irradiation in neonatal animals relative to mice irradiated later in life.

There can be no doubt that all of the developmental experiences of the animal, as well as its genetic endowment, have interacted with each other to produce the animals as it is at any moment in time. They have acted together to determine the constitution of the individual. From a conceptual view, therefore, brain damage can be interpreted as producing a change in this constitution and, in some ways, this change is no different from ones that could have been produced by a different gene structure. Brain damage alters the structure and constitution of the animal at the time of surgery to produce effects that can find expression in different ways; both genes and lesions act upon the macro- and microstructure of the individual. It is upon these structures that behavior is ultimately based.

But genes do not govern the development of any structure in any absolute sense. Their effects are always modified by the micro- and macroenvironment from the time that the egg and sperm are united. In this sense the genes issue invitations for structural development, not commands.

However, even though the interaction of heredity and environment determines structure, the behavior of the individual is not specificable unless the factors of the immediate environment are taken into consideration. For convenience it is easier to lapse into a more psychologically oriented language at this point, but it should be remembered that this is for convenience only. It does not indicate that anatomical structures of physiological functions are being neglected. Rather, it provides another way to describe them.

The reactions of an individual in any given situation are determined by (1) a general orientation and (2) specific reactions developed in identical or similar situations in the past. General orientations or dispositions of an individual develop over the entire life span of the individual and can be considered as tendencies to be active or passive, aggressive or fearful, and optimistic or pessimistic; this includes the tendency to approach new situations with certain strategies. The importance of general behavioral dispositions for learning was shown by Brutkowski (1959) who found that some dogs with prefrontal neocortical lesions were able to master a complex inhibitory reaction while others were not. This difference between impaired and nonimpaired dogs could not be explained on the basis of the size of the lesions, since increasing the size of the lesion in the nonimpaired animals only led to a temporary impairment with subsequent full recovery. The conclusion was reached that successful performance on the problem with or without surgery depended upon the temperament of the animal and that brain lesions produce modifications in some aspects of these temperamental differences.

General orientations may be considered to include a hierarchy of hypotheses the individual has acquired which is used in dealing with the world. Some people treat every new experience with fear and caution; others welcome new experiences and plunge into them with joy. Some mice eagerly explore a new environment; others remain immobile in a corner of the maze. Some people behave in accordance with the hypothesis that the world is a benevolent place; others, that it is an evil jungle. Some rats approach a new learning problem ''believing'' that the spatial location of rewards will be critical, while others only pay attention to ''sign posts'' indicated by colors (Isaacson & Kimble, 1972).

It must also be recognized that each of us has many different dispositions.

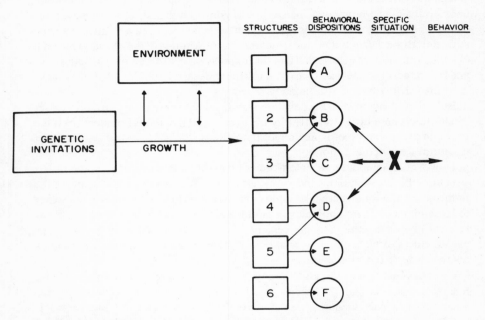

FIG. 1. Schematic drawing of the way in which genetic and environmental influences interact to produce a set of structures and "behavioral dispositions" in individual, A. See text for further explanation.

Different situations and different people evoke different orientations. Past experiences in a variety of situations and the conditions of the moment affect us toward one or another general approach. An animal trained in tasks based on the avoidance of pain will approach a new problem differently than one that hasn't had that experience. For the animal previously punished, returning to its home cage will evoke a different reaction than that evoked in an animal returning from a romp.

These general dispositions toward behavior are biologically represented by the composition and structure of the brain, but they are the consequences of a constant interplay among major structural units. There is no "hypothesis center," no "mood region," nor any "strategy system." Therefore, due to our ignorance of just how structures interact with each other, we must fall back upon a behavioristic language. In Figs. 1 and 2 I have tried to indicate some of the complexities of the situation by indicating the contributions of different structures to general behavioral dispositions by the arrows connecting the squares (representing structural units) with the circles (representing general behavioral dispositions).

This response of an individual in a given situation, represented by the "X" in the drawings, is determined by the relationship of "X" to the past experiences of the individual as it affects the various dispositions and the second factor determining behavior: the specific responses acquired in the same or similar situations in the past. In different individuals the same situation could call out quite different general dispositions and quite different specific responses. A given situation will not have the same relationship to general dispositions in all individuals. This is shown by the arrows of different thickness connecting "X" and the circles.

Two individuals can differ in both anatomical systems and behavioral dispositions, and in the relationships between these and the specific, immediate environment.

The effects of brain damage in such a scheme can be seen in Figs. 3 and 4. Let us consider blocks 3 and 4 to be the damaged regions. Let us further assume that these blocks are more or less similar "major structures" in the two brains. By assuming the completely arbitrary rules that a disposition will be altered if it has a reduction in input from the associated structural units, and eliminated completely if it has none, the result of the lesion in individual A could eliminate disposition C and alter dispositions B and D. In individual B, on the other hand, elimination of regions 3 and 4 altered dispositions B, C, D, and E but did not eliminate any. If we consider elimination of areas 3 and 4 to represent damage to what are commonly called "comparable areas," the model then shows how easily the "same" brain damage can produce divergent effects in two individuals.

INDIVIDUAL   B

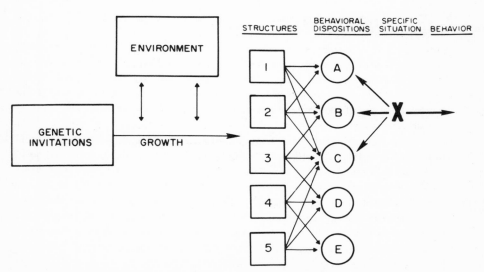

FIG. 2. Schematic drawing of development of structures and "behavioral dispositions" in individual, B.

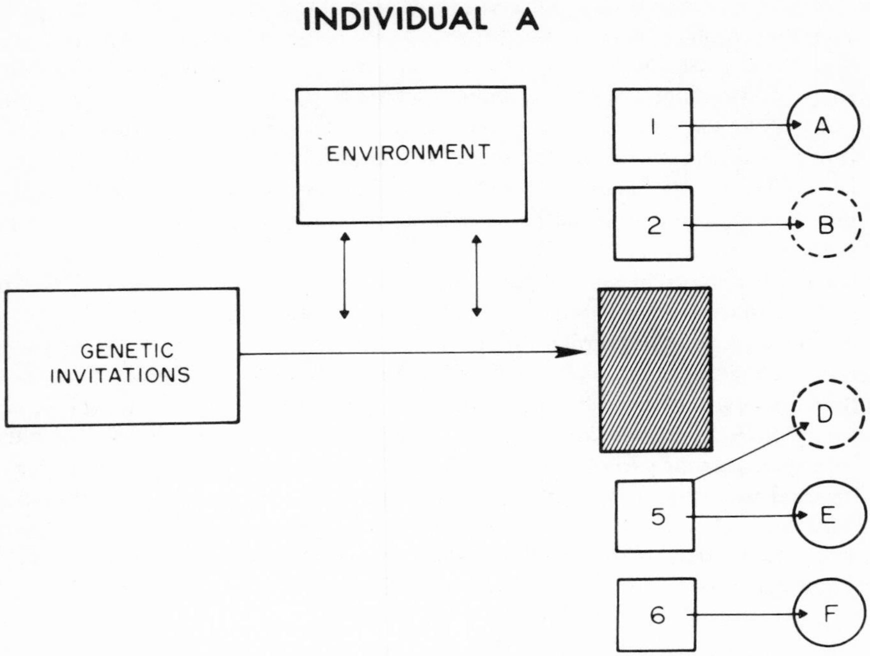

INDIVIDUAL A

FIG. 3. The hypothetical effects of brain damage in individual A. Structural units 3 and 4 have been removed, producing a loss of behavioral disposition C and a change in dispositions B and D.

This approach can help us understand the "recovery" seen after brain damage. This is shown in Fig. 5. In this figure the damage to areas 3 and 4 is assumed to have temporarily reduced activity in regions 2 and 5. This results in a much greater effect on the number of behavioral dispositions available to the individual (middle part of figure). As blood supplies are increased, edema is reduced, glia reactions change, etc., regions 2 and 5 again begin to achieve near-normal functions. As a result, the total effects of the damage are reduced (right part of figure).

The effects of brain damage early in life are also susceptible to analysis along these same lines. The infant has fewer anatomical systems and behavioral dispositions established than does the mature individual. The effect of damage is to produce a loss of some established systems and structures but also to produce an abnormal structure which is the special consequences of early brain damage. This is shown in Fig. 6. Some of the structures existing in a more or less functional form at the time of the damage can be influenced as can some that will develop afterwards. The structural anomalies induced by the destruction of area 2 in the infant are shown by the diamond-shaped figures in the bottom drawing. Therefore, the effect of early brain damage is likely to be more complicated and widespread than that found after later brain damage. This would account for the fact that the behavior of an animal with early brain damage is likely to be affected on a larger number of tasks than his adult-lesioned counterpart (see Hebb, 1949, pp. 289–294).

This type of analysis suggests that the effects produced by brain damage *at any age* should be dependent upon the genetic endowment, developmental history, and the age at which the lesion occurs. Furthermore, it not only helps us understand why the effects of brain damage can often only be considered in a probabilistic manner.

The effects of brain damage in adulthood are always probabilistic in nature. A certain form of brain damage always produces its "usual" effects upon behavior in a less than certain fashion. As an example, of 20 lesioned animals, 18 or 19 of them will show the expected behavioral changes in a particular behavioral test. One or two will not. On the other hand, one or two of twenty control animals without lesions will seemingly be impaired just as if they had had the brain damage.

The probabilistic nature of the behavioral effects of brain damage presents a theoretical problem only if the differences among the animals before the damage are ignored. Individual differences arise from differences in the genetic endowments of the animals as they interact with developmental experiences. For the most part, the animals used in experiments are of a mixed genetic background. The use of inbred strains reduces the variability of behavior in a number of tasks. However, genetic inheritance only involved the events occurring at the union of the sperm and the egg. After that, environmental factors make their presence felt. The result is a group of animals with widely different general dispositions in their behavior. Some of these dispositional factors operate to make the acquistion of a behavioral task difficult

INDIVIDUAL B

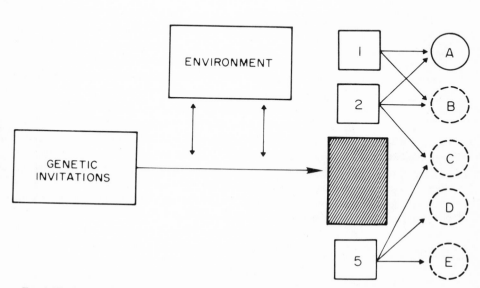

FIG. 4. The hypothetical effects of brain damage in individual B. Again, structural units 3 and 4 have been destroyed. In this case no behavioral disposition is lost, but all except A have been altered.

INDIVIDUAL A

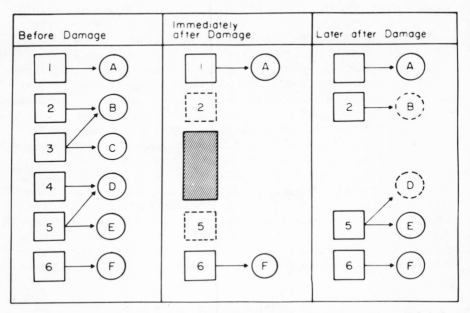

FIG. 5. Schematic drawing of the recovery that could be shown after early brain damage. Only the structures and behavioral dispositions of previous figures are given. Structural units 3 and 4 were lost at the time of damage, and units 2 and 5 temporarily were suppressed due to secondary reactions (middle portion of figure). This produces a temporary loss of behavioral dispositions B and E. As these secondary reactions subside, activity in units 2 and 5 is restored and behavioral dispositions B and E return but in altered form (right side of figure).

under some conditions but easy under others. It may be that a particular constitutional anomaly might preclude finding a solution to a task at all.

The changes in individual dispositions in the brain damaged animals will make some tasks easy, others difficult. Yet, the fact is that animals or people with brain damage often fail to solve problems that are capable of solution in many different ways and thus should be soluble. They often start to solve a problem by means of an incorrect strategy and fail to change their reactions in order to improve performance. They continue to respond inappropriately while most intact people or animals change to new ways of responding. This perseverative quality of behavior needs to be given additional consideration.

PERSEVERATION AFTER BRAIN DAMAGE

Part of the constitutional endowment of the individual includes emotionality and reactions to frustration. Differences in behavioral dispositions include the threshold for frustration reactions as well as their intensity. It is a commonplace that both animals and people differ greatly in their emotionality and reactions to frustrating events. There are constitutional differences in the tolerance of an individual to frustrating events. Brain damage would affect these general attributes of behavior as well as any others.

The work of Maier (1949) established that perseverative responding was a hallmark of frustration-instigated behavior. When a problem becomes insoluble, the animal responds in a perseverative manner without regard to the availability of reward. Everyone has been similar perseverative, nonproductive behavior in people subjected to extreme frustration. According to Maier's work, if a frustration reaction occurs, it does so in an all-or-none fashion. It is a "threshold" phenomenon.

If the reactions of an animal to frustration-inducing circumstances are determined by a threshold reaction, then behavioral anomalies based upon frustration should be of an all-or-none quality. This all-or-none quality of reactions of brain-damaged animals has been found in animals with lesions made in infancy and adulthood.

INFANT C

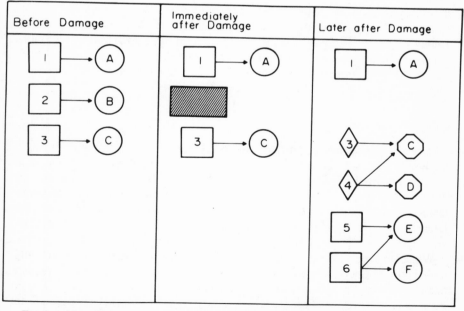

FIG. 6. A schematic drawing of the possible effects of brain damage early in life. The smaller number of completed structural units and behavioral dispositions available to the infant are represented in the upper two panels. After damage to structural unit 2, the immediate effect is a loss of structural unit B, but this loss also affects the future development of other units, e.g., 3 and 4 in the drawing. These abnormal structures are indicated by diamond-shaped figures. The abnormal behavioral dispositions that result are indicated by hexagons.

Thomas (1971) found such reactions after lesions of the fornix, and we have found it after other damage to the limbic system (e.g., Isaacson & Kimble, 1972; Nonneman & Isaacson, 1973). All-or-none effects have also been found in the behavior of retarded people working on a delayed response problem Isaacson & Perkins, 1973). Very often there is a complete absence of graded effects. For example, in the report of Nonneman and Isaacson (1973) animals with neonatal destruction of the hippocampus either had starting latencies in a passive avoidance task of less than 1.3 sec or beyond 20 sec. No animals had latencies in between. This reinforces the view that the presence or absence of a behavioral deficit is determined, in part, by the emotional constitution of the animal, as modified by the brain damage, as it interacts with past and present experiences.

According to this hypothesis, many brain damaged individuals would be capable of excellent performance on tasks "diagnostic" for a particular brain lesion, but the occurrence of an impairment depends upon the circumstances of the testing and upon the individual's initial orientation toward the problem. For example, if the individual begins the problem "on the wrong foot" and experiences nonreward, frustration and frustration-instigated perseverative responding could follow.

If a brain lesion alters an animal's ability to tolerate frustrating conditions, this change could interact with other behavioral dispositions related to the ways in which the animal is motivated, the value of incentives provided, the penalties for incorrect responses, the relative degree of successes and failures early in training, and the animal's training history. The more intense the circumstances of training, the more likely it is that frustration-based behavior will be exhibited. Since some of these factors may vary from day to day or from moment to moment, whether or not an impairment is found may be an "accidental" manner.

CONCLUSIONS

When I began my research in the mid-1960's on the effects of early brain damage, I believed that it was possible to show recovery or sparing of functions if the brain damage occurred early enough in life. Furthermore, I felt that the behavioral recovery was associated with a *decreased* amount of structural abnormality. It has taken a decade for me to change my views. Now, it seems clear that damage to the infant brain produces greater anomalies in structure and behavior than are found after damage to the brain of mature or juvenile animals.

Whatever recovery does occur after early brain damage seems to reflect only those natural processes related to the great number of changes of a direct and indirect nature occurring after brain damage. These processes are not mysterious. Indeed, many have been well-studied by neuropathologists and anatomists. They require no explanation based upon the ability of one area to "take over" the functions of another.

The variability of behavior after brain damage in adult or infant is understandable once we give up the absurd view that the structure of each and every brain is identical. By accepting the obvious differences among individuals due to their genetic and environmental backgrounds, it is easy to anticipate and accept the wide diversities of behavioral alterations found after brain damage. The suggestion to consider brain damage effects as if they were genetic effects was made to stress the difference between structural damage (genotypic alteration) and its phenotypic consequences.

Even though this approach stresses the permanent sequelae of brain damage, it is by no means of pessimistic approach. Instead, it should help us to focus our attention on methods that could limit or decrease secondary, indirect effects of brain damage and to find new ways in which the residual capacitites of the individual can be utilized. Such a direct approach seems preferable to basing out hopes upon ''vicarious functioning'' which is beyond our knowledge and from my point of view almost certainly does not exist.

REFERENCES

Akert, K., Orth, O. S., Harlow, H. F., & Schiltz, K. A. Learned behavior of rhesus monkeys following neonatal bilateral prefrontal lobotomy. *Science,* 1960, **132,** 1944–1945.

Baisden, R. Behavioral effects of hippocampal lesions after adrenergic depletion of the septal area. Unpublished doctoral dissertation, University of Florida, 1973.

Bernardis, L. L. Hypophagia, hypodipsia and hypoactivity following dorsomedial hypothalamic lesions. *Physiology and Behavior,* 1972, **8,** 1161–1164.

Bland, B. H., & Cooper, R. M. Posterior neodecortication in the rat: Age at operation and experience. *Journal of Comparative and Physiological Psychology,* 1969, **69,** 345–354.

Brutkowski, S. The şolution of a difficult inhibitory task (alternation) by normal and prefrontal dogs. *Acta Biologiae Experimentalis,* 1959, **19,** 301–312.

Bucy, P. C. The delusion of the obvious. *Perspectives in Biology and Medicine,* 1966, **9,** 358–368.

Cornwell, P., Cornwell, G., and Overman, W. Effects of unilateral and bilateral striate lesions in neonatal kittens on visual discrimination. Unpublished manuscript, The Pennsylvania State University, 1972.

Cornwell, P. and Overman, W. Effects of early rearing conditions and neonatal striate lesions on visually guided behavior in kittens. Unpublished manuscript, 1972.

Cornwell, P., Overman, W., and Nonneman, C. Photically evoked activity in extrastriate cortex after striate lesions. Unpublished manuscript, The Pennsylvania State University, 1972.

Cornwell, P., Overman, W., and Ross, C. Deficits in visually guided behavior in cats after neonatal lesions. Unpublished manuscript, The Pennsylvania State University, 1972.

Cornwell, P., Ross, C., Overman, W., and Levitsky, K. Effects of lesions of the visual cortex on performance on the visual cliff. Unpublished manuscript, 1972. The Pennsylvania State University.

Dawson, R. G., Conrad, L., & Lynch, G. Single and two-stage hippocampal lesions: A similar syndrome. *Experimental Neurology,* 1973, **40,** 263–277.

Doty, R. W. Functional significance of the topographical aspects of the retino-cortical projection. In R. Jung & H. Kornhuber (Eds.), *The visual system: Neurophysiology and psychophysics.* Heidelberg: Springer-Verlag, 1961.

Doty, R. W. Survival of pattern vision after removal of striate cortex in the adult cat. *Journal of Comparative Neurology,* 1971, **143,** 341–369.

Douglas, R. J. The development of hippocampal function: Implications for theory and for therapy. In R. L. Isaacson & K. H. Pribram (Eds.), *The hippocampus: A comprehensive treatise.* New York: Plenum, 1975.

Finger, S., Walbran, B., & Stein, D. G. Brain damage and behavioral recovery: Serial lesion phenomena. *Brain Research*, 1973, **63**, 1–18.

Glassman, R. B. Similar effects of infant and adult sensorimotor cortical lesions on cats' posture. *Brain Research*, 1973, **63**, 103–110.

Goldman, P. S. Functional development of the prefrontal cortex in early life and the problem of neuronal plasticity. *Experimental Neurology*, 1971, **32**, 366–387.

Goldman, P. S. An alternative to developmental plasticity: Heterology of CNS structures in infants and adults. In D. Stein, J. Rosen, & N. Butters (Eds.), *CNS plasticity and recovery of function*. New York: Academic Press, 1974.

Goldman, P. S., & Rosvold, H. E. The effects of selective caudate lesions in infant and juvenile rhesus monkeys. *Brain Research*, 1972, **43**, 53–66.

Goldstein, K. *Human nature in the light of psychopathology*. Cambridge, Mass.: Harvard University Press, 1940.

Goodman, D. C., & Horel, J. A. Sprouting of optic tract projections in the brain stem of the rat. *Journal of Comparative Neurology*, 1966, **127**, 71–88.

Greene, E., Stauff, C., & Walters, J. Recovery of function with two-stage lesions of the fornix. *Experimental Neurology*, 1972, **37**, 14–22.

Harlow, H. F., A. J. Blomquist, C. I. Thompson, K. A. Schlitz, & M. K. Harlow. Effects of induction age and size of frontal lobe lesions on learning in rhesus monkeys. In R. L. Isaacson (Ed.), *The neuropsychology of development*. New York: Wiley, 1968. Pp. 79–120.

Hebb, D. O. The effect of early and late brain damage upon test scores and the nature of normal adult intelligence. *Proceedings of the American Philosophical Society*, 1942, **85**, 275–292.

Hebb, D. O. *The organization of behavior*. New York: Wiley, 1949.

Hicks, S. P., & D'Amato, C. J. Motor-sensory behavior after hemispherectomy in newborn and mature rats. *Experimental Neurology*, 1970, **29**, 416–438.

Isaacson, R. L., & Kimble, D. P. Lesions of the limbic system: Their effects upon hypothesis and frustration. *Behavioral Biology*, 1972, **7**, 767–793.

Isaacson, R. L., & Nonneman, A. J. Early brain damage and later development. In P. Satz & J. J. Ross (Eds.), *The disabled learner*. Rotterdam: Rotterdam University Press, 1972.

Isaacson, R. L., Nonneman, A. J., & Schmaltz, L. W. Behavioral and anatomical sequelae of damage to the infant limbic system. In R. L. Isaacson (Ed.), *The neuropsychology of development*. New York: Wiley, 1968.

Isaacson, R. L., & Perkins, M. A. Delayed response performance of mentally retarded patients. *American Journal of Mental Deficiency*, 1973, **77**, 737–747.

Johnson, D. A. Developmental aspects of recovery of function following septal lesions in the infant rat. *Journal of Comparative and Physiological Psychology*, 1972, **78**, 331–348.

Johnson, D. A., Poplawsky, A., Bielauskas, L., & Liebert, D. Recovery of function on a two-way conditioned avoidance task following septal lesions in infancey: Effects of early handling. *Brain Research*, 1972, **45**, 282–287.

Kennard, M. A. Age and other factors in motor recovery from precentral lesions in monkeys. *American Journal of Physiology*, 1936, **115**, 138–146.

Kennard, M. A. Reorganization of motor function in the cerebral cortex of monkeys deprived of motor and premotor areas in infancy. *Journal of Neurophysiology*, 1938, **1**, 477–496.

Kennard, M. A. Relation of age to motor impairment in man and in subhuman primates. *Archives of Neurology and Psychiatry*, 1940, **44**, 377–397.

Kennard, M. A. Cortical reorganization of motor function: Studies on series of monkeys of various ages from infancy to maturity. *Archives of Neurology and Psychiatry*, 1942, **47**, 227–240.

Kling, A., & Tucker, T. J. Effects of combined lesions of frontal granular cortex and caudate nucleus in the neonatal monkey. *Brain Research*, 1967, **6**, 428–439.

Kurtz, R. G., Rozin, P., & Teitelbaum, P. Ventromedial hypothalamic hyperphagia in the hypophysectomized wealing rat. *Journal of Comparative and Physiological Psychology*, 1972, **80**, 19–25.

Lawrence, D. G., & Hopkins, D. A. Bilateral pyramidal lesions in infant rhesus monkeys. *Brain Research*, 1970, **24**, 543–544.

Lawrence, D. G., & Kuypers, H. G. J. M. The functional organization of the motor system in the monkey. I. The effects of bilateral pyramidal lesions. *Brain*, 1968, **91**, 1–14.

Liu, C. N., & Chambers, W. W. Intraspinal psrouting of dorsal root axons. *Archives of Neurology and Psychiatry*, 1958, **79**, 46–61.

Lund, R. R., Cunningham, T. J., & Lund, J. S. Modified optic projections after unilateral eye removal in young rats. *Brain, Behavior, and Evolution*, 1974, in press.

Lynch, G., Deadwyler, S., & Cotman, C. Post-lesion axonal growth produces permanent functional connections. *Science*, 1973, **180**, 1364–1366.

McCough, G. P., Austin, G. M., Liu, C. N., & Liu, C. Y. Sprouting as a cause of spasticity. *Journal of Neurophysiology*, 1958, **21**, 205–216.

Maier, N. R. F. *Frustration: The study of behavior without a goal.* New York: McGraw-Hill, 1949.

Miller, E. A., Goldman, P. S., & Rosvold, H. E. Delayed recovery of function following orbital prefrontal lesions in infant monkeys. *Science*, 1973, **182**, 304–306.

Moore, R. Y., Björklund, A., & Stenevi, U. Plastic changes in the adrenergic innervation of the rat septal area in response ot denervation. *Brain Research*, 1971, **33**, 13–35.

Murphy, E. H., & Stewart, D. L. Effects of neonatal and adult striate lesions on visual discrimination in the rabbit. *Experimental Neurology*, 1974, **42**, 89–96.

Nash, D. J. Effects of neonatal irradiation and genotype on postnatal growth in mice. *Biologia Neonatorum*, 1971, **18**, 17–28.

Nonneman, A. J. Anatomical and behavioral consequences of early brain damage in the rabbit. Unpublished doctoral dissertation, University of Florida, 1970.

Nonneman, A. J., & Isaacson, R. L. Task dependent recovery after early brain damage. *Behavioral Biology*, 1973, **8**, 143–172.

Raisman, G. Neuronal Plasticity in the septal nuclei of the adult rat. *Brain Research*, 1969, **14**, 25–48.

Sperry, R. W. Split-brain approach to learning problems. In G. C. Quarton, L. Melnechuk, & F. O. Schmidt (Eds.), *The neurosciences.* New York: Rockefeller University Press, 1967.

Stein, D. G., Rosen, J. J., Grazaidei, J., Mishkin, D., & Brink, J. J. Central nervous system: Recovery of function. *Science*, 1969, **166**, 528–530.

Stewart, D. L., & Riesen, A. H. Adult versus infant brain damage: Behavioral and electrophysiological effects of striatectomy in adult and neonatal rabbits. In G. Newton & A. H. Riesen (Eds.), *Advances in psychobiology.* New York: Wiley, 1972. Pp. 171–211.

Tanaka, D., Jr. Sparing of an escape response following serial prefrontal decortication in the monkey. *Brain Research*, 1974, **65**, 195–201.

Teuber, H. L., & Rudel, R. G. Behavior after cerebral lesions in children and adults. *Developmental Medicine and Child Neurology*, 1962, **4**, 3.

Thomas, G. J. Maze retention by rats with hippocampal lesions and with fornicotomies. *Journal of Comparative and Physiological Psychology*, 1971, **75**, 41–49.

Thompson, C. I., Harlow, H. F., Blomquist, A. J., & Schiltz, K. A. Recovery of function following prefrontal lobe damage in rhesus monkeys. *Brain Research*, 1971, **35**, 37–48.

Thompson, V. E. Visual decortication in infancy in rats. *Journal of Comparative and Physiological Psychology*, 1970, **72**, 441–451.

Tsang, Y. C. The functions of the visual areas of the cerebral cortex of the rat in the learning and retention of the maze. I. *Comparative Psychology Monographs*, 1934, **10**, 1–56.

Tsang, Y. C. The functions of the visual areas of the cerebral cortex of the rat in the learning and retention of the maze. II. *Comparative Psychology Monographs*, 1936, **12**, 1–41.

Tsang, Y. C. Maze learning in rats hemidecorticated in infance. *Journal of Comparative Psychology*, 1937, **24**, 221–254. (a)

Tsang, Y. C. Visual sensitivity in rats deprived of visual cortex in infancy. *Journal of Comparative Psychology*, 1937, **24**, 255-262. (b)

Tucker, T. J., & Kling, A. Preservation of delayed response following combined lesions of prefrontal and posterior association cortex in infant monkeys. *Experimental Neurology*, 1969, **23**, 491–502.

2

FUNCTIONAL ADAPTATION
AFTER BRAIN INJURY
AND MALFORMATION
IN EARLY LIFE IN RATS[1]

Samuel P. Hicks
Constance J. D'Amato
University of Michigan Medical Center

INTRODUCTION

Normality. Normal has been defined as a rule or reference standard, and abnormal as deviation or aberration from it. For a population of humans or rats or some other species, normal is the attributes of form and behavior of the members of the population who have been able to reproduce the species in the course of evolution. These attributes may change with variations in genes and environment, but they are regarded as normal as long as they insure adaptability of the species to perpetuate itself. They become abnormal when they extinguish the species.

Such an absolute evolutionary definition of normal and abnormal applies to a population of a species, not individuals. The central tendencies of a variety of physical, mental, physiologic, and other attributes of such a successful population can be determined, and called normal because they are typical. But as soon as these evolutionary criteria are applied to the individual, disparities begin to appear. As one example, a successful population harbors a variety of diseases and disorders that are also typical. Although they do not threaten the species with extinction, they are usually branded as abnormalities in an individual. Another example lies in the marauding, aggressive behavior of many animal and human populations that has made them successful. In many circumstances when such behavior is exhibited by an individual, it is regarded as abnormal or aberrant, but sometimes, depending

[1] Present research is supported by USPHS grant NS 10531, and earlier work by AEC Contract (11-1) 1201 and USPHS grant NS 03861.

27

on the observer, it is held to be normal. Thus any definition of normal and abnormal involves value judgments.

Studies of aberrant development. Against this background of how organisms struggle to survive and reproduce, many laboratories are studying development in animal models, and sometimes human models, toward a better understanding of nervous system adaptability and what is normal and what is aberrant. Some assess the relative contributions of genes and early environmental influences to the formation of adult behavior patterns, including those concerned with aggressiveness and docility (Dennenberg, 1969; Ginsburg, 1971). Others investigate the effects of hormones on the development of reproductive behavior and adaptive social interactions (Money & Ehrhardt, 1972). Experiments in still other laboratories deal empirically with the altering effects of teratogenic agents on the growth of behavior, or search for the neural mechanisms by which the effects are mediated (Joffe, 1969). Our laboratory has been interested in the range of capacities of young nervous systems of animals and humans to compensate morphologically and functionally in the presence of deviations from what we call normal development. We have explored effects of metabolic inhibitors, anoxia, certain mutant genes, and especially, as we report here, radiation and surgical injuries on the developing nervous system in rats. In the experiments the nervous system has certainly been made abnormal, but the morphologic and functional responses have reflected some of its basic adaptive capacities, and we attempt to emphasize that aspect.

In the following we summarize some of our earlier experiments in which responses to radiation or surgical injury of the developing nervous system were observed, and then consider more fully more recent and current work on functional responses to malformation of the retina, or removal of motor–sensory cortex, at birth.

RESTITUTION AFTER PRENATAL INJURY OF THE NERVOUS SYSTEM

Early embryo. Radiation (x-rays) selectively killed or altered the growth of certain primitive and differentiating cells in the embryo, and by controlling the dose and the stage of development when it was given, one could produce an array of highly reproducible patterns of malformation of the nervous system and other organs (Hicks & D'Amato, 1961, 1966; Hicks, D'Amato, & Lowe, 1959). Vulnerability in the rat extended from the period of formation of the body axis of the embryo, the beginning of organogenesis, to more than a week after birth. Histologic studies in a series of animals removed from a litter at intervals after irradiation provided a stepwise picture of the response to injury and the morphogenesis of the malformative and restitutive processes.

Such experiments showed that the mammalian embryo had the same powers of restitution of damage and the same susceptibility to profound malformation that the amphibian embryo had displayed in classic experimental embryological studies. The point of interest in respect to adaptation here was that during some periods in the earliest stages of organogenesis, losses of more than half the cells in the embryo (caused by 150 r[2]) could be restituted and an apparently normal animal still developed (Hicks & D'Amato, 1966).

Morphologic restitution and functional adaptation after injury to the fetus. Remarkable restitution of cell losses could occur in the primitive cell populations in certain places in the later fetus, too, though it was quite limited in scope. Perhaps the most dramatic restoration was demonstrated after irradiation with 100 to 200 r around the 12th day of gestation, the stage of some 25 to 35 pairs of somites and earliest formation of the cerebral vesicles (cerebral hemispheres). Vast numbers of primitive cells were killed in this dose range. It was virtually impossible to see any abnormality in the animals that grew up after 100 or 150 r, and after 200 r the volume of the mantle might be a little reduced on direct gross and microscopic comparison with brains of normal animals. As in the very early embryo, though, this kind of morphologic adaptation after injury was exceptional, and in most stages malformation was the rule.

Radiation–induced malformations are among the most reproducible responses that can be produced by teratogens, and they seemed to provide an opportunity to correlate developmental abnormalities of brain structure with altered behavior. A number of investigators have shown relations between the stages of radiation during fetal development and constellations of altered behavior that developed later. In these studies it was virtually impossible to attribute the behavior to involvement of particular brain systems (Fowler, Hicks, D'Amato, & Beach, 1962; Furchgott, 1963). One reason for this lack of specificity was that radiation applied during fetal life altered diverse regions of the nervous system.

Can malformed cortex function? Falk and collaborators (Falk & D'Amato, 1962; Hicks, D'Amato, & Falk, 1962) investigated the relation between malformation and function by attempting to determine whether abnormally developed brain tissue functioned at all. Cerebral cortex took on a number of patterns of malformation, depending on the stage of development and dose of radiation. Using visual pattern discrimination tasks, he showed that rats with several kinds of defective and severely scrambled cortices could discriminate the patterns. This kind of detail vision was assumed to be a cortically dependent function. Knowledge of the morphogenesis and architectural detail of the abnormal cortices, however, did not explain why they functioned, and the obvious conclusion had to be made that enough organization had been built into the malformed cortices to subserve the function.

In summary, severe cellular damage of the very early embryo could be completely restituted at certain stages, and comparable restitution of damage to the

[2]Radiation factors in experiments described here were 250 kV, 3 mA, 70 cm, 50 r/min, or 250 kVcp, 9 ma, 70 cm, 60 r/min; details in Hicks and D'Amato (1966) and Hicks *et al.* (1959).

early cerebral mantle occurred. Another kind of adaptation was shown by apparent function of cerebral cortex when it was histologically malformed.

MALADAPTIVE RESPONSES TO INJURY OF THE INFANT CEREBELLUM

Radiation malformation. The cerebellum put in its appearance between 15 and 16 days of fetal life, and primitive cells that formed it continued their building activities into the third week after birth. It was still in a very early stage of development at the time of birth in the rat. Restitution after radiation injury (200 r) during the earliest stage of fetal cerebellar growth, 15 or 16 days, was complete. After that, grossly visible malformation could be recognized when radiation was given at any stage up to 10 or 12 days after birth. A series of especially distinctive patterns of malformation of the cerebellum could be produced by irradiating the infant rat with doses of 200, 300, or 400 r on one of the first six days after birth (Hicks & D'Amato, 1966; Hicks *et al.*, 1959; Hicks, D'Amato, French, Klein, & Austin, 1969). By appropriate shielding, the effects of the radiation could be largely confined to the cerebellar region. Disorders of locomotion in the form of slight incoordination resulted from 200 r. Three hundred or 400 r given at 1 or 5 days of age produced extremely severe incoordination of locomotion. The radiation could also be confined in an approximate way to regions of the cerebellum at these two ages, malforming lateral, intermediate, or middle regions. Incoordination, less severe than that after irradiation of the whole cerebellum, resulted, and there was no distinction between the functional effects of irradiation on one part or another.

Cerebellectomy. It was possible to make some comparisons of effects of aberrant development of cerebellar cortex (malformation) with effects of ablating parts or all of the infant cerebellum at 1 or 5 days of age (Hicks, *et al.*, 1969). Superficial ablations that resulted in failure of formation of parts of the folia (essentially the cerebellar cortex) produced no functional abnormalities. This contrasted with the effect of malformation. When the ablations resulted in complete or nearly complete absence of the deep cerebellar nuclei, which was necessarily associated with nearly completely absent folia, locomotion and staying upright were profoundly impaired as the animals grew up. (There was no difference in effects between those operated on at 1 or 5 days.) Essentially, the animals could stand up only momentarily, and they walked and ran upright only a few steps and then fell over. As juveniles they played vigorously, in their way, with normal or affected littermates, falling over backwards if they reared up, and crawling most of the time on their sides or bellies. They showed momentary episodes of extensor spasms of the limbs and trunk during vigorous play. At maturity there was no improvement of locomotion or ability to stand. Nonetheless, one affected pair managed to mate successfully, if awkwardly, and the female raised two litters. (Adult rats subjected to cerebellectomy were also severely incapacitated, principally by being unable to stand or stay upright, moving about like the animals operated on in infancy. They showed no "spasms." Over a period of several months they were able to walk short distances, though precariously.)

In summary, animals with aberrantly developed cerebellar cortex caused by radiation showed locomotor incoordination. A relatively small region of severely malformed cerebellar cortex could induce general locomotor incoordination. Ablations that led to defects of parts of the cerebellar cortex produced no visible disorder of function. Animals surgically deprived of deep cerebellar nuclei in infancy were unable to maintain an upright position as they grew up, but they made certain compensatory adjustments of motor function.

VISUAL FUNCTION IN MALFORMED RETINAS

Malformation of the retina by radiation. The retina is part of the brain, and its relatively isolated situation offered an opportunity to malform one part of the brain whose function is distinctive without affecting other parts. The mechanisms and morphology of retinal malformations induced by radiation in the rat have been studied (Hicks & D'Amato, 1963, 1966). Like the early embryo and cerebral mantle, the retina was capable of virtually perfect restitution after extensive destruction of cells in a certain few stages (30 to 40 pairs of somites, for example), but throughout most of its development until a week after birth it was subject to a variety of malformations when exposed to radiation.

The malformations, like others produced by radiation, were quite time and dose specific. In the neonatal period, their patterns reflected the progressive differentiation of the members of the retinal cell layers from undifferentiated primitive cells. By the time of birth the ganglion cells and a few of the innermost members of the bipolar layer (shorthand for inner nuclear layer of bipolar and amacrine cells) had begun to differentiate. These latter were not known to be appreciably harmed by radiation. The remaining primitive undifferentiated cells, whose task it was to proliferate and differentiate into the rest of the bipolar layer cells and the photoreceptors, were radiosensitive. Two hundred r killed large numbers of them, but the residual cells still manufactured the remaining retina, moderately deficient in numbers of cells and architecturally somewhat distorted into a rosette pattern.

Six hundred r was far more devastating to the primitive cells, but from the few remaining a retina was completed. The resulting retina had a ganglion cell layer, but cells of what would have been bipolar and photoreceptor cell layers were extremely deficient in numbers and so chaotically intermingled that no normal layering was recognizable (Fig. 1). Because the periphery of the postnatal retina was less differentiated than was the center, fewer cells had formed peripherally than centrally. The whole eye was smaller than normal after 600 r owing not only to effects on the retina, but also on the growing periorbital tissues. The optic nerve was about half to two-thirds normal diameter, because optic nerve fibers (ganglion

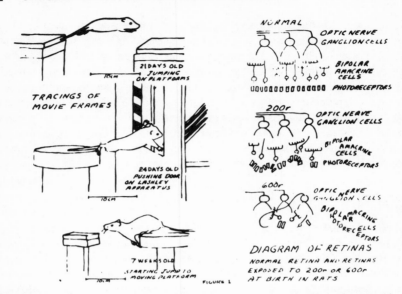

FIG. 1. At left, tracings of movie frames of performing rats, showing visual behavior tests. Above, a rat 21 days old jumping spontaneously from one large platform to another. Middle, a rat 24 days old pushing down a striped card in a doorway of a Lashley apparatus. Below, a rat seven weeks old anticipating a short jump to a moving platform.

At right, diagrams based on histologic preparations of retinas of a normal mature rat and mature rats whose eyes were exposed to 200 or 600 r at birth.

cell axones) formed aberrant bundles that remained in the retina. This was regarded as a consequence of disorder of retinal growth rather than a direct effect of radiation on ganglion cells.

(The role of the stage of retinal differentiation in determining the pattern of malformation at a given dose level was illustrated by two examples. At 5 or 6 days after birth, when only photoreceptors were being made, the deficiencies and rosettes resulting from 200 r involved only photoreceptors. At 14 or 15 days of fetal life, when little differentiation had occurred yet, the deficiencies and rosettes involved all retinal layers.)

Three hundred or 400 r in the newborn produced malformations that could be epitomized as lying between 200 and 600 r effects in severity. Nine hundred r was so devastating to primitive cells, and also damaged or killed some of the more differentiated retinal cells, that the resulting retinas were rudimentary.

The radiation in these experiments was confined, by shielding, almost to the eyes alone, but with some exposure of the adjacent olfactory bulbs and the extreme frontal regions of the cerebral hemispheres. Serial histologic sections of the whole eyes at the end of the experiment were made to check whether any part of the retina was spared.

Methods of visual behavioral tests. The rats used here, and in the subsequently described cortex ablation studies, were black animals with white feet, the

F1 cross between black-selfed nonagouti males and albino females of Wistar origin. Both parent lines had been brother–sister mated 50 to 70 generations.

We had observed that juvenile rats whose eyes had received 200, 300, or 400 r at birth accurately jumped variable distances up to 30 or 40 cm from one platform to another in different directions. We, therefore, tested visually guided behavior extensively in juvenile rats whose eyes had been exposed to 200, 300, 400, 600, or 900 r. There were two animals at each dose level except 6 in the 600 r group. (Two additional 400-r animals and one 600-r animal had small patches of unirradiated retina on serial section, the result of shielding.)

Vision in the rats was studied in several ways (Fig. 1). Most of the methods were similar to standard procedures commonly used by behavioral scientists, only the training of rats at a very young age, as described later, being novel. Because the 600-r animals had extremely deformed and deficient retinas but showed an unexpected capacity for visually guided jumping and visual pattern discrimination, we give in some detail the procedures used. The animals were tested jumping spontaneously variable distances from one platform to another in the light, or to a very dimly lighted platform in the dark, and to a platform mounted on the edge of a record turntable moving in a circle. They were tested in visual pattern discriminations on an apparatus closely modeled after that designed by Lashley (1930) many years ago. The apparatus presented two doorways in which matching pairs of patterns were reciprocally displayed on cards: vertical versus horizontal black and white stripes, upright versus inverted white outline equilateral triangles on black ground, etc. In training, the negative stimulus card was locked in the doorway; the positive stimulus (''correct'') card was unlocked. If the animal chose the correct door, it could push through, knocking the card down to get on the platform behind it. Criterion in these tests was the attainment of 20 consecutive errorless trials in one session. The animals were further tested on their discrimination between upright and inverted triangles, without differential reinforcement, both cards left unlocked in doorways, and by two observers; for equivalence with several reciprocal pairs of fractions of the outline triangle, such as the base, one side, both sides, and on solid triangles; with pairs of traingles of unequal size; with a pair of equal size triangles, one gray and one white; and with transilluminated triangles of equal size. They were then still further tested with the triangles but with eyelids sutured closed (sutures were placed under ether anesthesia) and the apparatus in a normal position; then, eyes still closed, with the apparatus rotated 180° in relation to surroundings; then still again with eyes open and the apparatus in normal position.

Training infant and juvenile rats. Our manner of training our rats in these tasks (and others described later) was to work with them from about thirteen days of age through to several weeks of age as necessary. Generally 2 to 6 animals in a litter were altered experimentally, as by irradiation here, and 2 to 4 normal littermates served as controls in the behavioral tests (Hicks & D'Amato, 1970). All were handled briefly almost daily from birth. They were first introduced to large jumping platforms and allowed to step across gradually increasing gaps. By weaning time at 21 days they were jumping enthusiastically from one stationary platform to another, a distance of 20 cm, about twice body length. At about this time a round jumping platform 13 cm in diameter and a landing platform 10 cm long by 7 cm wide were substituted. The round platform was regularly used for the Lashley apparatus. All platforms were 20 cm high. Foam cushions protected the animals from possible injury in falls.

In the mid or latter part of the third week, the rats were introduced to the Lashley apparatus and allowed to push light-weight cards, one black and one white, with the black locked, for several days. Criterion performance was not sought here, and the somewhat heavier vertical versus horizontal stripe cards began. Juvenile rats generally reached criterion on stripes in two to four sessions, and then triangles in three to five (Hicks & D'Amato, 1970).

The dimly lighted platform was like the 10 by 7 cm landing platform but built like a chimney with a translucent top, and a small rheostatically controlled light inside. Jumping was observed in the dark by seeing the rat's silhouette against the top. The test was done in a single session, varying the distance jumped, when the animals were about five or six weeks old.

Reinforcement was the exploration and activity involved in these situations, and being handled a great deal by the experimenters, which the animals often sought during the proceedings. When they were several weeks old, particularly the normals, they sometimes lost their enthusiasm for rapid decisions in the later discriminations in the series on the Lashley apparatus. This could be restored by depriving them of water for several hours or overnight and offering it both sweetened and plain in small dishes on the apparatus platform behind the doorways. They drank relatively little here, doing most of it afterwards in the home cage.

Results of visual behavior tests in irradiated rats. There was essentially no difference between normals and irradiated animals in the 200 to 600-r groups in discriminating patterns and jumping on the stationary platforms in the light and dark. The 900-r animals did not learn to discriminate patterns nor did they ever "jump" from one platform to another if they could not first contact the landing platform with whiskers. They behaved essentially like rats blind from early infancy, as we describe in later paragraphs.

In the pattern discrimination tests the animals (except the 900-r pair) attained criterion on stripes and triangles in a few sessions, saw various triangle fractions as equivalent, were not confused by a gray triangle paired with a white one, by pairs of triangles of unequal size, or by transilluminated triangles. With eyes closed their choices on triangles were random, but returned to criterion or nearly criterion as soon as they were opened. With eyes closed and the setup rotated 180°, they occasionally jumped toward where the doors would have been, after some searching movements, or they did not jump. If brought close to the doors on the jumping platform with eyes closed, they did not attempt to go through the doors until whisker contact was made, thus seeming not to use olfactory cues.

That radiation impaired the ability of animals to track and jump to the moving platform could be supported by considering performances of normals and 200-r rats as one group and 300-, 400-, and 600-r rats as another. It was reinforcing to juvenile animals to step onto the moving platform when first introduced to it around three weeks and later jump a short distance to it and ride on it for a turn and be taken off. A common distance for rats four to six weeks old to jump was 12 to 15 cm as the rotating platform came nearest the jumping platform at about half maximum speed, 15 rpm. Normal rats also jumped to the platform variable distances as it was receding, or approaching the near point, and did so when it was traveling maximum speed, 30 rpm, estimated at about 50 cm per second. They rarely jumped to the platform at the far point of its course, about 35 cm. The 200-r rats behaved as normals, but as a group the more heavily irradiated animals confined their jumping to the shorter ranges. One 600-r rat jumped much like the normals, and another never jumped more than about 10 cm and always to the near point. The animals behaved as though they were tracking the platform visually. Even the shortest jumps were out of vibrissae contact reach, and auditory cues did not seem to be a factor.

Additional experiments with four animals suggested that 600-r was the level beyond which increasingly severe impairment of vision would occur. They were excluded from the 600-r group because the radiation factors were different, though they might appropriately have been included. In one pair, the olfactory bulbs and rostral tips of the cerebral hemispheres adjacent to the eyes were not shielded at all, and in the other two, the x-rays were of different potential, 100 kV. Three of these animals learned stripes; one did not after many sessions. None learned triangles. They jumped variable distances on the stationary platforms, and to the nearest point on the path of the rotary platform.

Behavior of rats blinded at birth. When the performances of the irradiated animals were compared with those of rats without eyes, considerable differences were found which strengthened our conclusion that the animals with extremely deformed retinas were using predominantly visual cues.

Rats whose eyeballs were surgically removed under ether anesthesia at birth (Hicks & D'Amato, 1970) were trained to jump from one platform to another. This required a long and patient period of training, beginning about age two weeks, during which the distance between platforms was lengthened by tiny increments, and the surroundings and conditions of the experiment, including the experimenter, kept constant. By the time the animals were about three months old, they were jumping 30 cm from one platform to another. Foam cushions were placed everywhere the animals could land to avoid harm to them and aversive stimuli. If the distance was shortened, the animals overshot on the next jump but then adjusted their jumps the following time to land on the platform. They could angle their jumps to the landing platform accurately when the jumping platform was moved 15 cm in either direction lateral to its normal position. After such a change of position, they first stood up on their hind legs as though they were "looking about" before jumping. Yet if the landing platform was removed entirely, after some hesitation and "looking about" movements, they still jumped to where the platform would have been in space. (Normal animals simply got down off the jumping platform in this circumstance.) If the whole setup was rotated 180°, the blind animals oriented themselves as usual and jumped as though the landing platform was in its customary place.

It was assumed that the animals were using many cues: a wall constantly to their left, ventilating air flowing into the room overhead, and regular ambient sounds could provide auditory, tactile, and vibratory stimuli, and perhaps (heat) radiation cues. Deafening the animals by removing the middle ear contents surgically under anesthesia, then closely cropping the hair and vibrassae, did not alter their jumping ability. Only when a 60 cm by 60 cm Plexiglas (to permit movies) "wall" was placed about 30 cm to the animal's right, parallel to the regular wall, was the direction of jumping completely disrupted.

On the Lashley apparatus, to which they were introduced early in life, as the irradiated animals had been, these blind rats performed enthusiastically over a period of several weeks. Their jumping position had to be brought within whisker-reach of the sills of the doors. Their choices were random; finding one doorway locked they switched instantly to enter the other. These animals did not track and jump onto the moving platform, though they would step onto it if it passed close enough to the jumping platform to touch them if they were facing it.

Does a malformed retina transmit malformed information? Some other experiments with 600-r retinas were done because we were curious to know whether a malformed retina transmitted "malformed" information to the brain. If the brain learned a pattern through a malformed eye would it recognize the pattern if it then saw the pattern through a normal eye? We irradiated one eye with 600-r at birth, then trained the rat to criterion on stripes or triangles, using the malformed eye alone while the lids of the normal eye were sutured closed, as described earlier. Then the normal eye was opened, the irradiated eye closed, and the animals were tested on the respective patterns. Six normal and four irradiated animals were used. All made several errors in the first session in which the normal eye was used. One irradiated and two normal rats then made perfect scores (criterion) in the second session. Another irradiated and two normals reached criterion in the third session, and the remaining irradiated and controls took four or more. Some developed conjunctivitis and keratitis with the protracted lid closure which might have contributed to the slow transfer in some animals. We concluded that the brain recognized a pattern it had learned through a malformed eye when it saw it later through a normal eye (Hicks & D'Amato, 1971).

Histologic studies of the irradiated retinas. The serial sections of the whole eyes kept in situ in the skull base were examined with conventional dye stains. Rat retinas have been peculiarly refractory to Golgi stains, but we have devised one that reveals many elements. With it, we are presently studying normal eyes and eyes exposed to 200- or 600-r. The 200-r retinas retained a good deal of the normal interrelations of the cells in the traditional layers despite the reduced numbers of elements in the inner nuclear layer and the rosette arrangement mentioned earlier. The 600-r retinas, extremely reduced in volume, yielded correspondingly few stained cells. These cells had the usual individual morphology, but were in disarray, with ganglion cell axones forming aberrant bundles, as noted before.

Remarks on functional adaptation in irradiated retinas. We are accustomed to think of extraordinarily complex circuits and precisely organized spatial relationships among the elements of the retina as it encodes information for the brain about pattern detail, moving objects, and relative distances in the visual world around it. The deficiencies and especially the spatial disarray of the retinal cells in the 600-r animals made it hard to believe that any appreciable function was possible.

In the rat, a major part of the optic nerve and tracts (ganglion cell axones) grew after birth, and most of their connections with the brain seemed to have been established over a period of three or four weeks after birth (Lund & Lund, 1972). The ganglion cells, which were not destroyed in the irradiated animals, would have been developmentally specified as to position in the retina at birth (Jacobson & Hunt, 1973) but the connections made by their axones could still have been altered. We hypothesized that this postnatal axone growth might somehow be a factor in functional adaptation of the malformed retina, that as vision developed in the third week, some modification of connections would make the eye more useful. The interocular transfer experiments seemed to have quashed that idea, as the brain viewed the code from an irradiated or normal eye as the same.

Though the histologic picture made it difficult, another view could be taken that, for all its disorder, the 600-r retina represented essentially a massive reduction of the amount of visual machinery. In this view, the animals' performances were not all that great, for in other experiments considerable visual function was retained in animals with other parts of their visual apparatus massively reduced. Lashley (1939), Isaacson and his colleagues (Lewellyn, Lowes, & Issacson, 1969), and Galambos, Norton, and Frommel (1967) had shown that animals with extensive removals of visual cortex or less than 2% of the optic tract fibers remaining were capable of considerable detail vision. In our own experiments (unpublished), rats from whom most of the visual cortex and superior colliculi were removed at birth performed the platform jumping exercises about as well as the 600-r animals, and reached criterion on stripes and triangles though they required many more trials.

In summary, the retina could be made severely deformed and deficient by irradiation at birth, yet manage to function. Comparisons of effects of (radiation) malformation on the development of function in different parts of the nervous system can only be very general because of the nature of the function of the parts: cerebellar malformations impair movement, retinal malformations reduce vision.

EFFECTS OF INJURY TO THE DEVELOPING MOTOR–SENSORY CORTEX–CORTICOSPINAL SYSTEM

Motor–sensory cortex and corticospinal tract. The motor–sensory cortex, which occupies much of the frontal half of the isocortex in rats, and the corticospinal tract system, one of its major outflows, are concepts based on an accumulation of anatomic, physiologic, and behavioral studies. Information about them and definitions of them are approximations, as they are for many other neural systems, and of course such systems do not operate in isolation. Ablation of the motor–sensory cortex is followed by degeneration of a vast population of axonal fibers (as seen in Fink–Heimer–Nauta silver stains for degenerating axones) that travel to myriads of destinations in other parts of the cortex, basal ganglia, thalamus, brain stem, and spinal cord. In the more caudal parts of the internal capsule the outflow becomes increasingly sharply defined. It forms the pyramids in the medulla, hence its other name, pyramidal tract, and crosses there decussating with its fellow tract from the other side, and ending in medullary nuclei or continuing caudalward to destinations in the spinal cord.

The corticospinal system in its more caudal reaches is but a fraction of the whole motor–sensory cortex outflow. The rat has one of the largest corticospinal tracts in proportion to brain size, among mammals, in respect to the medullary and spinal cord parts. Surgical section of the medullary pyramids in rats (Barron, 1934) or cats (Liddel & Phillips, 1944) abolished tactile placing reactions which are best regarded as reflexes concerned with positioning the feet on terrain during locomotion. The corticospinal system has come to be considered as a guidance and facilitating system for movement, exercising this governance in large measure through posterior column and spinal trigeminal nuclei, the medullary reticular formation, and spinal interneurons.

We are studying this system in the rat, particularly its growth in relation to developing motor function. We are interested in how infant and mature rats adapt functionally after ablation of all of the motor–sensory cortex, as well as we can define it, or of specific portions of it. We are interested in what anatomic modifications of the cortex and corticospinal tract, that could be called plasticity, may follow these ablations. We summarize some results of our experiments thus far, and then indicate some directions in which experiments now being done may lead.

Hemispherectomy in newborn and mature rats. Studies had shown that hemispherectomy in newborn rats did not paralyze them, nor did it have any neurologic effects that our examinations could show until the middle of the third week (Hicks & D'Amato, 1970). Then in a period of about a day, usually during the 17th day, the animals lost their tactile placing responses in the limbs opposite the lesions, permanently. In one litter with four such animals, the loss developed almost exactly simultaneously among the four within a 20-hr period on the 17th day: the responses became progressively less and less likely to be elicited until they simply no longer occurred.

Tactile placing could be demonstrated in several ways, which we consider later, but in the hemispherectomized animals, we relied principally on the following two ways. One was the laboratory procedure of touching the lateral aspect of the rat's forefoot in a lateral direction to the vertical side of a level board or similar ledge.

The normal response was a brisk raising of the limb and placing the foot precisely on top of the board. The animal was prevented from seeing the ledge or touching it with whiskers by the experimenter's finger or a cloth face mask, since stimuli through these channels could elicit placing. The second way was to observe the natural function of tactile placing, the positioning of the feet on the ground in locomotion, particularly if the terrain was irregular. For example, a young mature rat hemispherectomized at birth appeared to walk or run virtually normally on a flat level surface, such as a board track, but the feet contralateral to the lesion easily slipped off the edge of the track; or if the animal jumped from one platform to another, which it did essentially as well as a normal rat, its feet also slipped if they came to the edge of the platform. The feet were fairly quickly retrieved, as a rule, but slipped repeatedly if they came to an edge. Normal rats almost never let the feet slip off such edges, and if they did retrieval was lightning quick.

In mature rats, hemispherectomy temporarily incapacitated the animals severely, but in a few days they closely resembled mature animals that had been hemispherectomized at birth, except in one aspect of stride which we mention later.

Ablation of motor–sensory cortex in newborn and mature rats. Removal of motor–sensory cortex on one side was expected to affect locomotion and tactile placing in a manner similar to that of hemispherectomy. It did in mature animals; as Phillip Bard originally showed, tactile placing was immediately lost in the limbs on the side contralateral to the ablation (Fig. 2). When the operation was done in the newborn, the placing loss on the 17th day was often less rapidly completed than after hemispherectomy. It sometimes faded out more gradually over a period of days or sometimes longer. Whether one considered hemispherectomy or motor–sensory cortex ablation alone, the ultimate question was, What mechanisms came into play in the third week to turn off a placing response that had been working well since the first week of infant life? Both cerebral hemispheres were involved, as the following experiments indicate, though we are far from understanding the mechanisms.

When motor–sensory cortex was bilaterally removed from newborn rats there was another paradox. The animals did not lose their tactile placing responses in the third week, or any time thereafter (with certain uncommon exceptions). They usually could not jump from one platform to another, but in a few instances, learned to jump only after many weeks. They turned awkwardly and sometimes backed up when initiating walking, but once started they could walk and run on the flat in a fairly normal manner. They might fall off a jumping platform in a vain effort to initiate a jump, but there was no slipping from loss of placing as in unilaterally ablated rats. (Some of these animals were tested on the Lashley apparatus described in the previous section and learned the visual pattern discrimination sequences, though in some cases more slowly than normals.)

When both motor–sensory cortices were removed from a mature rat, it immediately lost its tactile placing responses on both sides (Fig. 2), but it could jump

REMOVAL OF MOTOR-SENSORY CORTEX

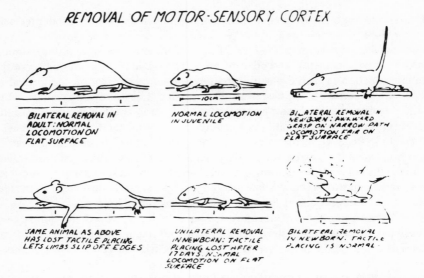

FIG. 2. Tracings of movie frames of performing rats, showing some effects of removing the motor–sensory cortex, and normal locomotion in a juvenile. The figures on the left are of a rat 8 weeks old a few days after both motor–sensory cortices were ablated. The upper middle figure is that of a normal juvenile just assuming the mature pattern of locomotion at 17 days. Below it, a rat 17 days old, hemispherectomized at birth, shows the effects of loss of motor–sensory cortex, letting its feet slip off the edge of a track. At right, above, a rat several weeks old traversing a narrow path with difficulty. Both of its motor–sensory cortices were removed at birth. Below it, a demonstration of tactile placing in a juvenile rat whose left forefoot had been touched to the edge of the track a moment earlier.

like a normal rat from one platform to another although its feet on both sides slipped off an edge as in unilateral ablation.

One might ask whether after motor–sensory cortex had been removed on one side at birth, removal of the opposite cortex as the animal matured would restore the placing that was lost as a result of the newborn operation. It did not restore it in the few experiments we have tried: The animal now had lost its placing on both sides. The turning off phenomenon exercised by the remaining ipsilateral cortex in the third week became permanently fixed.

Functional and morphologic growth of the corticospinal tract system. Some developmental events that occurred in the infant and juvenile period related to the altered placing responses just discussed.

In the middle of the third week there was a rapid transition from an infantile pattern of locomotion to the adult pattern of walking and running, in which the precisely sequenced, progressive movements of the limbs and placing of the feet on the ground took over (Hicks & D'Amato, 1970). The change was relatively rapid. The animal's locomotion on the 16th day was still the infant's awkward mixture of crawling and walking, something like that of a salamander. During the 17th day, or sometimes between the 17th and 18th day, this was all pulled together into the extremely smooth action of the adult pattern, coordinating every part of the body from head to tail (Fig. 2). The normal rat 16 days old would still let its hind limbs dangle over the edge of a track, but from the 17th day on this was virtually never allowed to happen. Slow motion movies showed this normal development, as well as deviations from it, particularly well, and indeed much of it could not be seen by eye alone. Galloping, in which the limb movement sequences were different from ordinary running and walking, did not seem to appear until some five or six weeks of age. It was an occasional part of playful running as well as a response to fright in these juveniles.

(In our notation here newborn was the first day of life and operations on the newborn were performed between 12 and 24 hr after birth. Centering attention on locomotion, infancy could be said to extend to about the 16th day. The juvenile period continued thereafter to about seven or eight weeks when reproduction could begin, heralding adulthood. Maturity was used more variously: a rat three to four weeks old was relatively quite mature as to locomotion, jumping, and beginning to discriminate visual patterns.)

A study of the growth of the corticospinal tract revealed that it too underwent its greatest development in the brain stem in the third week (Hicks & D'Amato, 1973a, b). Using conventional histologic methods and Fink–Heimer–Nauta preparations after appropriate cortex ablations in series of rats of various ages from birth to adulthood, we found that a small number of pilot fibers had reached the caudal medulla, decussated there, and entered the cervical spinal cord at the time of birth. In the next several days these pilots had extended to the lumbar spinal cord levels, a growth rate of a little less than a centimeter a day. Then between 10 and 14 days, the tract in the caudal part of the cerebral peduncle and in the pons had enlarged considerably owing to increasing numbers of fibers, and enlargement in the medullary pyramids was greatest between 10 and 21 days. Growth in cross section in the spinal cord lagged a little behind the medulla, the increase continuing into the fourth week. Myelination of the tract was protracted and still incomplete at 25 days. Thus it did not contribute substantially to the growth described here. It hardly needs to be said that there were other coincidences between growth of parts of the nervous system and locomotor development in the juvenile period: growth of ascending fiber systems in the spinal cord paralleled that of the corticospinal tract, and the cerebellum was undergoing a major part of its development in this period. We have centered attention on the corticospinal system because of the functional relationships between it and the placing and positioning responses that were an integral part of locomotion. Further experiments, which we mention later, may bring these relationships closer.

Plasticity in the growth of the corticospinal tract and motor-sensory cortex. The capacity of the infant nervous system to change the direction of its growth and differentiation was illustrated in two phenomena that follow motor–sensory cortex ablation in the newborn rat. They are of interest to us because, as examples of morphologic plasticity in the growth of the corticospinal

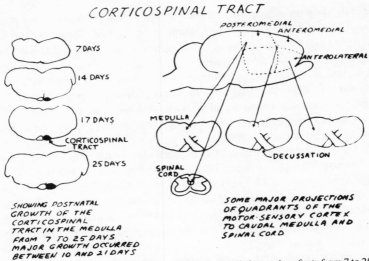

FIG. 3. At left, tracings of frontal sections of the mid-medulla in a series of rats from 7 to 25 days old to show the growth of the corticospinal tract which forms one of the pyramids (black) in the medulla at this level. At right, the quadrants of the motor–sensory cortex are diagrammed on an outline of a mature rat's brain. The arrows indicate some major areas of projection of the corticospinal tract to the caudal medulla and (cervical) spinal cord.

tract and differentiation of the isocortex, they suggested hypothetical mechanisms for functional plasticity.

The first was the response of the developing corticospinal tract to unilateral ablation of the motor–sensory cortex or to hemispherectomy in the newborn. In the normal rat, the corticospinal tract in the caudal medulla is completely crossed. After the ablation in the newborn, a considerable number of axones did not cross but formed a miniature uncrossed corticospinal tract whose fibers terminated, as far as our methods can reveal, in the same nuclei in the caudal medulla and spinal cord as normal crossed fibers would have. This aberrant response could be stimulated by ablation in rats five days old, but by nine days it was scant, and by two weeks we could not longer detect it (Leong & Lund, 1973). Older animals did not form the uncrossed tract (Hicks & D'Amato, 1970). The time sequence of the development of the aberrant, uncrossed tract paralleled that of the normal as far as we have studied it, progressing through the medulla in the third week.

Whether the little tract functioned usefully was not established. About the only difference we could find between rats hemispherectomized at birth or maturity was the length and character of stride during running on a measured track as shown in slow motion movies (Hicks & D'Amato, 1970). A normal part of the rat's stride was a forward thrust of the forefoot, fanning of the digits, and then precise downward placing of the foot, digits first, on the ground (Fig. 2). Animals operated on as infants retained these characteristics, whereas those hemispherectomized at maturity lost some of the thrust and had a shorter than normal stride. We suggested that the uncrossed tract in the animals operated on as infants, by providing bilateral corticospinal tract representation, might have spared the stride, but this is wholly speculative at present.

The other alteration following ablation of motor–sensory cortex in the newborn was a transformation in the differentiation of the isocortex adjacent to the site of the ablation. It was seen regularly in the medial dorsal isocortex in all animals in a series with subtotal motor–sensory cortex ablations: what would normally have differentiated into medial isocortex instead became an extension of the cingular cortex. Cingular cortex, forming the medial cortex of the hemisphere, has a peculiarly distinctive cytoarchitecture, including among other features, a condensation of small neurons in layer 2. The result of the ablations was that the area of this kind of cortex was considerably increased, rising lateralward toward the vertex. The experiments emphasized how immature and modifiable the infant cortex was, and recalled that many young neurons continued to migrate into the cortex during the early postnatal period (Hicks & D'Amato, 1968), and that many afferent and efferent fiber connections as well as local synapses were yet to be formed.

The cingular cortex transformation led one to think that regions of cortex normally destined for one functional role might be altered to take on another one. Two rats of a dozen that had had both motor-sensory cortices removed at birth retained their tactile placing reflexes as expected, but after several months these reflexes began to fade out. In one animal they were lost unilaterally; in the other, they were lost bilaterally. The possibility is being investigated that posterior cortex might have been transformed into aberrant motor–sensory cortex whose slowly forming "corticospinal" axones had turned off the responses. Ablations of this supposedly transformed cortex with Fink–Heimer–Nauta techniques are the first step toward examining the hypothesis.

Morphologic and functional aspects of different parts of the motor-sensory cortex. Much of what we believe we know about the function of the nervous system is inferred from the effects of surgical ablations of parts of it or the consequences of disease in animals and humans. Mechanisms for some functions are certainly concentrated in particular parts, but the nervous system is not an aggregate of independent units that do this or that, but of closely interlocked systems. Ablation of a part may tell us by the resulting functional deficits what machinery resided there, but the deficits may also reflect the expression of mechanisms situated elsewhere that are no longer held in check by what was ablated.

To find out more about how the two motor–sensory cortices and their derivatives, the corticospinal tracts, governed the placing and positioning of limbs in locomotion, we have begun to search for relations between the anatomic projections of the corticospinal tract from different parts of the motor–sensory cortex and disturbances of motor functions resulting from ablation of those parts. We have divided the cortex arbitrarily into quadrants (Fig. 3), and we are studying the anatomy and function from birth to three weeks, and to about seven weeks. We have preliminary results from these experiments that can be summarized as follows.

The more caudal projections, with which we will be concerned here, from the anterior lateral quadrant went largely to the spinal trigeminal and lateral reticular nuclear regions of the caudal medulla. There was very little projection to posterior column (gracile and cuneate) nuclei or into the spinal cord. This quadrant overlapped the cortical regions mapped by Woolsey (1952) and his colleagues, in which motor and sensory functions involving head, face, mouth, and probably forefoot were partly represented. Woolsey's cortical regions were mapped by recording potentials evoked in the cortex by stimuli over the body surface, or by stimulating the cortex directly and recording movements of various parts of the body. When we ablated this anterior lateral quadrant on one side in the newborn, or in three- or seven-week-old rats, tactile placing or locomotion on a flat track were not impaired, and direct observation did not reveal any handicap in traversing a narrow path, but movies of this activity remain to be analyzed.

The anterior medial quadrant projected predominantly to the dorsal column nuclei. Tactile placing laterally with the forefoot was sluggish after ablation of it and sometimes could not be elicited. The hind foot opposite the lesion was retrieved somewhat awkwardly when it slipped off the narrow pathway (normal animals slipped, too, but retrieved instantly). The quadrant overlapped the head, mouth, and forelimb motor region of Woolsey. The projections from the posterior medial quadrant, which included some of both motor and sensory representations of the posterior half of the body in Woolsey's topography, went to the posterior column nuclei and the spinal cord. Of all quadrants, ablation of this one, on one side, affected tactile placing responses and locomotion on irregular terrain the most seriously. If the animal was carefully placed on the edge of a flat track, it would let the limbs opposite the lesion dangle over the side until it initiated walking again, resembling the animal at left in Fig. 2. On a narrow path these limbs, contralateral to the lesion, slipped off easily, grasped awkwardly, and were retrieved clumsily. On a falt surface, walking and running appeared normal.

Anatomic data are not yet complete on the posterior lateral quadrant, but ablation of it, on one side, impaired placing and locomotion to about the same degree the anterior medial quadrant ablation did, and so far as our experiments have progressed, affected reflexes only on the side contralateral to the lesion. The region corresponded partly to the sensory cortex, called somatic sensory 2, that had some bilateral representation of the body surface in Woolsey's topography.

We mentioned reliance earlier on testing lateral tactile placing and observation of placing and positioning of limbs in natural locomotion. We have used or explored a variety of examinations, including other tests of tactile placing, visual placing, hopping, stepping, running on horizontal ladders and on narrow longitudinal strips, climbing, and such elements of a neurologic examination that can be applied to a rat (Hicks & D'Amato, 1970; Hicks et al., 1969). One cannot be sure in advance that one has selected proper tests for an experiment, but in the present studies we have continued the tactile placing tests with fore and hind limbs, observations of locomotion on a board track, and walking and running along elevated narrow pathways (Fig. 2). The latter were a length of wood strip a half-inch wide and two approximated parallel quarter-inch dowels. Traversing these latter was just difficult enough for normal rats to slip a foot or a limb off occasionally and to magnify deficits in animals with ablations. Whether the ablations were performed at one day, three weeks, or about seven weeks, the subjects were members of a litter that were introduced to the experimental apparatus at about 13 days of age and allowed to explore it in daily sessions (but less often after they were about five weeks old) until termination of the experiment. Two to four members of a litter were operated on and two or more normal littermates went through the same performances as controls. The animals ran across or otherwise negotiated (Fig. 2) the track and narrow pathways enthusiastically (or at least persistently) by the middle of the third week. Even quite handicapped animals persisted at this activity.

Besides contributing to the preliminary results of the quadrant ablations just outlined, this approach suggested that there were differences in effects of similar ablations at the three different ages, and differences in effects of bilateral ablations depending on what quadrants were removed. Seven-weeks-old rats seemed to show more flagrant dangling of the limbs contralateral to certain unilateral lesions than animals operated on at the earlier ages (Fig. 2). Our first experience with ablation of the posterior medial and the posterior lateral quadrants, sparing the anterior quadrants, on both sides showed that the dysfunction following this partial ablation differed from that following removal of all four quadrants. With removal of the whole motor–sensory cortex, the animal though awkward in initiating locomotion, as noted earlier, tactually placed with both forelimbs, and also visually placed. The animal with the posterior quadrants bilaterally removed, but the anterior ones spared, not only retained tactile placing in all four limbs, but the responses were much exaggerated and the limbs over-shot the mark considerably. It did not place visually, ignoring a ledge on either side until limbs or whiskers touched it. Its locomotion was on a wide base and awkward, and it had great difficulty negotiating the narrow pathways, being almost unable to get across. When the animal was several weeks old, it could visually place, but the character of its locomotion and exaggerated placing remained about the same.

Remarks on the growing motor–sensory cortex–corticospinal system. The experiments illustrated how much nervous system development went on after birth, both structurally and functionally, and how potentially plastic some of this postnatal growth was. Major development of the corticospinal system and its functions occurred in the third week, coinciding with a rapid transition from infantile to mature patterns of locomotion.

That a developmental defect in infancy might not show itself functionally until some time later was illustrated by the loss of placing reflexes 17 days after motor–sensory cortex ablation at birth. The difficulty of determining "localization of function" in the brain by ablations, especially in early life, was also illustrated in this latter experiment. The loss of function involved mechanisms, not at all understood presently, in both the growing cortex that had been removed and the growing cortex that remained. The problems of localization of function and predicting what kind of adaptation may follow an injury were further illustrated by the bilateral ablations in the newborn. The disturbances of function that might be attributed to ablation of one part of the cortex depended very much on whether other parts were present or absent.

REFERENCES

Barron, D. H. The results of unilateral pyramidal section in the rat. *Journal of Comparative Neurology*, 1934, **60**, 45–55.

Dennenberg, V. H. Experimental programming of life histories in the rat. In A. Ambrose (Ed.), *Stimulation in early infancy*, New York: Academic Press, 1969.

Falk, J. L. & D'Amato, C. J. Automation of pattern discrimination in the rat. *Psychological Reports*, 1962, **10**, 24.

Fowler, H., Hicks, S. P., D'Amato, C. J., & Beach, F. A. Effects of fetal irradiation on behavior in the albino rat. *Journal of Comparative and Physiological Psychology*, 1962, **55**, 309–314.

Furchgott, E. Behavioral effects of ionizing radiation. *Psychological Bulletin*, 1963, **60**, 157–199.

Galambos, R., Norton, T. T., & Frommel, G. P. Optic tract lesions sparing pattern vision in cats. *Experimental Nuerology*, 1967, **18**, 8–25.

Ginsburg, B. E. Developmental behavioral genetics. In N. B. Talbot, J. Kagan, & L. Eisenberg (Eds.), *Behavioral science in pediatric medicine*. Philadelphia: Saunders, 1971.

Hicks, S. P., & D'Amato, C. J. How to design and build abnormal brains using radiation during development. In W. S. Fields & M. M. Desmond (Eds.), *Disorders of the developing nervous system*. Springfield: Thomas, 1961.

Hicks, S. P., & D'Amato, C. J. Malformation and regeneration of the mammalian retina following experimental radiation. In L. Michaux & M. Field (Eds.), *Les phakomatoses cerebrales, deuxieme colloque international, malformations congenitales de l'encephale*. Paris: S.P.E.I., 1963.

Hicks, S. P., & D'Amato, C. J. Effects of ionizing radiations on mammalian development. In D. H. M. Woolman (Ed.), *Advances in teratology*. London: Logos Press, 1966.

Hicks, S.P., & D'Amato, C.J. Cell migrations to the isocortex in the rat. *Anatomical Record*, 1968, **160**, 619–634.

Hicks, S. P., & D'Amato, C. J. Visual and motor function after hemispherectomy in newborn and mature rats. *Experimental Neurology*, 1970, **29**, 416–438.

Hicks, S. P., & D'Amato, C. J. Visual function of rat retinas malformed by irradiation at birth (Abstract and exhibit), Society for Neuroscience, Proceedings of 1st Annual Meeting, Washington, D.C., October, 1971.

Hicks, S. P., & D'Amato, C. J. Effects of ablation of motor-sensory cortex are different in newborn and mature rats. (Abstract) Society for Neuroscience, Proceedings of 3rd Annual Meeting, San Diego, November, 1973.   (a)

Hicks, S. P., & D'Amato, C. J. Normal and aberrant development of corticospinal tract in rat. (Abstract and exhibit) Michigan Chapter: Society for Neuroscience, Proceedings of the 4th Annual Spring Meeting, University of Michigan, Ann Arbor, May, 1973.   (b)

Hicks, S. P., D'Amato, C. J., & Falk, J. L. Effects of radiation on structural and behavioral development. *International Journal of Neurology*, 1962, **3**, 535–548.

Hicks, S. P., D'Amato, C. J., French, B. C., Klein, S. J., & Austin, L. L. Effects of regional irradiation or ablation of the infant rat cerebellum on motor development. In M. R. Sikov & D. D. Malum (Eds.), *Radiobiology of the fetal and juvenile mammal: Ninth annual Hanford biology symposium.* Oak Ridge, Tenn: USAEC Div. Tech, Inform. Extension, 1969.

Hicks, S. P., D'Amato, C. J., & Lowe, M. J. The development of the mammalian nervous system. I. Malformations of the brain, especially the cerebral cortex, induced in rats by radiation. II. Some mechanisms of the malformations of the cortex. *Jouranl of Comparative Neurology,* 1959, **113**, 435–469.

Jacobson, M., & Hunt, R. K. The origins of nerve cell specificity. *Scientific American,* 1973, **228**, 26–35.

Joffe, J. M. *Prenatal determinants of behavior.* Oxford: Pergamon, 1969.

Lashley, K. The mechanism of vision. I. A method for rapid analysis of pattern-vision in the rat. *Journal of Genetic Psychology,* 1930, **37**, 453–460.

Lashley, K. The mechanism of vision. XVI. The functioning of small remnants of the visual cortex. *Journal of Comparative Neurology,* 1939, **70**, 45-67.

Leong, S. K., & Lund, R. D. Anomalous bilateral corticofugal pathways in albino rats after neonatal lesions. *Brain Research,* 1973, **62**, 218–221.

Lewellyn, D., Lowes, G., & Isaacson, R. L. Visually mediated behaviors following neocortical destruction in the rat. *Journal of Comparative and Physiological Psychology,* 1969, **69**, 25–52.

Liddel, E. G. T., & Phillips, C. G. Pyramidal section in the cat. *Brain,* 1944, **67**, 1–9.

Lund, R. D., & Lund, J. S. Development of synaptic patterns in the superior colliculus of the rat. *Brain Research* 1972, **42**, 1–20.

Money, J. & Ehrhardt, A. A. *Man & woman, boy & girl: The differentiation and dimorphism of gender identity from conception to maturity.* Baltimore: Johns Hopkins University Press, 1972.

Woolsey, C. N. Patterns of localization in sensory and motor areas of the cerebral cortex. In *The biology of mental health and disease; The 27th annual conference of the Milbank memorial fund.* New York: Hoeber, 1952.

3

SOCIAL RESPONSES
TO BLIND INFANT MONKEYS[1]

Gershon Berkson
Illinois State Pediatric Institute

In *The Descent of Man* (p. 475), Darwin stated that herds of animals sometimes gore or worry to death a disabled member of the group so that his presence will not attract a predator. Social selection for defects has since been more or less assumed to be an obvious aspect of natural selection in animals. However, instances of one animal of a group killing a defective individual who is not already moribund are difficult to find in the literature. More commonly, it is believed (Wynne-Edwards, 1962, p. 547) that density-dependent social mechanisms, such as competition for territory, force disabled individuals into situations where they are more vulnerable to predation or starvation (Errington, 1967). Intraspecific contributions to mortality are therefore generally indirect.

In the same passage, Darwin described social compensation for defects. He cited instances in which birds kept a blind member of a flock alive by feeding him. Disabled animals apparently do sometimes survive in natural habitats (Berkson, 1974; Schultz, 1956), and it is likely that they benefit from the same social forces that protect normal individuals. Survival of disabled animals seems likely to the degree that protective social behaviors are characteristic of the group in which the animal lives. More specifically, it seems that animals who live in permanent social groups that have low intrinsic fertility rates and that raise dependent young for long periods are likely to tolerate and compensate for defects in group members (Berkson, 1973a).

Most species of higher primates fulfill these criteria, and it appears that they do compensate for defects in infants and tolerate them in older animals. Rumbaugh (1965) and more recently Rosenblum and Youngstein (1974) have shown that monkey mothers compensate for temporary experimentally produced disabilities

---

[1] I am especially indebted to Lilian Tosic, Linda Massen, and Russell Puetz who did the observations and analyses.

in their infants, and Lindburg (1969) and Berkson (1973b) indicate that this is also true of permanent defects.

Studies preliminary to the one I am going to describe have shown that infant monkeys with a visual acuity deficit survived until seven months of age in a natural habitat in Thailand. While they were alive, their group adapted its behavior to the infant's deficit (Berkson, 1970). A repetition of this experiment (Berkson, 1973b) in a free-ranging monkey colony where food is freely available and predators absent has thus far shown that partially blind animals have survived until almost three years of age. For practical reasons, it has not been possible to examine intensively social responses to these monkeys. However, I have been able to do a longitudinal study of totally and partially blind individuals in four laboratory groups of monkeys. We have recently completed the first year of observations which show relatively normal social development in the home cage.

METHOD

The animals were part of four crab-eating monkey troops *(Macaca fascicularis)* housed in 4.8-m × 3.9-m × 1.7-m cyclone fence cages, each troop in a separate room. Food and water were freely available. The troops were initially composed of an adult male, four adult females, and two 1.9–2.6-kg male juveniles. Each adult female was pregnant when the troop was formed, and their offspring were the experimental and control groups. Within three weeks after birth, six infants were made partially blind (Berkson & Karrer, 1968). In addition five infants were made totally blind and eleven infants underwent a control operation. The experimental and control groups were randomly distributed to the four troops (Table 1).

The troop was observed on three days every two weeks, with eight momentary observations of 37 categories of behavior taken on all animals on each observation day. Percentage of agreement on occurrences averaged 95 for the various categories. In addition to the routine observations which continued throughout the year, each group was exposed to a series of "stress tests" every three months to determine the response of the stressed troops to the experimental and control animals. Detailed quantitative data were collected and log books were kept of both routine and stress observations. Only the data on the routine quantitative observations will be reported here.

RESULTS

In our previous study, partially blind animals survived in a free-ranging environment where food was plentiful and there were no predators. No mortality was therefore expected in the first year in this laboratory study, even though the visual deficit was more severe and the density of the animals very high. This expectation

TABLE 1
Composition and Characteristics of the Groups on February 15, 1974

No. Group	Sex	Birth	Mother	No. Group	Sex	Birth	Mother
Room I				Room II			
01 Adult	M			01 Adult	M		
02 Adult	F			02 Adult	F		
03 Adult	F			03 Adult	F		
04 Adult	F	(Died 4/25/72)		04 Adult	F		
05 Adult	F			05 Adult	F		
06 Juv	M			06 Juv	M		
07 Juv	M			07 Juv	M		
08 Partial	M	1/ 3/70	04	08 Control	F	9/12/71	02
09 Control	M	1/29/70	02	09 Partial	F	10/31/71	03
10 Partial	M	4/17/70	03	10 Total	M	8/ 6/72	04
11 Control	M	7/28/70	05	11 Partial	M	12/ 2/71	05
12 Control	M	8/19/71	03	12 Total	M	9/18/72	02
13 Control	M	5/10/72	05	13 Control	F	10/17/72	05
14 Adult	F	Replaced 04		14 Control	F	4/ 6/73	03
15 Total	M	12/10/72	02				
Room III				Room IV			
01 Adult	M			01 Adult	M		
02 Adult	F			02 Adult	F		
03 Adult	F			03 Adult	F		
04 Adult	F			04 Adult	F		
05 Adult	F	(Died 2/12/74)		05 Adult	F		
06 Juv	M			06 Juv	M		
07 Juv	M			07 Juv	M		
08 Control	F	1/12/72	04	08 Total	M	6/10/72	04
09 Partial	F	1/24/72	05	09 Partial	F	8/ 2/72	03
10 Control	M	5/19/72	03	10 Control	M	11/25/72	05
11 Total	M	2/17/72	02	11 Control	F	11/30/72	02
12 Control	F	10/31/72	05	12 Control	F	8/27/73	04
13 Control	M	6/23/73	02				
14 Control	F	7/20/73	04				

was confirmed: No animal died in its first year. We therefore have no evidence of social selection for visual deficit in macaque monkeys in the first year of life.

Despite the fact that they were blind, all experimental animals learned to feed themselves by eating the easily available monkey biscuits and drinking at one of the six watering faucets in the cage. Even the totally blind infants knew their way around the cage. Although they were obviously awkward in traveling, they were able to get to the vicinity of the faucet, feel their way to its exact location, and drink normally. Initially we thought that locomotion paths were more stereotyped in

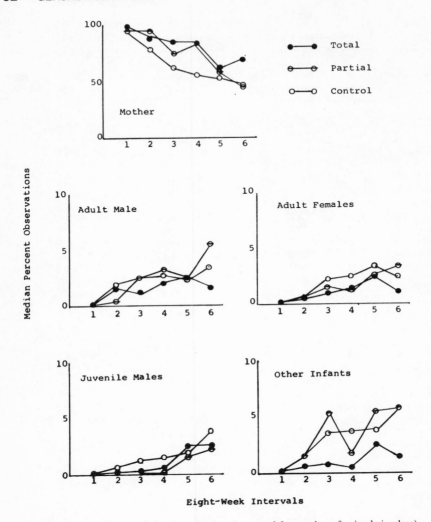

Fig. 1.   Animal closest to infant by role class (corrected for number of animals in class).

blind than control animals, but a series of intensive observations did not confirm this. The relatively normal interaction with the environment was also reflected in a general lack of difference between the three groups of infants in their amount of independent walking and interaction with the physical environment.

It is therefore not very surprising that the social differences of the three groups were negligible. Although there were normal age changes in sociability and although the groups ordered themselves in the expected ways on the social measures, in no case was the blindness variable or its interactions with age statistically significant.

Figure 1 portrays the proportion of time the infants of each group were closest to members of various age–sex role classes. The totally blind animals became independent of their mothers somewhat more slowly than controls and also developed relationships with other animals more slowly. However, these group differences were not significant.

Figure 2 shows the relationship with the mother in more detail. The blind infants clung to their mothers and were in contact with her somewhat more. The mother also groomed and cared for the blind infant by retrieving it, preventing it from leaving her, punishing it, and carrying it on her back slightly more than controls.

In our study in a free-ranging monkey colony, it was shown that certain animals other than the mother would care for the blind animals. Figure 3 shows that this also occurred in this experiment. However, it was clear that this kind of care was sporadic and as much related to characteristics of the caretaker as of the infant. Two adult males spent an appreciable amount of time carrying infants. However, they were the only males to do so, and they were seen with both normal and blind infants. Adult females other than the mother did sometimes stay close to infants,

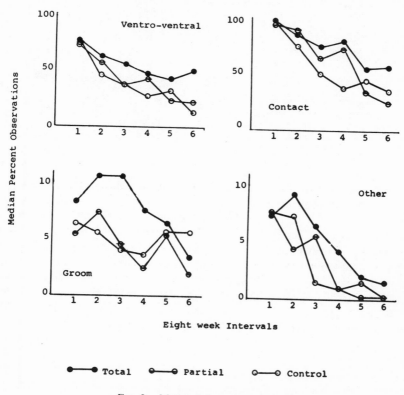

FIG. 2.   Mother–infant relationship.

FIG. 3.   Adult male holding infant.

but in only three two-week periods was an individual female the closest animal to a baby more than 10% of the time.

Figure 4 shows that with age social activities of infants with animals other than the mother increased. Totally blind animals were somewhat slower than normals in this regard. However, again, only the age effect was statistically significant.

Sinc the totally blind animals were more awkward than the controls, one might expect that they would be in the way of other animals more often and would as a consequence be the object of aggression more frequently. Figure 4 shows that aggression toward all infants was low and that, if anything, the totally blind animals were less subject to aggressive acts than controls.

DISCUSSION

Vision is clearly an important sense mode in macaque monkeys. In a natural habitat, partially blind infants do not survive the first year. However, having normal vision is not apparently necessary for normal social integration during that

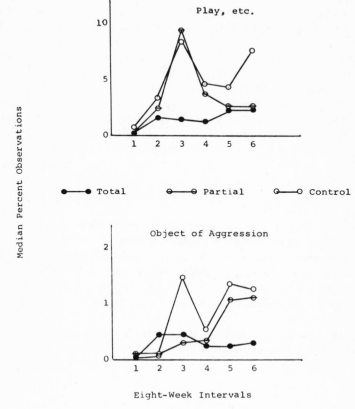

FIG. 4.   Infant social behavior.

period. It may be that social communication is not mediated by vision in any important way in the first year. More likely is that other sense modes can substitute for vision (viz. Latané, Joy, Meltzer, Lubell, & Cappell, 1972), and other animals modify their behavior to compensate for the visual defect.

Certainly there is no evidence of social selection for a visual deficit in monkey infants. Compensatory care seems to be the rule but seems to depend on the extent to which the environment makes the visual defect obvious. Social responses to blind infants do not differ qualitatively from those to normals. To the extent that the visual deficit makes them more awkward, they behave like younger infants and are responded to as if they were younger. It is not yet clear what are the limits of compensatory care, although there undoubtedly are some, and they probably reside in changes in maternal responsiveness (Rosenblum & Youngstein, 1974).

The blind infant survives partly because it benefits from the general protection afforded by permanent group living. Predators are warded off by the group, and having a number of animals traveling together probably increases the likelihood of finding food. In macaque monkeys, the main direct caretaker of the young is the mother. Other animals in the group also participate by carrying the baby and can therefore help to compensate for a defect. However, this participation by other group members is generally sporadic. Only certain animals in the group are prone to take care of the infant, and when this occurs, the care is extensive only in exceptional cases.

We are continuing our studies of blind animals in monkey groups by asking whether compensatory care turns to social selection as the mother–infant relationship declines and social relationships with peers normally take a greater proportion of the day. In this study, blind infants socialized with other animals somewhat less than controls, and we expect this difference will increase. We do not believe that the blind animals will be killed or excluded by the group, but we do think that they will be increasingly isolated within it.

Applying the results of these studies with monkeys to human response to disability depends on the assumption that there are certain universal features of human society that are a product of primate evolution. Most people live in relatively permanent social groups. All have low intrinsic fertility rates, and all raise small numbers of dependent young for long periods. Even severely disorganized human societies have these properties (Turnbull, 1972). These are the characteristics of subhuman primate societies mentioned above. To the extent then that monkey and human societies have similar social organizations, it is possible that patterns of compensatory care and social selection for defects are also similar. It would then be possible to consider social responses to disability as grounded not only in traditions that vary from culture to culture, but also in behavior patterns that evolved prior to man.

REFERENCES

Berkson, G., & Karrer, R. Travel vision in infant monkeys: Maturation rate and abnormal stereotyped movements. *Developmental Psychobiology,* 1968, **1**, 170–174.

Berkson, G. Defective infants in a feral monkey group. *Folia Primatalogica,* 1970, **12**, 284–289.

Berkson, G. Animal studies of treatment of impaired young by parents and the social group. Paper presented at Symposium of American Foundation of the Blind, New York, 1973.

Berkson, G. Social responses to abnormal infant monkeys. *American Journal of Physical Anthropology,* 1973, **38**, 583–586.

Berkson, G. Social responses of animals to infants with defects. In M. Lewis & L. Rosenblum (Eds.), *The effect of the infant on its caregiver.* New York: Wiley, 1974.

Darwin, Charles. *The origin of species and the descent of man.* New York: Modern Library.

Errington, P. L. *Of predation and life.* Ames: Iowa State University Press, 1967.

Latané, B., Joy, V., Meltzer, J., Lubell, B., & Cappell, H. Stimulus determinants of social attraction in rats. *Journal of Comparative and Physiological Psychology.* 1972, **79**, 13–21.

Lindburg, D. G. Behavior of infant rhesus monkeys with thalidomide-induced malformations. *Psychonomic Science,* 1969, **15**, 55–56.

Rosenblum, L., & Youngstein, K. Developmental changes in compensatory dyadic response in mother and infant monkeys. In M. Lewis & L. Rosenblum (Eds.), *The effect of the infant on its caregiver.* New York: Wiley, 1974.

Rumbaugh, D. M. Maternal care in relation to infant behavior in the squirrel monkey. *Psychological Reports*, 1965, **16**, 171.

Schultz, A. H. The occurrence and frequency of pathological and teratological conditions and twinning among non-human primates. *Primatologia*, 1956, **1**, 965–1014.

Turnbull, C. M. *The Mountain People*. New York: Simon and Schuster, 1972.

Wynne-Edwards, V. C. *Animal dispersion in relation to social behavior*. Edinburgh: Oliver and Boyd, 1962.

4

VULNERABILITY FOR ABNORMAL DEVELOPMENT: PREGNANCY OUTCOMES AND SEX DIFFERENCES IN MACAQUE MONKEYS

Gene Sackett
Richard Holm
Sharon Landesman-Dwyer
University of Washington

In this contribution we will consider the possibility of a nonhuman primate model for the experimental study of the causes, consequences, and possible prevention of poor pregnancy outcomes. Our primary concern is to identify prenatal, perinatal, and early postnatal factors related to abnormal or retarded behavioral development. To this end we will assess the outcomes of high risk pregnancies, such as prematurity and low birth weight, and the differential effects of various early environments on males and females. Considerations include (a) the human data on the causes and effects of poor pregnancy outcomes and sex differences in susceptibility to abnormal development; (b) the results of an epidemiological study of pregnancies in a pigtail macaque breeding colony, and related human data; and (c) the differential effects of privation rearing conditions on male and female rhesus monkeys.

RISK RELATED TO PREGNANCY OUTCOME AND SEX IN HUMANS

Pregnancy Outcomes

Hundreds of published studies consider factors correlated with poor pregnancy outcomes and the subsequent development of high risk infants. Although we cannot review these studies here, we will discuss certain maternal and infant characteristics that are well documented in connection with abnormal development and that may help to identify important causal factors.

The high risk pregnancy outcomes considered in this paper include spontaneous abortion, stillbirth, premature birth (lower end of the gestational age distribution), small-for-date birth (lower end of the weight distribution for a given gestational age), immature birth (characterized by physical, neurological, and behavioral signs for a given gestational age), and neonatal death. Many factors have been correlated with these high risk pregnancy outcomes, including genetic and chromosomal abnormalities (Sterling, 1970; Wolanski, 1970), maternal nutrition (Bergner & Susser, 1970; Manocha, 1972), maternal age, size, parity, and marital and socioeconomic status (Emanuel, 1972), maternal psychological stress (Ottinger & Simmons, 1964; Sontag, 1941), maternal diseases, infections, and physical trauma, and mechanical and physiological complications during labor and delivery (reviewed by Kappelman, 1971), and maternal medication and drug usage (Bowes, Brackbill, Conway, & Steinschneider, 1970; Brazelton, 1971). Unfortunately, most of these factors do not elucidate actual mechanisms responsible for poor fetal and infant development. Furthermore, there are many problems inherent in these correlative and retrospective studies related to sampling techniques, reliable data collection, and analytic methods. Nonetheless, the factors listed above have been significantly correlated with poor pregnancy outcome in a variety of studies over many years in different parts of the world.

Experimental studies of rodents (reviewed by Joffe, 1969) have demonstrated that preconceptual and prenatal "stress" to a mother significantly affects the development of her offspring. Furthermore, the offspring of stressed mothers are themselves at high risk for producing abnormal offspring. This intergenerational effect is difficult to assess precisely in humans, although epidemiologic studies have related the mother's early development (indexed by birth weight, nutrition, socioeconomic status, etc.) to poor pregnancy outcomes (Emanuel, 1972).

Consequences of poor pregnancy outcomes. Prematurity, low birth weight, and immaturity have been correlated with a variety of physical, physiological, and behavioral abnormalities. Despite serious methodological limitations (Braine, Heimer, Wortis, & Freedman, 1966), the overall evidence confirms that low-birth-weight, premature, or immature infants are at higher risk for abnormal postnatal development than are full-term, normal-birth-weight infants. The biomedical data supporting this conclusion are from many sources, including electrophysiological studies (Lundstrom & Elder, 1971; Metcalf, 1970), neurological testing (Illingworth, 1970; Sainte-Anne Dargassies, 1966), longitudinal assessment of physical and skeletal maturation (Fitzhardinge & Stevens, 1972), neuroanatomical data (Kosmarskaya, 1963), and epidemiological investigations of incidence of malformations, disease, and mortality (Miller, 1968). Behavioral and clinical data support the conclusion that these infants have more frequent and more serious brain damage, as seen in the rates for mental retardation, cerebral palsy, minimal cerebral dysfunction, perceptual–motor and learning problems, speech disorders, visual impairment, auditory hypersensitivity, lower performance on IQ and development tests, and poor school performance (reviewed by Wright, 1971). Many other behavioral patterns, such as more frequent parental rejection and abuse, have been related to prematurity and low birth weight (Hultin & Ottosson, 1971; Klein & Stern, 1971). Concerning physical growth, small perinates usually exhibit a "catch-up phenomenon" in height, weight, and bone age by two or three years of age, although *very* low-birth-weight infants are more likely to remain smaller than normal throughout their lives (Fitzhardinge & Stevens, 1972).

Clearly, there are many developmental problems associated with poor pregnancy outcomes. However, not all studies find immediate or long-term effects of prematurity or low birth weight. In fact, there appears to be considerable variability in the development of infants who are exposed to similar preconceptual, prenatal, perinatal, and neonatal variables. What innate or unidentified environmental factors contribute to the "buffered" or apparently normal development of certain high risk individuals? As discussed below, we feel that study of sex differences in vulnerability to abnormal development may further our understanding of individual differences in general. Studies that are primarily correlational and retrospective cannot adequately control the variables necessary to make valid conclusions about the causes or prevention of abnormal development. What is needed is an *experimental* methodology to study the contribution and interaction of genetic, parental, prenatal, perinatal, and early postnatal factors to subsequent physiological, physical, and behavioral development.

Sex Differences in Vulnerability to Abnormal Development

There are many reliable sex differences reported in susceptibility to abnormal development. Overall, males appear more vulnerable than females to adverse developmental effects of poor pregnancy outcomes (Miller, 1968). The one notable exception concerns rates of congenital malformations, particularly major central nervous system abnormalities, which appear to be higher in females. In general, the behavioral and physical development of males is slower and more likely to be deviant than that of females, from the time of prenatal differentiation on. Obviously, there are many fundamental biological differences between males and females. Which of these differences are responsible, and to what degree, for the differential vulnerability of the sexes to environmental influences is not known. Although many hypotheses have been advanced to account for particular differences, such as activation levels and cognitive performance, experimental confirmation is lacking. Briefly, we will present some of the sex differences in response to prenatal stress factors, physical trauma and disease, and behavioral and psychological status.

Stott (1957) studied the effects of prenatal maternal stress on the susceptibility of offspring to nonepidemic diseases during infancy. Stress was defined by psychological factors such as marital discord, personal difficulties with relatives, and chronic "anxiety" states reported by mothers during interviews. Significantly more males had nonepidemic illnesses during infancy (23%) than did females (12%). Of 245 males whose mothers were stressed during pregnancy, 41% developed illnesses during infancy. However, of 205 females whose mothers were similarly stressed, only 25% developed illnesses during infancy. In another sample, Stott found that nearly 50% of retarded children had mothers who were stressed during pregnancy, whereas only 15% of their normal siblings were subjected to prenatal stress factors.

Stevenson (1966) reviewed eight studies reporting sex differences in spontaneous abortion rates. From the second to ninth months of pregnancy, significantly more males were aborted than females. Overall, the average ratio reported was 2.3 abortions to 1 female abortion. Postnatally, males have higher mortality rates for all ages, averaging 1.3 deaths to every female death (Childs, 1965).

Concerning exposure to extreme environmental conditions, extensive studies of radiation at Hiroshima and Nagasaki (Greulich, Crimson, & Turner, 1953) show that boys were significantly more retarded in stature and skeletal age than were females, relative to the norms for each sex. Furthermore, females recovered to a greater degree than males by 8 years of age. This is consistent with Tanner's (1970) conclusion that on a variety of physical measures females are better "canalized" than males, i.e., following potentially adverse environmental, nutritional, or disease and trauma conditions, females are more likely to return to their projected growth curves than are males.

There are many provocative statistical differences in psychological status between adult males and females. Kramer, Pollack, Redick, and Lock (1972) reported on some of these, including (a) admission to mental hospitals (2.3 males:1.8 females); (b) mental illness rates (more males than females, except schizophrenia which, however, claimed more males in the 15- to 34-year-old range); (c) alcoholism rates (males 5–9 times higher than females); and (d) suicide rates (males 5–10 times higher than females). Regardless of whether these statistics represent innate or cultural differences, males exhibit more extreme behavioral deviations than females.

Collectively, these studies and many others support the following hypothesis: under normal circumstances, males are at higher risk for abnormal development than are females; and males appear to be more vulnerable to adverse effects of stressful or atypical prenatal and postnatal environments.

Epidemiology of Poor Pregnancy Outcome in a Primate Breeding Colony

In order to establish a valid experimental model to study pregnancy outcomes, we assessed the pattern of pregnancies in a colony of pigtail monkeys (*Macaca nemestrina*). The Regional Primate Research Center at the University of Washington maintains a breeding colony of 800 pigtail monkeys at Medical Lake, Washington. Breeding and medical history records, which have been computerized for 12 years, contain information on more than 1100 births. For our

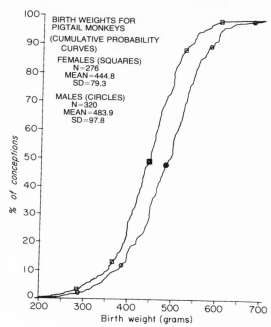

FIG. 1. Cumulative percentages for birth weights of liveborn male and female pigtail monkeys.

TABLE 1
Pregnancy Outcomes, Medical Treatments to Mothers, and Sex
Distribution of Births for 759 Pigtail Monkey Births

Variable	Category		
Pregnancy outcome	Living 72.7%	Stillborn or aborted 14.4%	Neonatal death 12.9%
Medical treatments	None 71.6%	Before conception 17.1%	During pregnancy 11.3%
Sex	Males 55.4%	Females 44.6%	

preliminary analysis, we excluded those births involving females who participated in experiments six months prior to or during pregnancy. This yielded 792 births sired by 94 male breeders with 412 females. Breeding occurs in harem groups containing three to seven females and one male. Many groups have remained stable over long periods, with occasional replacements for delivering mothers or animals who die. Delivery occurs in a group of pregnant females only, and

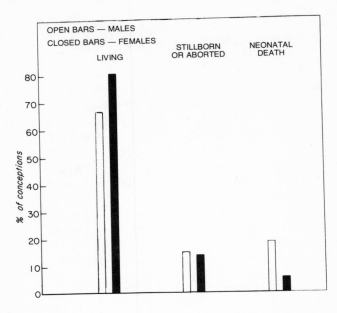

FIG. 2. Pregnancy outcome percentages for male and female conceptions.

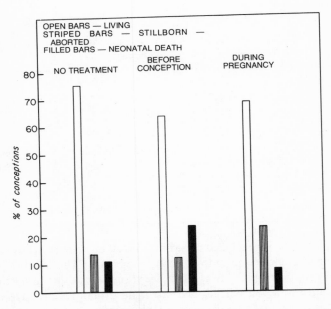

FIG. 3. Percentage of conceptions for each pregnancy outcome type as a function of medical treatments.

maternal rearing occurs during the first three months of life until the infants were weaned. At that time, the females are returned to their harem groups.

The cumulative percentage curves for the 596 birth weights reliably recorded in the colony are presented in Fig. 1. As expected, the average birth weights for males were greater than for females. However, the *lowest* birth weights recorded were for males, and the *highest* ones were for females. The curve for female birth weights reflects a more normal distribution than the male curve which is skewed toward low birth weights ($p < 0.025$ by goodness-of-fit test to a normal distribution).

Gestation age averaged approximately 167 days for live births ($\overline{X} = 166.6$ days for 211 females; $\overline{X} = 167.6$ for 245 males). Table 1 shows percentages for (a) pregnancy outcomes (living, stillborn or aborted, and neonatal death); (b) medical treatments (none, before conception, or during pregnancy); and (c) male and female births. Over 12 years, more males than females were born. Of the recognized conceptions, 27.3% resulted in abortion, stillbirth, or neonatal death. Furthermore, 28.4% of the breeders were treated medically during the period six months prior to conception or during pregnancy.

Figure 2 shows the percentages of male and female conceptions that resulted in live birth, stillbirth or abortion, or neonatal death. Fourteen percent more females lived than males ($p < 0.01$). Although there were no significant differences between male and female stillbirths and abortions, 13% more males died neonatally than did females ($p < 0.025$).

Figure 3 presents percentages of conceptions that were not treated or were treated medically prior to or during pregnancy. Breeders receiving medical treatment at any time had significantly fewer live births ($p < 0.01$), with the worst prognosis for breeders treated *before conception*. For breeders receiving no medical treatment, there were no significant differences in prenatal versus neonatal death rates. However, breeders treated before conception had more neonatal deaths among their offspring ($p < 0.025$), while those treated during pregnancy produced more stillborn or aborted offspring ($p < 0.025$).

Figure 4 presents sex differences for the medical treatment groups. This was a double-blind test, since neither the breeder nor the experimenter knew the sex of the fetus before delivery. Breeders carrying male fetuses were *not treated* as often as those carrying females (8% lower incidence rate) ($p < 0.05$). Breeders treated before conception delivered more males than females, although this was not statistically significant. However, breeders treated during pregnancy had a threefold higher rate of carrying a female fetus than a male fetus ($p < 0.01$). This startling finding (discussed below) indicates that pregnant pigtail monkeys are less likely to require medical treatment if they are carrying a male fetus.

An examination of the reasons for medical treatment revealed that 80% of all treatments were for bite wounds. Pigtail monkeys living in social groups exhibit a dominance hierarchy in which subordinate animals are more frequently harassed and bitten. Theoretically, females who are bitten severely enough to require

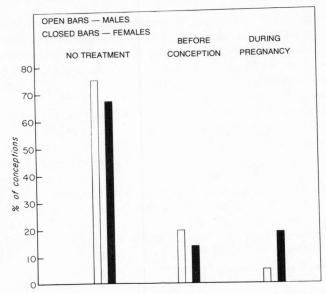

FIG. 4. Percentages of male and female conceptions for each medical treatment category.

medical attention are under greater social "stress" than untreated females. In our data, medical treatments during the first half of pregnancy did *not* differ as a function of the sex of the fetus, but did during the second half when 78% of all treatments occurred.

Resko (1970) measured circulating testosterone in rhesus monkeys (closely related to pigtail macaques) throughout gestation. When male sexual differentiation begins (approximately 100 gestational days), the fetal gonads begin secreting testosterone. At the same time, there is a sharp increase in maternal circulating testosterone, suggesting transplacental activity of male hormones. Thus, there is some preliminary evidence that the differential response of other monkeys in the group toward the female carrying a male fetus has an underlying hormonal basis. It seems likely that adults in the harem group perceive a change in the way breeders carrying male fetuses smell, look, or behave, and this results in different behavior toward those carrying male fetuses during the second half of pregnancy.

To summarize, we found that 25–30% of our breeding females were at high risk for delivering premature, low birth weight, stillborn or aborted, or neonatally dead offspring. Further, we have identified at least two factors related to degree of risk: sex of the offspring and need for medical treatment.

Table 2 shows average birth weights and length of gestation for male and female offpsring in each of the pregnancy outcome and medical treatment categories. Unequal N analysis of variance revealed significant three-way interactions for both measures ($p < 0.001$). These data correspond generally to the expectations from the human data, with a few unexpected findings.

Birth weight. 1. *Surviving* males and females showed effects of medical treatments to their mothers. Males whose mothers were treated before conception weighed significantly less than average ($p < 0.01$), while females whose mothers were treated before conception weighed significantly more than average ($p < 0.01$) and females whose mothers were treated during pregnancy weighed significantly less than average ($p < 0.01$).

2. *Stillborn* or *aborted* males and females weighed less if their mothers received medical treatment ($p < 0.05$).

3. *Neonatal deaths* showed an unusual pattern. Males and females whose mothers were treated during pregnancy weighed more than those whose mothers were not treated or were treated before conception ($p < 0.01$).

Gestation. Unfortunately, many colony records did not contain estimates of gestational age, or the estimates seemed unbelievable for a given birth weight. After applying criteria to screen for such errors, the resulting sample size was reduced considerably ($N = 399$). The overall correlation in this final sample for birth weight and gestational age was $+0.79$. We found that:

1. *Surviving* males and females had significantly shorter gestational periods if their mothers were treated during pregnancy ($p < 0.05$) compared with infants born of mothers that received no treatment, or received treatment before conception.

2. As expected, *stillborn* or *aborted* males and females had shorter gestational periods than liveborn animals ($p < 0.001$). Furthermore, males and females whose

TABLE 2

Mean Birth Weights and Gestation Age
for Males and Females in Each Pregnancy
Outcome and Medical Treatment Group

Pregnancy outcome	Medical treatment	Birth weight (grams)				Gestation age (days)			
		Male		Female		Male		Female	
		N	mean	N	mean	N	mean	N	mean
Surviving	none	138	490	107	448	103	167.4	84	167.3
	BC	40	458	21	472	31	166.0	20	166.6
	DP	11	502	9	415	11	163.5	7	158.4
Stillborn	none	16	427	11	448	13	162.2	10	149.7
aborted	BC	7	394	6	365	8	160.7	9	147.7
	DP	19	424	5	316	6	143.3	7	138.7
Neonatally	none	23	467	28	429	20	166.8	26	165.1
dead	BC	19	424	11	426	16	162.4	10	166.3
	DP	7	553	6	455	8	171.3	9	171.7

None = no treatment; BC = treated before conception; DP = treated during pregnancy.

TABLE 3

Independent Variables and their Percentage of
Total Variance in the Regression Equation Used
to Predict High- and Low-Risk Pregnancy Outcomes

Independent Variable	Parent	
	Mother	Father
Days in social group before conception	1.8 ($p < 0.01$)	not included
Birth order of conception since breeder entered colony	4.7 ($p < 0.001$)	not included
Change in body weight during 6 months prior to conception	0.2 n.s.	not included
Body weight in 6 months before conception	1.6 ($p < 0.01$)	1.1 ($p < 0.05$)
Percentage of previous offspring in high risk categories	5.1 ($p < 0.001$)	3.2 ($p < 0.01$)
Year of entering colony	2.1 ($p < 0.01$)	0.7 ($p < 0.05$)
Nonexperimental medical treatment	4.0 ($p < 0.001$)	not included
Year conception occurred	2.6 ($p < 0.01$)	

mothers were treated during pregnancy had the shortest gestational periods ($p < 0.001$).

3. *Dead neonates* again showed an unexpected pattern. Gestational ages for no-treatment and before-conception-treatment groups were close to normal. However, for males and females whose mothers were treated during pregnancy, gestational ages were significantly longer than average within each sex ($p < 0.025$).

Thus, both gestational age and birth weight data show that liveborn monkeys who die neonatally appear to be *postmature*, compared with animals who survive.

Outcome of pregnancy in pigtail monkeys appears to be influenced by preconceptual and prenatal factors. However, the relationships among preconceptual and prenatal stress, length of pregnancy, birth weight, and sex are complex.

Regression analysis approach. The independent variables entering into a multiple regression equation used to predict poor pregnancy outcome are presented in Table 3. The dependent variable is pregnancy outcome, high risk (coded as 1) or low risk (coded as 0). High risk was defined by one or more of the following criteria: (*a*) birth weight in the lower fifth of the colony, (*b*) gestational age in the lower fifth of the colony, (*c*) stillbirth or abortion, or (*d*) death within the first 30 postnatal days. The multiple correlation for this equation was $r = .52$.

Table 3 also shows the percentage of non-error variance (27.1%) accounted for by each of the 11 variables in the equation. The significant factors in this regression equation were (*a*) percentage of previous high risk conceptions, (*b*) birth order, (c) type of medical treatment received by the mother, (d) year mother entered the colony, (e) number of days before conception that female entered the harem group, and (f) weight of the female six months prior to conception. Thus, certain maternal background variables relate to risk for poor pregnancy outcome. Age and physical maturity of the mother (as indexed by birth order variable) showed that younger females, often ones having their first births in the colony, were at greater risk than older females or those who had more previous colony births. These findings agree with the human epidemiological data on births to women who are very young or primiparous. Year-of-entry into the colony and weight prior to conception may also reflect the biological maturation of the breeder. Other significant factors in this prediction equation were medical treatment and being a relative newcomer to a social group, since treated females and females recently introduced to a group were at greater risk for poor pregnancy outcomes.

Two paternal variables contributed significantly in this equation. One was fathers' incidence of previous high-risk offspring. In one striking example, a male sired 47 offspring, 22 of whom met our high-risk criteria. The second was father's weight before conception, a factor correlated with age. Fathers who weighed less (i.e., probably were younger) had more high risk offspring.

The final variable weighing significantly in the equation was the year when conception occurred. This may reflect differences in introduction of wild-captured animals into the colony, increasing disease possibilities and social stress, or differences in colony record keeping, which improved over time.

The predictive validity of these variables was tested on the complete data base using a discriminant analysis technique. Table 4 shows the predicted risk scores and the actual outcomes for first borns (based on parental characteristics before and during pregnancy) and second borns (based on outcome of first pregnancy, plus parental characteristics before and during pregnancy). Predicted scores were arranged in centiles, and the number of surviving or deceased animals was calculated within each centile range. The equation performed reasonably well on the data used to derive it. For first borns, 95% of those predicted to be in the *lowest* risk group did, in fact, have normal outcomes; and 71% predicted to be in the *highest* risk group had poor pregnancy outcomes. For second borns, the predictions were even more accurate, with 86% of those predicted to be in the *highest* risk group showing low birth weight, prematurity, stillbirth or abortion, or neonatal death. As a more stringent application, the prediction equation was applied to 72 births during 1972–1973 that did not enter into the derivation of the equation. Fifty-five percent of the conceptions in the upper 20 centiles actually exhibited high risk characteristics, compared with the chance value for the colony of 27.3%. Only 12% of the births with predicted scores in the lower 20 centiles had high risk characteristics. Although this equation is far from precise, it predicted twice as accurately as chance expectation.

Characteristics of surviving high-risk monkeys. To date, we have not

TABLE 4

Discriminant Analysis Results for Predicting Pregnancy Outcomes

	Centiles of predicted pregnancy outcome scores					
	0–10	11–20	21–50	51–80	81–90	91–100
First borns						
Frequency high risk	2	8	33	47	19	29
Frequency low risk	37	31	84	70	20	12
Percent high risk	5.1	20.1	28.3	40.2	48.7	70.7
Second borns						
Frequency high risk	1	3	6	12	10	18
Frequency low risk	20	17	52	45	11	3
Percent high risk	4.8	15.0	10.3	21.2	47.5	85.7

Note.—Predicted scores in the upper centiles indicate expectation of high risk pregnancy, and those in the lower centiles are expected to be at low risk. The observed frequency of high- and low-risk outcomes at each centile range is given for first and second coneptions, and percentages of observed high risk outcomes among all conceptions in each centile range are indicated (e.g., for first borns there were 2 high- and 37 low-risk outcomes, yielding 5.1% high risk out of these 39 cases).

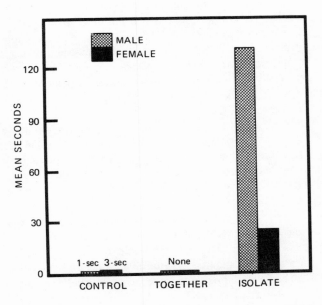

FIG. 5. Average time spent in stereotyped, self-directed behaviors by normal, peer-raised, and isolate rhesus monkeys.

systematically studied low birth weight and premature pigtail monkeys for comparison with human data. However, our experience with 40 high-risk infants reared in our laboratory nursery confirms that these animals had comparatively poor reflex development, muscle tone, and alertness. During the first three months of life, their physical growth was retarded. Behaviorally, these infants were slow to become self-feeding. Normally, full-term infants in our nursery are self-feeding by 10–15 days old. However, none of these high risk infants were self-feeding before 23 days old, and most were not self-feeding even by 30 days old. In the breeding colony, most of these high risk infants die, although in our nursery 80% survived beyond the neonatal period.

The nonhuman primate model. The data for this pigtail breeding colony confirm that pregnancy outcomes are influenced by a variety of preconceptual and prenatal factors similar to those reported in the human literature. By using monkeys living in relatively stable environments, social stress factors, genetic variables, and length of gestation can be experimentally manipulated or controlled. Since pigtail monkeys also reveal sex differences in susceptibility to certain environmental factors, compatible with the human evidence, it seems plausible that identifying important causal mechanisms in monkeys may be relevant to humans.

SEX DIFFERENCES IN VULNERABILITY OF MONKEYS TO ABNORMALIZING EFFECTS OF REARING CONDITIONS

Infant rhesus monkeys reared under conditions of social-sensory deprivation are usually atypical or abnormal in their behavioral development. These effects seem to be some of the best documented facts in the area of animal behavioral development. Reviews by Harlow and Harlow (1965) and by Mason (1968) show that rhesus monkeys reared alone in totally isolated and enclosed cages, or raised alone in wire cages allowing only distal stimulation from other animals, have persistent abnormalities in personal, exploratory, social, maternal, and sexual behaviors. Some of the more dramatic effects appear in personal behavior. Isolates spend much of their day engaged in repetitive stereotyped behaviors directed toward parts of their body or toward parts of the environment. Such animals are hyperaggressive, show abnormal reactions to painful stimulation, fail to perform in learning tasks, and often show self-abusive behavior. In many ways the responses of these monkeys resemble those of severely retarded or emotionally disturbed children.

Less well known, however, are findings that many of the qualitative and quantitative effects of isolation depend on the sex of the monkey subject. Briefly we will summarize some of the studies that show male rhesus monkeys to be more vulnerable to the negative effects of isolation rearing than females.

Sexual behavior. Sexual performance of adult monkeys reared in isolation was compared with that of feral controls born in India (Harlow, 1965). Subjects were

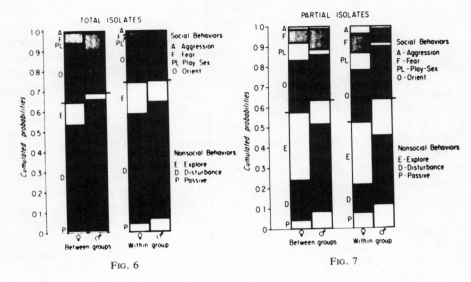

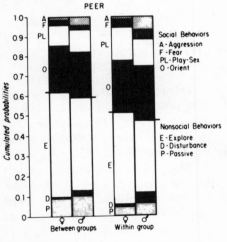

FIG. 6. Percentage of time male and female total isolate rhesus monkeys spent in social and nonsocial behavior.

FIG. 7. Percentage of time male and female partial isolate rhesus monkeys spent in social and nonsocial behaviors.

FIG. 8. Percentage of time male and female peer-raised rhesus monkeys spent in social and nonsocial behaviors.

paired with sexually sophisticated partners of the opposite sex. During 30-min tests conducted over 12 months, both male and female isolates showed significantly less appropriate sexual activity than controls. However, female isolates did show some appropriate sexual behavior and some were impregnated. None of the 16 isolate males showed appropriate sexual behaviors or any evidence of improvement over the 12-month testing period.

Self-aggression. Gluck and Sackett (in press) studied self-aggression in adult rhesus monkeys reared in partial isolation (wire cages) or with mothering and physical contact with peers. During test sessions in a novel, empty cage, mother-peer subjects showed almost no self-aggression. However, partial-isolates did show self-aggression, with males averaging 5.5 self-aggressions per 5 min and females averaging less than 2.5. Thus, under similar rearing and testing conditions, females were significantly lower than males on this self-aggressive tendency.

Exploratory behavior. Adult rhesus monkeys reared under different conditions show differences in their exploratory behaviors (Sackett, 1972). In measuring latency to leave start position and overall activity, as well as exploratory behaviors, animals reared in complete or partial isolation or with surrogate mothers performed worse than those reared in the wild or with mothers in the laboratory. The sex differences were striking in the various isolation groups. Males took more than five times longer to leave the start area in a novel situation. Males were significantly less active than females reared under similar privation groups. Finally, even though males reared in the wild or under normal social laboratory conditions explore more than females, females reared in isolation conditions were more active than males reared in similar environments.

Stereotyped and self-directed behaviors. In another testing situation with toys in a novel situation, sex differences were again found in isolation reared animals. Figure 5 shows average time spent in stereotyped or self-directed behavior during four trials. Animals reared with mothers or peers spent almost no time in these behaviors. Isolation reared monkeys, however, spent a considerable amount of time engaged in these behaviors, with males spending more than five times as much time as females in self-directed, stereotyped behaviors.

Social behavior. Pratt (1969) studied social behavior in two-year-old rhesus monkeys reared with peers (a) in wire cages where they could see, hear, and smell other animals, and (b) in total isolation chambers for the first eight months of life. Although group data show patterns typical of the "isolation syndrome," a breakdown within groups reveals important effects of sex. Figure 6 shows that females reared in isolation had significantly less disturbance ($p < 0.025$), more environmental exploration ($p < 0.01$), more positive social orientation ($p < 0.05$), and less social fear ($p < 0.01$) than males reared in isolation. Figure 7 shows that sex differences were even more striking for animals reared in wire cages or partial isolation conditions. The males reared in partial isolation appear quite similar to males reared in complete isolation, while the females reared in partial isolation behave more like normal peer-raised females. Female partial isolates had lower probabilities of disturbance, fear, and passive behavior ($p < 0.01$) and higher probabilities of exploration and social play ($p < 0.001$) than males reared under identical conditions. Figure 8 shows few behavioral differences between males and females reared with peers.

Survival of isolation-reared monkeys in a free-ranging environment. A final study of sex differences concerns adult rhesus monkeys (7–8 years old) released onto Guayacon Island off the southwest coast of Puerto Rico (Sackett,

Westcott, & Westcott, in preparation). The 15 animals included (*a*) feral animals brought into the laboratory before two years of age, (*b*) laboratory-born animals reared with mothers and peers, and (*c*) laboratory-born animals reared in complete or partial isolation. Seven of nine females survived and two of these were from the isolate groups, one having shown years of stereotyped, abnormal behaviors in the laboratory. This one female continued her atypical patterns of behavior on the island, but was accepted by a group of nine adult animals. However, only two of the six males survived and these both were from the normal, socialized rearing groups. Apparently, deviant females can survive under conditions that lead to death in deviant males.

Females: The buffered sex. These studies can be summarized as follows. Under various social-sensory deprivation conditions, females are "buffered" against permanent rearing-induced deficits and are more able to modify their behavior in species-typical ways. Such adaptive changes are rarely seen in males reared in isolation conditions. Controlled studies of the physical, physiological, and behavioral development of male and female monkeys may elucidate factors responsible for these observed differences. Furthermore, such a model may reveal factors that make a given animal more or less susceptible to abnormal or retarded development, regardless of sex.

CONCLUSION

We have presented some of our ideas concerning the appropriateness of an experimental, nonhuman primate model to study risk factors involved in abnormal human development. For humans, poor pregnancy outcomes are correlated with subsequent high risk for abnormal or retarded development. In general, male humans are more likely to show developmental deviancy than are females. The results of a study on pregnancies in a pigtail macaque breeding colony reveal that factors similar to those in humans are correlated with poor pregnancy outcomes. Finally, we have presented evidence that male monkeys are at a substantially greater risk for abnormal development following postnatal deprivation conditions. The reasons responsible for this sex difference in vulnerability to adverse effects of deprivation may help identify general causes of susceptibility to or buffering against abnormal development. We are now designing a series of investigations with pigtail macques at the Medical Lake breeding colony and in our own nursery and laboratory conditions. We hope to report on our findings within the next three to five years.

ACKNOWLEDGMENTS

Epidemiology study and manuscript preparation were supported by NIH grant RR00166 to the Regional Primate Research Center at the University of Washington. We thank (i) Mr. Arthur Davis for heroic efforts in assembling our data base from colony computer records, (ii) Dr. Orville A. Smith for making high-risk neonates available to us for study, and (iii) ourselves for the obsessive-compulsive behavior required to overcome entry errors, omission errors, and computer errors to arrive at a usable data base from a record file not designed for specific scientific investigations but rather for purposes of record keeping ("Charlie Brown, you won't believe it, but it can be done").

REFERENCES

Bergner, L., & Susser, M. W. Low birth weight and prenatal nutrition: An interpretative review. *Pediatrics*, 1970, **46**, 946–966.

Bowes, W. A., Brackbill, Y., Conway, E., & Steinschneider, A. Obstetrical medication and infant outcome: A review of the literature. *Monographs of the Society for Research in Child Development*, 1970, **35** (4, No. 137).

Braine, M. D. S., Heimer, C. B., Wortis, H., & Freedman, A. M. Factors associated with impairment of the early development of prematures. *Monographs of the Society for Research in Child Development*, 1966, **31** (No. 106).

Brazelton, T. B. Influence of perinatal drugs on the behavior of the neonate. In J. Hellmuth (Ed.), *Exceptional infant*. Vol. 2: *Studies in abnormalities*. New York: Brunner/Mazel, 1971. Pp. 419–431.

Childs, B. Genetic origin of some sex differences among human beings. *Pediatrics*, 1965, **35**, 798–812.

Emanuel, I. Some preventive aspects of abnormal intrauterine development. *Postgraduate Medicine*, 1972, **51**, 144–148.

Fitzhardinge, P. M., & Stevens, E. M. The small-for-date infant. I. Later growth patterns. *Pediatrics*, 1972, **49**, 671–681.

Gluck, J., & Sackett, G. P. Self-aggression and frustration in social isolate monkeys. *Journal of Abnormal Psychology*, in press.

Greulich, W. W., Crimson, C. S., & Turner, M. L. The physical growth and development of children who survived the atomic bombing of Hiroshima and Nagasaki. *Journal of Pediatrics*, 1953, **43**, 121–145.

Harlow, H. F. Sexual behavior in the rhesus monkey. In F. A. Beach (Ed.), *Sex and behavior*. New York: Wiley, 1965.

Harlow, H. F., & Harlow, M. K. The affectional systems. In A. M. Schrier, H. F. Harlow, & F. Stollnitz (Eds.), *Behavior of nonhuman primates*. Vol. 1. New York: Academic Press, 1965.

Hultin, M., & Ottosson, J. O. Perinatal conditions of unwanted children. *Acta Psychiatrica Scandanavica*, 1971 (suppl.) **221**, 59–67.

Illingworth, R. S. Low birth weight and subsequent development. *Pediatrics*, 1970, **45**, 335–339.

Joffe, J. M. *Prenatal determinants of behavior*. New York: Pergamon, 1969.

Kappelman, M. M. Prenatal and perinatal factors which influence learning. In J. Hellmuth (Ed.), *Exceptional infants*. Vol. 2: *Studies in abnormalities*. New York: Brunner/Mazel, 1971. Pp. 155–171.

Klein, M., & Stern, L. Low birth weight and the battered child syndrome. *American Journal of Disadvantaged Children*, 1971, **122**, 15–18.

Kosmarskaya, E. Peculiarities of the structure of the brain in premature infants. In B. Klosovskii (Ed.), *The development of the brain and its disturbance by harmful factors*. New York: Macmillan, 1963.

Kramer, M., Pollack, E. S., Redick, R. W., & Lock. B. *Mental disorders in suicide*. Cambridge, Mass.: Harvard University Press, 1972.

Lundstrom, N. R., & Elder, I. Ultrasound cardiography in infants and children. *Acta Paediatrica Scandanavica*, 1971. **60**, 117–128.

Manocha, S. L. *Malnutrition and retarded human development.* Springfield, Ill.: C. C. Thomas, 1972.

Mason, W. A. Early social deprivation in the nonhuman primate: Implications for human behavior. In D. C. Glass (Ed.), *Biology and behavior: Environmental infleunces.* New York: Rockefeller University Press, 1968.

Metcalf, D. R. EEG sleep spindle ontogenesis. *Neuropediatrie,* 1970, **1**, 428–433.

Miller, H. C. Prematurity. In R. E. Cooke (Ed.), *The biologic basis of pediatric practice.* New York: McGraw-Hill, 1968.

Ottinger, D. R., & Simmons, J. E. Behavior of human neonates and prenatal maternal anxiety. *Psychological Reports,* 1964, **14**, 391–394.

Pratt, C. L. The developmental consequences of early social stimulation. Unpublished doctoral dissertation, University of Wisconsin, 1969.

Resko, J. A. Androgens secreted by the fetal and neonatal rhesus monkey. *Endocrinology,* 1970, **87**, 680–687.

Sackett, G. P. Exploratory behavior of rhesus monkeys as a function of rearing experiences and sex. *Developmental Psychology,* 1972, **6**, 260–268.

Sackett, G. P., Westcott, J. T., & Westcott, R. Behavior of laboratory-born rhesus monkeys in a semi-natural environment. In preparation.

Sainte-Anne Dargassies. Neurological maturation of the premature infant, 28 to 41 weeks gestational age. In F. Falkner (Ed.), *Human development.* Philadelphia: Saunders, 1966.

Sontag, L..W. The significance of fetal environmental differences. *American Journal of Obstetrics and Gynecology.* 1941, **42**, 996–1003.

Sterling, H. M. Disabilities of genetic origin. *Archives of Physical Medicine,* 1970, **51**, 291–296.

Stevenson, A. C. Sex chromatin and the sex ratio in man. In K. L. Moore (Ed.), *The sex chromatin.* Philadelphia: Saunders, 1966.

Stott, D. H. Physical and mental handicaps following a disturbed pregancy. *Lancet,* 1957, **272**, 1006–1012.

Tanner, J. M. Physical growth. In P. H. Mussen (Ed.), *Carmichael's manual of child development,* New York: Wiley, 1970. (3rd ed.)

Wolanski, N. Genetic and ecological factors in human growth. *Human Biology,* 1970, **42**, 349–368.

Wright, L. The theoretical and research base for a program of early stimulation care and training of premature infants. In J. Hellmuth (Ed.), *Exceptional infant.* Vol. 2: *Studies in abnormalities.* New York: Brunner/Mazel, 1971.

5

AN ANIMAL MODEL FOR THE SMALL-FOR-GESTATIONAL-AGE INFANT: SOME BEHAVIORAL AND MORPHOLOGICAL FINDINGS [1]

Victor H. Denenberg
Darlene DeSantis[2]
Univeristy of Connecticut

In the Laboratory of Developmental Psychobiology of the Department of Biobehavioral Sciences, we have recently initiated a program to develop animal models of several human perinatal and neonatal events. One major impetus for developing this program is the presence of a human infant research group within the Laboratory, under the direction of Dr. Evelyn Thoman. It is our belief that the understanding of the processes underlying development will advance most rapidly when researchers and students alike have available to them human infants for developmental investigations and animal models that can be experimentally manipulated. As we travel the pathway from the animal laboratory to the nursery and back, we anticipate finding interesting developmental vistas that cannot be seen as easily or as clearly from within the confines of either research facility.

This is our first report on an animal model for the small-for-gestational-age infant. This infant is defined in the human clinical literature as one who is full term but underweight, falling in the weight range of 1700–2500 grams. There are various medical reasons for the occurrence of the small-for-gestational-age condition. However, most reasons center around the inability of the fetus to obtain sufficient nutrition to grow and develop normally.

In developing an animal model for this condition, we considered several procedures for reducing the supply of nutrients to the fetus. One widely used method is to place the pregnant mother on a reduced diet. We decided not to use this technique because the dietary restriction has effects upon the mother's care and feeding of her pups after birth, thus requiring a cross-fostered control group.

[1]Supported, in part, by NIMH Research Grant MH-19716.
[2]Trainee on NIMH Training Grant MH-12489.

Another technique we considered, and finally adopted, is described by Wigglesworth (1964, 1968), who was able to retard growth in the fetal rat by ligating the main uterine vessels to one horn on day 16 of pregnancy (Wigglesworth, 1968). This procedure reduced the blood supply to the experimental horn, and Wigglesworth found that the fetuses near the vaginal end of the ligated horn were considerably retarded in their growth.

This technique appealed to us because (1) the experimental intervention does not occur until late in pregnancy, and so we do not interfere with embryonic development; (2) the surgical procedure is simple, taking approximately 10–15 mins; (3) the overall effect upon the mother appears to be less than the effects of prolonged dietary restriction; (4) the time of impact of the intervention is known exactly and can be systematically varied; and (5) since the rat has two independent uterine horns, it is possible to ligate one and not the other, thus giving us an exquisite control group for studies in which we use Caesarian deliveries.

Our purpose is to describe our first three experiments investigating the feasibility of this technique as a method of generating small-for-gestational-age animals.

METHOD

Subjects

The subjects were Wistar rats maintained in our closed colony by random breeding since 1949. Males were placed with adult females overnight. The following morning the males were removed and vaginal smears were taken to determine whether insemination had occurred. If the sperm test was positive at this time, this was considered to be Day 1 of gestation. Pregnant rats were group housed until they were removed for surgery, after which they were placed singly into stainless steel maternity cages. These cages had shavings on the floor and external food and water hoppers.

Surgery

On the scheduled date for ligation females were anesthetized with ether. A longitudinal incision was made on the ventral surface, beginning at about the third set of nipples from the vagina and continuing anteriorly for about ⅝ inch. The same incision was made in the muscle layer. The two uterine horns containing the fetuses were gently pulled out through this opening and the branches of the common iliac artery to each horn were ligated at the vaginal end. Then the fetuses and uteri were carefully returned to the abdominal cavity, after which both the muscle and skin layers were sutured.

The same procedure was followed with the sham controls except that the arteries were not ligated.

The number of fetuses in each horn was noted during surgery for each mother.

EXPERIMENT I:
EFFECTS OF UNILATERAL LIGATION
ON DAYS 18, 19, 20 AND 21 OF PREGNANCY

The purpose of our first experiment was to determine the efficacy of the ligation technique at different gestational ages to (1) reduce birth weight and (2) still produce viable young. In deciding at what ages to do the ligations we consulted with our colleagues in the Laboratory of Endocrinology who had been doing experiments on pregnant rats. One of the difficulties in doing the ligation very late in pregnancy is the danger of dislodging the placentae, while surgery too early in pregnancy would result in complete loss of the fetuses. Based upon the advice of the endocrinologists, we decided to do the ligations on Days 18, 19, 20, and 21 of gestation. (In our colony mothers deliver, on the average, 23 days after impregnation.)

Since this was our first study we decided to use a unilateral ligation and then deliver the pups by Caesarian section, thus giving us an intramother control for each experimental group. Within each age group we alternated between ligating the right and left ovarian horns.

Caesarian sections were performed on the morning of Day 23 of gestation. The animals were anesthetized with ether. The original incisions were re-opened and the pups and uteri gently removed. At this time the ligations were inspected to be certain they were still intact. One horn at a time was delivered of its pups, and the animals were counted and weighed as they were delivered. The experiment was terminated at this point.

Results

Table 1 summarizes the survival and birth weight statistics for the ligated and control horns at the four gestation ages. For the 4 females ligated on Day 18 of gestation we found 89% of the fetuses were alive at delivery while all the fetuses in the control horns were born alive. The survival percentage of the ligated horn dropped markedly on Days 19, 20, and 21.

The birth weights were obtained by taking all the liveborn pups from an experimental and a control horn and getting the mean weight for that horn. Thus, for each mother there were two weight values, one based upon the pups from her ligated uterine horn and the other from the control horn (except in three instances where all the fetuses from the ligated horn had been resorbed, as indicated in Table 1).

An analysis of variance of the birth weights of the ligated horns among the four ages groups found a significant effect for gestation age ($F = 5.09$, $df = 3/9$, $p < .05$). Subsequent analyses found that the body weights of the groups ligated on

TABLE 1

Survival Percentages and Birth Weights of
Caesarian Delivered Pups from Mothers Ligated on
Days 18, 19, 20, and 21 of Pregnancy

Gestation age at ligation (days)	No. of litters	No. of fetuses	Ligated horn			Control horn			
			No. live-born pups	Fetuses live-born (%)	Mean birth weight (gm)	No. of fetuses	No. live-born pups	Fetuses live-born (%)	Mean birth weight (gm)
18	4	18	16	89	4.28	15	15	100	5.92
19	6	28	11	39	4.31*	32	32	100	6.01
20	3	7	3	43	6.12**	10	9	90	6.39
21	3	15	5	33	5.82**	14	9	64	5.67

*Based upon 5 litters since all fetuses in ligated horn of one mother had been resorbed.
**Based upon 2 litters since all fetuses in ligated horn of one mother had been resorbed.

TABLE 2

Birth Weight (gm) of Pups from Ligated and Control Horns by Position in
the Uterus

Treatment of uteri	Position in uterus relative to ovarian end			
	1	2	3	4
Ligated Horn	4.42	4.58	3.99	4.96
Control Horn	5.98	6.00	6.20	5.98

Days 18 or 19 did not differ from each other, nor did the groups ligated on Days 20 and 21. However, the average birth weight of the combined Days 18 and 19 groups were significantly less than the mean birth weight of the combined Days 20 and 21 groups ($t = 3.88$, $p < .01$).

A similar analysis of the birth weights of the control horns among the four age groups did not find any evidence of an effect ($F = 0.81$).

On Days 18 and 19 there were nine litters for whom mean weights for both the ligated and control horns were available. In all nine cases the mean weight of the pups from the ligated horn was less than that of its respective control horn ($p < .01$ by binomial test). For the four litters ligated on Days 20 or 21 for whom similar information was available, we found that the pups from the ligated horn weighed more in three of the four instances.

The final analysis of these data was concerned with the pup's weight relative to its position in the uterus. Wigglesworth (1964) had found that the fetuses toward the vaginal end of the ligated horn, where the blood supply was poorest, weighed the least, but there was little stunting at the ovarian end. We had four females from the Day 18 and 19 groups that had four or more pups in the ligated horn, and four females from the same two groups that had four or more pups in the control horn. When the pups were removed, their position, relative to the ovarian end of the uterus, was noted. The mean birth weights for the first four positions, moving away from the ovarian toward the vaginal end, are given in Table 2. As can be seen, there is no evidence of a gradient here. Indeed, for all four ligated horns, we found that the pups in position 4 (nearest the ligation) weighed more than the pup nearest the ovarian end, a finding in opposition to that of Wigglesworth. However, an analysis of variance of the birth weights of the pups from the ligated horn failed to find a significant effect ($F = 2.10$, $df = 3/9$).

The discrepancy between our findings and those of Wigglesworth may be due to the time parameters involved. In his 1968 review Wigglesworth stated that he did his ligation on Day 16 and that he removed his fetuses on Day 20. However, in his original paper, Wigglesworth (1964) reported these values as Days 17 and 21, respectively. In either case, his times differ from ours by at least one to two days and so the studies are not directly comparable.

EXPERIMENT II:
EFFECTS OF LIGATION ON DAYS 18 AND 19 OF PREGNANCY UPON VAGINAL DELIVERY

The data from Experiment I rather clearly show that the ligations should be performed on Days 18 or 19 in order to obtain an underweight animal. In addition to this finding, the failure to obtain a significant difference in birth weight among the four gestation age groups from the control horns is encouraging since it indicates that the age of ligation does not affect growth of the controls. There was the possibility that ligating one branch of the iliac artery would cause more blood to flow through the other branch, and in this way affect birth weight. Our data show no evidence of this happening.

Thus, the technique of unilateral ligation and Caesarian delivery appeared to be successful. Though it is an elegant procedure, the technique has two disadvantages: (1) a second operation must be performed upon the mother, and (2) most human small-for-gestational-age infants are vaginally delivered. Therefore, in our next experiment we investigated the effects of ligations on Days 18 and 19 upon vaginal delivery. In this study we followed the pups through weaning.

Procedure

Pregnant female rats received bilateral ligations of the two uterine horns on Day 18 or Day 19. They were allowed to deliver normally, and the body weights of all live pups were obtained. When there were more than six pups in a litter, that litter was reduced to six by keeping the six heaviest pups and trying to maintain a sex

TABLE 3

Survival Percentages of Pups of Mothers Ligated on Day 18 or Day 19 of Pregnancy

Group	No. of litters[a]	No. of fetuses	No. live-born pups	Fetuses liveborn (%)	No. of pups alive at weaning	Pups alive at weaning (%)
Day 18	8/8	106	32	30.2	28/32	87.5
Day 19	5/8	85	27	31.8	24/27	88.9

[a]Numerator: Number of litters delivering liveborn pups. Denominator: Total number of litters treated originally.

TABLE 4

Body Weights of Pups of Mothers Ligated on Day 18 or Day 19 of Pregnancy

	No. of litters	No. of pups	Mean litter weight (gm)
Birth weight			
Day 18	8	29[a]	6.00
Day 19	5	27	4.94
Weaning weight			
Day 18	8	28	48.23
Day 19	4	24	36.52

Note.—Average birth weight of colony controls = 6.9 gm; average weaning weight of colony controls = 55.0 gm.

[a]Three of the 32 liveborn pups died before birth weights were obtained.

ratio of 4 males to 2 females. If the litter size was six or less, no foster pups were added. The pups were then returned to the maternity cage. The mothers and litters were left undisturbed until weaning at which time the body weights of all live pups were recorded. No sham controls were included in this study since we simply wanted to determine whether we could obtain liveborn pups that would survive to weaning.

Results

Tables 3 and 4 summarize the data of this study. The survival statistics in Table 3 indicate that surgery on Day 18 or Day 19 yields equivalent results: In both groups approximately 30% of the fetuses were born alive, and approximately 88% of the liveborn pupus survived to weaning. All the litters operated upon on Day 18 had viable young, while 5 of the 8 litters that had surgery on Day 19 had liveborn pups.

The body weight data in Table 4 show a slightly different picture: The birth weight of pups whose mothers were ligated on Day 19 was significantly less than the weight of those ligated on Day 18 ($F = 4.97, df = 1/11, p < .05$). Though this difference persisted to weaning, the significance disappeared ($F = 2.32, df = 1/10$). [The birth weight data of Table 1 cannot be directly compared to the data in Table 4 (or Table 6 below) because the weights of Experiment I were obtained 23 days after impregnation while the weights in Experiments II and III were obtained 24 days post impregnation, that is, one day after birth.]

EXPERIMENT III:
EFFECTS OF LIGATION ON DAY 18 OF GESTATION UPON BODY WEIGHT AND OPEN-FIELD BEHAVIOR

Experiments I and II established that ligating the uterine arteries on Day 18 of pregnancy would reduce the birth weight of the pups. From Experiment II we found that the mother could deliver vaginally, and viable young would survive to weaning. Our next step was to compare a ligation group with a sham-operated group. We decided to do our surgery on Day 18 of gestation. In addition to the survival and body weight statistics, we followed the offspring into adulthood and measured their open-field behavior.

Procedure

The same procedure as described in Experiment II was followed here through weaning. When weaned, the pups in Experiment III were housed with one or two littermates of the same sex until 50–60 days of age, at which time all animals were housed singly in stainless steel laboratory cages. The animals were not disturbed again until 76–77 days when some of the rats were tested in the open field.

Open-field testing. The field consisted of a 45-inch square plywood base with wood walls 18 inches high. The whole field was painted flat black except for thin white lines that divided the floor into 9-inch squares. A square compartment was formed by placing a wooden L-shaped unit into one corner, and the subject was placed inside this square. Ten seconds later the L-shaped unit was removed, and the rat was free to move about the field for 3 min. The number of squares entered was recorded, and also the number of boluses defecated. The procedure was followed for each animal for four successive days.

The animals were weighed after the first day of open-field testing.

Results

Survival. Table 5 summarizes these data. Both groups averaged approximately ten fetuses per mother, but only 20.4% of those from ligated mothers were born

TABLE 5

Survival Percentages of Pups of Ligated and Sham-Ligated Mothers

Group	No. of litters [a]	No. of fetuses	No. live-born pups	Fetuses liveborn (%)	No. of pups alive at weaning	Pups alive at weaning (%)
Ligation	11/20	216	44	20.4	29/44	65.9
Sham	16/16	166	139	83.7	84/86	97.7

[a]Numerator: Number of litters delivering liveborn pups. Denominator: Total number of litters treated originally.

TABLE 6

Body Weights of Pups of Ligated and Sham-Ligated Mothers at Birth and Weaning

	No. of litters	No. of pups	Mean litter weight (gm)
Birth weight			
Ligation	11	41	5.41
Sham	16	139	6.56
Weaning weight			
Ligation	8	29	57.53
Sham	16	83	51.85

TABLE 7

Body Weight at 76 Days of Rats Whose Mothers Were Ligated or Sham Ligated

	Males		Females	
	N	Weight (gm)	N	Weight (gm)
Ligation	10	300.00	13	188.23
Sham	14	310.86	13	191.00

alive while the incidence was 83.7% in the sham-ligation group ($p < .01$). There was also significantly greater mortality in the ligation group between birth and weaning: 65.9% of liveborn ligated pups survived as compared to 97.7% of pups from the sham group ($p < .01$).

Body weight. The body weights at birth and weaning are given in Table 6. The ligated group was found to weigh significantly less at birth than the sham controls ($F = 12.58$, $df = 1/25$, $p < .01$), but there was no significant difference at weaning ($F = 3.07$, $df = 1/22$). We also failed to find a significant weight difference between the groups at 76 days when the animals were tested for open-field performance. The 76-day weight data are listed in Table 7.

Open-field performance. Table 7 lists the N's used in the open-field study. An unweighted means analysis of variance procedure was used to evaluate open-field activity. The analysis found significant effects for Sex ($F = 13.11$, $df = 1/46$, $p < .01$), Days ($F = 14.67$, $df = 3/138$, $p < .01$), Days × Treatment ($F = 3.51$, $df = 3/138$, $p < .05$), and Days × Treatment × Sex ($F = 3.79$, $df = 3/138$, $p < .05$). The significant interactions are plotted in Figs. 1 and 2.

The Days × Treatment curves in Fig. 1 show that the activity of the two groups was the same on the first day of open-field testing and that the shams showed a sharp drop on Day 2 with subsequent recovery while the ligated group continued to drop and then leveled off with no recovery.

In Fig. 2, which further breaks down Fig. 1 by sex, the same drop and recovery is found with both the males and females from the sham group, while neither sex in the ligation group shows a recovery in activity as a function of days. The cause of the significant triple interaction is due to the sex disparity in the ligation group: Females of ligated mothers had the highest profile of any of the four groups while males showed the lowest activity over the four test days.

No differences were found among the groups on the defecation measure in the open field.

DISCUSSION

In Experiment I the Days 18 and 19 pups from the ligated horn weighed 4.30 gm, while the controls averaged 5.96 gm, a loss of 28%. In Experiment III the pups from the ligation groups weighed 18% less than control pups. These significant weight losses establish that the ligation procedure is able to produce smaller liveborn young, the first requisite for a small-for-gestational-age animal model. We also found that all animals within the ligated horn, regardless of position, were affected. This finding differs from that of Wigglesworth who reported a gradient effect. Our procedure differed from his in that he made two ligations around the main branch plus a third in the mesometrium at right angles to the main branch, whereas we performed a single ligation on the main branch between the vagina and the first pup. This difference in procedure plus the differences in age at surgery and age at which the pups or fetuses were weighed may account for the lack of

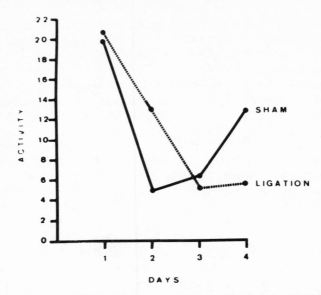

FIG. 1. Open-field activity of offspring of mothers ligated or sham ligated on Day 18 of pregnancy.

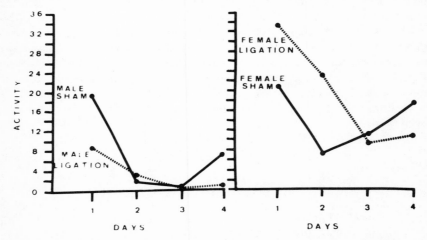

FIG. 2. Open-field activity of offspring of mothers ligated or sham ligated on Day 18 of pregnancy (broken down by sex).

agreement between the studies with respect to the weight characteristics of the pups in the ligated horn.

It is apparent that our technique has a drastic effect upon the viability of fetuses since only 20–30% of the fetuses from the ligated mothers were born alive in the two vaginal delivery experiments, in contrast to the survival value of 83.7% for the sham group in Experiment III. In view of these findings, the 89% survival rate for the Day 18 ligation pups in Experiment I is surprisingly high.

There appears to be a discrepancy between Experiments II and III with respect to the percentage of liveborn pups from the ligation group that survive to weaning. In Experiment II approximately 88% survived while 66% survived in the third study. This difference is significant at the .02 level ($\chi^2 = 6.14$ using Yates' correction). This discrepancy can be directly related to the mean litter weight at birth. In Experiment II the mean weight of the lightest litter was 4.45 gm, and in that experiment all litters except one (which contained only a single pup weighing 5.65 gm) had one or more pups that survived through weaning. In Experiment III there was complete mortality in 3 of the 11 litters. In the remaining 8 litters there was a single death in 2, and no deaths in 6. The mean birth weights of the pups in the 3 litters where all died were 4.03, 4.35, and 4.60 gm, respectively. The first two litters were the lightest ones in both experiments. These data suggest that dying is an all-or-none characteristic of the litter, and is probably based upon the mean litter weight, with a threshold for survival somewhere in the vicinity of 4.50–4.75 gm.

It is important to note that the conclusion suggested above is characteristic of the litter, not of the individual animal. In litters in which there was complete survival through weaning, we had pups whose birth weights ranged from 3.3 to 3.9 gm—values below the means of the litters that died. This observation suggest that the mother's behavior toward her pups may be the critical element in determining the viability of the litter.

One indication of the quality of maternal care in Experiment III is our finding that the weaning weight of the ligation groups did not differ from that of the sham group. These data are similar to our data in Experiment II for the Day 18 group where the mean weaning weight was 48.23 grams. We are not able to account for the lighter body weight of the Day 19 group in Experiment II, and it is obvious that we have to repeat Experiment III using 19-day ligated mothers.

In the third experiment we obtained behavioral differences in the open-field activity pattern of the two groups over days (Fig. 1), and we also found that the ligation procedure differentially affected males and females (Fig. 2). We also found no differences in body weights between our two groups at the time of open-field testing. These findings are important for two reasons: (1) we have been able to demonstrate a behavioral effect from our ligation procedure, and (2) the behavioral effect was present even though the body weight differences had disappeared, thus showing that recovery of weight to the normal level does not, of necessity, eliminate other differences.

In conclusion, we feel that the ligation procedure for generating "small-for-gestational-age" animals is yielding interesting behavioral and morphological data, and should be further investigated.

SUMMARY

In an attempt to generate an animal model for the small-for-gestational-age infant, we ligated the main artery supplying blood to the uterine horns of the rat at various ages late in pregnancy. Ligations on Days 18 or 19 of gestation resulted in significant weight retardation at birth. Between 20% and 30% of the fetuses in our ligation groups were born alive by vaginal delivery, as compared to an incidence of 84% in a sham-ligated group. The pups of ligated mothers weighed significantly less at birth, but the weight differences was not present at weaning or in adulthood. Between 66% and 88% of liveborn pups of ligated mothers survive until weaning, while approximately 98% of the sham-ligated pups were alive at weaning. In adulthood the groups were given the open-field test, and the activity pattern of the ligated group differed significantly from that of the sham group. In addition, the ligation procedure differentially affected the activity pattern of males and females.

REFERENCES

Wigglesworth, J. S. Experimental growth retardation in the foetal rat. *Journal of Pathology and Bacteriology,* 1964, **88**, 1–13.

Wigglesworth, J. S. Dysmaturity in the experimental animal. In J. H. P. Jonxis, H. K. A. Visser, & J. A. Troelstra (Eds.), *Aspects of praematurity and dysmaturity.* Springfield, Ill.: Thomas, 1968. Pp. 119–126.

6

BEHAVIORAL DEVELOPMENT VIEWED IN TERMS OF CONSPECIFIC COMMUNICATION

Gilbert W. Meier
College of Medicine, University of Nebraska

Let us look at our developmental problems anew. We have learned from a half century and more of laboratory research that no single cause of mental retardation exists and that any sharp and acute, or low-level and sustained, departure from normal physiologic conditions during prenatal and infantile life can effect such serious changes in developmental adaptability as can be called developmental or mental retardation (Meier, 1970b, 1973). With such a variety of agents with demonstrated potential for disabling the developing organism we are, indeed, impressed with the perilous journey from conception to maturity. However, we are only sometimes aware but never overly impressed by the great numbers of individuals who despite exposure to these hazards seemingly achieve that blessed state of mediocrity and are called "normal." Therefore, while we conclude that no single factor or agent can be designated as *the* cause of mental retardation, so must we also conclude that given survival no single factor is universally or invariably disabling. Consequently, we must search for and analyze those conditions that diminish the effectiveness of the hazards, that is, those conditions that mitigate the long-range effects once these agents have created an at-risk state.

For openers, I recommend the careful scrutiny of parent-offspring interactions during the early infantile and childhood periods. Although I recognize that similar suggestions have been made previously (e.g., Meier, 1970a; Richards, 1970; Rivinus & Katz, 1972), I believe that our current level of information about such interactions, gleaned from a wide variety of comparative-developmental sources, makes the recommendation even more meaningful at this time and promises new understanding and effective remediation. Additionally, I find that these more recent researches have revealed potent species-specific interaction mechanisms depicted in terms of adult-offspring contingencies. Together, these present the fundamentals for parent-offspring relations and the basis for mammalian communication. Because these relations constitute a dual process with both offspring and parent inextricably involved, our prospects for remediations are at least doubled; because one of the two is our age peer with whom we can communicate more readily, our prospects for thoughtful and willing intervention could be bright.

For any mammalian generation, the social beginning is birth. (Unquestionably, the mammalian female responds to the fetus she carries; the fetus, conversely, responds to the activites of the mother and to her environment as filtered by her body. However, this is a peculiar dyadic relation in which individuality and identity are not sharply defined.) As a newborn the individual, now anatomically and physiologically separated from the mother, immediately becomes uniquely intertwined behaviorally with her and others. The newborn appears with a series of patterns of behavior and reactivity which afford the foundation of his interactions with his caretakers and of the ontogenesis of the seemingly incredible complexity of communications—social-emotional behaviors—which typifies his species in its particular ecological niche. To the ethologically-inclined, these behaviors may qualify as "releaser mechanisms" (Rivinus & Katz, 1972). In a predictable sequence, new behaviors develop in the infant, the functions of which evolve thereafter, for the initial appearance of these behaviors seems to be without purpose or function. Their display in the ubiquitous social context may be followed by socially-produced contingencies that increase, or decrease, the probability of immediate repetition, as determined by their timing in that social situation, its current structure, and its ongoing activities. In short, two features of the ontogeny of behavior are being identified here: (1) the variety and abundance, the superabundance even, of neonatal and infantile behaviors; and (2) the selection pressure provided by environmental contingencies. Together, in their social context, these constitute a communicative sequence whereby the "message" of the infant's "signal" is the response it elicits among the caretakers around him. Some of these responses, e.g., smiles, cries, attentive looks, will be followed by parental orientation and interaction and, thereby, will increase in frequency of occurrence; others will be avoided (or ignored) and will, appropriately, decrease in likelihood of appearance, or presumably disappear. The first become the rubric for further elaboration of the communication between the child and his environment; the second are forgotten if not lost.

This presentation is not a recapitulation of the many recent studies on communication, particulary those on nonverbal and comparative aspects, whose numbers at this time are considerable and rapidly increasing (see, for example, Altmann, 1967; Harrison, Cohen, Crouch, Genova, & Steinberg, 1972; Peters & Ploog, 1973; Sebeok, 1968). It is, instead, a plan to go beyond that limited subset of the domain of communication defined by "words and things" and view the very substance of social interactions whereby the behaviors of two (or more) organisms are progressively and sequentially modified as the response of the one becomes the contingent stimulus to the response of the other. It is an effort to bring the focus of the developmentalist to bear upon the communication phenomena in the newborn and the infant, and to foster an appreciation of the essential nature of these interactions with the expectation that through their manipulation, either by experimenter or by clinician, at-risk developmental sequences can be allayed.

My own awareness of these interactions and some of their implications began with the observations of mother–infant pairs of rhesus monkeys. In one study (Meier, 1965b), I viewed the interactions of adult females, some laboratory-reared in partial isolation (see Sackett & Ruppenthal, 1970) and some feral-reared, with their offspring all of whom had been surgically delivered. In contrast to the isolate-reated females with vaginally delivered infants (Meier, 1965a), the isolate-reared females carefully avoided or clearly rejected their surgically delivered offspring who were presented to them in their own conventional cages within an hour of delivery, and repeatedly rejected them over the next 3 days. Yet, all of the feral-reared mothers vigorously accepted *their* surgically delivered infants and quickly brought them to a satisfactory nursing position. Parity and mothering experience did not seem to be related to the occurrence or intensity of these behaviors. I saw these differences as being related, in part, to the characteristic low activity and vocalization levels of the surgically delivered infant (Meier, 1964). In effect, so I thought, the infant "shaped" the maternal behaviors of the adult female as determined by its own repertoire at initial contact; with a high-risk mother (the isolate-reared female) this shaping went beyond the capability of the surgically delivered infant.

Other data on the behavior development of surgically-delivered rhesus infants (Meier & Garcia-Rodriquez, 1966) revealed the Treatment (mode of delivery) × Experience (repeated exposure) interaction made possible by a repeated measures experimental design. Vaginally born infants exposed immediately after birth to the conditioning protocol of that study demonstrated significant carry-over effects to subsequent exposures (at 30, 60, and 90 days) whereas the surgically delivered infants showed no such transfer of exposure at 30 days, whether it was the first or second exposure. Clearly, the neonatal experience with response-contingent stimulation modified the subsequent developmental sequences of behavior for one group of infants but was without significance for the other.

At the time those observations were reported (in the mid-1960s), and subsequently, the notion that the infant is an effective stimulus to parental behavior was becoming recognized in a variety of settings and in a number of species (e.g., Meier & Schutzman, 1968; Moss, 1967; Rheingold, 1969; Richards, 1966). Although the effectiveness of certain infantile features was indicated, especially those behavioral features that seemed to be species-specific, the interaction—the contingency relation—was not. Nor, for that matter, was the changing character of that interaction realized. We had not then accepted, as we do now, the consequence of that interaction whereby *both* mother and infant are progressively modified; that is, their successive responses are changed and, therefore, so are the stimuli that each presents to the other.

Recently, P. F. Chappell and I (Chappell & Meier, 1974) scored the mother-infant interactions of an isolate-reared female with her vaginally delivered infant in a playpen situation with other pairs in which the mothers were feral reared. Although the isolate mother's behaviors were adequate for the survival of the infant, they were bizarre in comparison with the behaviors of the other females and with other playpen configurations previously reported (Chappell, 1972). First, although the delivery was normal with typical activity on the part of the adult female during parturition and in the support of the infant thereafter, grooming of the infant was rarely seen, certainly not in the usual frequencies or durations. Second, the female failed to respond appropriately (by retrieval) to the infant's geckering on Postnatal Days but, rather, increased her aggressiveness toward the infant (without inflicting injury, however). This infraction of normal nurturant behavior was seen on several subsequent observation periods but not after Day 8. Third, although the female showed a remarkable reduction in stereotypic behavior (prancing and cage-strumming, in this case) with the delivery of the infant, she resumed this behavior on Day 34, occasionally trodding upon or pushing away the infant. The infant soon learned to avoid the mother at these times and to occupy itself with other aspects of the cage environment, although it would return promptly to the mother upon cessation of the episode. With the death of the infant at 4 months—the cause was apparently not related to the experimental conditions—the adult female resumed her stereotypic behaviors in full variety and intensity. Where the behaviors with the infant were of short duration and frequency, the stereotypic behaviors were greatly extended in the period following its death and approached, presumably, the prepartal levels. Although the infant did interact with the other infants in accord with our age norms, it remained close to the mother and did not enter the playpen as did infants in other pairs.

A prototype of the experimental research advocated here is the recent study by Bell, Nitschke, Bell, and Zachman (1974). In that study, the investigators monitored the ultrasonic vocalizations—species-specific responses—of infant rats in response to exposure to low ambient temperatures, and the maternal behaviors shown to those vocalizations. The nature of these vocalizations and some of the experimental conditions that elicit them have been well established. Moreover, their character and frequency of occurrence have become recognized as species and age specific (see Noirot, 1972). The incidence and possible significance of a reduction in body temperature for the understanding of the action of early manipulation of laboratory rodents upon subsequent development have been satisfactorily demonstrated by Schaefer (1968). Specific patterns of reactivity shown by the adult female rodent (laboratory rat and mouse) to manipulated offspring have been described by several authors (Hudgens, Chilgren, & Palardy, 1972; Noirot, 1969; Sherrod, Connor, & Meier, 1974). Bell and his associates in this study, however, showed that the differential responding by the rat mothers to their infants correlated (curvilinearly) with the duration of exposure to cold (5–6°C; 2 or 5 min) and, more specifically, to the nature of the infants' vocalizations. The maternal responses, for example, grooming ånd nursing pups, cage exploration, self-grooming, however, usually lasted less than 10 minutes and invariably less than 40 min; moreover, they could be elicited on Days 1–5, less so on Day 10, and not at all on Day 15. Obviously, both mothers and infants had changed by the last date.

A series of studies—no one was "complete" for the purposes of this presentation—with developing monkeys revealed the influence of environmental factors on dyadic relations between mother and infant. Jensen, Bobbitt, and Gordon (1968, 1973) reported that pairs of pig-tailed macaques maintained in essential isolation sustained close physical proximity but showed little aggressive or punitive behavior, or even retrieval behavior, either by the mother or by the infant to the mother. Instead, the infants spent much of the time climbing on the mother or manipulating her in a nonspecific fashion. However, similar pairs, maintained in similar cages but "enriched" through the addition of devices for handling and/or climbing and placement in the open laboratory, revealed much greater physical distance and greater amounts of specific manipulation of the mother and of retentive behavior toward her, but lower frequencies of restraint behaviors (e.g., prolonged looking) directed by the mother to the infant. In sharp contrast, however, were the pairs maintained in a social group (Wolfheim, Jensen, & Bobbitt, 1970). These last revealed the closest proximity of the three conditions and the lowest incidence of punitive behaviors. (These observations corroborate those of Hinde and Spencer-Booth, 1967, with rhesus macaques; Kaplan, 1972, has since extended them to the squirrel monkey as well).

A situation analysis of the daily recordings of mother-infant pairs in a simulated natural troop (Meier & Devanney, 1974) revealed that the occurrence of bouts of social play behavior was a compromise between the attractiveness of the immediate environment to the immediate environment to the infant and the proximity of the infant to the mother. Whereas activity and object play occurred early and in the presence of the mother, playful interactions with others (peers and siblings, especially) occurred only at distances greater than an arm's length from the mother and, usually, at distances greater than 3 meters or out of the mother's sight entirely. Such behaviors, or course, increased markedly in frequency from the third month on, consonant with the maturation of the infant's motor facility. In effect, the force of the mother's behavior was to restrict this form of infant social behavior to periods of quiescence of the troop when peer interactions (at all age levels) were maximal.

Something of the nature of the communication processes operative in these situations was shown by Meier, Izard, and Cobb (1971). They observed the group behaviors of six adult rhesus monkeys all of whom were devoid of certain facial expressions having had bilateral sectioning of the facial nerve (VII). The progressive changes in the aggressive (an increase) and nonaggressive (a decrease) behaviors noted over the course of the study (2 years) failed to match in kind or amount the change (from expectation) in the behaviors of the infants born to the 4 females in the group. All infants moved away from their respective mothers with fewer attempts toward retrieval by the mothers and interacted with the adult males, the females without infants at the time, and with the other infants as available, at much earlier ages than observed in intact, balanced groups of this species (Devanney, 1973).

Elsewhere, Jensen and Gordon (1970) described the effectiveness of the LEN, a species-typical facial display, in controlling mother–infant distance in pig-tailed macques. They observed that in isolation with the infant, the mother showed a progressive decrease in the frequency of this behavior over the course of the first 15 weeks postpartum (the period of the study), but that the most probable setting for its occurrence was during periods of separation of the mother and infant, contingent upon the infant looking directly at the mother. The consequence of this display was the movement of the infant toward the mother and thereafter making contact, if not immediately then upon repetition of the display by the mother.

From a playpen study of the interactions of mother-infant pairs of rhesus monkeys over the first four months, Chappell (1972) concluded that the spatial patterns of the members of each pair are situational in nature rather than an essential characteristic of the mother or infant involved, that is, they are deter-mined by "state" rather than "trait." After viewing the pairs over an extended period and mapping the baseline interactions between the individuals, the inves-tigator introduced physical barriers into the playpen whereby the infants were able to retain their mobility but the adult females were denied visual access to each other, or to the infants in certain locations. Contrary to expectations, Chappell noted that the mother-infant distance was significantly reduced with the introduc-tion of the barriers, as shown most vividly in the infants' behaviors but also in the maternal behaviors when specifically related to those of the infants.

The conclusion appears unavoidable that communication through postural and facial expressions is a dominant force in "controlling" maternal behavior in the social group, a force absent in the isolated pairs of Jensen et al. (1968) and in the nerve-sectioned group of Meier et al. (1971). Under the conditions of this degree of social control, the mother restrains the infant—inhibiting it—during the first 6 months (at least) from "free" interaction with others in the social group and with other "attractive" features in the immediate environment. Nevertheless, the contribution of other channels of communication cannot be discounted at this time. Michael, Keverne, and Bonsall (1971) have discussed and verified the considera-ble significance of olfaction for adult reproductive behaviors; Kaplan and Russell (1974) have reported upon olfactory cues important for the recognition of identity and place by the infants of these species. Unfortunately, despite the reports from Jensen and Tolman (1962), Simons, Bobbitt, and Jensen (1968), and Simons and Bielert (1973), definitive study of the development of macaque oral–aural com-munication has yet to be undertaken. The reported studies tend to show little, if any, communication through this medium. However, the conditions were such that the problem could not be examined fully. The nature of the equipment and of the sound analysis was restricted to a narrow segment (up to 6–8 kHz) of the animal's sound repertoire despite the evidence cited by Masterton, Heffner, and Ravizza (1969) that the rhesus macaque responds to frequencies up to 40 kHz. (Repeatedly over the last three years, my colleagues and I have detected in rhesus monkeys a variety of adult and infant vocalizations with significant components in this range of ultrasonic frequencies.)

We see in these nonhuman primate studies, reported on several species from several laboratories, the interactions between the mother and infant, evolving with the maturation of the infant, and the progressive changes in the stimuli and contingencies offered by each under the overall influence of the environment. With modifications in that environment—the presence or absence of playthings, the presence or absence of a social group—the behaviors of the mother and the infant are predictably and reliably altered. Although the description of the stimuli—the communicative responses and the social–environmental factors—is still grossly inadequate in comparison to the data provided by Bell and others working with laboratory rodents, we do appreciate the transaction—the interaction with progressive change—of the mother and infant behaviors as well as the impossibility of arranging for the laboratory and feral primates "neat" experimental situations of the genre of the rodent studies. Nevertheless, we are provided a basis for the extension of our approach to the human situation with some intimation as to how and where to look for appropriate behaviors.

So, let us examine the human situation, specifically a distinctly human perinatal problem; the short- and long-term effects of obstetric analgesics and anesthetics. Complications of delivery have long been recognized for their adverse effect on infant and childhood development (Little, 1861). Moreover, the very rapid increase during this century in the use of medications during pregnancy, especially at the time of delivery, has led many to question their safety for the mother and for the infant (see Bowes, 1970, for review). Noting that earlier investigators (e.g., Brazelton, 1961; Stechler, 1964) had reported significant differences in certain aspects of behavior in the newborn which were attributable to perinatal medication, Conway and Brackbill (1970) evaluated the behavior of 23 full-term, clinically-normal infants at 2 days, 5 days, and 1 month postpartum. They related the infants' Apgar ratings and their performances on the Graham Scales (Muscle Tension, Vision, and Maturation), a test of the extinction of the orienting reflex (to a 2-sec burst of white noise), and the Bayley Scales (Psychomotor Development Index and Mental Development Index) to the extent or "potency" of perinatal medication as independently judged by two experienced obstetricians. Significant correlations were found at all ages on all scales except for the Graham Maturation Subscale and the Bayley Mental Development Index. The investigators believed the Apgar ratings to be biased and declared the nonsignificant relation with the type of anesthesia used (none, local, general) to be invalid. (Drage and Berendes, 1966, analyzed data from a much larger sample collected by trained, disinterested observers and reported significant relations of the order sought by Conway and Brackbill.) Additional follow-up observations on this sample at 20 weeks (now much reduced through attrition) suggested persistent effects of the perinatal medication, especially on the orienting reflex measure.

Two directly-related mechanisms could explain the observed effects in the Conway and Brackbill study. (The authors suggested none.) First, the action of the drugs could be direct and short acting. The effect of this action would be detected at delivery and, possibly, at 2 days of age. (Continued direct effect at 5 days of age seems extreme, but this would be an estimate drawn from the effect of the drug on the mother and is, therefore, not necessarily valid for the infant.) Second, the action of the drugs could be indirect, through the responses of the parents and other caretakers to the drugged infant and the subsequent interactions between the adult and child in the 4th to 20th week. (A third possibility, i.e., profound CNS damage made transient through an autonomous, internal regenerative process, begs the question of definition and verification and, thus, will not be considered here.) The supposition of these two mechanisms is consistent with existing information. Together they can be substantiated as follows.

The most obvious effect of the direct action of the drug would be on the infant's sleep–wakefulness patterns, that is, on the infant's "state." State and state-related phenomena have been of increasing interest to the research exploring infant development. Notable among the comprehensive reports have been those by Roffwarg, Muzio, and Dement (1966) and by Wolff (1966). Critiques of research with infants, such as offered by Bell (1963), have urged the careful consideration of infant state for the analysis of patterns of reactivity, a point underscored with substantive data by Moss (1967) in his analysis of subject variables in research with infants. Not sufficiently recognized in these reports, much less in those that have built upon them, is the fact that, fisrt and foremost, state as operationally defined is a behavioral construct. Fundamentally, it is a pattern of behaviors that can be clearly and reliably recorded by an adult observer and can be shown to be both predictable and cyclic (see, for example, Reynard & Dockeray, 1939, and more recently, Boismier, 1970, and Chappell, 1970). Presumably, those behaviors recorded by a trained observer are the self-same behaviors that could be responded to by an involved and alert adult, particularly a mother or another charged with the immediate care of the infant.

The role of the mother in infant care and other interactions has been richly explored, having been given impetus by the writings of J. Bowlby (1951), which have associated a variety of psychiatric problems with aspects of maternal separation and deprivation. More recently, Levy (1958) has examined, still within the same (psychoanalytic) framework, the mother-infant interactions in the early postnatal feeding situations and has related those interactions to maternal attitudes concerning infant care.

Taking an eclectic approach, Klaus and his associates (Klaus, Kennell, Plumb, & Zuehlke, 1970; Kennell & Klaus, 1971) have observed in great detail the first interactions between the mother and her new offspring in the first 12 hr or so following its birth. They have found from their time-lapse photography of the first 10 min of maternal contact with the infant that the mothers demonstrated "an orderly and predictable pattern of behavior" toward their newborns, beginning with hesitant fingertip exploration of the infant's extremities to confident palmar massaging, carressing, and encompassing of the head and trunk. During this interval the mother's excitement increased, indicated especially by her verbalizations, but her rate of smiling decreased; her striving to waken the infant and to achieve an "en face" position (eye-to-eye contact with the axes of the mother's and infant's heads in the same plane and orientation) also increased substantially over the period of observation. In contrast with the mothers and full-term infants, mothers of premature infants, first observed 1–3 days following delivery under the constraints of the nursery (rather than on the mother's bed as with full-term infants), were much more subdued in their responses to their offspring. These mothers followed the same progression as that shown by the mothers with full-term infants but much more slowly and cautiously. They did not demonstrate the progression from finger-tip to palmar manipulation even within the first 3 visits with the child but demonstrated, instead, significant increases in fingertip contact during this period. They did show considerable interest in maintaining the "en face" position with the infant, as did the other mothers. Although not scoring such effects directly, Klaus et al. (1970) acknowledged that "maternal anesthesia might also have altered [in other studies or in the clinic routine] the effective state of either the mother or infant—a limp, sleepy unresponsive infant whose eyes were closed would not provide the same stimulus as an active, wide-awake baby [pp. 190–191]." The rapid progression from finger-tip to palmar manipulation of the infant by the mother, they recognized, may have been due in part to the presentation to the mother of the nude infant rather than the clothed infant; it may also have been due to presentation of the infant in a prone or lateral, rather than supine, posture. (Both postures [prone or lateral] of the infant have been shown by Konner, 1972, to be the "natural" postures in regard to the mother among certain hunter-gather peoples in which mother–infant contact is intimate and, for long-periods, continuous. Additionally, Brackbill, Douthitt, and West, 1973, have reported marked differences in durations of sleep and of crying between the two postures such that the infant in the prone position of the Klaus et al. 1970 study could have been more attractive [i.e., quiet and not crying] to the parent.)

We should also recognize that the human infant is not without its specific patterns of reactivity related to parent-offspring interaction during this early period. Eisenberg (1969), for example, has reported lower response thresholds to patterns and frequencies more representative of the adult (female) voice than for patterns without these characteristics or frequencies beyond (above and below) this range. Condon and Sander (1974) have described the synchronization possible between adult speech (male or female, direct or taped) and movement of the newborn (supine or held upright). In their sample, the patterns and discontinuities of infantile movement were in rhythm, with high probability of coincidence, with the articulated structure of adult speech. Such synchrony may be the basis for the concordances of mother and infant vocalizations reported by Jones and Moss (1971). The latter noted that the patterns of infantile vocalization varied with age such that at 2 weeks the amount of vocalization was related (positively) to the amount of maternal speech directed to the infant, whereas at 3 months of age, the amount of infant vocalization was related to the amount of maternal speech that was contiguous upon the infant's vocalization. (The data were analyzed in 2-second samples. They showed differences in amount as related to age—3 months more than 2 weeks—and state of the infant—active awake more than passive awake. Moreover, the incidence of infant vocalization decreased, while in the active state at least, in the presence of the mother; as could be expected, the time spent in the passive awake state was significantly greater than time in the active state. The overall influence of the mother was to increase both rate of vocalization and level of activity of the infant.)

Sander (1969) has related the activity levels of neonates to the caretaking activities, in an effort to understand the development of regulation of function. Monitoring crying and gross activity ("motility"), he showed cycles of activity evident by the sixth day which appeared sensitive to environmental conditions and routines (nursery versus home). Further, the overall level of crying and motility over the first 10 days was higher for the infant maintained in the hospital nursery than for the infant maintained with a single caretaker in a rooming-in situation. Under the latter conditions the short (about 4 hr) periods of activity and quiescence were not so evident. Under the latter conditions, only, was a 24-hr cycle evident by the end of the period of study. (See, for cross-cultural comparison, Konner, 1972.) Having shown considerable variation in frequency of crying during the first 10-day period, Sander noted that these differences were predictably modified by the subsequent caretaker (Nurse A or Nurse B, in this case). Those cared for by Nurse B showed an immediate reduction in crying in contrast to those cared for by Nurse A. (Nurse A, however, actually responded more promptly and more frequently to the infants cries than did Nurse B.) No such change in frequency of crying occurred during this period from 11–29 days of age under Nurse B's care if Nurse A had been the sole caretaker during the first 10 days. Thus, these data on crying illustrate "the complex interaction of infant differences, caretaking influence, and age effects in respect of a single measure" (Sander, 1969, p. 326). Moreover, such Infant × Caretaker interactions were reflected in the establishment of sleep-wake cycles. In this instance, infants cared for by Nurse B from 11–28 days had significantly longer periods than those cared for by Nurse A. (An account of infant differences reflecting prenatal influences has been provided by Kraemer, Korner, and Thoman, 1972. Infants of multiparous mothers required many more feeding intervals of the staff nurse at the first feeding 12 hr postpartum than did those of primiparous mothers. These differences disappeared on subsequent feedings when the mothers themselves fed the infant. The primiparous mothers, who tended to use more feeding intervals than did the multiparous mothers, used fewer intervals at the end of the 3-day period of the study. The multiparous mothers also showed some decline—from an initially lower level—but at a significantly lower rate [Thoman, Barnett, & Leiderman, 1971].)

As part of an elaborate observational study, Richards and Bernal (1972) noted that infants born to mothers medicated with Pethilorfan (a combination of two drugs, pethidine and levallorphane) were more likely to be depressed at birth and to have longer latencies to the first cry and to regular breathing. On Day 8 or 9, these infants were more likely to show certain neurologic signs (which indicated at-risk conditions) and a diminished sucking rate under test conditions. The authors concluded from observations of these mother–infant pairs as related to obstetric drug practice and to mode of feeding (breast versus bottle) that using an analysis of patterns of interaction:

> . . . we can show, at least tentatively, that Pethilorfan given to the mother during labour will alter the infant's behaviour and so in turn influence the mother–infant interaction. The consequences of this may be profound because it is possible that the 'style' of interaction is determined in this early phase. So, even if the direct effects of the drug on the infant's mother may continue, this could have developmental consequences for the infant. This is one of the possibilities that only longitudinal studies can investigate [p. 193].

Although neither conclusive nor definitive, the studies cited above (and possibly others) raise the interpretation of the Conway-Brackbill study offered here to the level of plausibility. I think that the interpretation has sufficient substance that we should now move from abstract consideration to active laboratory experimentation directing and augmenting our efforts with researches using other methodologies whereby the descriptions of the infant–adult(s) interactions be made more complete and the relevance to later behavior events shown. Additionally, we should carefully review the correlational studies on the role and influence of the extended family, on the incidence and effectiveness of siblings and grandparents as parents, on the implications of parental age for effective parental behaviors, and on the environmental (situational, architectural) constraints on parental behavior.

I find encouragement for the approach advocated here in an avowedly pragmatic study of the care of mongoloid infants, children whose prognosis for substantial behavior adaptation is extremely poor. In one study, reported by Kugel (1970), 7 infants 4–17 months of age with Down's syndrome were removed from an institutional setting and placed in a special environment which provided:

> . . . a homelike atmosphere, enough staff members to make . . . possible for each child to be assigned a staff 'substitute mother,' and continuous stimulating and physically strengthening exercises for each child. . . . Although [at the same of their introduction to the program] four of the seven children were at least 12 months old, only one child could sit alone or crawl. Four of the children had little or no head control; five had habitually open mouths and protruding tongues; and three turned their palms out awkwardly in a posture characteristic of autistic children. . . . One 12-month-old child related very well to others; another year-old child seemed happy but did not relate well. The rest of the children were extremely lethargic; they barely looked at interesting or moving objects and barely responded to the advances of adults or other children. . . . [By the end of 12 months in the program] the children were functioning up to age in gross motor activities; in fine motor activities they were slightly below the norm for their chronological age. For most of the children, adaptive behavior and even language development were appropriate for their ages; most of them had developed some self-help skill in feeding, dressing, and undressing; and some were beginning to show a little progress in toilet training. [pp. 188–192]."

This study, limited in scope (a pilot study with no control group) and duration (18 months), has been followed by a much more ambitious study at the University of Washington (Dr. Alice H. Hayden, personal communication). In this second program, interaction with the mongoloid children was even more extensive (it included scholastic activities) and enduring (from neonatal period to 6 years of age). The results, appropriately, have been even more impressive with linguistic capabilities of the order of reading with sufficient comprehension and skill that audiences may comprehend, as well. Sensorimotor and academic performances at ages 5 and 6 equaled, at least, those of normal, nonmongoloid children.

These efforts with the mongoloid children have been unabashedly eclectic in orientation, endeavoring to provide the children with as much of a variety of sensory and manipulative experiences as possible. While possibly unaware of the pitfalls of such intervention programs (Miller, 1968), the innovators provided additional inputs by way of social stimulation, as well. Kugel, for example, repeatedly acknowledged the leadership of the Skeels and Dye (1939) study and emphasized social factors in the selection and activities of the staff in his study. These adults were carefully instructed to work (interact) *with* the children in their care rather than minister *to* them. Moreover, recognizing the rapidly changing repertoires and demands of the children, the supervisory personnel held review-instruction sessions with the staff at frequent intervals (weekly). (In the Washington study the parents participated in the remediation program, by necessity. They were strongly encouraged to interact with the child at all levels—and ages—in the elaboration of his behavior.)

I am encouraged, also, by reports such as that by Herbert and Baer (1972) on the effectiveness of training parents to be behavior modifiers for children diagnosed as psychotic or organic–psychotic. I see in such approaches as those advocated by Hayden (the University of Washington project) and Herbert and Baer, for example, the tabulating of specific behaviors or the counting of attending responses to appropriate child behaviors, the possibilities for a program of remediation for developmental disabilities, one however, which will have to be carefully researched in that the particular behaviors and the age-dependent parental responses (the reinforcers) cannot now be identified.

But where do we go from here in our design of a program of intervention-remediation for parents of an at-risk newborn? If only we knew upon which infants, and which parent–infant pairs, we should direct our clinical attention! If only we knew which behaviors, both from infant and from adult, are to be encouraged (or discouraged) in the high-risk dyad! If only we could identify those caretaking situations which the epidemiologists tell us (after the fact, of course) are those that provide the "stimulating environment" as determined by the boggled statistical analyses pertaining to trends on infantile trauma and childhood development. You must recall, of course, that at present the prognosis for the at-risk infant, much less the high-risk infant, is far from precise, that many such infants survive and subsequently develop into individuals otherwise not differentiated from the rest of their society. You will agree, I am certain, that effecting any meaningful parental intervention by a rational-linguistic approach ("jawboning") by which we tell the parents that their infants need more Tender Loving Care is a notoriously poor maneuver. The goals of our research efforts should be the accumulation of more precise information on high-risk potentials and at-risk conditions, on the behaviors of infants and parents under those conditions, and on the behavioral and situational aspects leading to satisfactory outcome when a poor neonatal prognosis has been given. Such information can only come from careful monitoring of behavior, with frequent measuring and counting over extended periods of time.

REFERENCES

Altmann, S. A. *Social communication among primates.* Chicago, Illinois, University of Chicago Press, 1967.

Bell, R. Q. Some factors to be controlled in studies of behavior of newborns. *Biologica Neonatorum,* 1963, **5**, 200–214.

Bell, R. W., Nitschke, W., Bell, N. J., & Zachman, T. A. Early experience, ultrasonic vocalizations, and maternal responsiveness in rats, *Developmental Psychobiology,* 1974, **7**, 235–242.

Boismier, J. D. A Markov analysis of behavioral arousals in the human newborn. Unpublished master's thesis, George Peabody College for Teachers, 1970.

Bowes, W. A., Jr. Obstetrical medication and infant outcome: A review of the literature. *Monographs of the Society for Research in Child Development,* 1970, **35** (4, Serial No. 137), 3–23.

Bowlby, J. *Maternal care and mental health.* Geneva: World Health Organization, 1951.

Brackbill, Y., Douthitt, T. C., & West, H. Neonatal posture: Psychophysiological effects. *Neuropädiatrie,* 1973, **4**, 145–150.

Brazelton, T. B. Effect of maternal medication on the neonate and his behavior. *Journal of Pediatrics,* 1961, **58**, 513–518.

Chappell, P. F. The validation of a behavioral inventory for assessing states of arousal in the human newborn. Unpublished master's equivalency paper, George Peabody College for Teachers, 1970.

Chappell, P. F. The dynamic proximal relationship of rhesus monkeys *(Macaca mulatta)* mother-infant pairs as affected by temporary installation of physical barriers. Unpublished doctoral dissertation, George Peabody College for Teachers, 1972.

Chappell, P. F., & Meier, G. W. Mutual modification of behavior of an isolate-reared rhesus female and her infant. *Developmental Psychobiology,* 1974, **7**, 296.

Conway, E., & Brackbill, Y. Delivery medication and infant outcome: An empirical study. *Monographs of the Society for Research in Child Development,* 1970, **35** (4, Serial No. 137), 24–34.

Condon, W. S., & Sander, L. W. Neonate movement is synchronized with adult speech: Interactional participation and language acquisition. *Science,* 1974, **183**, 99–101.

Devanney, V. D. A developmental study of operant behavior acquired by infant monkeys in a social group. Unpublished master's thesis, George Peabody College for Teachers, 1973.

Drage, J. S., & Berendes, H. Apgar scores and outcome of the newborn. *Pediatric Clinics of North America,* 1966, **13**, 635–643.

Eisenberg, R. J. Auditory behavior in the human neonate: Functional properties of sound and their ontogenetic implications. *International Audiologist,* 1969, **7**, 34–35.

Harrison, R. P., Cohen, A. A., Crouch, W. W., Genova, B. K. L., & Steinberg, M. The nonverbal communication literature. *Journal of Communication,* 1972, **22**, 460–476.

Herbert, E. W., & Baer, D. M. Training parents as behavior modifiers: Self-recording of contingent attention. *Journal of Applied Behavior Analysis,* 1972, **5**, 139–149.

Hinde, R. A., & Spencer-Booth, Y. The effect of social companions on mother-infant relations in rhesus monkeys. In D. Morris (Ed.), *Primate ethology*. London: Morrison and Gibb, 1967. Pp. 267–286.

Hudgens, G. W., Chilgren, J. D., & Palardy, D. D. Mother-infant interactions: Effects of early handling of offspring on rat mothers' open-field behavior. *Developmental Psychobiology*, 1972, **5**, 61–70.

Jensen, G. D., Bobbitt, R. A., & Gordon, B. N. Effects of environment on the relationship between mother and infant pig-tailed monkeys *(Macaca nemestrina)*. *Journal of Comparative and Physiological Psychiatry*, 1968, **66**, 259–263.

Jensen, G. D., Bobbitt, R. A., & Gordon, B. N. Mothers' and infants' roles in the development of independence of *Macaca nemestrina*. *Primates*, 1973, **14**, 79–88.

Jensen, G. D., & Gordon, B. N. Sequences of mother-infant behavior following a facial communicative gesture of pig-tailed monkeys. *Biological Psychiatry*, 1970, **2**, 267–272.

Jensen, G. D., & Tolman, C. W. Activity level of the mother monkey, *Macaca nemestrina*, as affected by various conditions of sensory access to the infant following separation. *Animal Behaviour*, 1962, **10**, 228–230.

Jones, S. J., & Moss, H. A. Age, state, and maternal behavior associated with infant vocalizations. *Child Development*, 1971, **42**, 1039–1051.

Kaplan, J. Differences in mother-infant relations of squirrel monkeys housed in social and restricted environments. *Developmental Psychobiology*, 1972, **5**, 43–52.

Kaplan, J., & Russell, M. Olfactory recognition in the infant squirrel monkey. *Developmental Psychobiology*, 1974, **7**, 15–19.

Kennell, J. H., & Klaus, M. H. Care of the mother of the high-risk infant. *Clinical Obstetrics and Gynecology*, 1971, **14**, 926–954.

Klaus, M. H., Kennell, J. H., Plumb, N., & Zuehlke, S. Human maternal behavior at the first contact with her young. *Pediatrics*, 1970, **46**, 187–192.

Konner, M. J. Aspects of the developmental ethology of a foraging people. In N. Blurton Jones (Ed.), *Ethological studies of child behaviour*. Cambridge: Cambridge University Press, 1972. Pp. 285–304.

Kraemer, H. C., Korner, A. F., & Thoman, E. B. Methodological considerations in evaluating the influences of drugs used during labor and delivery on the behavior of the newborn. *Developmental Psychology*, 1972, **6**, 128–134.

Kugel, R. B. Combatting retardation in infants with Down's syndrome. *Child*, 1970, **17**, 188–192.

Levy, D. M. *Behavioral analysis*. Springfield, Ill.: Thomas, 1958.

Little, W. J. On the influence of abnormal parturition, difficult labours, premature birth, and asphyxia neonatorum, on the mental and physical condition of the child, especially in relation to deformities. *Transactions of the Obstetrical Society (London)*, 1861, **3**, 293–344.

Masterton, B., Heffner, H. E., & Ravizza, R. J. Evolution of human hearing. *Journal of the Acoustic Society of America*, 1969, **45**, 966–985.

Meier, G. W. Behavior of infant monkeys: Differences attributable to mode of birth. *Science*, 1964, **143**, 968–970.

Meier, G. W. Other data on the effects of social isolation during rearing upon adult reproductive behavior in the rhesus monkey *(Macaca mulatta)*. *Animal Behaviour*, 1965, **13**, 228–231. (a)

Meier, G. W. Maternal behaviour of feral- and laboratory-reared monkeys following the surgical delivery of their infants. *Nature*, 1965, **206**, 492–493. (b)

Meier, G. W. Editorial: In the name of communication. *Developmental Psychobiology*, 1970, **3**, 3–4. (a)

Meier, G. W. Mental retardation in animals. In N. R. Ellis (Ed.), *International review of research in mental retardation*. Vol. 4. New York: Academic Press, 1970. Pp. 263–309. (b)

Meier, G. W. Mental retardation. In G. H. Bourne (Ed.), *Primates in biomedical research*. New York: Academic Press, 1973. Pp. 431–465.

Meier, G. W., & Devanney, V. D. The ontogeny of play within a society: Preliminary analysis. *American Zoologist*, 1974, **14**, 289–294.

Meier, G. W., & Garcia-Rodriguez, C. Continuing behavioral differences in infant monkeys as related to mode of delivery. *Psychological Reports*, 1966, **19**, 1219–1225.

Meier, G. W., Izard, C. E., & Cobb, C. Facial display in primate communication. Paper presented at the meeting of the Southeastern Psychological Association, Miami, Florida, 1971.

Meier, G. W., & Schutzman, L. H. Mother-infant interactions and experimental manipulation: Confounding or misidentification? *Developmental Psychobiology*, 1968, **1**, 141–145.

Michael, R. P., Keverne, E. B., & Bonsall, R. W. Pheromones: Isolation of male sex attractants from a female primate. *Science*, 1971, **172**, 964–966.

Miller, J. O. Cultural deprivation and its modification: Effects of intervention. In H. C. Haywood (Ed.), *Social-cultural aspects of mental retardation*. New York: Appleton-Century-Crofts, 1968. Pp. 451–489.

Moss, H. A. Sex, age, and state as determinants of mother-infant interaction. *Merrill-Palmer Quarterly of Behavior and Development*, 1967, **13**, 19–36.

Noirot, E. Selective priming of maternal responses by auditory and olfactory cues from mouse pups. *Developmental Psychobiology*, 1969, **2**, 273–276.

Noirot, E. Ultrasounds and maternal behavior in small rodents. *Developmental Psychobiology*, 1972, **5**, 371–387.

Peters, M., & Ploog, D. Communication among primates. *Annual Review of Physiology*, 1973, **35**, 221–242.

Reynard, M. C., & Dockeray, F. C. The comparison of temporal intervals in judging depth of sleep in newborn infants. *Journal of Genetic Psychology*, 1939, **55**, 103–120.

Rheingold, H. L. The social and socializing infant. In D. A. Goslin (Ed.), *Handbook of socialization: Theory and research*. Chicago: Rand-McNally, 1969. Pp. 779–790.

Richards, M. P. M. Infantile handling in rodents: A reassessment in the light of recent studies of maternal behaviour. *Animal Behaviour*, 1966, **14**, 582.

Richards, M. P. M. The development of behaviour and its social context. *New Scientist*, 1970, **46**, 638.

Richards, M. P. M., & Bernal, J. F. An observational study of mother-infant interaction. In N. Blurton Jones (Ed.), *Ethological studies of child behaviour*. Cambridge: Cambridge University Press, 1972. Pp. 175–197.

Rivinus, H. A., & Katz, S. H. Evolution, newborn behavior and maternal attachment. *Comments on Contemporary Psychiatry*, 1972, **2**, 95–104.

Roffwarg, H. P., Muzio, J. N., & Dement, W. C. Ontogenetic development of the human sleep-dream cycle. *Science*, 1966, **152**, 604–619.

Sackett, G. P., & Ruppenthal, G. C. Development of monkeys after varied experiences during infancy. In S. A. Barnett (Ed.), *Ethology and development*. London: Spastics International Medical Publications, 1970. Pp. 52–87.

Sander, L. W. The longitudinal course of early mother-child interactions: Cross-case comparison in a sample of mother-child pairs. In B. M. Foss (Ed.), *Determinants of infant behaviour IV*. London: Methuen, 1969. Pp. 189–227.

Schaefer, T. The search for a critical factor in early handling. In G. Newton & S. Levine (Eds.), *Early experience and behavior*. Springfield: Thomas, 1968. Pp. 102–141.

Sebeok, T. A. *Animal communication: Techniques of study and results of research*. Bloomington: Indiana University Press, 1968.

Sherrod, K. B., Connor, W. H., & Meier, G. W. Transient and enduring effects of handling on infant and maternal behavior in mice. *Developmental Psychobiology*, 1974, **7**, 31–37.

Simons, R. C., & Bielert, C. F. An experimental study of vocal communication between mother and infant monkeys *(Macaca nemestrina)*. *American Journal of Physical Anthropology*, 1973, **38**, 455–462.

Simons, R. C., Bobbitt, R. A., & Jensen, G. D. Mother monkey's *(Macaca nemestrina)* responses to infant vocalizations. *Perceptual and Motor Skills,* 1968, **27**, 3–10.

Skeels, H. M., & Dye, H. B. A study of the effects of differential stimulation on mentally retarded children. *Journal of Psycho-Asthenics,* 1969, **44**, 114–136.

Stechler, G. Newborn attention as affected by medication during labor. *Science,* 1964, **144**, 315–317.

Thoman, E. B., Barnett, C. R., & Leiderman, P. H. Feeding behaviors of newborn infants as a function of parity of the mother. *Child Development,* 1971, **42**, 1471–1483.

Wolff, P. H. The causes, controls and organization of behavior in the young infant. *Psychological Issues,* 1966, **5** (Whole No. 17).

Wolfheim, J. H., Jensen, G. D., & Bobbitt, R. A. Effects of group environment on the mother-infant relationships in pig-tailed monkeys *(Macaca nemestrina). Primates,* 1970, **11**, 119–124.

7

PARADOXICAL EFFECTS OF AMPHETAMINE ON BEHAVIORAL AROUSAL IN NEONATAL AND ADULT RATS: A POSSIBLE ANIMAL MODEL OF THE CALMING EFFECT OF AMPHETAMINE ON HYPERKINETIC CHILDREN

Byron A. Campbell
Patrick K. Randall
Princeton University

The hyperkinetic syndrome in children is characterized by high levels of motor activity, lack of coordination, short attention span, inability to concentrate, lack of impulse control, nonresponsiveness to social influence, and labile emotionality. Characteristically there are no "hard" neurological signs of cerebral damage, EEG activity is within normal limits, and there is no consistent pattern of dysfunction on perceptual and cognitive tasks. Overall intelligence scores fall within the normal range, and in most cases the dysfunction disappears or is greatly attenuated as the child enters adolescence (Wender, 1971).

One of the most unusual aspects of the hyperkinetic child is the calming effect of a number of stimulants, particularly amphetamine and methylphenidate. This effect is usually described as paradoxical in that adult organisms, human as well as infrahuman, show marked increases in behavioral arousal in response to such agents. The neurochemical basis for calming is unknown and has not been observed in "normal" infant animals using typical tests of drug-induced locomotor activity. In developing rats, for example, hyperactivity to amphetamine is one of the earliest drug-induced responses to appear ontogenetically, and the effects of amphetamine-related compounds are, if anything, more pronounced in young animals. A higher maximal response is obtained, the dose-response curve is

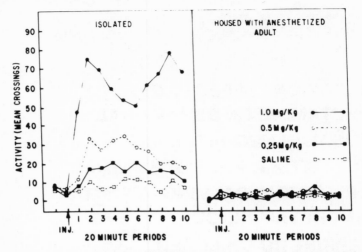

FIG. 1.   Time course of locomotor activity for different doses of *d*-amphetamine in 15-day-old rats housed with or without an anesthetized adult.

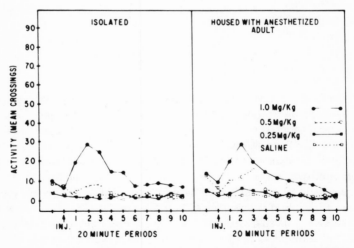

FIG. 2.   Time course of locomotor activity for different doses of *d*-amphetamine in 30-day-old rats housed with or without an anesthetized adult.

to the left of that of the adult, and there is a prolonged time course relative to adults (Campbell, Lytle, & Fibiger, 1969; Lal & Sourkes, 1973).

    There is, however, a distinct parallel between human and rat development. Both are altricial, with a large part of physical and neurological development occurring in the postnatal period, and both pass through periods of intense hyperactivity in the normal course of development. When the rat is tested in isolation, hyperactivity commences around 10 days of age, reaches a peak at 15 days, and declines precipitously to the lower levels of activity characteristic of adults by 20 or 25 days of age (Campbell et al., 1969; Moorcroft, Lytle, & Campbell, 1971).

Although the data are much less complete, it appears that young children pass through a similar period of hyperactivity. Gesell and Ilg (1943), for example, describe the 18–24 month period as follows: "charged with run-about compulsion . . . he lugs, tugs, dumps, pushes, pulls, and pounds with gross motor activity taking the lead over the fine motor . . . his attention, like his body activity, is mercurial [p. 141]." Recently, Routh, Schroeder, and O'Tauma (1974) have shown that number of squares crossed in an open field situation adapted for children decreased sharply from three to five years of age. Thus it appears that the normal human infant, like the rat, passes through a phase of relative quiescence in the early postnatal period followed first by the intense behavioral excitation described by Gesell and Ilg, and then by a decline in nondirected activity described by Routh and associates.

Many child psychiatrists interpret the hyperkinetic syndrome as a neuro-psychological lag in development. As noted there is no obvious neurological deficit and the child frequently outgrows the syndrome as he enters late childhood or adolescence. In addition, the behavioral profile is extremely reminiscent of the behavior of a child in the 18–24 month age range. It is as if the hyperactive child is slow to pass through the period of hyperkinesis that occurs during the normal course of ontogenesis. If this interpretation is correct, one might expect to see a calming effect of amphetamine on normal children in the 18–24 month range and, in the case of rats, calming at 15 days of age. The first information is difficult to obtain for social and ethical reasons and is not observed in the 15-day-old rat when tested in isolation. We have, however, recently found a discrete set of environmental conditions in which the young rat's behavioral response to amphetamine may be analogous to that of the hyperkinetic child. The details of these experimental findings are as follows.

Rats of different ages were observed in an 8 × 16 inch polyethylene cage either alone or housed in the presence of an anesthetized adult female. Injections of isotonic saline or 1.0 mg/kg d-amphetamine sulphate were administered to 10-, 15-, 20-, 25-, or 30-day-old rats ($n = 8$ in all groups) in both housing conditions, and dose-response curves with 0, 0.25, 0.5, and 1.0 mg/kg were obtained at 15 and 30 days ($n = 8$ in all groups). Behavior, number of times Ss crossed the middle of the cage, and time spent in contact with the anesthetized animal was monitored on a time lapse video tape recorder (record 1.5 fields/sec; playback 60 fields/sec). This allowed an observer to score a 5 hour session in 15 to 20 minutes. The time course of the activity in isolated 15- and 30-day rats at different doses is depicted in the left panels of Figs. 1 and 2. The younger animals, as previously described, show a much greater increase in activity across doses and respond to lower doses than do the 30-day rats. The prolonged time course is also evident with the 15-day Ss, with hyperactivity continuing throughout the entire 200-min session.

The effect of the presence of an anesthetized adult is dramatic. Plotted in the right-hand panels of Figs. 1 and 2 is the activity of 15- and 30-day-old rats housed

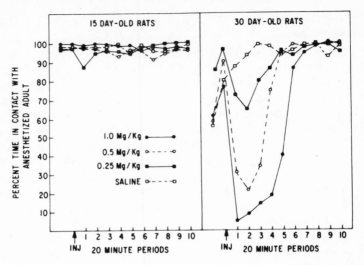

FIG. 3.   Percent of time spent in contact with anesthetized adult by 15- and 30-day-old rats at different doses of *d*-amphetamine.

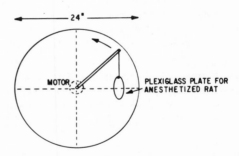

FIG. 4.   Schematic diagram of open field containing motor-driven lever that pulls an anesthetized animal 90° every 2 min. Behavior is recorded on a time-lapse video tape recorder.

with an anesthetized adult. In the 30-day-old group (Fig. 2) there is no difference between the amphetamine activity in the two housing conditions: Both show a dose-related increase in random locomotor activity. In the 15-day-old group, however, there is complete inhibition of amphetamine-induced locomotor activity in those animals housed with the adult, whereas the isolated animals show the hyperresponsivity characteristic of that age.

Further analysis of the video tape records confirm this finding. Amphetamine administered to 15-day-old rats in the presence of an adult appeared to potentiate behaviors incompatible with random locomotor activity, namely, approach and contact with the anesthetized animal. The simplest measure of this amphetamine effect, time spent in contact with the anesthetized adult, is shown in Fig. 3 for both the 15- and 30-day-old subjects. Here it is evident that amphetamine markedly reduces, dose dependently, time spent in contact with the anesthetized adult in

30-day-old rats, but does not decrease contact time in 15-day-old animals. Both saline and amphetamine treated neonates spend nearly all of the 4-hour session in contact with the anesthetized animal.

While these data demonstrate that amphetamine does not disrupt contact behavior at 15 days of age as it does at 30, we were not able to estimate or measure the vigor of the approach and contact response with any confidence. In order to determine if amphetamine had a potentiating effect on approach and contact in the 15-day-old rat we constructed a circular open field (2 ft in diameter) and installed a motor-driven arm in the center which moved the anesthetized animal 90° every 2 min. Figure 4 depicts the apparatus schematically.

With this procedure, most 15-day-old rats spent relatively little time in contact with the periodically moving anesthetized animal. Instead, after a few abortive efforts to stay next to it, they appeared to fall asleep or become quiescent. Of interest is the observation that they were not as active in the presence of the moving anesthetized animal as they were when placed alone in the apparatus.

When 15-day-old neonates were given amphetamine in this experimental situation, a remarkably different pattern of behavior emerged. Each time the anesthetized animal was pulled a quarter turn, the amphetamine-treated animal became alert, engaged in a burst of activity until it regained contact, and then either became quiescent or indulged in what appeared to be vigorous rooting and/or investigative behavior. Often after 2 or 3 hr the neonatal rat had learned to sit or lie on the anesthetized animal, thereby receiving a free ride every 120 sec. Riding on the anesthetized animal often persisted long after the drug had worn off.

In order to examine the following behavior *per se,* uncontaminated by this "riding" effect, we covered the stimulus animal with a second piece of plexiglass. This prevented the pup from riding on the fur of the anesthetized rat but left the lateral flanks of the stimulus animal exposed. This further minimized the tendency of the saline-treated animals to approach the stimulus animal but had little effect on the amphetamine treated group. Using this procedure we studied the effects of amphetamine on approach and contact in 15- and 30-day-old animals. The behavior scored was time spent in contact with the periodically moving animal. Eight animals were run in each group and the amphetamine dose was 1 mg/kg.

The results of this experiment are shown in Fig. 5. Here it is evident that amphetamine markedly increases the time spent by the 15-day-old rat in contact with the anesthetized animal, but had no effect on the approach and contact response in the 30-day-old rat. Instead, at 30 days of age amphetamine simply increased "random" locomotor activity. The moving anesthetized animal was completely ignored by both saline and amphetamine treated rats at that age. This transition from directed or "canalized" arousal to generalized arousal is extremely rapid and most likely reflects an age dependent change in central nervous system function.

In man, a similar transition may take place. Early in the normal course of development—and in those children showing a neurodevelopmental lag—amphetamine may serve to direct behavior toward ethologically relevant stimuli, resulting in decreased locomotor activity, increased attention span, less

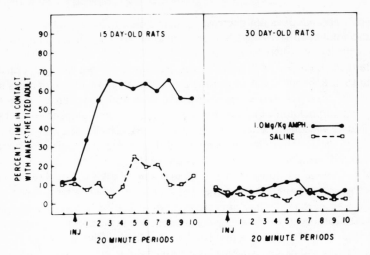

FIG. 5.   Effect of 1.0-mg/kg *d*-amphetamine on time spent in contact with rotating anesthetized adult.

labile emotionality, and so forth. With continued cerebral maturation, the directing and organizing effects of amphetamine may diminish and the generalized arousal-inducing properties emerge and become dominant.

The tendency for amphetamine to direct behavior is probably not restricted to amphetamine and its derivitives. On the basis of tentative pilot data it appears that many other stimulant conditions that produce generalized, non-directed arousal in the adult, including food deprivation and electric shock, increase approach and contact in the neonatal rat. This may also be true of the human infant. Bridger (1962) reports, for example, that immersing the child's foot in cold water increases nursing.

In both rat and man these sequences of development are closely correlated with, and presumably controlled by, central nervous system development. The brains of both develop in a caudal to rostral direction, the brainstem being far more mature at birth than the forebrain. In man, many of the reflexes of infancy which are organized at the brainstem level (e.g., rooting, suckling, Babinski) are known to be actively inhibited by maturation of specific regions of the cortex and to reappear following injury to those areas (Paulson & Gottlieb, 1968). For the rat it is similarly assumed that the reflexive behaviors of infancy which disappear during ontogenesis are inhibited by analagous regions of the brain, although direct experimental evidence on this point is lacking.

Given this interrelation between maturation of the central nervous system and the sequential emergence and disappearance of neonatal reflexive behaviors, it is tempting to assume that a comparable process mediates the transition from canalized arousal to generalized arousal. In the rat, forebrain areas such as the cortex and hippocampus are known to exert a high degree of inhibitory influence on behavioral excitability in the adult. In particular the hippocampus, a structure that at birth contains a large number of mitotic cells (Altman & Das, 1965), is neurochemically incomplete (Mathews, Nadler, Lynch, and Cotman, 1974), and is particularly sparce in synaptic clefts (Crain, Cotman, Taylor, and Lynch, 1973), has been implicated repeatedly in the control of arousal. Lesions of this area typically produce an animal that is chronically hyperactive, as well as hyper-responsive to phasic factors (e.g., estrous, food deprivation) normally resulting in locomotor activity increments (Altman, Bruner, & Bayer, 1973; Douglas, 1967). Frontal cortex, another area slow to mature, is believed to be involved in the suppression of reactive increases in arousal. Ontogenetically, lesions of these structures have no effect on activity prior to the period of decreasing normal activity subsequent to 15 days of age (Moorcroft, 1971). During the subsequent 5 days very rapid growth and development occurs, both anatomically and electrophysiologically, so that by 25 days the hippocampus has essentially adult characteristics (Crain et al., 1973; Myslivecek, 1970). Furthermore, pharmacological agents producing an effect on activity through cholinergic or serotonergic action do not become effective until ages at which hippocampal and frontal lesions produce adult-like effects (Fibiger, Lytle, & Campbell, 1970; Campbell & Mabry, 1973). In this connection there is good evidence that at least some components of the hyperactivity seen in hippocampal animals is a result of the disruption of a serotonergic projection from the raphe nucleus to the hippocampus (Trimbach, 1972).

The limbic system, and particularly the hippocampal complex, has been implicated in the control of emotional arousal. Furthermore, in humans it seems as well to be involved in attentional and short-term memory processes. In view of this and its extensive postnatal development as demonstrated by both anatomical and lesion techniques, the limbic system seems a good candidate for the neurological substrate of hyperkinesis. Late maturing structures, such as the hippocampus, may be particularly susceptible to neurotoxins of many sorts, for example, lead, which may play a role in the etiology of some forms of hyperkinesia. It is well-known that stresses of all sorts have a greater effect on rapidly developing organs than on mature structures (see Dobbing, 1970). Lastly, limbic system involvement seems particularly appealing since a general intellectual deficit is not a critical characteristic of the syndrome. If there were a general neurodevelopmental lag in the CNS, including cortex, one would also expect slower intellectual development. Instead, the hyperkinetic child seems plagued by impulsiveness, hyperactivity, and short attention span with minimal impairment of intellectual function.

Two recent studies in infrahuman primates tend to further support this analysis of juvenile behavior and its dependence on neurological development. First, infant chimpanzies have been reported to cease exploratory or play behavior and to cling to the mother following amphetamine administration (Mason, 1971). Second, lesions of the cortex are said to severely delay the normal transition from neonatal to juvenile behavior in the rhesus monkey. In particular, clinging and contact with the mother was prolonged in the lesioned animals.

These two observations offer further support for the view that amphetamine does indeed produce a different if not "paradoxical" effect on behavior in the neonatal animal and that the disappearance of this paradoxical effect is dependent upon further maturation of the central nervous system.

REFERENCES

Altman, J., Bruner, R. L., & Bayer, S. A. The hippocampus and behavioral maturation. *Behavioral Biology*, 1973, **8**, 557–596.

Altman, J., & Das, G. D. Autoradiographic and histological evidence of postnatal hippocampal neurogenesis in rats. *Journal of Comparative Neurology*, 1965, **124**, 319–336.

Bridger, W. H. Ethological concepts and human development. *Recent Advances in Biological Psychiatry*, 1962, **4**, 95–107.

Campbell, B. A., Lytle, L. D., & Fibiger, H. C. Ontogeny of arousal and cholinergic inhibitory mechanisms in the rat. *Science*, 1969, **166**, 637–638.

Campbell, B. A., & Mabry, P. D. The role of catecholamines in behavioral arousal during ontogenesis. *Psychopharmacologia*, 1973, **31**, 253–264.

Crain, B., Cotman, C., Taylor, D., & Lynch, G. A quantitative electron microscopic study of synaptogenesis in the dentate gyrus of the rat. *Brain Research*, 1973, **63**, 195–204.

Dobbing, J. Undernutrition and the developing brain. In W. A Himwich (Ed.), *Developmental neurobiology*. Springfield, Ill.: Thomas, 1970. Pp. 241–261.

Douglas, R. J. The hippocampus and behavior. *Psychological Bulletin*, 1967, **67**, (6), 416–442.

Fibiger, H. C., Lytle, L. D., & Campbell, B. A. Cholinergic modulation of adrenergic arousal in the developing rat. *Journal of Comparative and Physiological Psychology*, 1970, **72**, 384–389.

Gesell, A., & Ilg, F. *Infant and child in the culture of today*. New York: Harper and Row, 1943.

Lal, S., & Sourkes, T. L. Ontogeny of stereotyped behavior induced by apomorphine and amphetamine in the rat. *Archives Internationales de Pharmacodynamie et de Therapie*, 1973, **202**, 171–182.

Mason, N. A. Motivational factors in psychosocial development. In W. J. Arnold & M. M. Page (Eds.), *Nebraska symposium on motivation*. Lincoln: University of Nebraska Press, 1971.

Mathews, D. A., Nadler, J. V., Lynch, G. S., & Cotman, C. W. Development of cholinergic innervation in the hippocampal formation of the rat. I. Histochemical demonstration of acetylcholinesterase activity. *Developmental Biology*, 1974, **96**, 130–141.

Moorcroft, W. H. Ontogeny of behavioral inhibition by forebrain structures in the rat. *Brain Research*, 1971, **35**, 513–525.

Moorcroft, W. H., Lytle, L. D., & Campbell, B. A. Ontogeny of starvation-induced behavioral arousal in the rat. *Journal of Comparative and Physiological Psychology*, 1971, **75**, 59–67.

Myslivecek, J. Electrophysiology of the developing brain-Central and Eastern European contributions. In W. A. Himwich (Ed.), *Developmental neurobiology*. Springfield, Ill.: Thomas, 1970.

Paulson, G., & Gottlieb, G. Development reflexes: The reappearance of foetal and neonatal reflexes in aged patients. *Brain*, 1965, **91**, 37.

Routh, D. K., Schroeder, C. S., & O'Tauma, L. A. Development of activity level in children. *Developmental Psychology*, 1974, **10** (2), 163–168.

Trimbach, C. Hippocampal modulation of behavioral arousal: Mediation by serotonin. Unpublished doctoral dissertation, Princeton University, 1972.

Wender, P. H. *Minimal brain dysfunction in children*. New York: Wiley, 1971.

8

THE CONCEPT OF A CUMULATIVE
RISK SCORE FOR INFANTS

Arthur H. Parmelee, M.D.
Marian Sigman, Ph.D.
Claire B. Kopp, Ph.D.
Audrey Haber, Ph.D.
University of California at Los Angeles

INTRODUCTION

For this discussion, the term risk is used to imply an increased probability of handicap in childhood. At present, we generally identify infants at biological risk for later sensory, motor, or mental handicaps on the basis of pregnancy, perinatal, and postnatal factors related to infant mortality. Justification for this procedure derives from the concept that a continuum of casualty exists which has both lethal and sublethal manifestations. The lethal components consist of abortions, still births, and neonatal deaths, while the sublethal manifestations include sensory, motor, and mental disabilities (Lilienfeld & Parkhurst, 1951; Parmelee & Haber, 1973; Sameroff & Chandler, in press).

This concept is helpful in identifying potentially important variables, but it does not aid us in determining the predictive power of these factors. Such information is not available from present studies. Correlations between single perinatal or post-natal events and later disabling sequelae have been very low in several large prospective studies (Buck, Gregg, Stavraky, *et al.* 1969; Niswander, Friedman, Hoover, *et al.*, 1966; Parmelee & Haber, 1973; Sameroff & Chandler, in press). Similarly, the English risk registers, which attempted to classify infants with items selected on the basis of clinical impressions, have failed because too many unimportant isolated events were included (Rogers, 1968).

Studies that have focused on more comprehensive "risk" events such as prematurity and neonatal asphyxia or anoxia have demonstrated greater incidence of disabling sequelae among infants who have suffered such trauma than among control infants. However, even these results have varied between studies because of the heterogeneity of the risk groups studied. In all follow-up studies of risk

113

factors, a broad spectrum of outcomes has been obtained rather than a bimodal distribution of normal and abnormal outcomes between groups. While this is consistent with the concept of a continuum of casualty, such results do not aid in the identification of the strength of relevant variables (Braine, Heimer, Wortis, & Freedman, 1966; Douglas, 1960; Drage & Berendes, 1966; Drage, Berendes, & Fisher, 1967; Drillien, 1964; Graham, Ernhard, Thurston, & Craft, 1962; Heimer, Cutler, & Freedman, 1964; Keith & Gage, 1960; Lubchenco, Delivoria-Popadopoulos, & Searles, 1972; Parmelee & Haber, 1973; Sameroff & Chandler, in press; Schacter & Apgar, 1959; Wiener, Rider, Oppel, & Harper, 1968).

One important recurring observation is that outcome measures are strongly influenced by the socio-economic circumstances of the children's environments, and this influence is often stronger than that of earlier biological events. However, there is also evidence that early biological problems lead children to be more vulnerable to adverse environments. Since health problems during pregnancy and early infancy are related to socio-economic status, the two variables must be considered inextricably interwoven (Braine *et al.*, 1966; Douglas, 1960; Drage *et al.* 1969; Drillien, 1964; Heimer *et al.*, 1964; Knobloch & Pasamanick, 1960; Parmelee & Haber, 1973; Sameroff & Chandler, in press; Werner, Simonian, Bierman, & French, 1968; Weiner *et al.*, 1968).

Thus, with our present information, we can discuss which groups of infants are at risk of later disabilities on the basis of socio-economic and/or biological indicators, but we cannot specify the degree of risk or identify the individual infant who will suffer a disability in childhood.

A CUMULATIVE RISK CONCEPT

The majority of the infants in any "risk" group so far identified do sufficiently well on all outcome measures later in childhood that they can not be considered truely handicapped. As a result, the manpower required for intervention programs with the truely handicapped infants is critically diluted by our inability to precisely identify these children. We would like, therefore, to devise more accurate predictive measures of the degree of risk for individual infants. Several studies have demonstrated that multiple factors may be considered as additive in determining degree of risk. Some have cumulated pregnancy, perinatal, and neonatal events and others have included socioeconomic factors (Braine *et al.* 1966; Drage & Berendes, 1966; Drage *et al.*, 1969; Drillien, 1964; Heimer *et al.*, 1964; Werner *et al.*, 1968; Wiener *et al.*, 1968). A recent study demonstrated high prediction of behavioral achievement at 7 years of age using a cumulative score of biological factors during pregnancy, birth events, socio-economic factors, and performance items during the first year of life (Smith, Flick, Ferriss, & Sellman, 1972).

On this basis, we decided to design a method of identifying infants at risk that used multiple assessments at different ages and measured a wide range of variables

(Parmelee, Sigman, Kopp, & Haber, 1974). In devising our risk scoring system we considered the following clinical observations and deductions:

1. Many perinatal problems cause only transient insult, rather than permanent brain injury. Thus, in the newborn period, babies may appear equally ill upon examination but some will recover completely.

2. Some pregnancy and perinatal problems cause brain injury that is not manifest in obvious ways in the neonatal period but the deviance becomes more evident as complex behaviors unfold during infancy.

3. Some parents appear intuitively able to provide an optimal environment for an infant with mild neurological deviances, allowing him to compensate.

With these points in mind a useful risk scoring system might be one that (a) scores pregnancy, perinatal, and neonatal biological events and behavioral performances in an additive fashion; (b) reassesses the infant in the first months of life to sort out those infants with transient brain insult from those with brain injury who remain deviant; (c) reassesses the infant again primarily on a behavioral basis later in the first year of life, providing time for environments to have an effect on developmental progress.

Cumulative Risk Score Design

Our cumulative risk score system is composed of five items in the neonatal period, four at three and four months, and five at eight to nine months, as follows:

Neonatal risk score items:
1. obstetric complications
2. postnatal events
3. newborn neurological examination
4. visual attention
5. sleep polygraph

Three- and four-month risk score items:
1. pediatric events and examination
2. Gesell test
3. visual attention
4. sleep polygraph

Eight- and nine-months risk score items:
1. pediatric events and examination
2. Gesell test
3. cognitive test
4. hand precision/sensory–motor schemes
5. exploratory behavior

Pilot studies were conducted on these measures to determine the range and distribution of scores. A range of performance scores from normal to abnormal was established for each test, and the raw scores were converted to standardized scores with means of 100 and standard deviations of 20. In this way, the scores could be treated as equivalent and all tests summed and averaged to obtain a cumulative risk score at nine months. We arbitrarily determined that infants having an average cumulative risk score of 96 or less at nine months would be designated as high-risk, and those with scores greater than 96 as low risk.

The significance of this cumulative risk score system can only be established through validation studies which relate scores at nine months to later performance. In other words, the cumulative risk score is an independent variable which must be compared with subsequent dependent measures. The dependent variables in the present study will consist of assessments made at two years of age. These outcome measures will include Bayley and Gesell developmental examinations, a cognitive test, measures of expressive and receptive language, and an assessment of exploratory behavior. In addition, we hope to continue collecting information on outcome at older ages so the predictive value of the cumulative risk score can be established.

The research flow plan is illustrated in Fig. 1.

Subjects

In order to test the validity at two years of age of our risk score system, a sample of infants is being followed from birth. The longitudinal sample consists of premature infants, of 37 weeks gestation or less with birth weights at 2500 gm or less, and a control group of full term infants, of 39–41 weeks gestation and a birth weight greater than 2500 gm. All infants are tested at equivalent conceptional ages, defined as gestational age plus age from birth. Gestational age is calculated from the onset of the mother's last menses. Thus, the newborn tests are administered at 40 weeks conceptional age, which is the expected date of delivery for the premature infants and the gestational age of the full-term infants. Date of testing for the later measures is calculated from the expected date of delivery for the prematures rather than the actual date of birth (Parmelee & Schulte, 1970).

Subjects will include infants from all socio-economic groups and attempts will be made to equalize the representation of different socio-economic groups within the risk categories. At present in our study socio-economic status signifies the level of education completed by the infant's mother. Several previous studies have demonstrated a correlation between the level of mother's education and the intellectual development of the child (Drage et al., 1969; Werner et al., 1968). Data is also being collected on other aspects of family background so alternative systems of classifying socioeconomic status can be used.

Every infant and family who participates in the longitudinal study receive medical, nursing, and social work help in an effort to provide support services

RESEARCH FLOW CHART

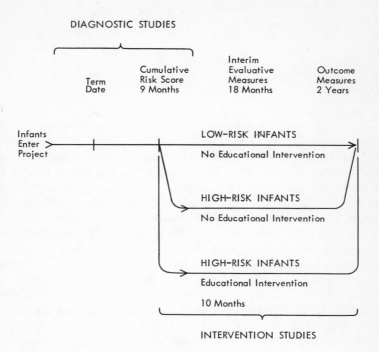

FIG. 1. Research flow chart.

regardless of risk category. The family is referred to special community resources whenever these are needed for the infant. A subgroup of "high-risk" infants is participating in a specialized educational intervention program from 10 to 24 months to test the value of such treatment (Kass, Sigman, Bromwich, & Parmelee, 1974).

Preliminary Results

These data are preliminary since we have tested about half the 200 cases to be studied before the final analyses. As of March 1, 1974, a total of 76 premature infants were assigned term risk scores. Of these, 65 babies had completed all tests through four months and thus, had four month risk scores as well. Only 39 babies had nine month risk scores.

The means and standard deviations of the three separate risk scores for the 39 babies who have completed all tests throughout the first nine months are reported in Table 1.

TABLE 1

Mean Risk Scores at Term, Four Months, and Nine Months
of Infants Completing All Measures

Risk scores	N	Mean	SD	% Infants classified as high risk
Term	39	96.15	10.91	56
Four months	39	100.13	9.46	33
Nine months	39	99.76	9.11	28

The results of an analyses of variance indicate that the Risk Scores are significantly lower (indication of higher risk) at term than at four and nine months $[F(2, 76) = 10.01, p < .01]$. In addition, among these 39 infants, more babies scored 96 or below at term and four months than at nine months. Thus, on the basis of term risk score, 22 infants would have been classified as high risk, and on the basis of four month risk score, 13 would have been classified as high risk. In comparison, 11 infants have been classified as high risk on the basis of the 9-months risk score.

In order to get a preliminary idea of which individual diagnostic measures most closely mirrored the aggregate risk scores, the correlation coeficients of each diagnostic measure with the risk scores at term, 4 months, and 9 months were examined (Table 2). Most of the early measures are significantly related to risk status at term and four months. Correlations may be somewhat inflated since the score on each measure is included in the total risk score. However, even at 9 months, where any one measure is a very small part of the cumulative risk score because of the greater number of diagnostic measures included, there are significant relationships between many measures and risk score.

DISCUSSION

The data presented in this paper are truly preliminary in that many of the correlations will probably change when all the data are analyzed. Furthermore, the really critical questions can not be addressed until information from the outcome measures is available. While it is interesting to determine the interrelationship between the measures comprising the high risk scale, the more significant problem concerns the relationship between the various measures in the high-risk score and outcome variables.

The cumulative risk system was designed to feature the use of multiple measures. In fact, we expect that the most valid predictions will be made using clusters of these measures. The strength of this approach is that it will make possible the identification of the contributions in predictive outcome made by the various measures independently and in combination. With this information, it may be possible to design a more effective system either by eliminating certain measures or utilizing a weighting system. In addition, the strength of the various components of each measure can be evaluated in relation to risk score and later performance so the individual measures can be improved.

As a separate part of our project, but not included in our present risk score, mother–infant interaction is observed in the home at one and eight months (Beckwith, 1974). A retrospective analysis will attempt to determine those qualities of mother–infant interaction which had an ameliorating effect on infants who were at risk early in infancy and improved by nine months or two years. In

TABLE 2

Correlations between Individual Diagnostic Measures
and Cumulative Risk Scores

Diagnostic measures	Cumulative risk scores		
	Term	4 Months	9 Months
Obstetrical	0.60*	0.55*	0.62*
complications scale **N =	76	65	39
Newborn	0.33*	0.32*	0.01
neurological	76	65	39
Term visual	0.471*	0.23	0.39*
attention	74	63	37
Term sleep	0.32*	0.37*	0.37*
polygraph	76	65	39
Postnatal	0.65*	0.57*	0.46*
factors	76	65	39
3-month	—	0.22	0.39*
sleep polygraph		65	39
4-month visual	—	0.48*	0.43*
attention		61	38
4-month	—	0.50*	0.50*
Gesell		65	39
4-month pediatric	—	0.53*	0.38*
examination		65	39
8-month precision and	—	—	0.49*
sensory–motor schemas			38
8-month exploratory	—	—	0.49*
behavior			38
9-month cognitive	—	—	0.54*
(Piaget)			34
9-month	—	—	0.43*
Gesell			38
9-month pediatric	—	—	0.62*
examination			39

*$p < 0.05$.
**N = Number of subjects in each correlational analysis.

addition, we will attempt to isolate those factors in mother–infant interaction which correlated with a decline in the infant's development. This information may enable us to identify environmental factors that should be included in the risk score. It will also be helpful in the selection of intervention procedures.

The subjects in the longitudinal sample include infants from all socioeconomic groups, so the relationship between socioeconomic status, biological risk, and mother–infant interaction can be examined. Our current hypothesis is that even though mother–infant interaction is related to social class, mother–infant interaction will have powerful effects on infant development irrespective of social class. Analyses will be done which will relate mother–child interaction and social class to each other, biological risk factors, and later development.

The need for follow-up studies is essential to any research of this nature. However, the general failure of long-term studies to demonstrate a direct relation between early medical events and later outcome suggests that another strategy is needed. Long-term studies fail to take into account the ongoing changes that affect outcome measures. In the past, most studies have attempted to predict development in early childhood from the neonatal period. An alternative strategy is that of repeated predictions over short periods of time. Such a strategy allows for the probable occurence of changes resulting from transactional processes between environment and individual and provides the opportunity to identify the nature of these processes. Our cumulative risk score was designed with this in mind, and our follow-up will continue this strategy.

ACKNOWLEDGMENTS

This research was supported by NIH Contract NO1-HD-3-2776 "Diagnostic and Intervention Studies of High-Risk Infants"; and NICHD Grant No. HD-04612, Mental Retardation Research Center, UCLA. Computing assistance was obtained from the Health Sciences Computing Facility, University of California at Los Angeles, sponsored by National Institutes of Health Special Research Resources Grant RR-3.

REFERENCES

Beckwith, L. Care giver—infant interaction and the development of the risk infant. Conference report. Early Intervention for High Risk Infants and Young Children. Chapel Hill, N. C., 1974.

Braine, M. D. S., Heimer, C. B., Wortis, H., & Freedman, A. M. Factors associated with impairment of the early development of prematures. *Monographs of the Society for Research in Child Development*, 1966, **31** (Whole No. 106).

Buck, C., Gregg, R., Stavraky, K., *et al.* The effect of single prenatal and natal complications upon the development of children of mature birthweight. *Pediatrics*, 1969, **43**, 942–955.

Douglas, J. W. B. "Premature" children at primary schools. *British Medical Journal*, 1960, **1**, 1008–1013.

Drage, J. S., & Berendes, H. W. Apgar scores and outcome of the newborn. *Pediatric Clinics of North America*, 1966, **13**, 635–643.

Drage, J. S., Berendes, H. W., & Fisher, P. D. The Apgar scores and four-year psychological examination performance. In *Perinatal factors affecting human development*. Pan American Health Organization Scientific Publication No. 185, 1969.

Drillien, C. M. *The growth and development of the prematurely born infant*. Baltimore: Williams and Wilkins, 1964.

Graham, F. K., Ernhard, C. B., Thurston, D., & Craft, M. Development three years after perinatal anoxia and other potentially damaging newborn experiences. *Psychological Monographs*, 1962, **76** (Whole No. 522).

Heimer, C. B., Cutler, R., & Freedman, A. M. Neurological sequelae of premature birth. *American Journal of Diseases of Children*, 1964, **108**, 122–133.

Kass, E. R., Sigman, M., Bromwich, R., & Parmelee, A. H. Educational intervention with high risk infants. Conference report. Early Intervention for High Risk Infants and Young Children. Chapel Hill, N. C., 1974.

Keith, H. M., & Gage, R. P. Neurologic lesions in relation to asphyxia of the newborn and factors of pregnancy: Long-term follow-up. *Pediatrics*, 1960, **26**, 616–622.

Knobloch, H., & Pasamanick, B. Environmental factors affecting human development before and after birth. *Pediatrics*, 1960, **26**, 210–218.

Lilienfeld, A. M., & Parkhurst, E. A study of the association of factors of pregnancy and parturition with the development of cerebral palsy. A preliminary report. *American Journal of Hygiene*, 1951, **53**, 262–282.

Lubchenco, L. O., Delivoria-Papadopoulos, M., & Searls, D. Long-term follow-up studies of prematurely born infants. II Influence of birthweight and gestational age on sequelae. *Journal of Pediatrics*, 1972, **80**, 509–512.

Niswander, K. R., Friedman, E. A., Hoover, D. B., et al. Fetal morbidity following potentially anoxigenic obstetric conditions. I. Abruptio placentae. II Placenta previa. III Prolapse of the umbilical cord. *American Journal of Obstetrics and Gynecology*, 1966, **95**, 838–845.

Parmelee, A. H., & Schulte, F. J. Developmental testing of preterm and small-for-dates infants. *Pediatrics*, 1970, **45**, 21–28.

Parmelee, A. H., & Haber, A. Who is the "Risk Infant"? *Clinical Obstetrics and Gynecology*, 1973, **16**, 376–387.

Parmelee, A. H., Sigman, M., Kopp, C. B., & Haber, A. Diagnosis of the infant at high risk for mental, motor or sensory handicap. Conference report. Early Intervention for High Risk Infants and Young Children. Chapel Hill, N. C., 1974.

Rogers, M. G. H., 1968. Risk Registers and early detection of handicaps. *Developmental Medicine & Child Neurology*, **10**, 651–661.

Sameroff, A. J., & Chandler, M. J. Reproductive risk and the continuum of caretaking casualty. In F. D. Horowitz, M. Hetherington, S. Scarr-Salapetek, & G. Siegel (Eds.), *Review of child development research*. Chicago, Ill.: University of Chicago Press, in press.

Schachter, F. F., & Apgar V. Perinatal asphyxia and psychologic signs of brain damage in childhood. *Pediatrics*, 1959, **24**, 1016–1025.

Smith, A. C., Flick, G. L., Ferriss, G. S., & Sellman, A. H. Prediction of developmental outcome at seven years from prenatal, perinatal and postnatal events. *Child Development*, 1972, **43**, 495–498.

Werner, E., Simonian, K., Bierman, J. M., & French, F. E. Cumulative effect of perinatal complications and deprived environment on physical, intellectual, and social development of preschool children. *Pediatrics*, 1968, **39**, 490–505.

Wiener, G., Rider, R. V., Oppel, W. C., & Harper, P. A. Correlates of low birthweight. Psychological status at 8 to 10 years of age. *Pediatric Research*, 1968, **2**, 110–118.

9
EARLY DEVELOPMENT OF SLEEPING BEHAVIORS IN INFANTS

Evelyn B. Thoman
University of Connecticut

An infant's behavioral state is his most continuous characteristic. He expresses his state by sleeping, wakefulness, or even by giving mixed signals of sleeping and wakefulness simultaneously. Along with the behaviors that indicate state, an infant may display additional spontaneous behaviors such as startles, jerks, rhythmic mouthing, sucking, smiles, frowns, etc. as well as crying which primarily occurs when the infant is awake. The purposes of our research are: (*a*) to describe the characteristics of behavioral states of newborn infants, (*b*) to identify changes that occur in state organization throughout the first weeks of life, and (*c*) to identify measures of behavioral states that characterize individual infants during these early weeks.

Researchers have been interested in infants' states for as long as they have been interested in studying infants. Crying or sleeping are obvious behaviors to record, and these general state categories are very useful in describing infants. Definition of "state" as a concept and as a research variable is still evolving, and a variety of sleeping and waking states are identified by various researchers (Ashton, 1973; Korner, 1972).

Interest in state behaviors has converged from two primary directions: (1) studies of the function and physiology of sleep, and (2) behavioral studies in which the infant's state is expected to account for variability in behavior.

Sleep researchers have produced an enormous literature on neural, autonomic, and endocrine changes associated with sleep states. Aserinsky and Kleitman (1955) and others have demonstrated the cyclical nature of sleep states. The ontogeny of sleep states has been studied by a number of investigators (e.g., Dittrichova, 1969; Dreyfus-Brisac, 1967; Parmalee, 1961; Parmalee & Stern, 1972; Roffwarg, Muzio, & Dement, 1966). From these studies two major categories of sleep have been identified: (1) an active sleep state, generally characterized by irregular respiration, low muscle tone, and the occurrence of

123

rapid eye movements (REMs); and (2) a quiet sleep state, characterized by a lack of motor movement, absence of eye movements, and regular respiration. Depending on the investigator, different labels have been applied with very little difference in referents. This situation was somewhat remedied by a conference (Anders, Emde, & Parmalee, 1971), at which nomenclature and criteria, behavioral and physiological, were agreed on for scoring of states of sleep and wakefulness in newborn infants. This was a major step in operationally defining the state concept, using a combination of behavioral and physiological parameters. The guiding principle for physiological definitions of states is that they are defined by the concordance of measures of physiological parameters observed, including EEG, EOG, EMG, heart rate, and respiration (Prechtl, Weinmann, & Akiyama, 1969).

Researchers interested in organization of the infant's behavior and behavioral development have applied the same notion, that is, concordance of behaviors, to define states. The classic example, and the most extensive system for defining behavioral states, was provided by Wolff (1966). For researchers who have a primary interest in behavior, physiological measures are not only irrevelant, but obtaining such measures by means of electrodes and other attachments are considered an intrusion and a possible interferences with the infant's most naturalistic behaviors. This is the position we maintain, as we are interested in the developing behaviors of the infant, how these behaviors may constitute stimuli for the mother, and modifications of behavior as a function of the infant's interaction with the mother.

If the concept of behavioral state is to be a useful one in research, a great deal more work is yet to be done in determining the most appropriate clusters of behaviors for defining state categories. This point was emphasized by Ashton (1973) in a recent review of the state literature. Our research is aimed at clarifying some of the issues with respect to the state concept. Justification for the definitions we use comes from our findings that infants show individual differences over the first weeks of life on the state measures employed for our systematic observations. Even more, our data are beginning to provide a basis for predicting some aspects of both behavioral and physiological development in infants. Consistency and predictive power are the basic requirements of any meaningful descriptive system. The following sections will describe both the consistencies and the consequences of behavioral states as we have observed them.

METHODS

Subjects

The subjects for these studies were selected as full-term, normal infants, without prenatal, perinatal, or postnatal complications. They include males and females, with mothers of varying parity. All are Caucasian. Our studies have been made at three hospitals located in different parts of the country. Although all infants were initially "normal" by medical standards, not all of these infants have remained in this category throughout their first months of life. One objective of our research is to identify the neonates that may have developmental difficulties which are not detected by the usual examinations given newborn infants.

Procedure

The categories of behavioral states and the criteria we use for their definition are as follows:

Quiet sleep A. The infant's eyes are firmly closed and still. There is little or no motor activity, with the exception of occasional startles or rhythmic mouthing. Respiration is abdominal and relatively slow (average around 36 per minute), deep and regular.

Quiet sleep B. All of the characteristics of Quiet Sleep *A* apply for this category except for respiration, which deviates somewhat from the slow regularity seen in *A*. In this state, the respiration check may be relatively fast, above 46, and show some irregularities, or the respiration may be slower but show some irregularities. Respiration is primarily abdominal in this state.

Active sleep without REM. The infant's eyes are closed, but slow, rolling movements may be apparent. Bodily activity can range from minor twitches to writhing and stretching. Respiration is irregular, costal in nature, and generally faster than that seen in quiet sleep (average of 46 per minute). Facial movements may include frowns, grimaces, smiles, twitches, mouth movements, and sucking (actually face movements are not very often seen in this category of active sleep).

Active sleep with REM. The infant's eyes are closed, and REM occur during the 10-sec epoch; other respiration and movement characteristics are the same as those just described for active sleep without REMs, except that the facial activity is highly likely to accompany REMs or to be interspersed between groups of REMs.

Active sleep with dense REM. Characteristics of this category are the same as those of the other two categories of active sleep; however, this one is distinctive for the continuous occurrence of REMs throughout the 10-sec observation epoch. REMs in this category are often accompanied by raising of the eyebrows and by eyeopening.

Drowsy state. The infant's eyes may either open and close or they may be partially or fully open, but very still and dazed in appearance. There may be some generalized motor activity, and respiration is fairly regular, but faster and more shallow than that observed in Quiet sleep.

Alert inactivity. The infant's body and face are relatively quiet and inactive, and the eyes are "bright and shining" in appearance (Wolff, 1966).

Waking activity. The infant's eyes are generally open, but may be closed. There is generalized motor activity, accompanied by grimacing, grunting, or brief vocalization.

Fussing. The characteristics of this state are the same as those for waking activity but mild, agitated vocalization is continuous; or one cry burst may occur.

Crying. The characteristics of this state are the same as waking activity, but generalized motor activity is more intense, and cry bursts are continuous.

Indefinite state. The infant's eyes may be closed, or opening and closing. There is generalized motor activity, but there are no sufficient criteria by which the infant's state can be classified as waking or sleeping.

There is much overlap between the behavioral state categories as we define them and the behaviors included in the physiological states as defined by Anders *et al.* (1971) for the newborn infant. Primarily, our changes consist of subdividing the sleep categories. Justification for these separate categories is derived from our studies which have shown individual consistency in the newborn period and individual differences over the early weeks of life in these behavioral states (Thoman, in press). Respiration is recorded by means of a small, portable analog chart recorder which derives a signal from a sensor placed under the infant's mattress pad.

In addition to the behavioral states listed above, we also record startles, jerks, rhythmic mouthing, sucking, smiles, frowns, grimaces, small body movements, large body movements, grunts, sneezing, hiccups, the occurrence of a bowel movement, gagging or spitting up, REM, eyes open during sleep states, vocalization during sleep states, and noncrying sounds made by the baby.

Data for the studies to be reported have been obtained from observations of newborn infants in hospitals and also from observations that have been made in the infant's homes. Home observations consist of a 7-hr day that is spent observing the mother and her infant once a week during the first four weeks after birth. These observations are part of a major project in which we are interested in the ongoing state behaviors of the infant, both when he is alone and in the crib and when the mother and infant are interacting. When the mother is holding the infant or is nearby, we record both mother and infant behaviors. Whenever the infant is out of the crib, sleep is recorded as "eyes closed," as it is impossible to note specific sleep states reliably under these circumstances. When the infant is in the crib, all of the sleeping and waking states are recorded along with respiration. Thus, on each day of observation, we obtain a total of 7 hr of the infant's state of which about 2.5 hr each time is sleep observed when the infant is in the crib. The sleep data from the crib observations will be the basis for the present report.

When the infant is observed in the hospital, he is taken to a separate research room, placed in a warmer, wearing only a diaper, and is maintained at neutral temperature. Under these conditions, the infant is observed until two hours of sleep has occurred or until time for the next feeding. States and state-related behaviors are recorded every 10 sec. This short time period is used in all of our research because (*a*) we have found that state durations in highly volatile infants may be extremely short, and (*b*) we have found this form of variability in behavior

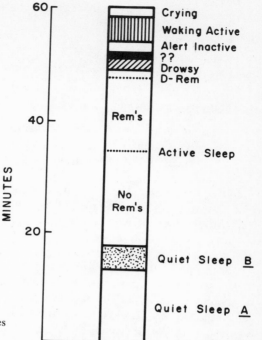

FIG. 1. Mena number of minutes per hour spent in each state.

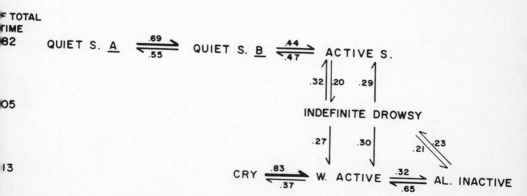

FIG. 2. Transition probabilities among eight states.

to be a significant measure of individual differences among infants. These findings will be described.

When the infants are observed in the home, they are placed in the crib dressed, wrapped and positioned as the mother chooses, as we do not intervene in any way with the interaction between the mother and the infant.

Results of Studies of Sleeping and Waking Behaviors in Neonates

Figure 1 presents the data on the study of 41 babies and indicates the distribution of time that infants spend in each sleep or wake state. About 40% of sleep time is spent in the two categories of Quiet sleep. Relatively small periods of time are spent in the waking states.

The sequence of states that an infant may have is not a random affair. Figure 2 presents a flow diagram, showing the highest probabilities of transitions among states. This diagram was derived from a sequence analysis of the data from the 14 newborn infants referred to above. Each subject was observed for 2 hr. The percent figures in the diagram indicate the probability of a change in state in the direction of the arrow. The highest probabilities are among the sleep states and among the wake states. Given that the baby makes a transition from sleep to wakefulness or vice versa, such changes are made primarily via either the Indefinite State or the Drowsy State. However, this transition is unlikely, and once the infant is asleep or awake, he is likely to stay in that category of states. As indicated by this diagram as well as the previous figure, 82% of the total observation time was spent in some form of sleep. Figure 2 depicts the transition probabilities among states for full-term normal infants. An infant that generally deviates from such a pattern may be considered as nonnormal in some respects. The significance of such deviations are, of course, not yet known.

In describing Fig. 1 we noted that approximately 40% of sleep time was spent in Quiet Sleep. Variability in infant populations in amount of Quiet Sleep is indicated in Fig. 3. Three groups of infants obtained in three different hospital showed varying amounts of quiet sleep. These differences may reflect a variety of factors. Infants from Hospital I were most stringently screened for weight, amount of maternal medication given during labor, length of labor, and other prenatal and perinatal factors. In addition, the infants at this hospital are born to parents from a higher socioeconomic level than those in the other two groups.

Since Quiet sleep may require more homeostatic control than Active sleep, and since it is a state which increases relative to active sleep with maturation, these data suggest that the advantages associated with the population of infants born at the hospital I may have influenced the state organization of these newborn infants. Much more study would be required to identify the specific factors that account for these differences as well as for the actual implications of such differences. At this time the data are simply descriptive.

Since babies are highly variable, a major question that arises is whether any

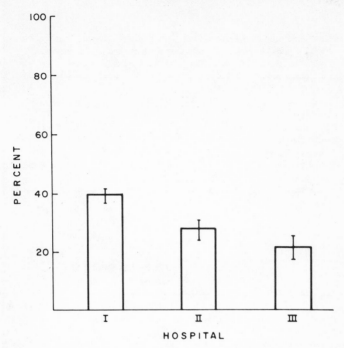

FIG. 3.   Amount of Quiet sleep as a percent of total sleep, subjects from three hospital populations.

particular observation is typical for a baby or simply a random sample from the total variable repertoire of his behaviors. Table 1 presents data on this issue. Two- and three-day-old infants were observed in the hospital mid-feeding in the morning and mid-feeding in the afternoon for one hour each time. Only infants that slept both hours are included in the data reported here. Correlations for the several sleep states that we have defined are indicated on this table. It is apparent that infants are highly consistent with respect to the amount of Quiet and Active Sleep they have at this age. There is also significant consistency in each of the three categories of Active Sleep. However, it should be noted that there is no consistency whatsoever $(r = .13)$ in the amount of Active Sleep taken as a single state. This is an important finding, because it points up the value of subdividing Active Sleep into these three specific components. A state category can be of little use if it occurs without any consistency.

The appropriateness of our subcategories of both Quiet sleep and Active sleep are also demonstrated in Table 2, which shows the rate of occurrence (per hour) of the various state-related behaviors recorded for each of the various sleep states. Differences in these rates among the several sleep categories were found to be significant. It is clear from the data presented that rates during quiet and active sleep are very different. They also differ for each of the three active sleep

TABLE 1

Mean Time (minutes) Spent in Each State During a.m. and p.m. Observations, Intraclass Correlations for a.m. and p.m. Durations
(N = 24 Babies)

	a.m.	p.m.	r
Quiet sleep A	15.8	15.3	.72
Quiet sleep B	8.7	6.1	.71
Active sleep	35.2	38.4	.13
without REM	19.5	20.6	.63
REM	14.4	15.8	.48
dense REM	1.3	2.0	.87

TABLE 2

Hourly Rates of State-Related Behaviors During Sleep
(N = 41 Babies)

	Smile	Frown	Grim-ace	Mouth-ing or sucking	Sigh sob	Startle	Jerk	Small move-ment	Large move-ment
Quiet sleep A	0.0	0.4	1.4	9.7	3.4	13.3	7.6	7.2	1.8
Quiet sleep B	0.0	0.7	2.5	8.3	3.4	4.3	5.4	13.7	5.7
Non-REM									
Active	2.8	7.4	25.0	31.6	5.6	0.7	8.8	45.1	42.3
REM Active	3.6	11.6	8.8	37.6	4.7	0.0	3.2	28.4	13.0
Dense REM									
Active	3.6	5.0	4.0	25.9	2.8	0.0	8.6	11.5	0.7

categories. For example, smiles, frowns, and grimaces rarely occur in Quiet sleep; mouthing or sucking, and body movements occur at much lower frequencies; and startles occur almost exclusively in Quiet sleep. In Quiet sleep B, the infant is less likely to startle and more likely to make small or large body movements than in Quiet sleep A. Among the Active sleep categories, there are more grimaces and more large and small body movements in Quiet sleep without REM and there are more frowns in Active sleep with REM.

The distinct rate of occurrence of the various behaviors in the subcategories of Quiet and Active Sleep states strongly suggests the appropriateness of using these separated state categories to describe infants.

Characteristics of Infants' States over the First Five Weeks of Life

Distribution of sleep state time. Figure 4 presents the mean percent of total sleep that is Quiet Sleep for each of 5 weekly observations. There are ten infants represented at each time point except for the 3-month observation, at which time

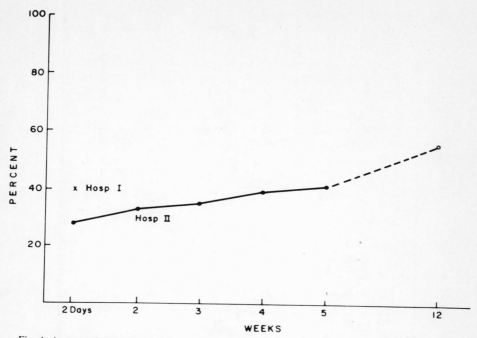

Fig. 4. Amount of Quiet sleep as a percent of total sleep, at 2 days and 2, 3, 4, 5, and 12 weeks of age.

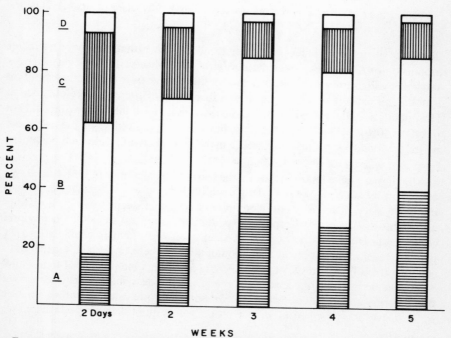

FIG. 5. Amount of time spent in each of the four categories of quiet sleep (expressed as a percent of total Quiet sleep), at 2 days and 2, 3, 4, 5, and 12 weeks of age.

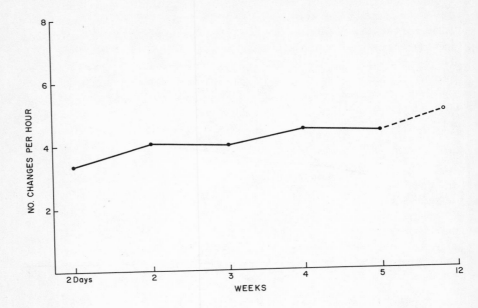

FIG. 6. Percent of Quiet Sleep spent in C and D combined by four subjects during each of the five weekly observations.

there are six infants. There is a clear trend for the infants to show a greater proportion of Quiet sleep over the period of time observed. However, there is sufficient variability among the infants that this change over the five-week period is not significant. It should be noted that this group of subjects were obtained at Hospital II, as indicated in Fig. 3. It can be seen that the infants in this study did not reach the 40% level for quiet sleep until they were 5 weeks old. Over the five-week period we found a significant difference in the individual infants in their percent of sleep that was Quiet $(F = 2.30, df = 9/27, p < .05)$.

Although we have reported thus far the use of two categories of Quiet sleep, we have recently subdivided Quiet sleep even further, using 4 subcategories including Quiet sleep A and B, as defined previously; Quiet sleep C, which is distinguished by a very erratic respiration pattern although all the other behavioral components are indicative, of Quiet sleep; and D, which is characterized by periodic respiration or apnea, even though all other behavioral components indicate that the infant is in Quiet sleep. Figure 5 presents the percent of total Quiet Sleep that is composed of each of the 4 categories just described, as they occur over five successive weeks of observation. Not only does quiet sleep A show a relative increase over this time period, but the proportion of quiet sleep C and D decreases consistently over time.

Infants are significantly different from each other in the amount of Quiet sleep A they show over this five-week period ($F = 2.22$, $p < .05$, F value required = 2.25). If A and B are combined, there is a significant increase in the amount of time spent in these states over the five-week period ($F = 4.31$, $df = 3/27$, $p < .01$). There is also a significant difference among individual infants on this combined measure ($F = 2.25$, df h 9/27, $p < .05$). If C and D are combined, there is a significant change (decrease) over the five-week period ($F = 4.23$, $df = 3/27$, $p < .01$). And there is a significant difference in the amount of time spent by individual infants in Quiet sleep C and D taken together over the five-week period.

These results indicate the appropriateness of the separate categories of Quiet sleep. They also suggest that three rather than four categories may be more appropriate, although it is not yet clear which combinations should be made. We are, therefore, continuing to use four categories for our observations until we can determine from additional data which combinations yield the most reliable results.

To illustrate the nature of individual differences in the amount of time spent in the two lower categories of Quiet sleep, Fig. 6 presents, for four of the infant subjects, the amount of time spent in these two categories of Quiet sleep combined, over the 5 successive weeks of observation. Marked differences among the 4 infants, both in total amount of time and in variability in amount of time spent in these combined subcategories of Quiet sleep, are apparent. Infant PO was taking sedative medication on weeks 3 and 4, and the amount of time in these sleep categories was possibly suppressed by this intervention.) Infant OB was later

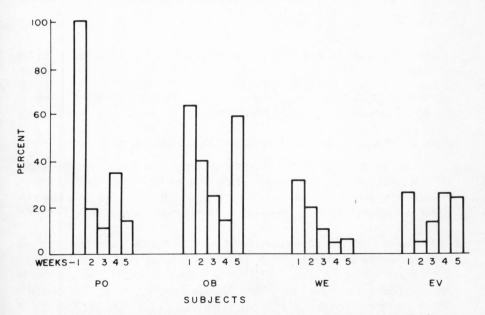

FIG. 7. Mean number of state changes per hour, at 2 days and 2, 3, 4, 5, and 12 weeks of age.

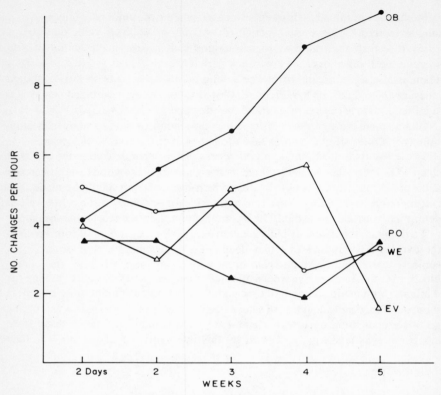

FIG. 8. Number of state changes per hour for five subjects during each of the five weekly observations.

found to be developing aberrantly; and our analyses suggested that PO may be likewise. This issue will be discussed later.

Rate of State Change as a Measure of Infant State Organization

Figure 7 presents the mean number of state changes per hour for 10 infants over the first 5 weeks of life, and then for 7 infants on week 12. There is not a significant change in the rate of state change over this period of time. However, there are significant differences among individual infants on this measure (F H 2.45, df H 2/27, $p < .05$).

An illustration of the individual differences as they may be found among infants on this measure is provided by Fig. 8. This figure presents the rate of state changes for 5 infants over the 5 weeks. Although individual differences are marginally apparent, the changes for one infant, OB, are striking. In fact, this dramatic change may have been part of a prelude to the infant's later fate—at 3 months of age this baby died of Sudden Infant Death (SIDS). Since we had made intensive observations of the infant over the first 5 weeks of life, we reviewed the data and found a picture of disorganization in state patterns throughout our observation period. Included among the aberrant measures obtained for this infant were his respiration characteristics. These are illustrated in Fig. 9, which presents the mean and range of respiration rates of OB and three other infants for the five successive weeks of observation. PO, obviously similar to OB, is an infant who showed state characteristics quite similar to those of infant OB. This is also seen in Fig. 9, in which these two infants were very deviant from normal infants in the amount of Quiet sleep C and D. These two infants showed a great deal more of the Quiet sleep states with respiration difficulties. As there were other characteristics of these infants that were similar, we have considered the possibility that their characteristics may suggest a susceptibility to SIDS. In such a case, infant PO might also be at risk. We have, therefore, in collaboration with the infant's pediatrician, placed infant PO on an apnea monitor for his protection.

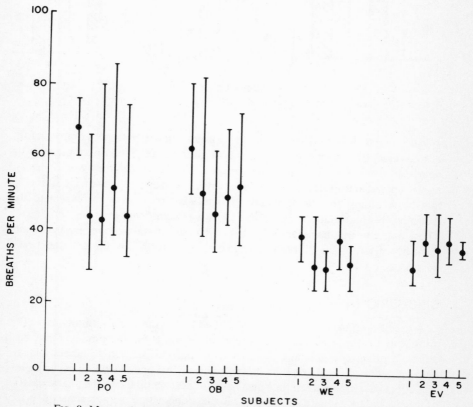

FIG. 9. Mean and ranges in respiration rates during quiet sleep for four subjects during each of the five weekly observations.

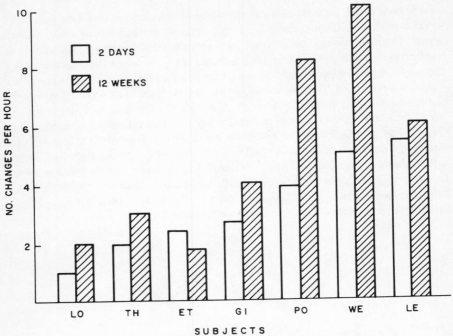

FIG. 10. Number of state changes per hour at 2 days and 12 weeks of age.

Returning to the rate-of-state-change measure, Fig. 10 presents a dramatic form of individual differences over the first 3 months of life. This figure presents the hourly rate of state-change seen in a group of 7 infants when they were 2 days of age compared to the rate of state-change they showed at 3 months of age. It is clear that these infants tend to maintain their relative position with respect to this measure. The correlation for the two ages was significant ($r = .81, p < .05$). These data confirm the meaningfulness of the rate-of-state-change measure since it clearly discriminates infants from the time of birth and through the first 3 months.

DISCUSSION

A major premise for the studies described is that there is continuity as well as variability in the development of infant behaviors. From the time of birth, each newborn infant is a unique individual with characteristics that interact with the environment and are affected by that interaction. An understanding of the factors that affect development requires measures for describing the initial characteristics of infants and then identifying changes in these characteristics as a consequence of encounters with the environment.

We have chosen to describe infants in terms of their state behaviors. An infant's state is a ubiquitous characteristic, which may elicit environmental stimulation (such as maternal caretaking activities), affect the nature of the response to stimulation, or change in response to stimulation. Changes in state may occur spontaneously also. Measures of state behaviors should, therefore, reflect in a basic way the infant's behavioral organization.

We have extended and modified previous classifications of sleeping and waking behaviors in infants (Anders *et al.*, 1971; Wolff, 1966), primarily by subdividing the Active and Quiet sleep categories. A rationale for these changes is provided by the results of the studies reported. First, Active sleep shows no consistency when newborns are observed, whereas the three subcategories we defined for Active sleep are each highly reliable measures of infant sleep states. The same holds for the subcategories of Quiet sleep as we have defined them. Further confirmation of the usefulness of these categories derives from the fact that there were different rates of occurrences during each of these various subcategories for the state-related behaviors such as smiles, grimaces, small and large movements, etc.

In addition to consistency during the newborn period in sleep states, we also found that our state categories discriminated individual infants throughout their first five weeks of life. These measures clearly meet the criterion of reliability.

Two infants were described who were markedly deviant in their state behaviors, and they were subsequently found to be deviant in their physical development. Additional cases of aberrant development have been identified in the course of our studies. Thus, our system offers the promise of predictive capability.

Further study of infant behaviors may provide a basis for elaboration or consolidation of the behavior clusters for a system of classifying infant sleep and waking behaviors. As they stand, however, our measures of state have provided evidence for continuity in infant behavior over the first weeks of life. We are now exploring the effects of infants' state behaviors on the mother-infant relationship and the effects of this relationship on the development of the infant's state organization.

ACKNOWLEDGMENTS

This research was supported by The Grant Foundation; by Public Health Service Grant HD-03591; and by Grant RR-81 from the General Clinical Research Center Program of the division of Research Resources. Several of the studies reported were carried out in collaboration with Margaret M. Poindexter, with invaluable assistance from Patricia T. Becker.

REFERENCES

Anders, T., Emde, R., & Parmelee, A. (Eds.) *A manual of standardized terminology, techniques and criteria for scoring of states of sleep and wakefulness in newborn infants.* UCLA Brain Information Service, NINDS Neurological Information Network, 1971.

Aserinsky, E., & Kleitman, N. A motility cycle in sleeping infants as manifested by ocular and gross bodily activity. *Journal of Applied Physiology*, 1955, **8**, 11–18.

Ashton, R. The state variable in neonatal research: A review. *Merrill-Palmer Quarterly*, 1973, **19**, 3–20.

Dittrichova, J. Development of sleep in infancy. In R. J. Robinson (Ed.), *Brain and early behavior*. London: Academic Press, 1969. Pp. 193–204.

Dreyfus-Brisac, C. Ontogenese du sommeil chez le premature humain: etude polygraphique. In A. Minkowski (Ed.), *Regional development of the brain in early life*. Oxford: Blackwell, 1967. Pp. 437–457.

Korner, A. F. State as variable, as obstacle, and as mediator of stimulation in infant research. *Merrill-Palmer Quarterly*, 1972, **18**, 77–94.

Parmelee, A. H., Jr. Sleep patterns in infancy. A study of one infant from birth to eight months of age. *Acta Paediatrica*, 1961, **50**, 160–170.

Parmelee, A. H., Jr., & Stern, E. Development of states in infants. In *Sleep and the maturing nervous system*. C. Clemente, D. Purpura, & F. Mayer (Eds.), New York: Academic Press, 1972. Pp. 199–228.

Prechtl, H. F., Weinmann, H., & Akiyama, Y. Organization of physiological parameters in normal and nuerologically abnormal infants. *Neuropadiatrie*, 1969, **1**, 101–128.

Roffwarg, H. P., Muzio, J. N., & Dement, W. C. Ontogenetic development of the human sleep-dream cycle. *Science*, 1966, **152**, 604–619.

Thoman, E. B. Organization of sleep and waking behaviors in neonates: Consistency and consequences. *Merrill-Palmer Quarterly*, in press.

Wolff, P. H. The causes, controls, and organization of behavior in the neonate. *Psychological Issues*, 1966 (Monograph 17) **5**(1).

10
CORRELATIONS BETWEEN SCORES ON THE BRAZELTON NEONATAL ASSESSMENT SCALE, MEASURES OF NEWBORN SUCKING BEHAVIOR, AND BIRTHWEIGHT IN INFANTS BORN TO NARCOTIC ADDICTED MOTHERS

Stuart L. Kaplan
Reuben E. Kron
Mitchell Litt
Loretta P. Finnegan
Marianne D. Phoenix
University of Pennsylvania

INTRODUCTION

The epidemic increase in use of opiates among women of child bearing age, the high incidence of disturbed states of CNS arousal reported among infants born to such mothers (Goodfriend, Shey, & Klein, 1956), and differences among experts regarding appropriate therapy for the neonatal abstinence syndrome (The Medical Letter of Drugs and Therapeutics, 1973), have led us to develop new objective methods for monitoring the effects upon newborn CNS function resulting from maternal addiction and neonatal narcotic withdrawal. Our goals are to refine diagnostic and treatment methods and to investigate the short- and long-term effects of maternal addiction on these infants. In this report we shall describe significant findings with regard to the neonatal abstinence syndrome as evaluated by the Brazelton Neonatal Behavioral Assessment Scale and by measures of sucking behavior (Kron & Litt, 1971).

EXPERIMENTAL METHODS

Sucking Measurements

An apparatus for measuring nutritive sucking behavior has been developed which consists of a reservoir for the nutrient, a metering device to regulate nutrient flow, a pressure transducer to record the sucking pulses, and a nipple from which the infant withdraws milk formula. The apparatus is designed to record subatmospheric intraoral pressure (sucks), while simultaneously rewarding the infant with a quantity of nutrient proportional to the area under the time-pressure curve of its sucking. Test feedings lasting 10 min each are carried out with this apparatus just prior to the routine nursery feedings. A number of sucking variables including rate (sucks per minute), volume of nutrient consumed (milliliters per minute), average and peak sucking pressures (millimeters mercury per suck), and the amount of time that the infant engages in sucking compared to the total time available for sucking (percentage of suck time) are recorded and computed from the pressure data. The details of this apparatus, the standard operating procedures, and the methods for analyzing the sucking data have been described in prior publications (Kron & Litt, 1971; Kron, Stein, & Goddard, 1965; Kron, Stein, Goddard, & Phoenix, 1967). The sucking instrument has been successfully applied to the study of drug effects in the newborn (Kron, Ipsen, & Goddard, 1968; Kron, Stein, & Goddard, 1966) and has provided objective evidence for CNS depressant effects upon the infant caused by routine amounts of obstetric sedation given to the mother during labor. These effects generally are not detected by standard clinical methods. Also, sucking studies of infants undergoing narcotic withdrawal have confirmed the value of this technique for monitoring the effects of narcotic abstinence and treatment (Kron, Litt, & Finnegan, 1973, 1974).

Brazelton Assessment

A Neonatal Behavioral Assessment Scale was developed by Brazelton (1972) with the recognition that routine pediatric neurological examination of the newborn is a poor predictor of later neurobehavioral performance. By assessing a wide range of behaviors found in the neonate, the Brazelton method attempts to measure those aspects of newborn behavior that may have better predictive value for later development than do standard neurological examinations. Seventeen neonatal reflexes are elicited and scored on a scale of 1 through 3, and the infant's initial and predominant CNS arousal states during the examination are scored on a scale of 1 through 6, ranging from deep sleep to active crying. The core of the examination consists of the assessment of 26 neonatal behavioral items each scored on a scale of 1 through 9. The infant's arousal state is taken into account when evaluating the behavioral items, and the examiner is required to perform a variety of maneuvers to insure that the infant's optimal performance has been elicited on each item. Brazelton indicates that the scores represent the infant's response to its interaction with the examiner. For example, in one test the crying infant is cuddled and consoled by the examiner, and in another it is subjected to a variety of graded stimuli, such as the sound of a bell, the shining of a light, removing bedclothes, and so on. The infant's response to these perturbations and interventions is scored. Other scores represent summations of the infant's behavior throughout the entire course of the examination. For example, the total number of changes in arousal states is scored as a measure of state lability. The Brazelton scale has been applied to the study of infants undergoing narcotic withdrawal (Soule *et al.*, 1973), and significant differences in the scores between such infants and a normal control group have been reported.

Population

The experimental group consisted of 23 infants born to narcotic addicted mothers. These infants entered the study on an ''as-you-come'' basis as they were admitted to the high-risk nursery at Philadelphia General Hospital (PGH). Prior to delivery, 21 of the addict mothers had been attending the methadone maintenance clinic associated with PGH, where a daily dose of methadone was administered; two of the mothers were street addicts maintaining themselves on heroin. During labor, the majority of the addict mothers received no general obstetric sedation or analgesia; however, seven were given analgesic medication within the 4-hour period preceding delivery. Local anesthesia was routinely administered to all mothers during the delivery.

The 23 infants born to the addict mothers were closely observed in the high-risk nursery where the pediatric staff prescribed medication for each infant in accordance with a clinical scoring system for rating the severity of the neonatal narcotic abstinence syndrome. Infants with low abstinence scores did not require treatment with pharmacologic agents. The neonatal narcotic abstinence scoring method and its clinical application have been previously reported (Finnegan, Emich, & Connaughton, 1973). On the basis of the abstinence scoring system, 13 of the infants were receiving drug treatment on the day of the Brazelton examination, while the remaining 10 infants had not required pharmacologic treatment. The 23 infants included eight who weighed less than 2500 gm.

A normal-weight control population was drawn from the same high-risk nursery at PGH as the experimental group. This selection provided a similar extrauterine environment for both experimental and control groups, and also provided controls from the same social class and racial background as the experimental babies. PGH serves the most disadvantaged population in a large urban center. The control infants were also selected on an ''as-you-come'' basis, excluding only those infants born to narcotic addicts, those under 2500 gm, and those considered by the pediatric staff to be ''too ill'' to participate in the study. Of the 10 infants in this control group, nine were considered to be ''at risk'' because of a variety of obstetric and neonatal conditions that might require close observation within the high-risk nursery; one was a ''normal'' infant boarded in the nursery. Two of the mothers had received general obstetric analgesia within four hours of delivery, and two received general obstetric anesthesia for cesarean section.

Procedure

The experimental and control infants were administered the Brazelton assessment between the third and seventh day of life. Sixteen of the experimental infants were also studied on the sucking instrument. Sucking behavior was measured on three consecutive days, on one of which the Brazelton was also given. The infant's sucking performance on the third day was used for comparison with the other variables in this study; the first two days were considered practice sessions. For the purpose of this paper only the results for % *suck time* will be reported, since it is representative of the other sucking measures.

The Brazelton evaluations were performed by two trained examiners who have achieved inter-rater reliabilities of .85 or higher on repeated testing. The Brazelton was performed with both examiners present, each recording his ratings independently. Therefore, each Brazelton examination also served as a retest for inter-rater reliability. The examiners were not blind to whether the infant belonged to the experimental or to the control group; however, they were blind to the infant's performance on the sucking instrument.

The Brazelton and sucking data were statistically analyzed as follows: Differences between the experimental ($N = 23$) and control ($N = 10$) group were tested for significance by comparing the groups' means for each of 21 Brazelton behavioral items.[1]

Within the experimental group proper, 16 infants were further tested on the sucking instrument in order to study the correlation between the behavioral items included in the Brazelton examination and measures of sucking behavior. Of the 21 Brazelton items subjected to detailed statistical analysis, 11 were found either to significantly distinguish between experimental and control groups, *or* to show a significant correlation with sucking behavior. On the basis of our interpretation of the clinical meaning of the various Brazelton items, these 11 significant items were grouped into 3 categories: *alertness, irritability,* and *motor.* Table 1 enumerates the items included in these categories. A combined score for each of the three Brazelton categories was calculated by algebraically summing the scores of the individual items making up each category.

Because of differences in weight distribution between experimental and control groups, the Brazelton and sucking data were also analyzed as a function of birthweight. This was done by correlating birthweight with the Brazelton scale and also with sucking measures (Table 2). In addition, a low birthweight control group consisting of 10 premature infants was obtained from the high-risk nursery at PGH. This group was selected on as "as-you-come" basis from among infants weighing under 2500 gm, born to nonaddicted mothers, and who were considered by the pediatric staff to be healthy enough to participate in the sucking studies.

---

[1] Items 1 through 5 of the Brazelton were excluded from our statistical analyses of the experimental group because approximately 50% of these infants did not provide scorable responses to these initial items. However, the experimental group had a high scorable response rate (mean 92%) during the remainder of the Brazelton (i.e., items 6 through 26). In contrast, the normal weight control infants exhibited a high scorable response level (mean 87%) throughout the 26 Brazelton items. A minimum criterion for inclusion of an individual Brazelton item in our statistical analysis was set at 75% scorable responses.

TABLE 1
Differences between Experimental and Control Groups on
Brazelton Items, and Correlations between Brazelton Items
and the Sucking Measures within the Experimental Group

Brazelton Item No.	Description of Item	Level of significant differences found between experimental and control groups ($p<$)	Brazelton item vs. sucking in experimental group ($n = 16$) $r =$	($p<$)
	Combined irritability items	.001		n.s.
16	Consolability	.35		n.s.
17	Peak of excitement	.35		n.s.
18	Rapidity of buildup	.05		n.s.
19	Irritability	.05		n.s.
21	Tremulousness	.35		n.s.
	Combined motor items	.05		
12	Motor maturity	.35	.499	.025
13	Pull to sit	n.s.	.522	.025
20	Activity	.35	.458	.05
			.520	.025
	Combined alertness items	—		
6	Response to rattle	n.s.	.567	.025
8	Response to voice	n.s.	.486	.05
10	Alertness	n.s.	.520	.025
			.463	.05
	Combined alertness plus motor items	—	.673	.005

TABLE 2
Correlations between Birthweight, Brazelton Items,
and Sucking Measures

	$r =$	$p<$
Experimental Population ($n = 16$)		
birthweight vs % suck time	.674	.005
birthweight vs combined motor items	.640	.01
birthweight vs combined alertness items	.442	.025
birthweight vs combined motor items plus combined alertness items	.542	.01
Normal Birthweight Controls ($n = 10$)		
birthweight vs combined motor items	.029	n.s.
birthweight vs combined alertness items	.148	n.s.
birthweight vs combined motor items plus combined alertness items	.149	n.s.
Low Birthweight Controls ($n = 10$)		
birthweight vs % suck time	.064	n.s.

This additional control group was included in order to better estimate the effect of birthweight (independent of maternal addiction) upon newborn sucking behavior.

The mother's dosage of methadone was correlated with her infant's birthweight, Brazelton scores, and sucking measures to study the influence of maternal narcotic dose upon these variables (Table 3).

TABLE 3

Correlations of Maternal Dose of Methadone with Sucking,
Birthweight and Brazelton Scores in the Experimental Group
($N = 16$)

Maternal dose of methadone correlated with	$r =$
% suck time	−.423
Birthweight	−.337
Brazelton scores:	
combined irritability items	+.285
combined motor items	+.209
combined alertness items	+.166

FINDINGS

Differences between experimental and control groups on the Brazelton examination were most clearly seen in the *irritability* and *motor* items (Table 1). In regard to *irritability*, the experimental group was more excited, more rapidly excited, more irritable, more tremulous, and less easily consoled than were controls. When these items were combined to generate an overall irritability score, the difference between experimental and control groups was significant at $p <$ .001. In regard to *motor* items, the addicts were less mature in motor function and more active than the controls.[2] When the motor items were combined to generate an overall score, the difference between experimental and control groups was found to be significant at the $p < .05$ level. None of the *alertness* items distinguished between the experimental and control groups.

The Brazelton items were correlated with *% suck time*. Table 1 summarizes the findings. The *irritability* items did not correlate with sucking measures. Both the individual and the combined *alertness* and *motor* items correlated significantly with sucking. An overall score computed by adding the individual scores of the *motor* plus *alertness* items correlated highly with sucking measures ($r = .673$). This value of the correlation coefficient implies that almost half of the variability of the motor and alertness behaviors measured by the Brazelton can be expressed in terms of a single sucking measure.

[2]Although the "pull to sit" item did not distinguish between the experimental and control infants, it did correlate with sucking within the experimental group and was therefore included in the *motor* category.

The weight of the experimental infants correlated with sucking behavior as well as with the scores achieved by the infants on the Brazelton (Table 2). The mean weight of the experimental group (2.8 kg) differed significantly ($p < .05$) from that of the normal birthweight control population (3.2 kg). *Alertness* and *motor* measures on the Brazelton correlated significantly with birthweight for the experimental group, but were independent of birthweight in the normal weight controls (Table 2); % suck time correlated significantly with birthweight for the experimental group, while the low birthweight controls showed no correlation between % suck time and birthweight.

Within the experimental group, correlation coefficients were calculated between the mother's prenatal methadone dosage and several of the infant variables (Table 3). Although correlations were found, the mother's dose of methadone did not explain a large portion of the variance. It is of interest however that both the % suck time and birthweight were negatively correlated with maternal dosage. This finding suggests that the higher the maternal dose of methadone, the lower the birthweight and sucking performance of the infant.

DISCUSSION

The behavior of passively addicted newborn infants on the Brazelton can be analyzed in terms of concomitant measures of the infant's sucking behavior, the infant's birthweight, and the mother's prenatal methadone dose level.

Irritability items of the Brazelton significantly distinguish between experimental and control infant populations. Irritability items have a high degree of face validity in regard to the expected clinical findings of the neonatal narcotic withdrawal syndrome, which includes many signs of CNS excitation. Thus, it can be predicted that infants undergoing withdrawal will score differently on irritability items than a normal control population. Therefore, our findings indicate that the irritability items are a valid measure of neonatal narcotic withdrawal.[3] Soule *et al.* (1973), in a comparable study applying the Brazelton to infants born to mothers taking methadone, also found increased irritability in their experimental populations vis-à-vis normal controls.

Irritability items do not correlate with sucking measures. A possible explanation is that sucking performance is related to CNS arousal as a U shaped function (Fig. 1). According to this model both the high and low levels of arousal will be expected to decrease the infant's sucking performance. Kron *et al.* (1966) have reported that infants born to mothers who have received obstetric sedation sucked poorly. The sucking performance of these sedated infants falls on the lower left side of the "U" curve in Fig. 1. Those infants with a high degree of CNS arousal

---

[3]Although there was a significant difference in mean birthweight between experimental and control populations, no differences were found in irritability scores within the experimental group proper when it was divided into high birthweight and low birthweight subgroups. Therefore, the Brazelton irritability scores are independent of birthweight.

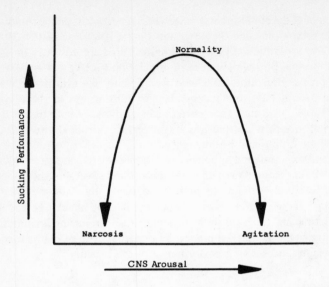

FIG. 1. The relationship between sucking performance and CNS arousal.

would fall on the right side of the curve. Infants undergoing narcotic withdrawal often demonstrate a high degree of CNS arousal, while those obtaining pharmacologic treatment (i.e., sedation) for the narcotic abstinence syndrome may be behaviorally depressed (Kron *et al.*, 1973, 1974). The irritability items are directly related to CNS arousal and therefore, as can be seen in Fig. 1, infants with either high or low irritability scores may demonstrate similar sucking behaviors.

   Motor items correlate with sucking measures, and also distinguish between experimental and control groups. A possible explanation of the former finding is the close relationship between measures of motor ability on the Brazelton and measures of sucking behavior, that is, sucking is a motor ability. In addition, motor items distinguish addicts from controls because narcotic withdrawal influences the quantity and quality of motor performance. For example, as illustrated in our data, infants undergoing withdrawal are more active than control infants. Therefore, a monotonic model of the linear relationship between sucking and motor items is suggested by our findings. This is supported by the regression equation for the actual data on the experimental group.[4]

   Alertness items fail to distinguish between addicts and controls. Nevertheless, they correlate well with sucking measures. A possible explanation for the correlation between alertness and sucking is that the Brazelton alertness items measure both the infant's initial orienting response to a stimulus and its ability to sustain attention to the stimulus. For example, the infant is presented with a ball, to test

----

[4]The equation for the regression of motor and alertness items versus % suck time: % suck time = .347 × combined scores + 20.

whether he alerts and then follows with his eyes and head. The infant's following the ball is a measure of its ability to maintain visual contact with the stimulus. This adhesiveness to stimuli may also be reflected by % suck time which is a measure of the relative amount of time that the infant spends actively attending to the nipple, i.e., sucking. The infant's general ability to adhere to a stimulus may therefore account for the high correlation found between Brazelton measures of alertness and % suck time.

The correlations between maternal dose of methadone, sucking measures, birthweight, and Brazelton scores in experimental infants, and the lack of correlation among controls, suggest that the behavior of passively addicted neonates depends upon an interaction between the maternal dose of narcotic drug and the birthweight of the infant. The precise definition of the variance explained by the mother's prenatal level of methadone dosage and the contribution of the infant's birthweight to newborn behavior awaits more refined statistical analysis.

CONCLUSION

Twenty-three infants born passively addicted to narcotics were studied on an instrument to measure infant sucking and on the Brazelton Neonatal Assessment Scale. Brazelton irritability items distinguished between the experimentals and controls ($p < .001$), but did not correlate with sucking measures. Brazelton alertness items did not distinguish between experimental and controls, but did correlate with sucking measures ($r = .567$). Brazelton motor items both correlated with sucking measures ($r = .449$) and distinguished between experimentals and controls ($p < .05$). The birthweight of the infants also correlated well with Brazelton motor ($r = .640$) and alertness items ($r = .442$). Weight also correlated highly with sucking measures ($r = .674$). In a high-risk non-addicted population, there were no correlations between groups of Brazelton items and birthweight. A second control population of low birthweight infants demonstrated a lack of correlation between birthweight and sucking. Thus, we conclude that the above findings are unique to the passively addicted infant population and are a result of the neonatal narcotic withdrawal syndrome.

ACKNOWLEDGMENTS

The studies described herein were performed within the Newborn Nurseries of the Philadelphia General Hospital, laboratories of the Departments of Psychiatry and Pediatrics of the University of Pennsylvania School of Medicine and the Department of Chemical and Biochemical Engineering of the University of Pennsylvania. We are grateful to the Departments of Obstetrics and Gynecology, and of Pediatrics, of the Philadelphia General Hospital for their support, and especially to Dr. John P. Emich, Director of the Department of Obstetrics, and the Staff of the Newborn Nurseries of the Philadelphia General Hospital, for their cooperation. Also, our thanks to Mr. Don Newman for help in data reduction. This work was supported in part by Research Grant HD-DA-06009 from the NICHD and the NIDA, Research Grant DA-00325 from the NIDA, and small Grant MH-19052 from the

NIMH; also, Research Contract 1674 from the Commonwealth of Pennsylvania Governor's Council on Drug and Alcohol Abuse, and the Department of Public Welfare through the Eastern Pennsylvania Psychiatric Institute.

REFERENCES

Brazelton, T. B. *Neonatal Behavioral Assessment Scale*. Unpublished manual, Harvard University, 1972.

Finnegan, L. P., Emich, J. P., & Connaughton, J. F. Clinical scoring system for the assessment and treatment of the neonatal abstinence syndrome. *Pediatric Research*, 1973, **7**, 91. (Abstract)

Goodfriend, M. J., Shey, I. A., & Klein, M. D. The effect of maternal narcotic addiction on the newborn. *American Journal of Obstetrics & Gynecology*, 1956, **71**, 29–36.

Kron, R. E., Ipsen, J. & Goddard, K. E. Consistent individual differences in the nutritive sucking behavior of the human newborn. *Psychosomatic Medicine*, 1968, **30**, 151–161.

Kron, R. E., & Litt, M. Fluid mechanics of nutritive sucking behavior: The suckling infant's oral apparatus analyzed as a hydraulic pump. *Medical & Biological Engineering*, 1971, **9**, 45–60.

Kron, R. E., Litt, M., & Finnegan, L. P. Behavior of infants born to narcotic addicted mothers. *Pediatric Research*, 1973, **7**, 64. (Abstract)

Kron, R. E., Litt, M., & Finnegan, L. P. Effect of maternal narcotic addiction on sucking behavior of neonates. *Pediatric Research*, 1974, **8**, 90. (Abstract)

Kron, R. E., Stein, M., & Goddard, K. E. A method of measuring sucking behavior of newborn infants. *Psychosomatic Medicine*, 1963, **25**, 181–191.

Kron, R. E., Stein M., & Goddard, K. E. Newborn sucking behavior affected by obstetric sedation. *Pediatrics*, 1966, **37**, 1012–1016.

Kron, R. E., Stein, M., Goddard, K. E., & Phoenix, M. D. Effect of nutrient upon the sucking behavior of newborn infants. *Psychosomatic Medicine*, 1967, **29**, 24–32.

Medical Letter of Drugs and Therapeutics, Treatment of neonatal withdrawal syndrome, 1973, **15**(No. 11), 46–48.

Soule, B., *et al.* Clinical implications of Brazelton Assessment. Presented at the Biennial Meeting of the Society for Research in Child Development, Philadelphia, Pa., 1973.

11
DEVELOPMENT OF FINE MOTOR BEHAVIORS: ISSUES AND RESEARCH

Claire B. Kopp
University of California, Los Angeles

I. INTRODUCTION

Development of prehension from the first tentative gropings of an infant to the use of a precise, refined grasp is one of the substantive accomplishments of infancy. To some theorists, hands represent tools that are used in conjunction with other sense systems to acquire knowledge; for others, hands, and the actions they represent, are the *sine qua non* of knowledge. This dichotomy is representative of a number of issues relating to development of prehension. Fortunately, we are again exploring this topic and are asking new questions about biological givens, development and organization of visual-motor systems, specific experiential effects, and the nature of fine motor behavior to infant learning (Bruner, 1968, 1970, 1973; Humphrey, 1969; Twitchell, 1970; White, 1970, 1971; White, Castle, & Held, 1964; White & Held, 1966). Developmentally it could be said that our investigations are still in a rather immature period, perhaps at the stage of "intense hand regard."

The history of research on grasp, though fascinating, is characteristic of descriptions of other infant behaviors in the early days of psychology. Preyer (1882), Shinn (1893), and Moore (1896) made naturalistic observations of the developmental sequencing of prehension and proposed stages of change. Watson and Watson (1921) and Jones (1926) also studied grasp; Watson even attempted to promote grasp by conditioning, but his subjects generally showed the same age acquisition as did non-conditioned infants. Brainard (1927) used a quasi-experimental model by conducting small experiments to test particular responses he observed in the eye-hand development of his daughter.

The most comprehensive study of grasp was made somewhat later by Halverson (1931) who was one of Gesell's associates. He used film for behavioral analysis and described the ontogeny of prehension in infants who were 16–52 weeks of age. He included analyses of visual-motor orientation, approach, positioning, and accuracy of reach, grasp, and release. Furthermore, Halverson took issue with those who suggested that learning to grasp was a function of training; instead, he declared it was mainly dependent upon growth of the body and maturation of the neuromuscular system. He stated that training a 20-week-old infant to grasp a cube could not produce approaches similar to those used by older infants. Castner (1932), another member of the Yale group, followed with some additional research on fine prehension, by using a similar approach and orientation. Then, with the exception of a few studies (Baruk, Leroy, Launay, & Vallancien, 1953; Zagora, 1959) the topic seemed exhausted as a research area.

The resurgence of interest in infancy that occurred in the sixties was coupled with renewed acceptance of Paiget's theoretical perspective and led to research on many facets of infant development, including prehension. White *et al.* (1964), using some of Piaget's (1952) ideas regarding the development of prehension, and his orientation, demonstrated the role of experiential factors in development of eye–hand behaviors. The group first studied the developmental sequence of visual pursuit, hand regard, and the onset of visually directed reaching with subjects as young as one month of age. The role of experience was tested by providing a group of institutionalized normal infants with an enrichment program that consisted of increased tactual—vestibular stimulation and enriched visual surroundings. The results indicated that experiential factors affected the development of some visual and motor grasp behaviors (White, 1971; White & Held, 1966).

Recently Bruner (1968, 1970, 1973), as part of his research in infancy, initiated studies of infant development of skill as an indication of how hands shape the instrumental intelligence of humans. His research encompasses studies of development of voluntary behavior, sequencing and organization of skill behavior, and the interrelationship of skilled prehension with other developing competencies.

This renewed interest in the acquisition, nature, and the integration of prehension is infused with new ideas and techniques, but is not without controversy, for some basic issues remain unresolved. The purpose of this paper is to discuss some of the issues concerning fine motor development as well as to introduce some of our own research currently in progress at the UCLA Infant Studies Project.

II. ISSUES

A. Motor Behavior and Cognition

Just as there is debate about the long range consequences of particular infant experiences (Wolff & Feinbloom, 1969) so there is controversy about the nature and extent of the relationship between development of fine motor behavior and infant cognition. There is essentially no disagreement that ontogenetically the development of prehension represents a significant change in abilities and that infant learning may be mediated by sensory–motor interactions. Differences arise in the emphasis placed on motor development with regard to mental development and are reflected in questions like the following: Is mental development a consequence of motor acts? Is mental development equivalent to motor development? Are motor responses effective ways to measure infant cognition? Is promotion of attentional and effectance behaviors the major role of grasp? As yet there are no answers to these questions, for there are little data, but there are some historical and theoretical perspectives that highlight the issues.

Historically, there has been an assumption that mental and motor development were closely related, as early description and diagnosis of infant development was completely dependent on measurement of motor performance. Although some new techniques for measurement of infant behavior have been developed, there is still reliance on the older methodology, and the assumptions that accompany it.

Piaget's (1952, 1954) observations and view of the infant as an active seeker of knowledge revitalized thinking about the nature of infancy and seemed to reinforce the assumption of a special relationship between motor behavior and cognition. Flavell (1963) noted that Piaget often stressed that "cognition is at all genetic levels a matter of real actions performed by the subject [p. 13]." Sensory-motor interactions, the foundations of later cognition, recently were emphasized again by Piaget (1970) when he stated that in order to know objects an infant "must act upon them and therefore transform them: he must displace, connect, combine, take apart, and reassemble them [p. 704]." This interaction of organism and object leads to knowledge that can not be obtained by just recording external information. Furthermore, Piaget states that activity has two components: that concerned with coordination of actions, and another involved with understanding the relationship of one's own actions toward an object. Actions have meaning attached to them when they are performed in the context of "physical" or "logicomathematical" experiences, and therefore lead to subsequent increases in knowledge. However, Piaget suggests that sheer repetition of movement is just "simple exercise" and does not lead to an increase in knowledge.

Piaget's position seems to be quite clear—overt or interiorized actions (operative thought) are knowledge. Therefore, we can infer that the sensory-motor behaviors of infancy lead to restructuring of information and are knowledge. However, some clarification seems necessary, for some interpret Piaget as meaning that "actions," "activity," "exercise," particularly in the sensory-motor period, imply only *motoric* behavior. But, does this suggest that knowledge is not to be gained from acts of looking and listening? Piaget's (1952) description of "looking activity" in the sensory–motor stage of *primary circular reaction* intimates an increasing elaboration of behavior through use of the visual system. However, Piaget certainly does seem to emphasize the role of movement as "activity" after the infant begins to combine use of his sense and motor systems e.g., looking and reaching. Escalona (personal communication) suggests that

Piaget's critics have oversimplified his statements "for listening and looking have a motoric component, they are sensory–motor acts in Piaget's sense." Escalona further states that Piaget thinks that sense and motor systems are a single indivisible entity from the beginning.

Obviously there are no conclusions to be drawn at this point from either research or theory except to state that Piaget's theory continues to prod us to try to understand infancy.

Some of the most active research in the development of skill behaviors and the nature of its relationship to cognition is being done by Bruner (1968, 1970, 1973). Infant development, Bruner suggests, provides a means to explore the way humans achieve adaptive and voluntary control of their environmental interactions. Bruner's research is wideranging and includes study of the source, structure, organization, and interrelationship of attention, play, imitation, language, and skilled action. Bruner (1968) describes his approach as trying to explore "not only what the infant and child are developing towards, but also what they have developed from [p. 5]." His interest in fine motor development is not in the hands per se but rather how hands shape and express instrumental intelligence. Bruner considers that the development of skill represents a type of problem solving and growth of competence. However, competence is not just of a manipulative nature but involves visual, attentional, locomotive, and interactional skills that allow the infant to initiate and sustain varied interactions.

Some of the prehension skills that Bruner's research has focused on include the infant's development of control of objects, complementary use of hands, detour reaching, and differentiation of power and precision grips. Much of this research is concerned with descriptions of how certain acts are performed by infants and young children at specified ages. From these observations Bruner suggests a developmental sequence of hand skill behavior that includes periods of consolidation, modularization, patterning, and finally regrouping of actions so that a qualitatively new type of infant–object interaction emerges. Bruner's research, still in its early stages, may provide clues to the nature of fine motor behavior and cognition. His conceptualizations and research on manipulative skills do not appear to ignore the development and role of other important behaviors of infancy (Bruner, 1973; Bruner & Koslowski, 1972).

The theory and research of Piaget and Bruner have been criticized by Kagan (1971). He challenges what he considers a traditional view about infancy, which implies a close relationship between infant cognition and motor behavior. He states that the relationship between these variables might be considerably less extensive than previously had been thought. Kagan suggests that Gesell, Piaget, and Bruner share a common belief that the child's level of intelligence covaries with precocity in motor behavior. Alternatively, Kagan considers maturity of sensory–motor coordinations to be imperfectly correlated with maturity of cognitive structures. The main thrust of his argument is that motor actions are not required to change behavior or to develop perceptual or conceptual structures. The young infant, as well as more mature individuals, can learn by attending. However, Kagan does affirm the importance of motor actions and overt practice for instrumental adaptations to the environment and as an aid for certain kinds of learning. In addition to questioning the causal relationship of motor behavior to cognition, Kagan also suggests that use of overt acts to infer infant cognition may produce an over- or under-estimation of actual cognitive competence. Concern about measurement techniques is not new for psychology, but the current course of research in infancy suggests that reminders are important (Charlesworth, 1969).

Kagan's statements appear both reasonable and persuasive. His own data (Kagan, 1970) as well as that of others (Jeffrey & Cohen, 1973) provide ample research evidence that demonstrates infant discrimination, primitive information processing, and evidence of memory long before infants can effectively interact with objects on a motoric level. The view that Kagan is promoting has implications for future studies of human infancy, but also may promote development of new techniques both to appraise and treat the atypical child. Too many professionals, for too long a period, have conceptualized intelligence, particularly for the young, mainly in terms of voluntary, controlled motor behaviors.

On the other hand, evidence that infant learning may be mediated by the distance receptors does not disprove a possible close relationship between motor behavior and cognition. However, data on this issue is sparse. Until the gap is filled it can be said that fine motor behaviors allow the child to bring some of his world to himself; this helps him focus his attention, and it allows him to explore. These may not be equivalent to knowing but they aid in the acquisition of knowledge. However, this is not to say that learning and knowledge can not develop in the absence or impairment of hand skills (Décarie, 1969; Kopp & Shaperman, 1973).

B. Individual Differences

The second issue relates to individual differences in manipulative abilities of infants. Actually there is more interest than controversy associated with this issue, for knowledge is meager. With the development of reach and grasp, infants increasingly bring certain objects to themselves for oral, visual, and manipulative inspection. Just as there are vast differences in the amount of oral and visual explorations that infants do, so there are marked differences in the amount, type, and execution of prehension behaviors. Gesell (1954) noted that infants had individualistic modes of movement that, although difficult to describe, included muscular and skeletal components as well as aspects of speed, synergy, smoothness, and precision of action. At present it is not possible to determine the ultimate significance for infant learning that might accrue from these behavioral variations. Cognizance must be given to the evidence, previously noted, that learning can occur even when motoric development is impaired. Furthermore, the fact that individual differences in fine motor behaviors may occur is probably meaningless in terms of long range implications, unless note is also made of individual motivational, attentional, and object and person interactional factors. Therefore, fine motor behaviors should be paired with other variables for analyses, as has been suggested for other studies of individual differences (Baltes & Nesselroade, 1973). With these caveats in mind, I want to pursue the issue of differences in fine motor behaviors by using the eight-month-old infant as an example.

Most eight-month-old infants respond to novel objects with alacrity and accuracy (Baruk et al., 1953). They appear to have reached the period where their grasp is executed with economy and minimum expenditure of energy (Bruner, 1970). Because of this the infant can direct his attention towards objects that have an enormous initial attentional attraction for him at this age period. However, there are infants of the same age who, although considered to be healthy and neurologically intact, are clumsy. When they reach and grasp objects their timing is slightly off, and they tend to drop the object more often than other infants. Nonetheless, they are interested and want the object, but are diverted by having to shift their attention to execution of grasp and back to object, or to repeated attempts to complete a specific act. At times their behavior is reminiscent of the six month old whose reach and grasp demands a high level of attention. However, the six month old's prehension does improve, and his attention does become free to focus upon objects.

The puprose of the preceding description and comparison was to show that individual differences in fine motor behaviors exist and to focus attention on the following questions: (a) Is clumsiness a transient phenomenon for some infants 8 to 10 months of age, i.e. do these infants need just a little more experience in order to handle objects with ease? (b) If clumsiness is relatively permanent, will it be a source of distraction and affect attention, or will it cause frustration and affect motivation? Might these outcomes be the real significance of individual differences in fine motor behavior? Again we can only emphasize that there are no data available, and speculations and implications must be stated with caution.

III. RESEARCH ON FINE MOTOR BEHAVIORS OF EIGHT-MONTH-OLD INFANTS

The previous discussion of issues focused on some "unknowns" in development of fine motor skills. I wished to pursue one of these unknowns, the nature of individual differences, as it might have potential significance for infant development. The first phase of the research was to differentiate the quality of movement of eight-month-old infants and then to try to relate this to their sensory-motor development. This required quantification of specific approach behaviors of infants who appeared to be neurologically intact and who grasped objects with thumb and fingers. A classification system was developed to separate, into two groups, those infants who appeared to be relatively coordinated in approach to an object from those who seemed to be clumsy. (It was anticipated that most infants would appear to be relatively coordinated.) The classification system included eleven items that were derived from clinical judgements,[1] developmental norms, and Halverson's (1931) study of prehension. Each item was operationally defined. Some examples of the behaviors quantified were the position of the arm and hand as the infant approached an object, speed and accuracy of approach, presence of extraneous movements, and finger spread.

In addition to fine motor approach behaviors the infant's sensory–motor schemas were recorded. Schemas consist of many kinds of manipulative and visual activities manifested by the infant as he interacts with objects. The specific schemas measured included mouthing, examining (turning the object around in the hands while looking at it; Uzgiris, 1967), waving and banging the object while holding it, and holding the object and looking around the room. These particular schemas were selected as they are common behaviors exhibited by eight-month-old infants.

The schemas evidenced by infants were to be used to establish the concurrent validity of the fine motor classification system. It was reasoned that the way infants *approach* objects relates to the way that they *use* objects.

Thirty-six full-term and premature infants (male and female) who met the health and developmental criteria and who were between 32 and 36 weeks of age from their expected date of delivery participated in the first study. Since fine motor behavior was the only criterion used to classify infants, the subject pool consisted of available full terms and prematures, irrespective of their social class.

The procedure involved one laboratory session, to make a video tape of the infant's approach and use of objects while he sat in a crib before a table top. The entire procedure was standardized.[2] At a later period, the first third of the tape was used to code the quality of fine motor behaviors evidenced by the infant as he *approached* an object. The codings were rated and used to place the infants into two groups, those exhibiting "good" fine motor behavior (GFMB) and those exhibiting "poor" fine motor behavior (PFMB). Twenty-four infants (21 full terms, 3 prematures) fell in the GFMB group and 12 infants (5 full terms, 7 prematures) fell in the PFMB group. The items that differentiated the two groups were specifically related to prepositioning of arm and hand as the infant reached for the object, accuracy, and speed of approach.

Following the coding of fine motor approach behaviors, a new examiner coded the type and duration of sensory–motor schemas showed by the infants as they played with and handled two other test objects. The examiner, who did not know the group placement of the infants, used the last two-thirds of the video tape for coding of schemas.

There were many similarities noted in the visual and manipulative schemas of both groups of infants although occasionally an infant, in either group, showed an

---

[1]A. H. Parmelee suggested two of the items and appreciation is extended to him.
[2]Detailed information about the procedure is available from the author.

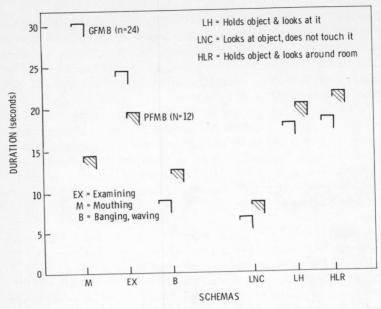

FIG. 1.   Duration of schemas evidenced by GFMB and PFMB groups.

idiosyncratic activity. Figure 1 gives the duration data for six commonly used schemas exhibited by the GFMB and PFMB groups. (There were no sex differences in use of schemas in either group so the male–female data were pooled).

These data show that the amount of time spent by the GFMB group of infants on oral and examining types of exploration was quite high, compared to their use of waving and banging the object. The former requires sustained, controlled actions and allows the infant to obtain a considerable amount of information about the object, whereas large quick actions such as waving and banging probably give little information about the object but do offer pleasurable proprioceptive feedback. The three "looking" schemas were not as prominent for the GFMB infants as was their oral and examining behaviors. In contrast, the data show the group of PFMB infants had a somewhat different pattern of schema use. In comparison to the GFMB group, they spent less time with oral and examining explorations and more time waving and banging the object. They also spent more time using the "looking schemas."

Therefore, it appeared that the fine motor classification system used to divide infants into two groups had concurrent validity, as differences in use of certain schemas had been demonstrated. However, two factors that had been ignored in the previous analyses had to be investigated. These factors were type of birth (full term or premature) and social class. It was possible that observed schema differences could be solely a function of premature-term differences in use of schemas. (However, one should not conclude that all full term infants evidence only "good" fine motor behavior and all premature infants only "poor" behavior. It is reasonable to expect that both similarities and differences in schema use would be found if a comparison were to be made between full term and GFMB groups, or with premature and PFMB groups.) Future analyses also had to account for possible social class variations in schema use as social class differences have been noted in schema use (Collard, 1971) and the incidence of later problems for prematures is partly a function of social class (Braine, Heimer, Wortis, & Freedman, 1966; Douglas, 1956).

Currently, additional studies and analyses are underway, with the use of the fine motor classification system, to examine individual differences in a sample comprised only of full term infants, and another only of premature infants. Similarly, schema performance as a function of birth and social class is being studied. Some preliminary data of this nature are presented next.

Infants who met the criteria of use of thumb and fingers for grasp and who had no apparent neurological problems were classified on the basis of type of birth and social class. Three groups were formed which consisted of full term–high social class (FT–Hi), premature–high social class (P–Hi), and premature–low social class (P–Lo). A small n precluded use of a full term–low social class group.

The first analysis consisted of a comparison of fine motor approach behaviors. There were a few differences that indicated better full term prepositioning and accuracy than demonstrated by both premature groups, whereas the P-Hi group exhibited fewer extraneous movements than did the other two groups. Small differences were noted in finger positioning and spread as a function of social class, but these were in opposite directions. These findings appear inconclusive. However, there does seem to be evidence that future analyses with larger samples may reveal a greater number of differences in fine motor approach behaviors between full terms and prematures than between infants of different social classes.

The second analysis consisted of group comparisons of the duration of use of selected schemas. Figure 2 shows the preliminary analyses of the duration data. Again, there are differences as a function of both type of birth and social class. However, the greatest differences are found between the full term and premature groups. Of particular interest is the finding that full terms spend more time than both premature groups in "examining" the object and less time "holding the object and looking at it." The former is a derivative of the latter (Uzgiris, 1967); therefore, "examining" could be considered an example of a more mature schema. The full terms also did considerably more "holding the object and looking around the room" than did the prematures.

When the schema uses are viewed as a function of social class, within the premature group, small differences are noted. However, it is unrealistic at this point to ascribe significance to these data as the sample sizes are too small to permit

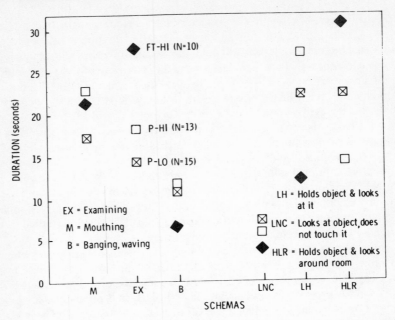

FIG. 2.   Duration of schemas evidenced by full terms and prematures as a function of social class.

definitive statements. Potential group differences will be explored with larger samples of infants.

IV. GROPING FOR UNDERSTANDING

Our review of issues and research has posed many questions and provided few answers. Understanding the development of prehension, in and of itself, is a complex and multifaceted problem. However, fine motor behavior is not a unitary system, so it demands to be analyzed in relation to other sense systems and other dimensions of behavior of the developing infant such as cognition, attention, motivation, etc. The research tasks are difficult, but as others have suggested, we can no longer use simple conceptions of infant behavior to explain development (McCall, Hogarty, & Hurlburt, 1972).

ACKNOWLEDGMENTS

[1]This research was supported by NIH Contract N01-HD-3-2776 "Diagnostic and Intervention Studies of High-Risk Infants"; and NICHD Grant No. HD-04612, Mental Retardation Research Center, UCLA.

REFERENCES

Baltes, P. B., & Nesselroade, J. R. The developmental analysis of individual differences on multiple measures. In J. R. Nesselroade & H. W. Reese (Eds.), *Life-span developmental psychology.* New York: Academic Press, 1973.

Baruk, H., Leroy, B., Launay, J., & Vallancien B. Les étapes du dévelopment psychomoteur et de la prehension voluntaire chez le nourrisson. *Archives Francaises de Pédiatrie,* 1953, **10,** 425–432.

Brainard, P. P. Some observations of infant learning and instincts. *Pedagogical Seminary,* 1927, **34,** 231–254.

Braine, M. D. S., Heimer, C. B., Wortis, H., & Freedman, A. M. Factors associated with impairment of the early development of the premature. *Monographs of the Society for Research in Child Development,* 1966, **31**(4).

Bruner, J. S. *Processes of cognitive growth: Infancy.* (Heinz Werner Lecture) Worcester, Mass.: Clark University Press, 1968.

Bruner, J. S. The growth and structure of skill. In K. J. Connolly (Ed.), *Mechanisms of motor skill development.* New York: Academic Press, 1970.

Bruner, J. S., & Koslowski, B. Visually preadapted constituents of manipulatory action. *Perception,* 1972, **1,** 3–14.

Bruner J. S. Organization of early skilled action. *Child Development,* 1973, **44,**1–11.

Castner, B. M. The development of fine prehension in infancy. *Genetic Psychology Monographs,* 1932, **12,** 105–191.

Charlesworth, W. R. The role of surprise in cognitive development. In D. Elkind & J. H. Flavell (Eds.), *Studies in cognitive development: Essays in honor of Jean Piaget.* London and New York: Oxford University Press, 1969.

Collard, R. R. Exploratory and play behaviors of infants reared in an institution and in lower and middle class homes. *Child Development,* 1971, **42,** 1003–1015.

Décarie, T. G. A study of the mental and emotional development of the thaledomide child. In B. M. Foss (Ed.), *Determinants of Infant Behavior IV.* London: Methuen, 1969.

Douglas, J. W. B. Mental ability and school achievement of premature children at 8 years of age. *British Medical Journal,* 1956, **1,** 1210.

Flavell, J. H. *The developmental psychology of Jean Piaget.* Princeton, N.J.: Van Nostrand, 1963.

Gesell, A. The ontogenesis of infant behavior. In L. Carmichael (Ed.), *Manual of child psychology.* New York: Wiley, 1954.

Halverson, H. M. An experimental study of prehension in infants by means of systematic cinema records. *Genetic Psychology Monographs,* 1931, **10,** 107–286.

Humphrey, T. Postnatal repetition of human prenatal activity sequences with some suggestions of their neuroanatomical basis. In R. J. Robinson (Ed.), *Brain and behavior.* London: Academic Press, 1969.

Jeffrey, W. E., & Cohen, L. B. Habituation in the human infant. In H. Reese (Ed.), *Advances in child development and behavior,* Vol. 6. New York: Academic Press, 1973.

Jones, M. C. The development of early behavior patterns in young children. *Pedagogical Seminary,* 1926, **33,** 537–585.

Kagan, J. Attention and psychological change in the young child. *Science,* 1970, **170,** 826–832.

Kagan, J. *Change and continuity in infancy.* New York: Wiley, 1971.

Kopp, C. B., & Shaperman, J. Cognitive development in the absence of object manipulation during infancy. *Developmental Psychology,* 1973, **9,** 130

McCall, R. B., Hogarty, P. S., & Hurlburt, N. Transitions in infant sensorimotor development and the prediction of childhood IQ. *American Psychologist,* 1972, **27,** 728–748.

Moore, K. C. The mental development of a child. *Psychological Monographs,* 1896, (Monogr. Suppl. 3), 150.

Paiget, J. *The origins of intelligence in children.* New York: International Universities Press, 1952.

Piaget, J. *The construction of reality in the child*. New York: Basic Books, 1954.

Piaget, J. Piaget's theory. In P. H. Mussen (Ed.), *Carmichael's manual of child psychology*. New York: Wiley, 1970.

Preyer, W. *Mind of the child*. New York: Appleton, 1882.

Schinn, M. W. *Notes on the development of a child*. (University of California Publications in Education), Berkeley: University Press, 1893.

Twitchell, T. E. Reflex mechanisms and the development of prehension. In K. J. Connolly (Ed.), *Mechanisms of motor skill development*. New York: Academic Press, 1970.

Uzgiris, I. Ordinality in the development of schemas for relating to objects. In S. Hellmuth (Ed.), *Exceptional infant: The normal infant*. Vol. 1. Seattle, Washington: Special Child Publications, 1967. **1**, Pp. 315–334.

Watson, J. B., & Watson, R. R. Studies in infant psychology. *Scientific Monthly*, 1921, **13**, 493–515.

White, B. L. *Human infants: Experience and psychological development*. Englewood Cliffs, N.J.: Prentice Hall, 1971.

White, B. L., Castle, P., & Held, R. Observations on the development of visually directed reaching. *Child Development*, 1964, **35**, 349–364.

White, B. L., & Held, R. Plasticity of sensorimotor development in the human infant. In J. F. Rosenblith & W. Allinsmith (Eds.), *Causes of behavior: Readings in child development and educational psychology*. (2nd ed.) Boston, Mass.: Allyn & Bacon, 1966.

White, B. L. Experience and the development of motor mechanisms in infancy. In K. J. Connolly (Ed.), *Mechanisms of motor development*. New York: Academic Press, 1970.

Wolff, P. H. & Feinbloom, R. I. Critical periods and cognitive development in the first two years. *Pediatrics*, 1969, **44**, 999–1006.

Zagora, E. Observations on the evolution and neurophysiology of eye-limbs coordination. *Ophthalmologica*, 1959, **138**, 241–254.

12

BEHAVIORAL EFFECTS FROM ANTENATAL EXPOSURE TO TERATOGENS

Richard E. Butcher
Karen Hawver
Thomas Burbacher
William Scott
University of Cincinnati
   and
Institute for Developmental Research

For the past few years we have been investigating the behavior of rats receiving subteratogenic or marginally teratogenic doses of drugs known to cause prenatal malformation of the central nervous system. The results of these studies together with those of several other investigators in the United States and Russia indicate that these substances produce deficient performance in learning tasks when administered in amounts at which no or very few malformations are found on examination of the twenty day fetus.

Taken together, these studies suggest the dose-response relationships (based on those of Dr. James Wilson) illustrated in Fig. 1. The center curve reflects the increase in the number of gross malformations usually associated with the administration of increasingly large doses of a teratogen during the sensitive period of CNS malformation. The right hand curve indicates a similar relationship for embryolethal effects. The left hand curve reflects the belief that in addition to embryolethal and teratogenic effects, a given dose of a CNS teratogen will produce functional effects, learning impairments, abnormal activity patterns, etc. A given dose, therefore, could result in a combined effect (in the center area): some animals dead, some grossly malformed, and some functionally impaired. At small doses (the area to the left of the dashed line) functional effects are found in the absence of gross malformation—some investigators have found behavioral effects at small fractions of the dose at which frank malformations are first seen. We have, for example, previously reported learning deficits in the offspring of

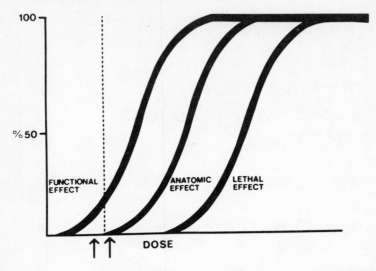

FIG. 1. Dose response relationships for agents teratogenic to the central nervous system (see text for details).

female rats receiving sodium salicylate (Butcher, Voorhees, & Kimmel, 1972) and hypervitaminosis-A (Butcher, Brunner, Roth, & Kimmel, 1970) at relative dose levels that lie between the arrows.

It is noteworthy that the belief that behavioral deficits are induced by low doses of teratogens has stemmed primarily from behavioral studies following treatment with substances teratogenic to the central nervous system, and the behavioral impairments observed have been attributed to neurologic dysfunction. We will present here a brief report of our behavioral testing of rats exposed in utero to hydroxyurea and acetazolamide (Diamox). Both are teratogenic substances, but hydroxyurea under the circumstances of the present study has a less obvious effect upon the CNS, and in rats Diamox affects the CNS only rarely.

EXPERIMENT I

Hydroxyurea (HU), a potent inhibitor of DNA synthesis, reduces the incorporation of (^{3}H) thymidine in embryos of pregnant rats receiving 250 mg/kg or more on the twelfth day of gestation (Scott, Ritter, & Wilson, 1971). This inhibition is associated with cell death in limb buds and neural tube. Although gross limb malformations are frequently found at term, those of the CNS are rare. This rarity, despite an appreciable amount of cell death in the ependymal layer of the neural tube, led to the proposal that functional consequences of defects in this system not detectable in standard teratological examinations of the 20-day fetus might appear postnatally. The first study was undertaken to determine whether such functional impairments would be evident in behavioral tests of rats exposed in utero to doses of HU large enough to produce cell death but not gross malformation of the nervous system.

Method

Pregnant Wistar rats were injected i.p. with 375 (HU 375) or 500 (HU 500) mg/kg HU on day 12 of gestation (date sperm found = day 0). Females were allowed to deliver normally, and all litters were examined at birth. Half of the experimental and control litters of each pair were exchanged (cross-fostered) on the day after birth.

All offspring were weaned at 25 days of postnatal age, housed individually, and allowed free access to Purina Lab Chow and water. Between 30 and 40 days of age subjects from all litters were tested for exploratory activity in an open field. Briefly, the subjects were placed in a corner of an enclosed, 45-inch-square surface painted flat black and divided by fine white lines into a checkerboard of 25 9-inch squares. The total number of squares entered with all four feet during 3 min of free exploration on each of 3 consecutive days was recorded for each subject. Observations of the physical condition and locomotor pattern of each animal were also recorded during this testing.

Ten days after open field testing all subjects were examined for their ability to swim and were then required to learn the route of escape from a water-filled multiple (6-unit) T maze (for details, see Butcher, Scott, Kazmaier, & Ritter, 1973). Two measures of maze performance were recorded: (1) errors (whole-body entries into blind alleys) and (2) elapsed time between entry into the water and contact with the exit ramp. For the final 2 days of testing the start and goal areas of the maze were reversed and the subjects were required to learn the reverse path through the maze.

Results

All litters were delivered normally and no evidence of reduced litter size or external malformation was found in any of the groups at birth.

The results of open-field testing indicated that differences between male and female subjects in the number of squares entered were not statistically significant (t test); the sex of the subject was therefore disregarded. An analysis of variance was performed on the data to examine the effects of treatment and cross-fostering. HU administration had no significant effect on exploration in the field ($p > .05$) nor did cross-fostered subjects enter significantly more squares than subjects nursed by their own mothers ($p > .05$). The interaction of these effects was not statistically significant.

During open-field testing two abnormalities were observed in a number of experimental subjects. These animals lacked normal neuromuscular control of the hind limbs, causing the feet to splay outward when rearing, resulting in an

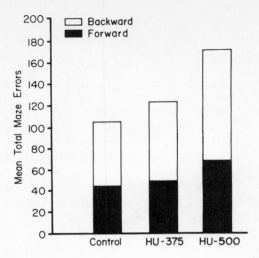

FIG. 2. Mean total errors made during maze testing by 50-day-old rats exposed prenatally to hydroxyurea (HU groups) and their controls.

unsteady locomotor pattern. Also, kinked tail, which had previously been observed in only 3% of the 20-day fetuses receiving 500 mg/kg HU on day 12 of gestation, was found in a substantial portion (47%) of the older experimental subjects examined in this study.

All subjects were weighed just before being maze tested. An analysis of variance performed on these data indicated significantly reduced weights in the HU-500 subjects ($p > .01$) and in female subjects ($p > .01$). All groups displayed a similar sex difference in weight, which was reflected in the analysis by a nonsignificant interaction term. No differences in weight between cross-fostered and non-cross-fostered subjects could be detected by directed t test for either sex ($t_{male} = 1.92$, $df = 49$, $p > .05$; $t_{female} = 0.09$, $df = 73$, $p > .05$).

No significant differences attributable to any of the experimental variables were indicated in an analysis of variance performed on the data from the swimming speed trials administered prior to maze testing. An analysis of variance performed on mean total errors for the 4 days of maze testing (Fig. 2) examined two principal effects (treatments and phase of testing) and their interaction. Administration of HU had a significant effect ($p = < .01$). Significantly more errors were made by all groups in learning the backward path through the maze than in forward-path testing ($p < .01$). A nonsignificant interaction term indicated that in all experimental groups the difference between the number of errors made during the forward and backward maze paths was similar. A posteriori (Scheffé, 1953) analysis indicated that the combined performance of experimental offspring was significantly poorer ($p < .01$) than that of the controls. Although the number of errors made by the HU-375 group was greater than those of the controls a direct comparison of these two groups approached but did not achieve statistical significance. The direct (Scheffé, 1953) comparison of the HU-375 and HU-500 groups, however, reached statistical significance ($p < .01$). Results consistent with those from the error data were obtained in an analysis of elapsed time (treatment, $p < .01$; testing phase, $p < .01$). To insure that the maze error results were not influenced by other experimental variables, two additional tests were performed which demonstrated that neither cross-fostering ($t = .751$, $df = 120$) nor sex ($t = .116$, $df = 120$) had significant effects upon maze errors. Separate t tests were also made to determine whether the physical impairments present in the HU groups led to poorer maze performance. These tests revealed that the number of errors of subjects with kinked-tail or locomotor impairments or both were not significantly ($p > .05$) greater than those of animals without these abnormalities in either the HU-375 or HU-500 groups.

EXPERIMENT II

A second series of experiments has examined the postnatal behavioral effects of prenatal Diamox administration. This substance rather uniformly produces deformity of the forepaw in rats (usually ectrodactyly and ulnar hemimelia of the right forepaw). Diamox is thought to affect the central nervous system only rarely (Wilson, Maren, Takano, & Ellison, 1968).

Method

We administered 500 mg/kg of acetazolamide subcutaneously to four pregnant Sprague Dawley rats on the afternoon of the tenth day and the morning of the 11th day of their pregnancy. This dose of Diamox was expected to produce forepaw malformation rates between 35–45%. Four additional control females received distilled water adjusted to a pH of 9.2 with NaOH. To provide positive control subjects, three additional groups of four females were prepared. These subjects received 500 or 625 mg/kg hydroxyurea or distilled water (negative control) i.p. on the twelfth day of pregnancy. Our previous investigation indicated that offspring of females treated with hydroxyurea in this way would show impaired performance on our learning tasks. Diamox, hydroxyurea, and control subjects were prepared and subsequently tested concurrently.

All litters were allowed to deliver normally, were reduced to number 10, and were examined externally for malformations at 5 days of age. Of the Diamox subjects 40% were observed to have a forepaw abnormality at this time. Litters were weaned and housed in individual cages at 21 days of age.

Results

At 30–35 days of age all subjects were examined in the open field test described previously. No difference in the amount of exploration was found. The malformed Diamox animals were observed to compensate for the affected limb and showed a "rocking" limp. Locomotor abnormalities, which included rear legs splaying

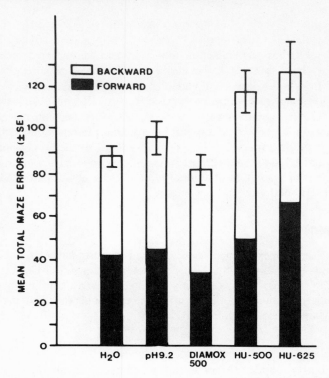

FIG. 3. Mean total errors made during maze testing by 50-day-old rats exposed prenatally to Diamox, hydroxyurea, and control solutions (H_2O and pH 9.2 groups).

outward and a hopping gait, were present in 40% of the hydroxyurea 500 and 66% of the 625 mg/kg hydroxyurea animals.

At 50–55 days of age all subjects were tested in the water filled six unit t-maze. No differences in preliminary swimming speed tests were noted. The results of this testing in terms of errors are displayed in Fig. 3. Approximately 30 subjects are represented in all groups except the hydroxyurea 625, which had 16. The performance of the Diamox animals was as good as either of the control groups prepared, while the hydroxyurea subjects made substantially more errors. An analysis of variance performed on these data indicated a statistically significant effect among the treatment groups ($p < .01$) and the comparison of individual groups (Scheffé, 1953) indicated that the Diamox subjects did not differ from the controls. The Diamox subjects, however, did perform significantly better than either of the hydroxyurea groups ($p < .01$ for all comparisons). The performance of malformed and normal Diamox was also compared by direct t test. No significant differences could be detected. Similar analyses performed on the elapsed time resulted in almost identical results.

Discussion

We have observed learning impairments without locomotor defects (sodium salicylate, hypervitaminosis-A) and with locomotor defects (hydroxyurea). Using Diamox we observe locomotor defects, but no learning impairments.

These results suggest that the behavioral impairments we have observed previously are not effects of muscular or skeletal defects alone. It appears that agents which cause malformation of or damage to the fetal nervous system will produce behavioral impairments in offspring when given in moderate amounts. It may also be that substances which do not have a major effect upon fetal central nervous system will not produce behavioral impairment even when administered in quantities that induce frank malformation.

ACKNOWLEDGMENTS

Supported in part by NIH grants HD00324, HD02792, and HD05221, and Contract No. 74-6 from the U.S. Food and Drug Administration.

REFERENCES

Butcher, R. E., Brunner, R. L., Roth, T., & Kimmel, C. A. A learning impairment associated with maternal hypervitaminosis-A in rats. *Life Sciences,* 1970, Part 1, **11**, 141-145.

Butcher, R. E., Scott, W. J., Kazmaier, K., & Ritter, E. J., Postnatal effects in rats of prenatal treatment with hydroxyurea. *Teratology,* 1973, **7**, 161–165.

Butcher, R. E., Voorhees, C. V. & Kimmel, C. A. Learning Impairment from maternal salicylate treatment in rats. Nature New Biology, 1972. **236**, 211–212.

Scott, W. J., Ritter, E. J. & Wilson, J. G. DNA synthesis inhibition and cell death associated with hydroxyurea teratogenesis in rat embryos. *Developmental Biology,* 1971, **26**, 306-315.

Wilson, J. G., Maren, T. H., Takano, K., & Ellison, A. Teratogenic action of carbonic anhydrase inhibitors in the rat. *Teratology,* 1968, 1(No. 1), 51–61.

Scheffé, H. A. A method for judging all possible contrasts in the analysis of variance. *Biometrika,* 1953, **40**, 87–104.

13

MORPHOLOGICAL AND BEHAVIORAL CONSEQUENCES OF CHEMICALLY INDUCED LESIONS OF THE CNS[1]

Patricia M. Rodier
William Webster
Jan Langman
University of Virginia

With the development of autoradiography, it has become possible to date the time of origin of cells in developing organisms. Through the work of many investigators, a chronology of the spinal cord and many brain regions has evolved. One effect of this work has been to push our estimates of the time when cell formation ceases past the time of birth. In the rat, for example, some neurons are formed as late as the onset of puberty, while some glia are still produced in mature adults (Altman, 1966). In man, as in rodents, many cerebellar neurons are produced after birth (Raaf & Kernohan, 1944; Rakic & Sidman, 1970). Teratologists have tended to focus on the period of organogenesis, when insults lead to gross malformations. The same insults late in pregnancy or early in postnatal life do not result in obvious abnormalities. Yet these periods include the birthdays of unique cell types in the CNS, and loss of even a few neurons could have serious consequences for an otherwise healthy animal.

We have used several drugs believed to interfere exclusively with cell prolifera-tion to eliminate specific cells in the developing CNS (Langman & Shimada, 1971; Andreoli, Rodier, & Langman, 1973). The treatments are systemic, but since they damage only those cells that are synthesizing DNA, they are extremely selective. Since the neurons destined for various adult structures are produced in a sequential pattern, the region of cell loss should depend on the time at which cell proliferation is interrupted. This is true not only of drugs that interfere with cell proliferation, but of x-ray, and, most important to those interested in congenital brain damage, of DNA viruses, such as measles. Our purpose, then, was to compare treated animals to controls, both morphologically and behaviorally, and

[1]Supported by NIH grant NS06188.

169

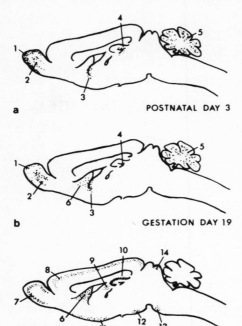

a   POSTNATAL DAY 3

b   GESTATION DAY 19

Fig. 1. (a) Adult position of heavily labeled cells in animals injected with tritiated thymidine on postnatal day 3 (2 inj. × 6 μC/g, 6 hr apart). (b) on gestation day 19 (2 inj. × 6 μC/g, 6 hr apart). (c) on gestation day 15 (2 inj. × 6 μC/g, 6 hr apart).

c   GESTATION DAY 15

further, to compare animals treated at different stages of development to one another.

The immediate effects of treatment with 5-azacytidine have been described by Langman and Shimada (1971). About 2 hr after a pregnant mouse was injected with azacytidine, a few abnormal mitotic figures appeared at the lumen of the neuroepithelium in the fetuses. Over the following hours the affected cells became more and more pycnotic and their number increased. Surprisingly, they migrated away from the lumen in an apparently normal fashion, but 24 hr after treatment many were disintegrating, and by 48 hr most had disappeared.

When animals treated with azacytidine are compared to those injected with tritiated thymidine, the regions of cell death match the regions of cell proliferation. When we have treated animals with azacytidine and labeled simultaneously it is clear that only labeled cells become pycnotic. Thus, the structures damaged by azacytidine should be the same as those labeled at the same stage of development.

Figure 1 shows the adult position of cells heavily labeled on postnatal day 3, embryonic day 19, and embryonic day 15. According to the labeling experiments, the cells undergoing their final division on PN 3 are: (1) glomerular layer cells of the olfactory bulb; (2) internal granular layer cells of the olfactory bulb; (3) subependymal cells; (4) granule cells of the dentate gyrus; (5) internal granular layer cells of the cerebellum and the cells surrounding the Purkinje cells.

The same areas were labeled by injection on E 19 as shown in Fig. 1b. More internal granular layer cells and fewer glomerular layer cells were involved by the earlier labeling, and the distribution of labeled cells in the cerebellum seemed more restricted to the vermis. Scattered labeled cells were observed in the corpus striatum (6).

On E 15 neurons for many structures were undergoing their final divisions (See Fig. 1c). Many cells in the corpus striatum were heavily labeled in adults after thymidine injections on E 15. Labeling in the olfactory bulb was almost exclusively related to mitral cells (7). Several layers of cerebral cortex (8) showed heavy labeling, along with many pyramidal cells of the hippocampus (10). The label in the olfactory tubercle was striking (11). Regions where cell proliferation must have been nearing completion were the septal nuclei (9), the inferior colliculus (14), the mammillary nuclei (12), and some pontine nuclei (13). The amygdala, especially the medial cortical nucleus, included many heavily labeled cells. It is too lateral to appear on the diagram.

The description of missing cells is considerably more difficult than the description of labeled cells. Some of the damage produced by azacytidine on E 15 is obvious. Figure 2a and b shows the thin, small cerebral cortex of a treated mouse, and in plastic sections, Fig. 2c and d, the gaps in the pyramidal cell layer of the hippocampus. The corpus striatum is not obviously affected, but its width in histological sections is consistantly reduced. Quantifying deficits in the scattered small cells involved by later treatments is extremely difficult. One cell type is amenable to counting, the large light-staining cells in the Purkinje cell layer, which may be Golgi epithelial cells. The number of these does appear to be reduced by azacytidine treatment on PN 3 (Figs. 2e and f).

Whatever their other characteristics, the azacytidine-treated animals are true small-for-date babies. Table 1 shows data on the physical development of the three experimental groups and controls. Weight differences between treated animals and controls were significant for all groups in infancy. The trend for body weights to decrease from controls to PN 3's to E 19's to E 15's persists into maturity, but only E 15's differ significantly from controls as adults. The same pattern of results occurs in measures of brain weight. The attainment of developmental landmarks was retarded in all groups, and the earlier the treatment the greater the delay. No gross malformations were observed in any of the animals studied—a total of several hundred.

All the animals used for behavioral testing were conceived on the same day. When any group received an azacytidine treatment (8 mg/kg in 2 injections, 6 hr apart) all other groups received saline injections. Prenatal treatments were administered intraperitoneally and postnatal injections were given subcutaneously. In contrast to the general retardation observed in physical characteristics, behavioral observation revealed different deficits in the different treatment groups. The pattern of behavioral abnormalities suggests that the functional changes observed are related to specific sites of cell loss, rather than the extent of cell loss.

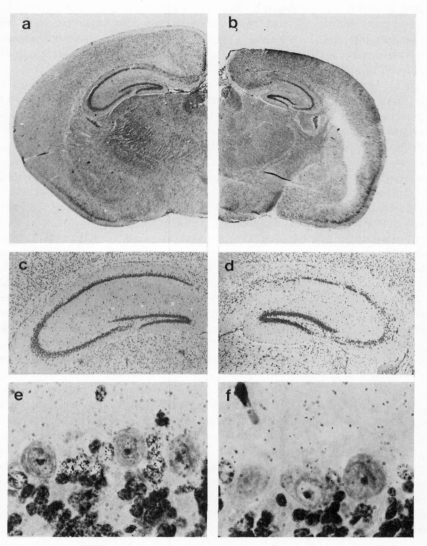

Fig. 2. (a) Paraffin section (4 μ) of adult mouse injected with saline on gestation day 15 (hematoxylin–eosin). (b) Paraffin section (4 μ) of adult mouse injected with 5-azacytidine (2 inj. × 4 mg/kg, 6 hr apart) on gestation day 15 (hematoxylin–eosin). (c) Methacrylate section (1 μ) of adult hippocampus after injection with saline on gestation day 15 (azure II). (d) Methacrylate section (1 μ) of adult hippocampus after injection with 5-azacytidine (2 inj. × 4 mg/kg, 6 hr apart) on gestation day 15 (azure II). (e) Paraffin section (4 μ) of adult cerebellum after injection with tritiated thymidine (2 inj. × 6 μC/g, 6 hr apart) on postnatal day 3 (hematoxylin–eosin). (f) Paraffin section (4 μ) of adult cerebellum after injection with tritiated thymidine (2 inj. × 6 μC/g, 6 hr apart) and 5-azacytidine (2 inj. × 4 mg/kg, 6 hr apart) on postnatal day 3 (hematoxylin–eosin).

Table 2 gives some examples of functional anomalies observed after azacytidine treatment.

On postnatal day 6, all animals were tested for righting responses. Time-to-right was greatly increased in the PN 3 and E 19 groups, but not in the E 15 group. Thus, the animals believed to have cerebellar damage had difficulty in righting, while the E 15's righted normally despite brain damage in many other areas. By the 9th day after birth all groups could right themselves almost immediately.

Pivoting is an infantile locomotor behavior in which the animal rests on a collapsed hind leg and moves the front legs with the result of spinning in place. This behavior persisted in PN 3's and especially in E 15's. Evidently damage in several motor areas can lead to this abnormality, for no damage to motor systems is common to the two affected groups. It is interesting that E 19-treated mice showed no locomotor impairment, and were even precocious in some ways. PN 3's showed a gait characterized by poor control of the hind limbs. Besides pivoting, they held the hind legs abducted and tended to walk on the medial side of the foot rather than on the sole. The forward excursion of the hind limbs was reduced, so that the feet were often posterior to the body during all phases of the gait. Early in development, E 15's had an efficient gait, but in the second week they began to show locomotor difficulties. Like the PN 3's, they pivoted and held the hindlimbs in abduction, but unlike the later treatment group, they walked on the soles of their feet and had an exagerated forward excursion of the limb. Some crossing of the front limbs was noted—a form of incoordination rarely seen in other groups.

Coarse intentional tremors were seen in all treatment groups. They appeared during the first week in E 19's and PN 3's and later in the E 15 animals. Although these axial tremors are a classic "cerebellar sign" they have also been associated with lesions of the basal ganglia (Martin, 1967).

General activity as measured by an induction coil activity meter (LKB Farad) demonstrated a clear dependence on time of treatment. Both E 15's and E 19's were significantly different from controls, but E 15's were hyperactive, while E 19's were hypoactive. Thus, the same treatment delivered on different days of development had opposite effects.

No physiological psychologist can resist the temptation to relate these behavioral anomalies to the brain structure damaged—one is reassured to see hippocampal damage associated with hyperactivity or cerebellar lesions associated with locomotor difficulties. Yet, with these combination lesions of several structures, a firm relation of structure to functional deficit is presumptuous. What is certain is that different patterns of cell loss do result in different syndromes of behavioral abnormalities. The description of such syndromes is directly relevant to human brain damage, for many insults interfere with cell proliferation and congenital brain damage must frequently involve the kinds of subtle, widespread lesions produced in these experiments.

If one considers the many experiments involving agents known to produce cell loss in proliferative populations, there is a wealth of evidence that suggests our

TABLE 1
Physical Development

	Control (N = 11)	PN 3 (N = 10)	E 19 (N = 11)	E 15 (N = 22)
Mean body weight at 5 days (gm)	3.7	3.5*	2.9**	2.1**
Mean body weight at weaning (gm)	21.4	22.2	21.9	15.8**
Mean body weight at 8 weeks (gm)a	38.4	35.8	33.6	24.3**
Mean brain weight at 8 weeks (gm)a	.555	.547	.534	.413**
Order of eye opening	1	2	3	4
Order of ear opening	1	2	3	4
Order of fur growth	1	2	3	4

*$p < .05$;   **$p < .01$.

aThese data were taken from groups prepared for antomical study only. Other figures are from animals prepared for behavioral study.

TABLE 2
Behavioral Development

	Controls (N = 11)	PN 3 (N = 10)	E 19 (N = 11)	E 15 (N = 22)
Proportion above median righting timeat 6 days	.090	.800**	.909**	.250
Mean seconds/minute pivoting at 8 days	5.9	10.9**	4.8	11.0**
Proportion showing tremor at 7 days	.090	1.000**	1.000**	.211
Proportion showing tremor at 17 days	.273	.600	.182	1.000**
Mean activity/2 minutes in adults	159.0	166.5	131.6**	201.3**

**$p < .01$.

results are part of a general picture of interference with late gestation and early postnatal life. Methylazoxymethanol treatment has been shown to cause deficits on a motor task (Ciofalo, Latranyi, & Taber, 1971) in rats. X-irradiation of E 15 rats produces hyperactive adults, as measured in tilt-cages (Furchtgott & Echols, 1958). Werboff, Havlena, and Sikov (1962) also found significant hyperactivity in rats irradiated on E 15. Some reports of treatment on E 15 include measures of brain weights. Reductions have been reported with methylazoxymethanol (Ciofalo *et al.*, 1971; Haddad, Rabe, Laqueur, Spatz, & Valsamis, 1969) and x-ray (Fowler, Hicks, D'Amato, & Beach, 1962). The histology presented in the latter paper is quite similar to that observed after azacytidine.

Less information is available for treatments that correspond to the E 19 group. One related finding comes from the x-irradiation series of Furchtott and Echols (1958). Hypoactivity was observed in animals treated on E 18 and after birth.

The first week of life, including PN 3, has been investigated extensively by Altman and his colleagues. While their studies involved more extensive damage, because of repeated treatments, and employed focal radiation to the cerebellum rather than systemic treatments, many of the behavioral results are similar to those resulting from azacytidine. For example, irradiation of the cerebellum led to tremor, righting difficulties, and an abnormal gait characterized by poor coordination of the hind limbs (Wallace & Altman, 1970a, 1970b). Rat virus infection in suckling hamsters damages the external granular layer of the cerebellum, like neonatal treatments with x-ray or azacytidine, and it leads to tremor and ataxia (Kilham & Margolis, 1964).

In summary, when azacytidine was injected at three stages of development, the treated mice differed from controls in weight and rate of development. The earlier the treatment, the greater the retardation. Histologically, cell loss in the CNS was obvious soon after treatment, but more difficult to demonstrate in adults. Where structures were abnormal after azacytidine treatment, they matched the areas labeled on the same treatment days. Behaviorally, each treatment period led to a syndrome of abnormal function, and each syndrome was different from the others. Thus, the effects on anatomy and behavior were dependent on the time of treatment. It is our hope that these animals may serve as appropriate models of congenital brain damage. By identifying the behavioral consequences of interference with cell proliferation at many stages of gestation and postnatal life, it may eventually be possible to specify the etiology of some brain damage syndromes.

REFERENCES

Altman, J. Autoradiographic and histological studies of postnatal neurogenesis. II. A longitudinal investigation of the kinetics, migration, and transformation of cells incorporating tritiated thymidine in infant rats, with special reference to postnatal neurogenesis in some brain regions. *Journal of Comparative Neurology*, 1966,**128**, 431–474.

Andreoli, J., Rodier, P.M. & Langman, J. Influence of a prenatal trauma on formation of Purkinje cells. *American Journal of Anatomy,* 1973, **137**, 87–101.

Ciofalo, V. B., Latranyi, M., & Taber, R. I. Effect of prenatal treatment of methylazoxymethanol acetate on motor performance, exploratory activity, and maze learning in rats. *Communications in Behavioral Biology,* 1971, **6**, 223–226.

Fowler, H., Hicks, S. P., D'Amato, C. J., & Beach, F. A. Effects of fetal irradiation on behavior in the albino rat. *Journal of Comparative and Physiological Psychology,* 1962, **3**, 309–314.

Furchtgott, E., & Echols, M. Activity and emotionality in pre- and neonatally x-irradiated rats. *Journal of Comparative and Physiological Psychology,* 1958, **51**, 541–545.

Haddad, R. K., Rabe, A., Laqueur, G. L., Spatz, M., & Valsamis, M. P. Intellectual deficit associated with transplacentally induced microencephaly in the rat. *Science,* 1969, **163**, 88–90.

Kilham, L., & Margolis, G. Cerebellar ataxia in hamsters inoculated with rat virus. *Science,* 1964, **143**, 1047–1048.

Langman, J., & Shimada, M. Cerebral cortex of the mouse after prenatal chemical insult. *American Journal of Anatomy,* 1971, **132**, 355–374.

Martin, J. P. *The basal ganglia and posture.* Philadelphia: Lippincott, 1967.

Raaf, J., & Kernohan, J. W. A study of the external granular layer in the cerebellum. *American Journal of Anatomy,* 1944, **75**, 151–172.

Rakic, P., & Sidman, R. L. Histogenesis of cortical layers in human cerebellum, particularly the lamina dessecans. *Journal of Comparative Neurology,* 1970, **139**, 473–500.

Wallace, R. B., & Altman, J. Behavioral effects of neonatal irradiation of the cerebellum. I. Qualitative observations in infant and adolescent rats. *Developmental Psychobiology,* 1970, **2**, 257–265.   (a)

Wallace, R. B. & Altman, J. Behavioral effects of neonatal irradiation of the cerebellum. II. Quantitative studies of young-adult and adult rats. *Developmental Psychobiology,* 1970, **2**, 266–272.   (b)

Werboff, J., Havlena, J., & Sikov, M. Effects of prenatal x-irradiation on activity, emotionality and maze learning ability in the rat. *Radiation Research,* 1962, **16**, 444–452.

14

CRITICAL PERIODS IN FETAL DEVELOPMENT: DIFFERENTIAL EFFECTS ON LEARNING AND DEVELOPMENT PRODUCED BY MATERNAL VITAMIN A EXCESS

Donald E. Hutchings
John Gibbon
John Gaston
Linda Vacca
New York State Psychiatric Institute

The theory underlying the work reported here first came to the attention of the senior author when he attended the 1966 Teratology Workshop held at the University of Colorado. A principle of teratology that appeared particularly relevant to psychology was the frequent observation that acute exposure to teratogenic agents during embryogenesis produces a specific type or pattern of malformation depending on the stage of development at the time of administration. What this describes, of course, is the notion of the critical period; that during embryogenesis specific organs or systems pass through a developmental period when they are maximally susceptible to damage. For example, in the rat, exencephaly and spina bifida can be produced only during the first half of embryogenesis, and cleft palate only during the last half.

Because the embryo becomes increasingly refractory to gross structural malformation as gestational age increases, studies of drug teratogenicity in the 1960s were quite understandably devoted almost exclusively to agents administered during organogenesis. However, at the conclusion of organogenesis fetogenesis begins, and the central nervous system undergoes finer histological development. It seemed likely that teratogenic agents administered at this time might very well interfere with this process, resulting in subtle brain damage and behavioral impairment. We further wondered, as the teratologists had so thoroughly documented for the embryonic period, whether there might be critical periods during fetogenesis when qualitatively different behavioral effects might be ob-

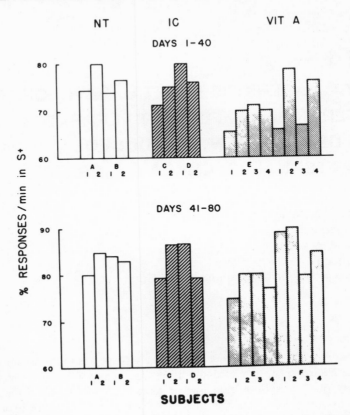

FIG. 1.   The mean proportion of total responses $S+$ for nontreated (NT), intubation controls (IC), and vitamin A (VIT A) animals averaged over the first 40 and last 40 days of discrimination training.

tained as a result of acute exposure to teratogenic drugs. We were unable to find any substantive work in which well-documented teratogenic drugs were administered during relatively circumscribed periods and behavioral effects measured later in life. It seemed to us that such work might have implications for a better understanding of such childhood disorders as mental retardation and minimal brain dysfunction, and we therefore initiated a program of research.

Initially we were faced with two problems: the choice of an appropriate teratogenic drug and the time in gestation to administer it. The latter problem was solved when a colleague mentioned the work of Dr. Samuel Hicks at the University of Michigan. When we saw the title "How to design and build abnormal brains using radiation during development" (Hicks & D'Amato, 1961), we felt we were on the right track. They irradiated rats at various times during the fetal period and described patterns of brain malformation that differed depending on the time of treatment. In addition, they had carried out collaborative work with psychologists investigating the behavioral correlates of these effects. We thought it would be interesting to compare the behavioral effects of irradiation and a teratogenic drug administered at comparable periods in gestation.

As to the selection of a drug, the problem seemed overwhelming. By this time, teratologists had amassed a vast armament of teratogens including azo dyes, vitamins, alkylating agents, antimetabolites, alkaloids, salycilates, antibiotics, antihistamines, and so on, all likely candidates to interfere with histogenesis. About this time, however, Langman and Welch (1967) presented findings that were critical to our subsequent work. They administered vitamin A excess, a well-known teratogenic treatment, to mice on 2–3 successive days during the early fetal period and examined brains at regular intervals up until 10 days of postnatal life. They found that the treatment inhibited DNA synthesis in the neuroepithelial cells of the cerebral cortex. This acted to prolong the cell cycle by approximately 40%, interfere with the differentiation of existing neuroblasts, and result in a cerebral cortex with a reduced cell density. This work provided us with convincing evidence that such a drug treatment could indeed produce subtle nonlethal brain damage, and we therefore decided to use vitamin A excess.

For our first study (Hutchings, Gibbon, & Kaufman, 1973) we administered a teratogenic dose of vitamin A to rats on Days 14 and 15 of gestation. Intubation controls received the vehicle alone, and nontreated mothers were not disturbed. All groups were fostered to untreated mothers after birth. Compared with controls, the vitamin-treated offspring showed a generalized retardation in growth as evidenced by a delayed onset of fur growth, eye opening, and reduced body weight. In adulthood, animals were tested on various operant conditioning tasks in order to assess learning ability. They were trained on a lever for continuous water reinforcement and then on an intermittent reinforcement schedule. No differences were found between treated and controls.

Following this, animals were tested on an auditory discrimination. In the presence of one auditory cue, $S+$, responding was reinforced on the intermittent schedule. $S+$ was altenated with another cue, $S-$, during which responding was never reinforced. Animals typically acquire such a discrimination by increasing responding in $S+$ while gradually extinguishing responding in $S-$. Both treated and controls did acquire the discrimination during the 80 daily training sessions. However, the treated group acquired it significantly slower because of a much slower extinction of $S-$ responding.

The data in Fig. 1 are averages of the proportion of total responses occurring in the $S+$ signal. The data are averaged over the first and last 40 days of discrimination training separately and are presented in the upper and lower panels, respectively, with litters (i.e., littermates) designated by letter and animals by number. During acquisition (Days 1–40) the mean performance of all the animals from treated litter E and animals 1 and 3 from treated litter F showed low proportions. This resulted from their higher rates of response in $S-$. During the last 40 days,

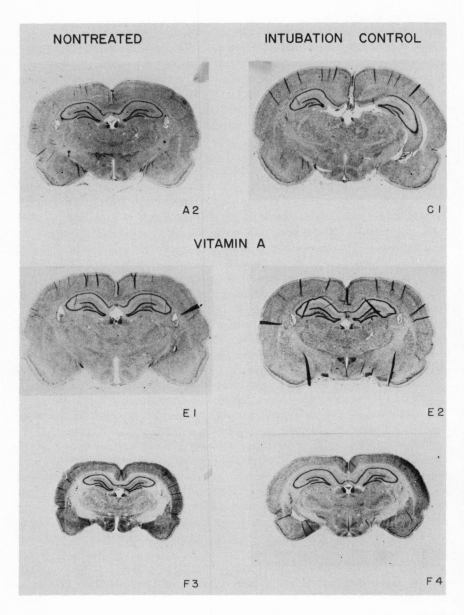

FIG. 2. Coronal sections at the level of the thalamus (Kluver-Barrera Luxol blue, low power).

which largely reflects asymptotic performance, the treated subjects are performing about as well as the controls.

The slower acquisition of the treated animals reflected a reduced ability to withold responding in the $S-$ signal. This is also evident in the latency of the first response in the $S-$ signal. As training continued the $S-$ latencies of the controls increased. That is, they learned to pause increasingly longer at the onset of the signal in which they were never reinforced. However, even at asymptotic performance when the treated had extinguished $S-$ rates of response to the level of the controls, their $S-$ latencies remained significantly shorter. This reduced ability to withold and delay responses in $S-$ was rather dramatically illustrated in the final phase of the study when for 40 sessions $S-$ responses were punished with mild shock. All subjects improved their performance by further extinction of $S-$ responding and longer $S-$ latencies, but the treated animals still failed to perform as well as the controls. Moreover, during 20 sessions when shock was eliminated, the treated, unlike the controls, reverted to their poorer preshock performance. Evidently, the aversive consequences for responding in $S-$ was necessary both to produce and maintain the improved discrimination performance. Measurement of water intake as an indication of drive level did not differ between groups.

Figure 2 shows representative sections of treated and control brains. Histological examination showed that none had any obvious abnormalities of cellular elements or structures. Sections from treated animals in litter E were not obviously different from the controls. Examination of sections from treated animals in Litter F showed that all were diffusely reduced in overall size. Some also showed a rather mild, diffuse enlargement of the ventricular system which was probably secondary to reduced brain size. Interestingly, however, a comparison of the amount of brain reduction with the discrimination performance shown in Fig. 1 fails to reveal any clear relationship. Of the two litters, litter E showed the slowest acquisition whereas litter F had the smallest brains. Thus, it is not at all clear what mechanism underlies the poorer performance of the treated animals.

The poorer performance of the treated animals suggested neither an auditory nor a generalized learning deficit. Their acquisition of the lever press and performance on the partial reinforcement schedule was no different from the control. Even though they were slower in acquiring the discrimination, the level of performance that they eventually achieved indicated that they could hear the signal and distribute their responses appropriately. They did have a diminished capacity, however, for witholding responding in the signal that indicated nonreinforcement. Direct observation of their behavior suggested a perseverative quality, as though they were not attending as carefully to the onset of the $S-$ signal. Interestingly, an inhibitory impairment in an operant discrimination, similar to that found here, has been reported by other workers following irradiation in rats at approximately the same gestational age that vitamin A was administered here (Fowler, Hicks, D'Amato, & Beach, 1962; Persinger, 1971) suggesting a critical period for

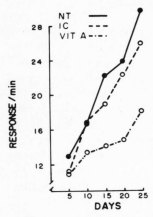

FIG. 3. The mean responses per min during the intermittent reinforcement sessions for nontreated (NT), intubation controls (IC), and vitamin A treated (VIT A) animals, averaged over 5-day blocks.

producing the impairment. However, one cannot reach such a conclusion until other periods are investigated, and this was the purpose of our next study.

For this, we investigated the effects of vitamin A excess on days 17 and 18 of gestation (Hutchings & Gaston, 1974). At this time the cerebellum is beginning active differentiation and it would not be surprising, therefore, if we observed motor impairment along with or independent of the kind of cognitive deficit observed when treatment was administered earlier. The same controls and testing procedures were used as in the previous study.

Unlike animals treated on days 14 and 15 there was no retardation in growth and development. On the operant measures we found that the treated animals had consistently slower rates of response compared with the controls. This is seen most clearly in Fig. 3, which shows rates of response during 25 sessions of partial reinforcement averaged over 5-day blocks. Throughout, both treated and controls acquired increasingly higher rates of response. The treated animals, however, increased much less rapidly and to levels significantly below that of the controls.

After day 25, animals were trained on the $S+$, $S-$ discrimination. The large rate differences observed previously were maintained in $S+$. However, treated animals extinguished responding in $S-$ just as rapidly as the controls. This is in sharp contrast to the failure to inhibit $S-$ responding of 14–15 day animals. Histological examination also showed no reduction in brain size or any obvious abnormality of cellular elements or structure.

Because no pathology was detectable by ordinary histological technique we undertook a preliminary study of the effects of vitamin A excess on S-100, a brain-specific protein. S-100 first appears around the time of birth, occurs in the cytoplasm of proliferating neuroblasts, and, because it increases with cell growth, it can be used as a cytochemical marker for differentiation (e.g., Sviridov, Korochkin, Ivanov, Maletskaya, & Bakhtina, 1972). Based on the observation of Langman and Welch (1967), that vitamin A delays cell division, we expected to observe a delay in the appearance of S-100, indicating an interference with differentiation.

Animals were treated with vitamin A excess on days 17 and 18 of gestation, and intubation controls were treated as described above. At birth and on postnatal days 5 and 10, animals were sacrificed, and their brains were removed and frozen. Sections were cut at 10 μ, fixed according to Hartman, Zide, and Udenfriend (1972), and stained by the indirect immunofluorescence procedure of Coons.

At birth the highest concentration of S-100 appeared in the cerebellum, indicating high proliferative activity. Figure 4 shows the amount of S-100 detectable in the cytoplasm of neuroblasts proliferating from the fourth ventricle. The darkened areas are the unstained neuronal nuclei, each surrounded by a thin rim of cytoplasm specifically stained for S-100. Compared with controls (left) the staining was considerably reduced in treated animals (right) indicating, as predicted, a significant lag in their development. By days 5 and 10 this lag was no longer detectable.

In related work, the same vitamin A treatment and histochemical techniques were employed, but a different cytochemical marker was used as a specific tag for the appearance of astrocytes. No staining was apparent at birth in either treated or controls, but by day 5 some distinct glial groupings were apparent in the brain stems of control animals. These were much less obvious, however, in treated animals, again indicating a delay in their development. By day 10 this pattern reversed. That is, the treated animals now showed the more obvious glial groupings, suggesting an overcompensation in response to the initial delay produced by vitamin A. A similar compensatory phenomenon has been observed by Rodier (personal communication).

The major behavioral finding was that the animals treated on days 17 and 18 of gestation failed to acquire a rate of response comparable to the controls. Just why, however, is not clear. Lower drive level was not indicated by water intake data. One possibility is that the treated animals had a minor motor disturbance which interfered with faster responding. In preliminary work we observed that some 17–18 day animals walk with a peculiar gait, possibly indicating a subtle motor deficit affecting fine motor coordination. Furthermore, Fowler, Hicks and D'Amato (1962) and Hicks and D'Amato (1966) found that rats irradiated on the same days that vitamin A was administered in our study were more sluggish in their placing reactions, move awkward in their general movements, and did not respond as rapidly as controls in a lever box. These observations nicely parallel our findings, and in future work we will investigate motor behavior more thoroughly. Our study further demonstrates, however, that such an impairment need not be associated with a learning deficit.

In view of the similarity of effect produced by irradiation and vitamin A, it is interesting that irradiation produces such severe and chronic damage to the developing CNS whereas vitamin A does not. Both Hicks and D'Amato (1966) and Hutchings *et al.* (1973) have emphasized the obscurity of the relation between teratogenetically produced brain damage and behavioral impairment. The similar-

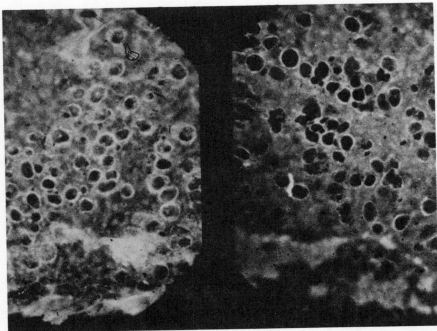

FIG. 4. Appearance of S-100 in the cytoplasm of proliferating neuroblasts detected at birth by immunofluorescence. Normal animal (left), vitamin A treated animal (right), fourth ventricle at bottom (× 630).

ity of impairment produced by both agents, however, suggests a common underlying mechanism. The results of our histochemical study has led us to speculate that since proteins define both the structure and function of cells, the behavioral effects possibly reflect biochemical imbalances in protein synthesis. An ontogenetic study of these processes may provide the link between prenatal drug exposure and adult behavioral function.

The results of our studies with vitamin A and similar studies using irradiation indicate that there are critical periods during fetogenesis when exposure to teratogenic agents produces a specific kind of behavioral effect. Additional studies using a variety of agents administered at different gestational ages will be required to determine whether this fundamental principle of teratology is applicable to behavioral effects.

Finally, we feel that these finding, as well as those of Drs. Butcher and Rodier, have important implications for the behavioral dimension of prenatal drug safety. We have been struck by the resemblance of the behavioral effects observed among our animals—inhibitory and motor impairments—to those so often described for children with minimal brain dysfunction. The extent to which drugs taken during pregnancy are implicated in this problem is not known, but clearly the first step is carrying out such research with animals.

ACKNOWLEDGMENTS

This research was supported by the General Research Support Grant RR-05650 to the New York State Psychiatric Institute, NIMH Grant DA00449, and NSF Grant GB 34095. The histochemical work was carried out while Dr. Vacca was on an NIMH Postdoctoral Fellowship, Department of Neuroscience, Dr. Maurice Rapport, Chief.

REFERENCES

Fowler, H., Hicks, S. P., D'Amato, C. J., & Beach, F. A. Effects of fetal irradiation on behavior in the albino rat. *Journal of Comparative and Physiological Psychology*, 1962, **55**, 309–314.

Hartman, B. K., Zide, D., & Udenfriend, S. The use of dopamine-β-Hydroxylase as a marker for the central noradrenergic nervous system in rat brain. *Proceedings of the National Academy of Sciences*, 1972, **69**, 2722–2726.

Hicks, S. P., & D'Amato, C. J. How to design and build abnomal brains using radiation during development. In W. S. Fields & M. M. Desmond (Eds.), *Disorders of the developing nervous system*. Springfield: Thomas, 1961.

Hicks, S. P., & D'Amato, C. J. Effects of ionizing radiation on mammalian development. In D. H. M. Woollam (Ed.), *Advances in teratology*. London: Logos Press, 1966. Pp. 195–250.

Hicks, S. P., D'Amato, C. J., & Falk, J. L. Some effects of irradiation on structural and behavioral development. *International Journal of Neurology*, 1962, **3**, 535–548.

Hutchings, D. E., Gibbon, J. The effects on vitamin A excess administered during the mid-fetal period on learning and development in rat offspring. *Developmental Psychobiology*, 1974, **7**, 225–233.

Hutchings, D. E., Gaston, J., & Kaufman, M. Maternal vitamin A excess during the early fetal period: Effects on learning and development in the offspring. *Developmental Psychobiology*, 1973, **6**, 445–457.

Langman, J., & Welch, G. W. Excess vitamin A and development of the cerebral cortex. *Journal of Comparative Neurology*, 1967, **131**, 15–26.

Persinger, M. A. Pre- and neonatal exposure to 10^{19} Hz and 0.5 Hz electromagnetic fields and delayed conditioned approach behavior. Unpublished doctoral dissertation, University of Manitoba, 1971.

Sviridov, S. M., Korochkin, L. I., Ivanov, V. N., Maletskaya, E. I., & Bakhtina, T. K. Immunohistochemical studies of S-100 protein during postnatal ontogenesis of the brain of two strains of rats. *Journal of Neurochemistry*, 1972, **19**, 713–18.

15

INFANT RECOGNITION MEMORY AS A PRESENT AND FUTURE INDEX OF COGNITIVE ABILITIES

Joseph F. Fagan III
Case Western Reserve University

I. INTRODUCTION

A. Objectives

The goal of the research reviewed here is to explore early cognitive functioning through systematic study of the human infant's capacity for visual recognition memory. The review is limited for the most part, to studies conducted at the Perceptual Development Laboratory of Case Western Reserve University. A more complete summary of the general literature pertaining to infant memory processes is contained in Cohen and Gelber (in press).

The plan of this contribution, following a discussion of the operational definitions of infant visual perception and recognition memory, is to review three aspects of infant recognition. The first concern is with the effects of age, stimulus characteristics, and study time on immediate recognition. The infant's capacity for delayed recognition and an identification of some factors that produce forgetting is then reviewed. Finally, the focus is on recognition memory as a source of early individual differences potentially important for the prediction of later cognitive functioning.

B. Operational Definitions

The chief methodological advance in the area of infant visual perception was made by Fantz (1956) who developed the "visual interest test." The response he chose to measure selective attention was the activity of the eyes themselves, the assumption being that if the infant consistently gazes at some stimulus more often than at others he must be able to perceive and differentiate among them. Visual "preferences" constitute an operational definition of selective attention and are

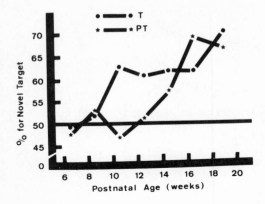

FIG. 1. Mean percent of total fixation to novel target for term (T) and preterm (PT) groups as a function of postnatal age.

obtained when, for example, one of a pair of targets receives significantly more than 50% of infants' fixation.

Attempts to discover if the infant retains information following selective visual exploration have assumed that an unequal distribution of attention between a novel and a previously exposed target indicates recognition memory. Two paradigms have been developed to test infant recognition. One procedure is to present a stimulus for a number of "trials" and then to introduce a new stimulus. Typically the infant's response to the repeatedly exposed target declines or "habituates" over trials but returns to a high level or "dishabituates" when a novel target is introduced. This habituation–dishabituation sequence indicates that the infant has noticed a change in the situation, presumably because he has stored some information about the repeatedly exposed stimulus. If, following the initial decline and recovery of response, the familiar target is reintroduced and the infant's response declines to its previous low level, there is some indication of delayed recognition.

A second procedure is to expose the infant to a target for a certain period of time, usually from one to two minutes, and then to present him with the recently exposed and novel target simultaneously. When tested with this paired-comparison approach, infants typically devote the greater part of their visual fixation to the novel target. Delayed recognition memory is easily tested by simply varying the time that elapses between the end of the familiarization period and the presentation of the test pairing. The studies to be reviewed were based on the paired-comparison approach to the testing of recognition.

II. IMMEDIATE RECOGNITION

A. Age

Three studies (Fagan, Fantz, & Miranda, 1971; Fantz, 1964; Fantz & Nevis, 1967) have traced age changes in differential responsiveness to paired novel and familiar stimuli. In all three reports the stimuli to be discriminated were abstract

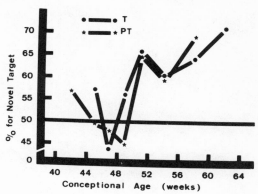

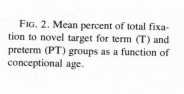

FIG. 2. Mean percent of total fixation to novel target for term (T) and preterm (PT) groups as a function of conceptional age.

black and white patterns varying along a number of dimensions. The initial studies of Fantz (1964) and Fantz and Nevis (1967) found preferences for novelty at and after, but not prior to 2.5 months of age. A more refined estimate of the age parameter was made by Fagan *et al.* (1971), who asked whether the development of immediate recognition is more influenced by the length of the infant's experience in the visual world or by the infant's general maturational level. The experiment by Fagan and co-workers provided pertinent data on this question by selecting samples of infants born at varying lengths of gestation and testing them at various postnatal ages ranging from 5 to 20 weeks. The results of this testing are presented in Figs. 1 and 2. In Fig. 1, responsiveness to novelty as a function of postnatal age is plotted for a group of infants born at term (T) and for another sample born preterm (PT). As one can see from Fig. 1, the curves for both groups are characterized by an initial chance (50%) level of responding, followed by a rapid rise to a stable preference for novelty. The T group, however, reached a reliable preference between 10 and 11 weeks; the PT group did not reach a reliable preference until one month later. Since these results questioned the value of postnatal age as a determinant of responsiveness to novelty, a second analysis compared the performance of the T and PT samples as a function of conceptional age. Plotting by conceptional age, in effect, matched both groups in terms of total maturation. In Fig. 2, the curves for the two samples are no longer displaced but, instead, are quite similar. Both show an initial chance level of response followed by a rapid rise to a reliable novelty preference at about 51 weeks of conceptional age.

In summary, paired-comparison testing tells us that infants demonstrate more interest in novel than in previously exposed targets by at least the third month of postnatal age, with total maturational level playing the more important role in determining when preferences for novelty will appear. This estimate of the beginnings of recognition memory, of course, does not deny the possibility that the infant may recognize a previously exposed stimulus prior to 51 weeks of conceptual age.

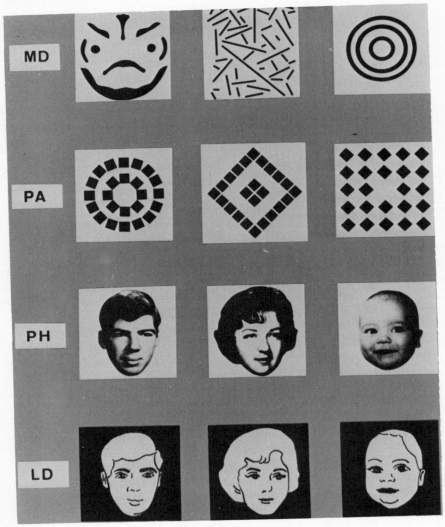

FIG. 3. Representative stimuli.

B. The Interaction of Age
with the Stimuli to Be Discriminated

In the following discussion it will be seen that the age at which the infant demonstrates immediate recognition depends on the nature of the previously exposed and novel targets that he is faced with. In general, targets differing along a variety of dimensions are differentiated at an earlier age than are stimuli varying along more restricted dimensions.

Examples of discrimination tasks which will be alluded to in the remainder of this paper are contained in Fig. 3. The first row of Fig. 3, labeled MD for "multidimensional," contains three abstract black and white targets which differ from one another along a number of dimensions (e.g., size, number of elements, length of contour, form of elements, ratio of black to white). Such MD patterns were employed in the study by Fagan and co-workers noted earlier, to estimate age trends in immediate recognition. The stimuli in the second row vary along the more restricted dimension of pattern arrangement (PA), each being composed of the same number and size of black squares, differing only in how the squares are arranged to form an overall pattern. The remaining targets in Fig. 3 are representations of faces, either achromatic photos (PH), or line drawings (LD) of the photos.

The age at which an infant will recognize which of two targets he has seen before varies with the nature of the discrimination confronting him. Memory for targets varying multidimensionally occurs at 2.5 months (Fagan *et al.*, 1971), while stimuli differing only in pattern arrangement are not recognized until 4 months (Fagan, 1970, Experiment I; Fagan & Fantz, 1971). Similarly, the difference between a rotated and an upright version of the same face photo, which may be considered a difference in pattern arrangement, is not shown until 4 months (Fagan, 1972, Experiment II; Fagan & Fantz, 1971). More difficult are distinctions between faces (e.g., between man and woman), not possible at 4 months but demonstrable at 5–6 months for either face masks or photos (Fagan, 1972). More difficult still are distinctions between line drawings of faces (e.g., man versus woman) or between two rotated faces, neither of which are possible at 5–6 months (Fagan, 1972).

Thus, if one asks at what age will an infant demonstrate recognition memory, the answer must be that it depends on what the infant is being asked to recognize. When an infant is faced with two targets that differ along a number of dimensions, attention to cues along any of those dimensions during familiarization may be sufficient to allow him to notice novel cues on recognition testing that will attract his attention. Observing those same dimensions during training may not stand him in good stead when he is subsequently presented with a target differing only in pattern arrangement. Presumably, general configurational aspects would have to be noted to allow such a discrimination. Even attention to general configurational differences, however, will not be sufficient if the infant is confronted with two faces. In fact, distinctions among faces would seem to require a period of perceptual learning during which the distinctive features demarking faces as a class of objects are acquired (Fagan, 1972).

Whatever the explanation for task differences in recognition memory, the point to bear in mind for our present purposes is that varying the nature of the stimuli to be discriminated and recognized reveals age differences in recognition memory from the second to the sixth month of life.

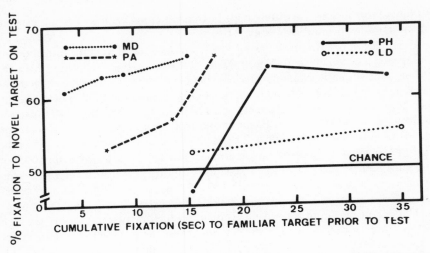

Fɪɢ. 4. Percentage of total fixation to the novel target on recognition testing as a function of amount of prior study of the familiar target for the discrimination tasks involving multidimensional stimuli, pattern arrangement, photos of faces, and line drawings of faces.

C. Study Time

In the research reviewed above, the amount of study time or the "familiarization" period allowed the infant prior to recognition testing ranged from one to two minutes, during which infants typically demonstrate 30–60 sec of fixation. A recent experiment (Fagan, 1974) asked whether briefer amounts of fixation during familiarization are effective in allowing recognition memory. A related question was whether the difficulty of the required discrimination demanded longer viewing during study time. Four types of discrimination tasks known to vary in difficulty as a function of age were given to 5–6-month infants. The tasks included, from earliest to latest recognition over age, a discrimination among multidimensional stimuli (MD), targets varying in pattern arrangement (PA), photos (PH) of faces (e.g., man versus woman), and line drawings (LD) of faces (e.g., man versus woman). Examples of each task are shown in Fig. 3. The general procedure, employing separate groups of from 18 to 48 subjects, was to allow the subjects a set study time, ranging from 5 to 60 sec over the four discrimination tasks, prior to recognition testing.

Plotted in Fig. 4, for each of the four tasks, is the percentage of total fixation time paid to the novel target on recognition testing as a function of the actual amount of time that the subjects devoted to the target exposed during the familiarization period. As is apparent from Fig. 4, the amount of study time necessary to elicit a novelty preference on recognition testing varied from task to task. As little as 3–4 sec of study time were needed to recognize a novel MD target, whereas a similar level of novelty preference was not reached for the PA task until 17 sec of study time had been used. Recognition of a novel face photo required at least 22 sec, and line drawings were not differentiated even after 35 sec of study time.

The facts that such brief periods of familiarization lead to recognition and that the order in which these four discriminations are solved over age can be recaptured at a single age by varying study time have interesting methodological and practical implications, which shall be pursued when the predictive value of infant recognition is discussed later in this paper.

D. Summary

The infant's tendency to devote more fixation to a novel than to a previously exposed target on tests of immediate recognition depends on interactions among the infant's conceptional age, the nature of the stimuli, and the amount of study time devoted to a target during familiarization. In general, discriminations between stimuli varying along a number of dimensions following long study times (e.g., 30–60 sec) are possible at 2.5 months of postnatal age for infants born at term. Given equivalently long study times, more subtle discriminations are not evidenced until 4 or 6 months of age. By 6 months, relatively brief amounts of study time are sufficient to allow immediate recognition, although more study time is needed for more difficult discriminations. In addition, the order in which stimuli are differentiated over age may be reconstructed within an age by varying study time for those discriminations.

III. DELAYED RECOGNITION AND FORGETTING

A. Delayed Recognition

As noted above, the 5–6 month infant, given sufficient study time, will demonstrate recognition of a previously exposed target some 5–10 sec after the end of the familiarization period. This section presents a summary of a series of experiments (Fagan, 1973) designed to explore delayed recognition on the order of hours, days, and weeks for a variety of discriminations on the part of 5–6-month infants. This series of experiments was prompted by earlier studies of 5–6-month subjects which demonstrated delayed recognition of MD targets after periods of 7 min (Fagan, 1971) and 2 hr (Fagan, 1970, Experiment II). The general procedure of Fagan (1973) was to expose the infant for 2 min to a particular target and then, some 5–10 sec later, to obtain a test of immediate recognition by pairing the previously exposed stimulus with a novel target. The infant then was revisited once either hours, days, or weeks later and was presented with the previously exposed and novel target as a test of delayed recognition.

In an initial experiment, the focus was on 24- and 48-hr delayed recognition for targets varying either multidimensionally or only in pattern arrangement. The

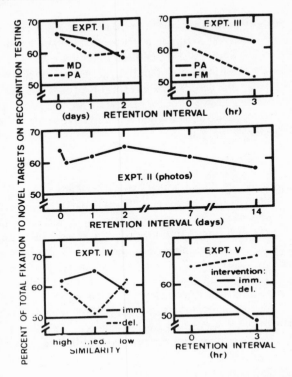

FIG. 5. Graphical summary of five experiments on delayed recognition and forgetting.

results of this first experiment are illustrated in the top left graph of Fig. 5. All points in the graph for Experiment I are reliably greater than a chance value of 50%. Analyses revealed no reliable effects or interactions among the factors of problems (MD, PA), sex, or time of testing (immediate, delayed). In short, the subjects in this initial experiment proved capable of recognizing which member of a pair of abstract black and white targets had been previously exposed as long as 48 hr ago, even for a discrimination as subtle as that of pattern arrangement.

A second experiment explored delayed recognition for photos of faces (e.g., man versus woman) at intervals of 3 hr, 1, 2, 7, or 14 days. Again the subjects were given an immediate as well as one delayed test. For 64 of the 98 infants in this second experiment simultaneous recordings were made by two observers on delayed recognition for most of the subjects tested at 1, 2, 7, or 14 days. The middle graph in Fig. 5 illustrates the results of the second experiment. All tests are significantly greater than chance. No reliable decline in preference for novelty occurred at any retention interval and no sex differences were observed. Interobserver reliability was on the order of .99.

Thus far, the series of experiments being considered reveals a remarkable exhibition of the 5–6-month infant's ability to recognize two-dimensional, achromatic, patterned stimuli following lengthy retention intervals, whether these stimuli are more (face photos) or less (abstract patterns) representative of naturally occurring objects. In a third experiment these tests of delayed recognition were extended to face masks as examples of more true to life representations of natural stimuli. Infants were given immediate and 3-hr delayed recognition tests on either face masks or PA targets. The results are shown in the top right graph of Fig. 5. Delayed recognition for PA targets was reliably greater than chance and did not differ from immediate recognition, a result fully expected on the basis of infants' performance at 24 and 48 hr for such stimuli in Experiment I. For the face masks (FM) the picture was quite different. Only reliable immediate recognition was shown. After a 3-hr delay, a significant decline to a chance level of 50% was obtained. The results of the third experiment, in short, gave an indication of an interesting phenomenon in infant recognition memory, that is, they sometimes forget. This lack of retention for face masks on the part of the infants in the third experiment led to attempts to specify the conditions producing forgetting, attempts reviewed in the next section.

B. Forgetting

The failure of the infants in the third experiment to demonstrate reliable differential responsiveness to novel face masks following a 3-hr delay stood in striking contrast to the demonstrated long duration of retention exhibited by the subjects in the first and second experiments. This decline in retention did not appear explicable on the basis of any obvious features of the data. One likely explanation of the infant's failure to differentiate novel from familiar face masks after a 3-hr delay lies in a consideration of the nature of the stimuli to be retained and the stimuli occurring between immediate and delayed recognition testing. Of the sets of targets employed in the three experiments, face masks are quite obviously most akin to patterned objects in the infant's natural environment, that is, real faces. Following immediate recognition testing, the infant would be bound to see people, and his attention to these people may have interfered with his subsequent ability to remember which of two masks he had seen before. The purpose of a fourth experiment was to test the possibility that exposure to perceptually similar material following immediate recognition testing might be a source of subsequent failure to distinguish novel from familiar targets. The stimuli employed for immediate and delayed recognition testing in the fourth experiment were photos of faces that infants had shown to be capable of recognizing after long time periods (Experiment II), yet still bore some degree of similarity to naturally occurring objects. In addition, the degree of similarity of intervening material to the targets to be recognized served as an additional variable in the fourth experiment.

The procedure in the fourth experiment was to expose infants for 2 min to a face photo and then obtain a test of immediate recognition. Some 60 sec following immediate recognition testing, a delayed test was made by again pairing the previously exposed with novel targets. Three different types of material were introduced for 30 of the 60 sec that occupied the period between immediate and delayed testing. For 30 of the 90 subjects, another set of face photos was shown as intervening material to constitute a "high" similarity intervention. A second group of 30 subjects were also presented with face photos, except that the photos were rotated 180°. The rotated photos were considered a "medium" similarity intervention. The remaining 30 subjects were exposed to "low" similarity targets consisting of line drawings of faces rotated 180°. The results of these various interventions are plotted in the lower left graph of Fig. 5. The only condition to result in forgetting was intervention with medium similarity material (rotated photos). The other conditions (upright photos, rotated line drawings) had no effect on delayed recognition. However one may wish to generalize such results to the forgetting of face masks that occurred in the third experiment, the findings of Experiment IV did reveal that delayed recognition could indeed be affected by exposure to certain stimuli. Further, these results emphasized the nature and perhaps the degree of similarity of the intervening to the original material as an important factor in loss of recognition on the part of the infant.

A fifth and final experiment in this series was conducted to explore two questions arising from the results of the fourth experiment. The first question was: Does the deleterious effect of immediate intervention persist, that is, would delayed recognition of upright photos still be affected following some appreciable delay (3 hr in Experiment V)? The second question was: How soon following immediate recognition testing must rotated photos be presented to disrupt delayed recognition? This second question was tested by presenting rotated photos to the subject 3 hr following immediate recognition testing but just prior to delayed recognition testing. Hence, two groups of subjects were given an immediate and a 3-hr delayed recognition test for properly oriented photos, with 30 sec of exposure to rotated photos intervening between immediate and delayed tests. For one group the intervention was immediate, that is, just after their initial recognition test. For the other sample intervention was delayed for 3 hr. As one can see from the data presented in the lower right graph in Fig. 5, the results were quite clear. Immediate intervention prevented delayed recognition. Delayed intervention had no effect. The results of the fifth experiment both replicated and extended the results of the fourth in finding that intervention with perceptually similar material will disrupt delayed recognition and, further, that this disruption lasts for an extended period and must occur soon after immediate recognition testing to have an effect.

C. Summary

Infants 5–6 months of age are capable of recognizing previously exposed visual targets after periods of hours, days, and even weeks. Failure of delayed recognition appears to be due to particular combinations of certain perceptual and temporal factors. Forgetting occurs when the infant is exposed to stimuli that bear some degree of similarity to previously acquired information. Not all similar stimuli lead to forgetting, and even those that do must be presented to the infant soon after he has acquired the original information.

IV. PREDICTING COGNITIVE ABILITY

A. Introduction

A paradigm measuring cognitive functioning attracts the attention of experimental psychologists in the field of mental retardation when two criteria are met. First, the paradigm must be sensitive to developmental status, that is, the older the child, the better the performance. Second, the paradigm must discriminate between individuals who differ on standardized intelligence tests, that is, normals would perform at a higher level under the paradigm than would retardates. Examples of such paradigms that are currently under much study with older children are discrimination learning (e.g., Fisher & Zeaman, 1973; Zeaman & House, 1963) and short-term recall (e.g., Ellis, 1970).

As has been shown (Section II. A, B) tests of infant recognition memory are sensitive to developmental status from the second through the sixth month of life; hence, the infant recognition paradigm meets the first criterion. Evidence to support the view that infant recognition also discriminates between ''normal'' and ''retarded'' infants will now be considered.

B. Differences in Recognition Memory for Selected Samples

The approach common to the studies to be reviewed here was to compare groups of infants on tests of selective visual attention when there was some reason to expect that one sample would differ from another in measured intelligence later in life. Perhaps the most obvious comparison, in this regard, is between normal and Down's syndrome infants. The latter condition is diagnosable at birth and almost certain to result in retarded intelligence later in life. Normal Down's syndrome comparisons will be considered below, but let us turn our attention now to an initial study by Fantz and Nevis (1967), which focused on changes in visual preferences from 1 to 6 months of age on the part of 10 home-reared offspring of highly intelligent parents (Case Western Reserve University faculty members) and 10 institution-reared offspring of women of average intelligence.

As part of their larger study concerned with changes in visual selectivity with age on the part of home-reared and institution-reared children of similar lengths of gestation, Fantz and Nevis (1967) included a test of the infant's differential responsiveness to a novel paired with a previously exposed target. The stimuli were abstract black and white patterns differing along a number of dimensions. A total of approximately 5 min of study time was allowed prior to a test of immediate recognition. The sample as a whole showed a growing preference for a novel over a previously exposed target, beginning at about 2–3 months. This preference developed earlier in age on the part of the home-reared infants, 8 out of 10 of whom preferred the novel target on all tests after 2 months of age. A novelty preference was not shown by the institution infants until about 3 months. A series of studies from our laboratory have compared Down's syndrome and normal infants on tests of recognition memory. In the first published results, Miranda (1970) reported that immediate recognition memory for abstract black and white patterns varying multidimensionally was present for both normal and Down's syndrome infants at 34 weeks of age. As an extension of this work, Fagan (unpublished manuscript) tested short-term delayed (1–7 min) as well as immediate recognition memory in younger Down's syndrome infants (median age about 22 weeks). The procedure employed by Fagan (1971), consisting of the presentation of three novelty problems during a single session, was repeated with 18 Down's syndrome infants. As in the Miranda (1970) study, the stimuli were abstract black and white patterns varying multidimensionally. The results indicated that Down's syndrome infants functioned about as well as normals (the subjects in Fagan, 1971) on such a task, showing reliable preferences for novelty on both immediate and delayed recognition tests for each of the three novelty problems with no reliable decline from immediate recognition testing to delayed testing.

These results were interpreted to mean that immediate and delayed recognition memory for stimuli varying multidimensionally was a relatively simple feat which could be accomplished by Down's syndrome as well as normal 5- to 8-month-olds. In other words, the tasks were too easy and resulted in "ceiling" effects. It seemed likely that more difficult recognition memory problems would reveal differences in functioning between normal and Down's syndrome infants. Results from an experiment by Miranda and Fantz (1974), which we will now consider, indicated that increasing the similarity among the targets to be discriminated and retained with concomitant variations in age did indeed reveal differences between normal and Down's syndrome infants in recognition memory.

In the Miranda and Fantz study, samples of normal and Down's syndrome infants were matched for sex, length of gestation, and level of parental education. Tests of immediate recognition following 30 to 60 sec of study time were made at each of the three ages: 13, 24, and 36 weeks. Three tasks were administered at each age: One problem employed abstract patterns varying along a number of dimensions (similar to the MD patterns in Fig. 3), another was based on targets differing in arrangement of pattern elements (the second and third PA targets in Fig. 3), and the third was a discrimination between face photos (woman versus baby). Preliminary testing indicated that the pattern detail contained in all the stimuli used by Miranda and Fantz were well within the acuity range of the Down's symdrome infants. The results from each task indicated a clear superiority on the part of the normal infants in recognition. Novel MD targets were recognized by the normals at 13 weeks, while Down's syndrome subjects did not accomplish this recognition test until 24 weeks. Distinctions among photos and between the PA targets were evidenced by 24 weeks for normals. The Down's syndrome infants distinguished one face photo from another at 36 weeks, but showed no recognition for PA targets at any age.

In short, the studies by Fantz and Nevis and Miranda and Fantz show that samples of infants who are likely to differ in measured intelligence later in life also differ in their ability to recognize familiar visual stimuli within the first 6 months of life. Given such differences early in life, it would seem worthwhile to obtain correlative data on selective attention to novel stimuli in infancy and later performance on standardized intelligence tests. As a first step in this direction a reliable test of individual differences in infant recognition memory must be developed. Although it has been shown that normals will discriminate novel from familiar targets within the confines of a particular task at an earlier age than Down's syndrome infants, it would not be feasible to conduct extensive longitudinal studies in the hope of finding the exact age that each of a number of infants exhibits a novelty preference in order to assign individuals a "memory score." As noted earlier (Section II.C), however, the order in which novel and familiar stimuli are discriminated over age for particular tasks may be recaptured within an age by varying study time for those discriminations. Hence, a more advantageous approach to the assessment of individual differences in early recognition memory may be to allow subjects a particular length of study time, a length somewhat less than necessary for recognition for the average infant of that age, and then test for novelty preferences. Following this procedure with a variety of tasks would allow an estimation of reliability. If reliable individual differences in recognition are demonstrated, subsequent tests of cognitive functioning at a later age may be given, and the predictive value of infants' responsiveness to novelty can be tested.

V. IMPLICATIONS

Throughout this paper examples have been given of the infant's ability to acquire, store, and retreive visual information. This knowledge has been gained by the simple paradigm of exposing the infant to a target and then pairing that target with a novel stimulus. Further research employing this paradigm will give a clearer picture of both the memory and perceptual capabilities of infants in the first half-year of life. In a more general sense the results of these and future experiments may have implications for theoretical questions concerning the psychology of memory. For example, it now may be assumed that human long-term visual recognition memory does not depend solely upon such factors as storage of verbal descriptions of pictorial stimuli or upon intentional strategies of encoding, since it occurs in infants without benefit of language and under what might be described as the perfect "incidental recall" conditions. The effect of "imagery" on memory, disruption of "consolidation," amnesic effects of interpolated novel material, the role of perceptual "similarity" in producing forgetting, facilitation of memory by orienting the subjects to particular aspects of the to-be-remembered material, all these are current questions being explored by students of memory. As a useful part of this exploration such questions may be approached in a context where verbal processes are not yet operational, where a large store and network of associations has not yet developed, and where the subject is not influenced by instructional sets, or a desire to please the experimenter or to do what he thinks is expected of him. The infant, faced with a novel and a previously exposed stimulus, is just such an ideal subject.

Further comparisons of recognition memory processes in normal and Down's Syndrome infants would be particularly valuable on both theoretical and practical grounds. It is probably fair to say that research on normal–retardate differences in memory represents a significant proportion of the effort expended over the past ten years by experimental child psychologists interested in mental retardation. As a result, a retardate inferiority in memory has been empirically established, and limited gains in theoretical explanations for this normal–retardate disparity have been achieved. Comparisons of normal and Down's syndrome subjects early in life will enable us to begin at the beginning, so to speak, in constructing a truly developmental explanation of the role that memory plays in intellectual deficit. On a practical level, tests of basic cognitive processes in infancy may accomplish what years of research on infant sensorimotor abilities has failed to do, that is, predict later intellectual functioning. An additional virtue of such research, which is often overlooked in the excitement of demonstrating a Down's syndrome deficit in early cognitive functioning, is that we will discover when and in what manner Down's syndrome infants *can* profit from their visual experiences. In other words, by asking such basic questions as what kinds of visual information can the normal infant acquire, how long can this information be retained, and what factors cause the infant to forget, we may be able to judge either the feasiblity or the impracticality of proposed remedial techniques aimed at infants who may be diagnosed early in life as likely to be deficient in their future intellectual functioning.

ACKNOWLEDGMENTS

Preparation of this paper was supported by a Career Development Grant (1 KO4 HD-70144) to the author from the National Institute of Child Health and Human Development.

REFERENCES

Cohen, L., & Gelber, E. Infant visual memory. In L. Cohen & P. Salapatek (Eds.) *Infant perception*. New York: Academic Press, in press.

Ellis, N. R. Memory processes in retardates and normals. In N. R. Ellis (Ed.), *International review of research in mental retardation*. Vol. 4. New York: Academic Press, 1970.

Fagan, J. F. Memory in the infant. *Journal of Experimental Child Psychology*. 1970, **9**, 217–226.

Fagan, J. F. Infants' recognition memory for a series of visual stimuli. *Journal of Experimental Child Psychology*, 1971, **11**, 244–250.

Fagan, J. F. Infants' recognition memory for faces. *Journal of Experimental Child Psychology*, 1972, **14**, 453–476.

Fagan, J. F. Infants' delayed recognition memory and forgetting. *Journal of Experimental Child Psychology*, 1973, **16,** 424–450.

Fagan, J. F. Infant recognition memory: The effects of length of familiarization and type of discrimination task. *Child Development.* 1974, **45**, 351–356.

Fagan, J. F., & Fantz, R. L. Infants' attention to novel stimuli as a function of postnatal and conceptional age. Appendices H and J in Progress Report to National Institutes of Health on Grant HD 04212, 1971.)

Fagan, J. F., Fantz, R. L., & Miranda, S. B. Infants' attention to novel stimuli as a function of postnatal and conceptional age. Paper presented at the meeting of the Society for Research in Child Development, Minneapolis, April, 1971.

Fantz, R. L. A method for studying early visual development. *Perceptual and Motor Skills*, 1956, **6**, 13–15.

Fantz, R. L. Visual experience in infants: Decreased attention to familiar patterns relative to novel ones. *Science*, 1964, **146**, 668–670.

Fantz, R. L., & Nevis, S. The predictive value of changes in visual preferences in early infancy. In J. Hellmuth (Ed.), *The exceptional infant*. Vol. 1. Seattle: Special Child Publ., 1967.

Fisher, M. A., & Zeaman, D. An attention-retention theory of retardate discrimination learning. In N. R. Ellis (Ed.), *Internation review of research in mental retardation*. Vol. 6. New York: Academic Press, 1973.

Miranda, S. B. Response to novel visual stimuli by Down's Syndrome and normal infants. *Proceedings of the 78th Annual Convention of the American Psychological Association*, 1970, **6**, 275–276.

Miranda, S. B., & Fantz, R. L. Recognition memory in Down's Syndrome and normal infants. *Child Development*, 1974, **45,** 651–660.

Zeaman, D., & House, B. J. The role of attention in retardate discrimination learning. In N. R. Ellis (Ed.), *Handbook of mental deficiency*. New York: McGraw-Hill, 1963.

16

INFANT VISUAL MEMORY:
A BACKWARD LOOK INTO THE FUTURE

Leslie B. Cohen
University of Illinois, Urbana-Champaign

I. INTRODUCTION

I am not completely certain why I was asked to contribute to this volume. Although our laboratory has been investigating infant recognition memory for some time, we have never conducted research on retardate memory, nor even systematically tested retarded infants. That does not mean we have been uninterested in aberrant memory development or in the comparison between aberrant and normal development, but we have been attempting to discover what we could about the processes underlying normal infant attention and memory before we began any comparative studies. It is one thing to show that retarded and normal infants differ in recognition memory, but quite another to show which processes are responsible for that difference.

After several years of research, both our procedures for investigating infant attention and memory and our understanding of the processes involved have advanced to the point where an examination of memory in the abnormal infant might prove fruitful. To that end we are currently trying to learn as much as possible about aberrant infant behavior and plan to begin some investigations of "high risk" and retarded infants.

II. HABITUATION AS A MEASURE OF INFANT MEMORY

Like Fagan (1970), we have assumed that, if an infant responds differentially to a novel and familiar stimulus, some type of recognition memory is involved. Unlike Fagan, we have used an habituation paradigm in which a single stimulus is repeatedly exposed and then changed, rather than a paired-comparison procedure in which two stimuli, either the same or different, are simultaneously presented.

In a traditional habituation experiment, the infant is repeatedly shown the same visual pattern for a fixed number of trials, and then one or more novel patterns are introduced. If the infant's response, usually visual fixation, decreases over trials, habituation is said to have occurred, and if the response increases again upon presentation of the novel stimulus, the response is said to have recovered or dishabituated. By varying the length of time between the end of habituation and the test for recovery, one can investigate long-term recognition. By manipulating the difference between familiar and novel stimuli, stimulus generalization and discrimination can be studied, and by inserting other stimuli in the interval between the end of habituation and recovery, one can examine the effects of interference.

Results from habituation and paired-comparison paradigms are usually quite similar. Both procedures have demonstrated immediate and delayed recognition. Both have shown that infants can discriminate colors, forms, and the arrangement of stimulus elements. A recent review of the infant habituation literature (Cohen & Gelber, in press) also revealed an interesting pattern of results from attempts to produce interference. Several experiments (Caron & Caron, 1969; Gelber, 1972; Martin, 1973) were unable to get interference, even following a considerable amount of potentially interfering material. In every case the interpolated material consisted of a number of different patterns, each presented for only a few trials. In contrast, the one habituation study to find clear evidence of interference (De-Loache, 1973) inserted a single second stimulus, immediately after habituation, and either for eight trials or until the infants habituated to it.

We hypothesized from these results that visual information will be stored accurately in long-term memory only after the infant has spent considerable time attending to it, and possibly, only when he habituates to it as well. In order for any new information to produce interference, it must enter long-term memory, and therefore, must also be extensively presented. Filling the retention interval with a number of novel stimuli, each exposed for a brief period of time, should not be sufficient for any of these stimuli to enter long-term memory and should produce little if any interference. However, filling the interval with the same repeated stimulus should be more likely to interfere with information stored earlier.

The assumption that an infant may not be storing information about a stimulus in long-term memory, even though he is attending to it, represents a departure from traditional models of habituation. Some of these models are discussed in more detail shortly, but most of them, in essence, assume that whenever an infant looks, he is storing some information about what he is looking at. If one assumes the infant may be looking but not remembering, a whole new set of questions becomes relevant. For example, how can one tell whether the infant is or is not storing information? On those trials when stimulus information is not entering long-term memory, is it being processed at all? If not, why does the infant look in the first place, and why does he look away after a few seconds? If the information is being processed, could it be stored in a short-term memory which quickly dissipates when the infant turns to look at something else, and are there individual differences in either short- or long-term infant memory? Much of our research is directed toward answering these questions, but before we get into a discussion of this research it might be worthwhile to examine methodological problems related to the study of infant habituation.

III. METHODOLOGICAL CONSIDERATIONS

One point we have stressed repeatedly (Cohen, 1973; Cohen & Gelber, in press) is that use of a fixed trial procedure, where a stimulus is presented for a predetermined length of time, may not provide an accurate reflection of the infant's interest in that stimulus. If the infant is looking somewhere else when the trial begins and the stimulus comes on, he may not turn to look at the stimulus until the trial is almost over. That does not necessarily indicate he is uninterested in the stimulus, just that he is preoccupied with something else. If he had looked at the start of the trial, he might have maintained his fixation for a much longer time. One way of avoiding this problem is to begin a trial only when the infant looks at the stimulus. (Friedman, 1972, for example, has used this technique successfully.) A second, related problem is associated with where the infant is looking at the end of a trial. If he is still looking at the stimulus when the trial terminates and the stimulus goes off, can one really assume that his interest in the stimulus ended with the end of the trial? Probably not. He might have looked considerably longer if just given the opportunity to do so.

We have circumvented these problems by devising a new procedure where the trial length is determined by the infant rather than the experimenter (e.g., Cohen, 1972). The infant, usually three to five months of age, is placed in an infant seat facing a vertical screen. The screen is blank except for a light located approximately $10°$ to the right or left of center. Each trial begins with the light blinking on and off until the infant looks at it. In this way we have control over the infant's head and eyes when we turn on the stimulus. As soon as the light is fixated, it goes off and a visual pattern appears on the opposite side. We record both the infant's latency in turning toward the pattern and his subsequent fixation time to it. The infant is allowed to look as long as he wishes, but as soon as he turns away, the pattern goes off, and the blinking light comes back on to start the next trial.

Using this procedure we not only get better estimates of infants' attention to patterns, but as a side benefit, have also noticed that the infants seem to enjoy the task more. Instead of losing about 40% of our subjects due to crying, irritability, or drowsiness, the attrition rate has fallen to approximately 25%.

We have also found that the factors determining how quickly an infant will turn to a pattern are quite different from those determining how long he will fixate the pattern once he has turned. In one experiment, for example (Cohen, 1972), 18 male and 18 female 4-month-old infants were exposed to checkerboard patterns varying in size and number of squares. The major finding was that the latency of turning toward the pattern was influenced more by the size of the checkerboard than by the number of squares. The duration of fixation, however, was more a function of number of squares than size. Other studies (Cohen, 1973; DeLoache, Wetherford, & Cohen, 1972) have shown that changes in latency of turning to a stimulus seem to reflect operant conditioning, while changes in the duration of a fixation reflect habituation. In fact we have even found infants speeding up their turning to a pattern at the same time they are decreasing their fixation time or are habituating to the pattern.

Evidence such as this has led us to propose two relatively independent processes in infant visual attention (Cohen, 1973): an *Attention-Getting* process, which determines whether an infant will orient his head and eyes toward a visual pattern, and an *Attention-Holding* process, which determines how long he will fixate after he has turned. Attention-Getting is more affected by the size, movement, or brightness of a pattern, or its distance in the periphery, while Attention-Holding is more affected by the complexity or novelty of the pattern. Thus the major function of the Attention-Getting process is to have the infant attend to a stimulus, so that the processing and storage of stimulus information can be done by the Attention-Holding process. Although Attention-Getting and Attention-Holding tend to operate independently, some evidence exists that infants may increase or decrease their speed of turning toward the stimulus, depending upon what they saw on previous trials. In one experiment reported by Cohen (1973), if the pattern was interesting or produced long fixations, four-month-old infants increased their turning speed; if it was uninteresting or produced short fixations, their speed slowed down.

The separation of infant attention into two processes points out the danger of using total fixation time per trial as a measure of habituation. Does the decrease one is likely to find over trials result from an actual reduction in the infant's looking at the stimulus, or from a slowing down of his turning to look? Most evidence from our laboratory suggests it results from a reduction in the duration of each fixation, but without separate measures of Attention-Getting and Attention-Holding one cannot know for certain.

IV. MODELS OF INFANT HABITUATION AND MEMORY

Most investigators in the area assume infant habituation implies infant memory. But, just because an infant decreases his response over trials does not necessarily mean he is habituating. The decrease could also have resulted from fatigue in the testing situation or from adaptation of the receptors. Fortunately, these interpretations are usually made less tenable by evidence of recovery to a novel stimulus or of delayed recognition. The only viable alternative remaining is that the infant responds less on later trials because the stimulus is becoming familiar. But to say that a stimulus is familiar is to say that it is remembered. Something about what he saw on earlier trials is being stored for use on later trials. Not only must there be some storage or memory, but the infant must also compare what he has remembered with what he is currently watching. To the extent that the comparison indicates he is watching something new, he is going to continue looking. To the

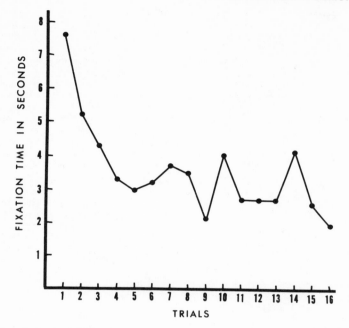

FIG. 1. A typical group habituation curve showing a gradual reduction in fixation time as the same stimulus is repeatedly presented.

extent that it indicates he is watching something old and familiar, he is going to stop looking.

The few existing models of infant habituation (Cohen, 1973; Lewis, 1971; McCall, 1971) assume both that a schema, engram, or representation of the stimulus is being stored while the infant attends, and that some comparator mechanism determines whether the infant will continue to attend to the stimulus or turn away. Although these models represent a starting point in our understanding of infant recognition memory, they also have several inadequacies. For one thing, details of how the stimulus information is stored and compared have not been explicitly given. For another, if taken literally, they would predict that the infant should take one long look at the pattern on the first trial and then stop completely, or at least should have nothing but short looks after that first trial. Even a cursory inspection of the infant data indicates that this prediction is incorrect. Some infants will produce several long fixations before they habituate. Others will repeatedly fixate on the pattern but never habituate. What does happen, according to the typical group habituation curve, is that fixations become successively shorter until some asymptote is reached. Figure 1 provides an example of one such curve. In this particular experiment 36 4-month-old infants were shown 16 repetitions of a checkerboard pattern. Subjects were actually divided into three groups with one group receiving a 2 × 2, the second an 8 × 8, and the third a 24 × 24 checkerboard. For purposes of this illustration the performance of these three groups have been combined in Fig. 1. Each trial began with the blinking light and

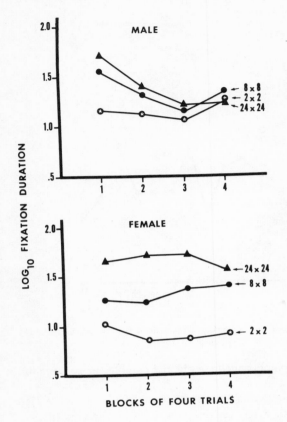

FIG. 2. Fixation time data from the checkerboard study presented separately for males and females (reproduced from Cohen, 1973).

ended when the infant turned away from the checkerboard pattern. Habituation was determined by a criterion. Infants were assumed to have habituated when their fixation time on three successive trials was equal to or less than one-half of their fixation time on the first three trials. Twenty-four of the 36 subjects met that criterion, and it is their performance that is shown in Fig. 1. As you can see, the infants initially looked for about 7.7 seconds, and over the next four or five trials dropped down to a final level of about 3 seconds.

It may be possible to modify current models of infant habituation to account for data such as these. For example, one could characterize an infant's memory as a bag full of marbles. Each marble represents information about a stimulus he has seen in the past. When he looks at some stimulus you have presented, the number or proportion of marbles in the bag representing that stimulus increase. At the same time the comparator is randomly selecting a subset of marbles from the bag. If the marbles it selects match the incoming stimulus, the infant will stop looking. If they do not match, the comparator continues picking other random subsets until a match occurs. On the first trial, very few marbles match what the infant is fixating, and so fixation times will be quite long. As the trials continue, however, the number of marbles in the bag that match the fixated stimulus should increase, fewer comparisons will be needed, and fixation times should become progressively shorter. Finally, asymptotic performance will be reached when each comparison produces a match and stops the infant's fixation.

Although the "marbles in the bag" or some similar probabilistic explanation might account for the behavior of infants who do decrease their fixation time over trials, it could not explain the behavior of those infants who may look several times but do not habituate during the course of the experiment. For example, in several studies (Cohen, 1973; Cohen, Gelber, & Lazar, 1971; Pancratz & Cohen, 1970) we have found that males habituate more than females. Figure 2 provides data from one of these studies (Cohen, 1973). It is the same checkerboard experiment described earlier, but now the data are broken down by stimulus and sex. Although on the first trial both males and females look at the stimuli approximately the same length of time, for some unknown reason, only the males seem to habituate. Whatever the reason for the sex difference, the point is that some infants look, even look longer, at a complex checkerboard than at a simple one, but they do not habituate. Before any model of habituation can be considered adequate, it must be able to explain both the behavior of those infants who do not habituate as well as those who do. In particular, it must be able to explain why an infant who does not habituate looks away from a stimulus, even though, presumably, that stimulus is not being stored in long-term memory.

What we have proposed in the past (Cohen, 1973) is that infants have two types of memory. While the infant is fixating, a short-term representation of the stimulus builds up to the point where it causes the infant to turn away. The more information in the pattern, the longer it will take for this short-term memory to develop an adequate representation of the pattern, and the longer the infant will fixate. As soon as the infant turns away, however, this short-term representation rapidly decays or is displaced by whatever he is currently fixating, so that on the next trial the process must start over once again, and he will look just as long as he did the first time. A second system, long-term memory, is more permanent. If and when stimulus information is transferred to long-term memory, the short-term memory will be superseded, and a relatively permanent reduction in attention will occur.

Thus, we have hypothesized that the length of an infant's fixation on any trial is a function of both short- and long-term memory systems. A match of the representation developed by either to the incoming stimulus will end the fixation. The short-term memory accounts for the infant's turning away from a stimulus when he is not habituating, and the long-term memory accounts for his turning away when he does habituate.

V. BACKWARD HABITUATION CURVES

The assumption that an infant makes use of two memory systems raises another question. Given that an infant's fixations do habituate over trials, how can one determine when the stimulus information first enters long-term memory? In other

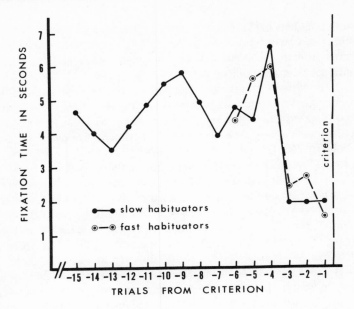

FIG. 3. Backward habituation for fast and slow habituators, from the colored form experiment.

words, do all infants who habituate begin to store information in long-term memory from their first look on the first trial, or do they vary in the number of looks that must elapse before long-term memory comes into operation?

Our attempt to answer this question has involved using a criterion to determine habituation and plotting the data a different way. The first thing we needed was a minicomputer that would allow us to set a criterion for habituation, so we could assess each infant's behavior at that point in time rather than after a fixed number of trials. We wanted to know when he habituated, not just whether or not he habituated sometime during the course of the experiment. Further more, since some infants will fixate longer than others, we wanted a proportional measure of habituation instead of one that assumes all infants habituate when they look less than some fixed amount. (See Cohen and Gelber, in press, for a more complete discussion of the hazards associated with selecting one criterion measure rather than another.) The computer we had built permitted us to do this. It summed the infant's first three looks, then compared that sum to each successive three looks, until the total was equal to or less than one-half of the original looking time.

Once we had developed a procedure that allowed each infant to reach his own criterion, we could assess habituation differently, namely, by plotting "backward habituation" curves. The argument for using a backward habituation curve is equivalent to the one for using a backward learning curve. It has been known for some time that group learning curves do not always reflect the acquisition rate for individual subjects. In retardate discrimination learning, for example, Zeaman and House (1963) have shown that even though a group curve may indicate a gradual increase in performance, individual subjects may actually solve the problem very rapidly. The gradual slope of the group curve results from individual differences in number of trials before the increase in performance begins, rather than from the rate of increase of any particular subject. Zeaman and House obtained a more accurate reflection of learning rate by constructing backward learning curves, that is, by equating the subjects at the point they reached criterion and then plotting performance on the preceding trials backward from that point.

The typical forward habituation curve (such as the one shown in Fig. 1) also indicates a gradual change in performance over trials, only in this case the change is a decrease rather than an increase. Perhaps this curve is just as misleading as the typical learning curve. Perhaps individual infants do not habituate gradually at all. Just as their counterparts in a discrimination learning experiment show rapid improvement once learning begins, so might infants show a rapid decrease in responding once habituation begins. Group habituation curves could be just as artifactual as group learning curves. They may reflect rapid habituation, but after a varying number of trials, rather than gradual habituation beginning on the first trial.

Thus far, we have reexamined the data from two experiments by plotting backward habituation curves. The results were somewhat surprising. In one study (DeLoache, 1973) 36 4-month-old infants were repeatedly shown a slide consisting of four simple colored geometric forms on a black background. The blinking light procedure described earlier was used, and each infant was allowed one look per trial. All infants were run to a criterion of one-half of their original fixation time. As soon as this criterion was reached, 24 infants were switched to a novel slide, and 12 continued to receive the same stimulus they had during habituation.

One surprising aspect of the data was that the infants appeared to be members of one of two distinct populations. They were either fast habituators, reaching criterion in eight trials or less, or slow habituators, requiring anywhere from 11 to 25 trials to reach criterion. The two distributions did not overlap, and approximately 50% of the infants fell into each category.

Other surprises came when we examined the backward habituation curves for fast and slow habituators. These curves are presented in Fig. 3. They were constructed by equating subjects on trials -1, -2, and -3, the trials on which they reached criterion. Performance on earlier trials was plotted backward from there. Since, even within the same group, some infants took longer to reach criterion than others, the number of scores making up each point on a curve varied somewhat, but in no case did any point contain fewer than one-half of the subjects in a group.

The inspection of these curves revealed, first, that the infants did not habituate gradually over trials. They did it all on a single trial. We knew habituation had actually occurred, since those infants who were subsequently given a novel

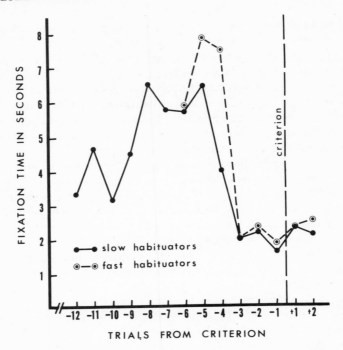

FIG. 4. Backward habituation for fast and slow habituators, from the checkerboard experiment.

stimulus significantly increased their responding, while those receiving the same stimulus did not increase.

Even more surprising was the peak in responding just before habituation. In fact, a significant increase in fixation time occurred from the first trial to the trial preceding habituation. At first we were concerned that this peak might be an artifact of our criterion procedure, but other evidence, to be presented shortly, indicated it was not.

The third interesting aspect of the data was that the behavior of fast and slow habituators was virtually identical. They both showed the peak, and both habituated on a single trial. The main difference between the two groups was the greater number of trials taken by the slow habituators before they showed the peak.

In order to verify these findings, we decided to take another look at the checkerboard experiment described earlier. As you will recall, 36 4-month-old infants were given 16 trials with either a 2 × 2, 8 × 8, or 24 × 24 checkerboard pattern. Twenty-four reached our habituation criterion sometime within the 16 trials, and it was data from these 24 that were shown in the forward habituation curve of Fig. 1.

Reexamining these data, but with separate backward habituation curves for fast and slow habituators, produced a very different picture. As seen in Fig. 4, these infants also showed the peak, rapid habituation, and little difference between fast and slow habituators. Performance on the two postcriterion trials, +1 and +2, indicated that the rapid decrease was not accidental. Fixation times remained low even after the criterion had been reached. A comparison of Figs. 1 and 4 reveals just how misleading the typical forward habituation curve can be. From Fig. 1, one would assume infants gradually decrease their fixation time as a stimulus becomes more familiar; from Fig. 4, however, one can see that they actually increase their fixation time initially and then abruptly decrease it.

In general, the results were quite similar in both experiments. One noticeable difference between them, however, was that the peak seemed more pronounced, including longer fixations over more trials, when checkerboards were presented than when simple colored forms were used. We began to wonder whether the peak might reflect the infant's processing and storage of information in long-term memory. If that were the case, one might expect the peak to be of greater magnitude and longer duration when the stimulus contained more information, edge, or was of greater complexity. Since infants in the checkerboard study had been exposed to either a 2×2, 8×8, or 24×24 pattern, we divided them into groups based upon the stimulus they had received, so we could examine their backward habituation curves separately. Figure 5 shows the result. As one can see, the largest peak occurred in the group receiving the 24×24 checkerboard. They looked moderately at first, increased their fixation time to over twice what it had been before, and then habituated on a single trial. The other two groups, receiving simpler stimulation, displayed little, if any, peak. We were unable to plot separate curves for fast and slow habituators at each stimulus level, since that would have left too few subjects per curve. Nevertheless, the results we did obtain were consistent with our hypothesis that the peak reflects the operation of infant long-term memory.

Our interpretation of these data is that fast and slow habituators do not differ from one another in the time needed to process and store information in long-term memory, but that they do differ in the number of trials or fixations before they *begin* to process the information. Some infants come into the experimental situation ready to go. They peak early and habituate almost immediately. Other infants take longer to get involved in the task. They may look without remembering for any number of trials. Once they do begin to store the information, however, they peak and habituate just as rapidly as the fast habituators.

As of now, research on backward habituation is so meager we do not even know if the difference between fast and slow habituators represents transient variations in state or persistent individual differences. That is one reason we hope to begin some studies of retarded infants in the near future. We also have no idea whether or not the infant is storing any information during the prepeak time. At least three alternative explanations are possible. He may be storing information in long-term memory, but just not showing it until he peaks. This alternative would be consistent with discrepancy theories of attention (e.g., McCall, 1971) which assume that

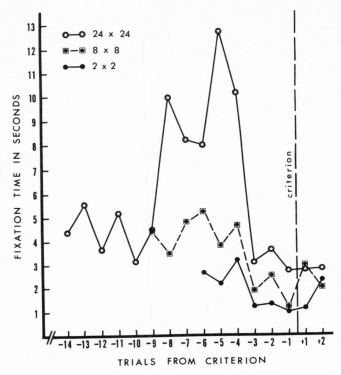

FIG. 5. Separate backward habituation curves for infants receiving repeated exposures to either a 2 × 2, 8 × 8, or 24 × 24 checkerboard pattern.

moderate discrepancies from existing engrams elicit the most attention. Perhaps, on the first few trials, the discrepancy is too great, and the infant will look for only a short time. The second alternative is that information is stored in short-term, but not long-term memory, on the prepeak trials. After all, even on these trials the infant looks and then looks away. Some sort of explanation is needed for why he ends his fixation. Perhaps, as we suggested earlier, a model of the stimulus does build up over these early trials, but then disappears when the infant turns away. The third alternative is that the infant does not process information at all on the prepeak trials. He looks away because he is simply getting tired of fixating on the same point in his visual field. We are currently planning research to determine which of these alternatives is correct, and within a year or two we should have a more definitive answer to what the infant is doing in the prepeak interval.

One thing is certain, however. Simple models of infant habituation and memory that say only that with repeated presentations of the same stimulus, infants process and store information are inadequate. A more elaborate model is needed, one that will explain what is happening during the prepeak time, what initiates and determines the magnitude of the peak, and what causes habituation to occur on a single trial.

VI. A LOOK INTO THE FUTURE

Our research on habituation has taken us to the point where we can say much more than that the infant is able to recognize familiar patterns. We now know that infant attention is not a simple response. It is a complex set of behaviors involving at least two identifiable processes: an Attention-Getting process that directs the infant toward a source of stimulation, and an Attention-Holding process that maintains his fixation once he has turned. We have evidence that Attention-Getting behavior may be a more sensitive indicator of conditioning, whereas, Attention-Holding behavior may be a more sensitive measure of habituation and recognition memory. Further, we have recently found that the gradual decrease in responding most people associate with habituation may not happen at all. Infants may actually fixate moderately at first and then increase their fixation time just before they habituate. This last finding may be the most important of all. If, as we suspect, the peak in attention immediately preceding habituation reflects the processing of stimulus information and the transfer of that information into long-term memory, we may actually have uncovered a behavioral measure of the onset and course of the encoding process in infants.

Evidence from several sources (e.g., Lewis, 1971; Miranda & Fantz, 1974; Sigman, 1973) indicates premature and retarded infants do not perform as well on recognition memory tasks as do full-term and normal infants. These sources, however, do not tell us why abnormal infants perform more poorly. Do they have difficulty learning to turn to a stimulus, or difficulty maintaining their fixation? Are they like our slow habituators who take longer to peak than our fast habituators, but once they do peak, will habituate just as rapidly? Or is there some fundamental difference in the ability of the aberrant infant to process and store information which will show up in the lack of a peak to complex stimuli and the absence of habituation? We have now developed the equipment and procedures needed to examine these questions. Hopefully, once the necessary experiments have been conducted, we will know considerably more about the differences between retarded and normal infants and about infant recognition memory in general.

ACKNOWLEDGMENTS

The research reported in this paper was supported in part by grant HD 03858 from the Institute of Child Health and Human Development.

REFERENCES

Caron, R. F., & Caron, A. J. Degree of stimulus complexity and habituation of visual fixation in infants. *Psychonomic Science*, 1969, **14**, 78–79.
Cohen, L. B. Attention-getting and attention-holding processes of infant visual preference. *Child Development*, 1972, **43**, 869–879.
Cohen, L. B. A two-process model of infant visual attention. *Merrill-Palmer Quarterly*, 1973, **19**, 157–180.

Cohen, L. B., & Gelber, E. R. Infant visual memory. In L. Cohen & P. Salapatek (Eds.), *Infant perception: From sensation to cognition*. Vol. I. *Basic visual processes*. New York: Academic Press, in press.

Cohen, L. B., Gelber, E. R., & Lazar, M. A. Infant habituation and generalization to repeated visual stimulation. *Journal of Experimental Child Psychology*, 1971, **11**, 379–389.

DeLoache, J. Individual differences in infant visual memory. Unpublished doctoral dissertation, University of Illinois, Champaign, 1973.

DeLoache, J., Wetherford, M., & Cohen, L. B. The effects of motivation and conditioned head turning on infant attention to patterns of varying complexity. Paper presented at the meeting of the Midwestern Psychological Association, Cleveland, May, 1972.

Fagan, J. F. Memory in the infant. *Journal of Experimental Child Psychology*, 1970, **9**, 217–226.

Friedman, S. Habituation and recovery of visual response in the alert newborn. *Journal of Experimental Child Psychology*, 1972, **13**, 339–349.

Gelber, E. R. The effect of time and intervening items on the recovery of an habituated response. Unpublished masters thesis, University of Illinois, Champaign, 1972.

Lewis, M. Individual differences in the measurement of early cognitive growth. In J. Hellmuth (Ed.), *Exceptional infant*. Vol. 2. *Studies in abnormalities*. New York: Brunner/Mazel, 1971. Pp. 172–210.

Martin, R. M. Long-term effects of stimulus familiarization. Paper presented at the meeting of the Society for Research in Child Development. Philadelphia, March, 1973.

McCall, R. B. Attention in the infant: Avenue to the study of cognitive development. In D. Walcher & D. Peters (Eds.), *Early childhood: The development of self-regulatory mechanisms*. New York: Academic Press, 1971. Pp. 107–137.

Miranda, S. B., & Fantz, R. L. Recognition memory in Down's Syndrome and normal infants. *Child Development*, 1974, **45**, 651–660.

Pancratz, C. N., & Cohen, L. B. Recovery of habituation in infants. *Journal of Experimental Child Psychology*, 1970, **9**, 208–216.

Sigman, M. Visual preferences of premature and full-term infants. Paper presented at the meeting of the Society for Research in Child Development. Philadelphia, March, 1973.

Zeaman, D., & House, B. J. An attention theory of retardate discrimination learning. In N. R. Ellis (Ed.), *Handbook of mental deficiency*. New York: McGraw-Hill, 1963. Pp. 159–223.

17

INFANT HABITUATION:
PROCESS, PROBLEMS AND POSSIBILITIES

Steven Friedman
George Peabody College

I. INTRODUCTION

One basic capability that the neonate possesses at birth involves use of his visual apparatus to scan and explore his visual world. As Walters and Parke (1965, p. 74) have said:

> Certainly, the capacity for visual and auditory responses, however rudimentary, is present soon after birth in the form of the orienting reaction (Berlyne, 1960; Lipsitt, 1963). This response may, in fact, be the primary foundation for the infant's social development, since it is accompanied by modifications of attention that frequently bring the infant into contact with the social agents who, at the commencement of his life, provide him with most of his visual and auditory stimulation. These modifications of attention also seem to be the forerunners of responses that have been previously labelled as "curiosity" and "exploration" of which attention is an essential component [Dember & Earl, 1957].

The newborn's searching and exploratory activity as reflected in eye-movement behavior may be the basis of gaining experience with (i.e., learning about) the visual world. This learning may involve familiarization with various forms and the ability to detect differences in visual input.

Investigations of the visual behavior of young human infants have reflected an interest in how information is *gathered* or *selected* from the immediate environment (Bond, 1972), and how this information is *processed* (e.g., Friedman, 1972; Friedman, Bruno, & Vietze, 1974; Lewis, 1971; McCall, 1971). Somewhat less attention has focused on how information is *regulated* in terms of the requirements of the infant (Brazelton, Koslowski, & Main, 1973; Stechler & Carpenter, 1967).

Information gathering refers to the infant's selection or rejection of specific visual events. This may be demonstrated as a stimulus preference (i.e., looking at one pattern longer than at another). Evidence for visual preferences in neonates and older infants has been reported extensively in the last 10 years (e.g., Fantz, 1963; Hershenson, 1964; Hershenson, Munsinger, & Kessen, 1965; Moffett, 1969; Stechler, 1964).

Besides merely selecting specific visual stimuli to view, the infant is capable of processing information contained in the array. Information processing involves storage, comparison, and retrieval of material and requires functional memory and discrimination capabilities. Demonstration of such memory and discrimination processes in infancy seems to be reflected dramatically with the habituation paradigm (e.g., Friedman, 1972; Jeffrey & Cohen, 1971). Habituation can best be defined in terms of two of its "parametric characteristics" (Thompson & Spencer, 1966): "*(a)* Given that a particular stimulus elicits a response, repeated applications of the stimulus result in decreased response and . . . . *(b)* . . . presentation of another . . . stimulus results in recovery of the habituated response . . . [p. 18]." If response recovery to the new stimulus is demonstrated, one can rule out adaptation of sensory receptors and/or effector fatigue as producing the decrement (Thompson & Spencer, 1966).

A waning of attention to a repeatedly exposed target is seen as concomitant with the build up of a schema or memorial representation of that visual array. In effect "habituation is the efficient response to stimulation that is no longer providing the organism with additional information" (Lewis, Bartels, Campbell, & Goldberg, 1967, p. 464). Following such a waning of attention, a new array, if introduced, may reinstate the attentive behavior originally observed, reflecting the infant's capacity to detect a mismatch between the already formed schema and the novel input. In effect, habituation reflects a buildup of an expectancy, and introduction of novelty, a violation of that expectancy. As Mackworth (1968) has said:

> The brain is continually constructing and modifying models of incoming stimuli and from these models it extrapolates into the near future. If the actual event agrees with the predicted event, then the neural responses to this event are reduced (habituation), but if the actual event differs sufficiently from the predicted event, then the neural responses are augmented . . . [p. 308].

Research on habituation provides information regarding a number of important issues:

(a) Behavioral Plasticity: Habituation is an example of an "exposure learning" whereby the organism comes to gain information through repeated exposure with some sensory event.

(b) Short-Term Memory: To quote from Germana (1968):

> Whenever it can be demonstrated that a system is capable of detecting differences between past and present events, then it would seem necessary to conclude: a) that the system is receiving information concerning the present event, b) that it already possesses information, in some form, of the past event, and c) that it possesses some mode of comparison [p. 615].

Demonstration of habituation indicates that storage and processing of information are part of the functional repertoire of the organism.

(c) Discrimination: Introduction of stimulus change following behavioral response decrement is in effect a test of the discriminatory capacity of the organism. The greater the difference between the standard event to which the organism

habituated and the new input, the greater the expectancy that the infant will detect the change.

The habituation paradigm therefore seems to be a valuable experimental procedure in investigating early discrimination and memory in the nonverbal human infant. Monitoring the infant's visual behavior to repetitive and novel visual stimuli gives the investigator some insight into the means by which this young organism extracts information from the environment, stores it, and uses this new information in interpreting and responding to familiar or discrepant events.

While the infant is attending to and processing visual information, he also exerts control over his reception of that input by use of nonattentive behaviors. Bond (1972) states: ". . . in many cases the time spent in looking at the stimuli is far less than the total time for which the stimuli are presented ⌊p. 241⌋." However, few investigators (Brazelton et al., 1973; Carpenter, Tecce, Stechler, & Friedman, 1970; Stechler & Carpenter, 1967; Stechler & Latz, 1966) have been concerned with what the infant is doing when he's not looking at some perceptual array. Studying both attentive and nonattentive behaviors (e.g., looking away, closing of eyes, turning the head or eyes away from the target) may lead to a better understanding of the process by which the infant exerts control over the intake of visual information.

The current report focuses on the habituation process in human neonates to repetitive visual stimulation as reflective of early information processing capacity. In addition, there is discussion of the usefulness of measures of infant habituation as an index of cognitive functioning. Finally, modes of regulating the intake of information are described, based on the responses of young infants to imposed visual stimulation.

II. HABITUATION TO VISUAL STIMULI

A. The Basic Process in Newborn Infants

Before presenting data on newborn habituation I would like to discuss the procedure we used in studying this process.

Subjects were randomly selected from populations of normal human newborn infants at Boston City Hospital and Nashville General Hospital, both city hospitals with patients of relatively low socioeconomic status. Infants were observed between about 7 and 9 a.m., prior to the morning feed. This time was found to be best in terms of finding infants who were awake, with eyes open, and not crying or sleepy. In both hospitals, infants studied ranged in age from about 24 to 96 hr. In some of the studies discussed, infants were required to reach an individually determined criterion as reflected in a decrement in visual attention. In others, a predetermined number of trials were presented to all infants. An experimental session was conducted in the nursery at the infant's crib where the newborn was

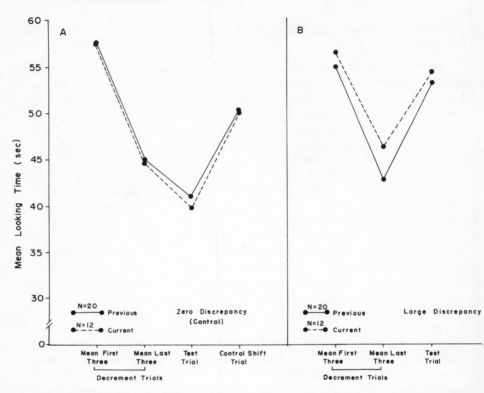

FIG. 1. Mean looking time (in seconds) at "familiar" and "novel" visual targets by newborns from a previously collected sample (Boston City Hospital) and a more current sample (Nashville General Hospital). Subjects in the zero discrepancy (or control) condition also received the novel target (control shift trial) (from Friedman *et al.*, 1974).

placed on his right side. A target was manually inserted against the inside of the infant's crib at approximately 19 cm from the infant's eyes. Two observers were positioned at the side of the crib behind the target, facing the infant. A Rustrak 4-channel event recorder with two silent remote buttons (each representing one channel on the recorder) was used in coding infant looking time. Recording of looking time began within 10 sec of presentation of the stimulus, when it was observed that the infant's eyes were oriented toward the target. Visual targets were manually presented on hardbacked cardboard and were nonglossy. Each target measured 6 × 6 inches with a 2-inch base for insertion between the mattress and the side of the bassinet. Trials consisted of 60-sec presentations of the target, separated by a 5–10-sec intertrial interval, during which time the target was removed. Interobserver reliability yielded Pearson correlations above .90. In studies using a criterion procedure, a Gra-Lab Timer was connected to one of the push-button switches and was activated when one observer depressed his button.

This provided the cumulative looking time by the infant on each trial so that a determination of when the infant had met the decrement criterion could be calculated. In the studies at Boston, instead of an event recorder, observers used cumulative stopwatches in recording infant looking time.

One experiment was an attempt to explore systematically whether the decrement in visual attention observed in earlier studies (Friedman, Nagy, & Carpenter, 1970a; Friedman, Carpenter, & Nagy, 1970b; Friedman & Carpenter, 1971) could be attributed to habituation. Of interest was the newborn's capacity for detecting a difference in the visual array after demonstrating response decrement. A counterbalanced design was employed in which the habituated stimulus and the novel stimulus were equated with regard to potency. Such a counterbalancing procedure had not been previously used in studies of newborn habituation to auditory (e.g., Bartoshuk, 1962b) and olfactory stimuli (Engen & Lipsitt, 1965).

When an infant reached a decrement criterion,[1] a random determination was made as to whether he would be presented with the *same* target to which he had shown decrement (control procedure) or a *new* target (experimental procedure). Thus, infants were presented with either the *same* or *new* target for one 60-sec trial, 5–10 sec after the last decrement trial. The experimental procedure specifically involved presentation of a 4-square black and white checkerboard target as the *new* stimulus to newborns who had shown decrement to a 144-square target, and vice versa.

Results indicated that the subjects receiving the same target to which they had been "familiarized" on the test trial showed no significant change in visual attention, whereas subjects receiving a new target showed a significant increase in visual attention. This habituation–recovery effect was subsequently replicated at Nashville General Hospital (see Fig. 1).

The results of these studies confirmed earlier findings (Friedman *et al.*, 1970a, b; Friedman & Carpenter, 1971), which indicated that a waning of visual fixation can be observed in a select sample of alert newborns with repeated exposure of a checkerboard target. Moreover, an increase in visual fixation (i.e., recovery) was demonstrated with the introduction of a stimulus change. Since a demonstration of recovery is a basic characteristic of a habituation process (see Thompson & Spencer, 1966), oculomotor fatigue and arousal effects were eliminated as possible explanations for the decrement effect. Based on the infants' recognition of stimulus change it appears that some alert newborns are capable of storing and processing redundant visual information and detecting variations in the input. If, as Fenz and McCabe (1969) point out, ". . . at least part of what is called

---

[1]Response decrement was determined by the following criterion: two consecutive trials on which the subject's visual fixations were eight seconds or less than the mean of his fixations on the first two trials. The 8-sec decrement criterion was empirically derived, based on pilot data that suggested that some infants do not display a decrease in looking time of more than 8–10 sec while remaining in a testable state. If a more stringent requirement is imposed, subject loss is increased primarily due to fussy behavior.

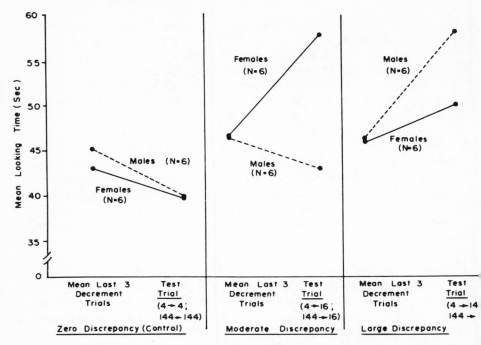

Fig. 2. Mean looking time (in seconds) of male and female newborns exposed to visual targets representing various degrees of discrepancy from a standard habituation target (from Friedman *et al.*, 1974).

'intelligence' is represented by the tendency of an individual to take notice and to react to minor changes in his environment [p. 1]," some newborn infants appear to be "intelligent" in this regard. Following decrement in visual attention, 29 of 40 babies in the Boston City Hospital sample and 18 of 24 babies in the Nashville General Hospital sample showed a 5-sec or greater increase in attention with introduction of stimulus change. However, since sizable numbers of infants were excluded from the above studies, mainly due to vigorous fussing sometime during the session, these results reflect the capacities of only a relatively small proportion of infants observed. In no way is the habituation process a general phenomenon in the newborn period.

These findings are consistent with newborn studies of habituation in other than the visual modality (e.g., Bartoshuk, 1962a, b; Engen & Lipsitt, 1965) as well as with findings of habituation to visual stimuli in infants beyond the neonatal period (e.g., Pancratz & Cohen, 1970), and suggest that the habituation process, as observed in some newborns, is demonstrable from birth.

Recently, Sigman, Kopp, Parmelee, and Jeffrey (1973) independently replicated the finding of response decrement in visual attention to repeated exposure of a checkerboard pattern, although they did not present a novel recovery target following decrement to defend their data against a fatigue explanation.

In order to study further the capacity of the newborn infant to discriminate between visual patterns, infants were exposed to either a 4-square, 16-square, or 144-square black and white checkerboard pattern following habituation to a 4-square or 144-square target. Using this design we could determine if the magnitude of response recovery following habituation is a function of the degree of discrepancy of the test stimulus from the standard habituation stimulus. Figure 2 displays the results of this study. As Fig. 2 reveals, detection of visual novelty was related to sex.

In the zero discrepancy group neither males nor females showed a recovery of attention on the test trial. In the moderate discrepancy condition, females demonstrated recovery but males did not. In fact, all six females in the moderate discrepancy group showed a 5-sec or more increase in looking time on the test trial, while only one male showed a comparable increase. In the large-discrepancy condition both males and females showed a significant increase in looking time with stimulus change.

These results may be interpreted as supporting the notion of greater female receptivity to sensory stimuli. Boismier (1970) and Berg, Adkinson, and Strock (1973) have indicated that newborn females are in states of alert inactivity for longer periods of time than are newborn males. Korner (1973), in a recent review of sex differences in the newborn period, reports that the female is generally more receptive and responsive to sensory stimulation than is the male. The increased periods of alertness found by Boismier (1970) and Berg et al. (1973) for females might permit increased exposure to environmental stimulation and could therefore lead to a greater opportunity for perceptual learning experiences in the female. Early differences in male and female perceptual receptivity and responsivity may be precursors of sex differences reported later in infancy (e.g., Olley, 1971).

However, these sex-related effects may also reflect differences in developmental rate. McCall (1973), in a study with 4- and 5½-month-old infants, has recently reported that the females displayed a preference for moderate stimulus change (corresponding to the "discrepancy hypothesis") at an earlier age than males. In addition, the pattern of visual response for the females at 4 months was comparable to that of the males at 5½ months. This study provides some evidence that rates of development for the two sexes are not in phase. In regard to the current study it is possible that males, a little older than those studied here, would also show evidence of detection of the moderate change, comparable to that for the females at the younger age. Further research, using longitudinal designs, is needed to look at this hypothesis.

Sex differences in infant attention pose some interesting questions regarding the use of a standard experimental procedure for both sexes in identifying infants at risk. If there is a developmental lag between the sexes in infancy, assessment procedures will need to be sensitive to this factor in interpreting results.

In addition, since detection of change is of biological significance in alerting the organism to environmental variation, further research using measures of dishabituation may provide information on the ability of individual infants to react to

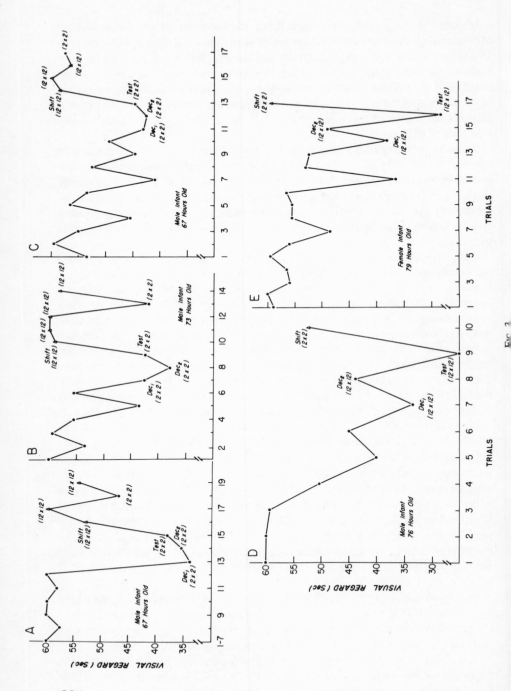

Fig. 2

224

stimulus novelty. In this regard, Bridger (1961) has reported differences in neonate reactivity to changes in auditory stimulation. Such individual variation may reflect differences among neonates in sensitivity to stimulus change. Studying infant dishabituation could be useful in detecting aberrant discrimination capacity in the neonatal period.

In addition to sex as a variable to be contended with in the neonatal period, age differences are also evident. As Bell (1963) has pointed out, "age differences are especially important in the newborn because of the rapid pace of development and the emergence from temporary early effects of the transition to extrauterine existence [p. 205]." Data collected at Boston City Hospital revealed age differences in degree of response decrement (Friedman & Carpenter, 1971), speed of reaching a decrement criterion (Friedman, 1972), and magnitude of response recovery to introduction of a novel target (Friedman, 1972). Older infants (mean age = 78 hr) showed a significantly greater degree of decrement with eight exposures of a patterned array than infants less than 48 hr old (mean = 38 hr) (Friedman & Carpenter, 1971). If a criterion method is used rather than the above procedure of imposing a set number of trials, older infants (>50.5 hr) were found to reach the criterion (i.e., habituate) more rapidly than younger ones (<50.5 hr). In addition, the magnitude of response recovery was significantly greater in the former age group than in the latter group.

It may be that these differences reflect recovery from effects of the birth process in the infant's transition from intrauterine to extrauterine functioning. Analyses relating these early age differences to amount of maternal medication received during labor, however, failed to indicate a significant influence of medication on infant visual attention. Since relatively low and fairly homogeneous drug dosages were administered, lack of a significant relationship may be attributable to lack of a suitable range of drug dosage levels from which to detect a relationship. However, such differences found between "younger" and "older" newborn infants may also reflect changes in the rate of perceptual processing over the first days of life. It may be that development is extremely rapid in the newborn period, with early sensory experiences rapidly facilitating perceptual learning. Studying visual habituation in the early days of life may be useful as a tool for monitoring recovery from birth related events, as well as monitoring differences in ability to process visual information.

B. Individual Differences

Differences have also been observed among newborns in the pattern with which they habituate (i.e., regular, gradual, or erratic), speed of habituation, and sensitivity to stimulus change.

Figure 3 shows the data from some exemplary subjects and illustrates various patterns of habituation. Some of these infants show a fairly erratic pattern of

FIG. 3. Looking time for individual newborn infants to exposure of the designated targets (from Friedman, 1971).

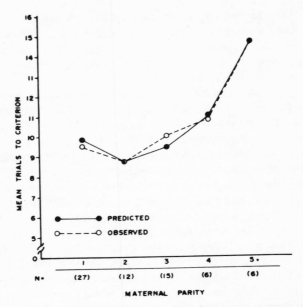

FIG. 4.   Mean trials to reaching a habituation criterion for newborns as a function of maternal parity. The solid line reflects the curve of best fit for the observed data. Due to the low frequency of occurences of parity above five all such occurences were combined as one category (5+).

habituation (particularly B, C, and E). One infant (A) shows a dramatic drop in looking time in meeting the decrement criterion; another (D) shows a more or less gradual decrease in attention over trials. It is interesting to note that (B), after showing recovery to presentation of the novel array, demonstrated a return to a low level of looking with re-presentation of the standard habituation stimulus, possibly reflecting a more long-term storage of the familiarized array.

In addition to various patterns of habituation, differences exist in speed of reaching a decrement criterion. Some infants are capable of rapidly habituating their visual attention to a repeatedly exposed pattern, while others fail to show habituation or do so relatively slowly. Some of these latter infants continue to visually explore the same stimulus pattern for 20, 30, and even 40 min (trials) without evidence of decrement in attention. Could it be that these slow-habituating infants have an inadequate short-term memory in which a stimulus trace quickly fades? With the assumption that differences in rate of habituation displayed might reflect stable behavior, Peggy Rogers and I asked if rate of habituation was in some way related to an infant's perinatal history.

One factor, maternal parity, was significantly related to the number of trials infants required in meeting the decrement criterion. Since several studies examining the relationship between maternal parity and children's cognitive functioning have reported that possibilities of maldevelopment, mental deficiency, and prematurity increase as a function of increasing parity (e.g., see Masland, 1958), a regression analysis was computed (Bottenberg & Ward, 1963) in order to test the predictive power of the parity variable in regard to speed of visual response decrement. In this analysis in order to have sizable numbers of infants at each level of parity, infants were included if they either met a standard decrement criterion as discussed above and remained in an alert and nonfussy state or showed a decrease in looking time due to vigorous crying which necessitated termination of the session. In the case of the latter infants "trials to criterion" was defined as number of trials completed prior to termination of the session.

Results revealed that parity significantly predicted trials to criterion. A quadratic model accounted for 17% of the variance; a linear model computed on the same data accounted for only 9% of the variance. Figure 4 displays the curve of best fit and observed mean trials to criterion scores at each level of parity.

In addition, since parity was highly correlated with maternal age a separate analysis was computed in order to determine if the maternal age variable would add to the predictive ability of the parity variable. This regression analysis revealed that the addition of maternal age information to the predictive equation increased the amount of criterion variance accounted for by only .3%. A quadratic function of maternal age alone accounted for about 12% of the variance.

After analyzing the Nashville General Hospital data we decided to go back and look at the data collected at Boston City Hospital, only to find that parity was not a variable that had been recorded from the babies' charts! However, having the opportunity to return to Boston, I did record the parity data for some of the Boston City Hospital babies.[2] Figure 5 compares, at each level of parity, infants from the two hospitals on the number of trials required in reaching a common decrement criterion. All the subjects included in this figure completed a session without vigorous crying. Although the Boston City Hospital data are not totally concordant with the Nashville General Hospital data, the trend still exists of increasing trials to criterion as a function of increasing maternal parity (see Fig. 5).

One possible explanation of the observed parity differences is that differential hormonal output by the mothers, transmitted to the baby, may influence the alertness and efficiency of the newborn in processing visual input. Gemzell (1954) found that the level of 17-hydroxycorticosteroids, a hormone secreted during times of stress, is higher in infants born of primiparae than in infants born of multiparae. The low-parity infant who is showing a higher level of this stress hormone may be more alert, less lethargic, and possibly more accessible to processing visual information.

Another possible mechanism that may explain the difference between infants from low- and high-parity mothers is associated with the potential of the uterus of the mother to effectively support the developing fetus. After many pregnancies, the uterus may become depleted and less effective in supporting the developing young (Eastman & Hellman, 1966), and this may be reflected in slower information processing in the newborn as observed in the above study.

Needless to say, research in this area is complicated since parity is confounded

[2]Special thanks go to Dr. Gerald Stechler for his help in retrieving these data.

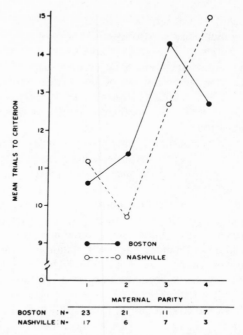

FIG. 5. Mean trials to reaching a habituation criterion for newborns at Boston City Hospital and Nashville General Hospital as a function of maternal parity. This figure includes only infants who met the criterion without engaging in vigorous fussing.

with other variables (e.g., maternal age). Further research will need to try to specify more clearly the effects of repeated pregnancies on perceptual processing and differentiate the consequences of high parity from other confounding variables.

C. The Need for Relativism

Only minimal attention has been directed at studying visual habituation in the newborn. This may be due to the belief that not only is the visual receptor apparatus immature but that visual habituation requires a highly developed cortical mechanism which the newborn lacks. Anatomical study of the newborn cortex (Conel, 1939) has provided evidence for its structural immaturity. Based on these factors, investigators have argued against pattern recognition and discrimination until after the second or third month of life (Bronson, 1969; Lewis, 1971; Munsinger, 1970). However, based on data presented above, such recognition and discrimination processes do appear to be functional in this young organism. As Sackett (1963) has pointed out, however, peripheral mechanisms cannot be excluded as responsible for such detection capabilities.

In addition to the supposed structural immaturity of the newborn visual system, another deterrent in studying his visual behavior is the difficulty in finding subjects who are in an open-eyed and alert state. Previous newborn habituation studies in other modalities (e.g., Engen & Lipsitt, 1965) have been criticized for using sleeping infants. In this regard it is interesting to note that early research on neonatal heart rate (HR) in response to stimuli from various modalities found an acceleration of HR with stimulus introduction, reflecting a "defensive" rather than "orienting" response (Graham & Clifton, 1966). This accelerative response reflects a "rejection of the environment"; in effect, an avoidance of sensory stimulation. In most of these studies the babies were in a sleepy or drowsy state. More current research (e.g., Pomerleau-Malcuit & Clifton, 1973; Porges, Arnold, & Forbes, 1973; Sameroff, Cashmore, & Dykes, 1973) has found that HR deceleration, reflective of attention and active processing, is demonstrable in neonates if certain conditions are met. As Berg (1974) points out ". . . while the infant may be capable of producing an orienting response very early in life, it occurs only under the most optimal conditions . . . [p. 311]."

What are those optimal conditions? For one, an awake, alert infant seems to be a necessary although not sufficient condition for obtaining HR deceleration in the young infant (Pomerleau-Malcuit & Clifton, 1973; Sameroff et al., 1973). Also of importance is whether the session is conducted before or after a feed, with the former condition having a greater probability of producing deceleration (Pomerleau-Malcuit & Clifton, 1973). A third critical factor is the complexity of the stimulus. Sameroff et al. (1973) found deceleration with a 144-square checkerboard pattern, whereas Gregg, Clifton, and Haith (1973) failed to obtain deceleration with a simpler visual array. It is interesting to note that all three of the above conditions, alert wakefulness, prefeed testing, and relatively "complex" visual arrays were used in the studies described above on neonatal habituation (e.g., Friedman, 1972).

Obviously, the infant's condition at time of testing affects the results obtained. Figure 6 illustrates the effect of state on the visual attention of a 2-day-old female presented with a 144-square checkerboard pattern. In the early testing the infant was awake but showing a great deal of both head turning and closing of eyes. As can be observed from the figure, visual behavior was extrememly variable. Forty-five minutes later, and following a vigorous bath, her visual attention was high and relatively stable. It is clear that differences in state of arousal were contributing to the differential results obtained. It seems necessary that investigators consider both the state of the infant and the procedural and stimulus factors imposed upon him in their interpretation of behavioral effects and of newborn competency.

With the habituation paradigm, evidence has been presented indicating that (1) habituation can be observed with some infants in the first days of life, reflecting fairly sophisticated short-term visual memory for simple patterns; (2) differences in sensitivity to stimulus novelty seem to be related to sex; (3) differences in rate and degree of habituation and sensitivity to stimulus novelty seem to be related to postnatal age; (4) differences in rate of habituation may be related to maternal

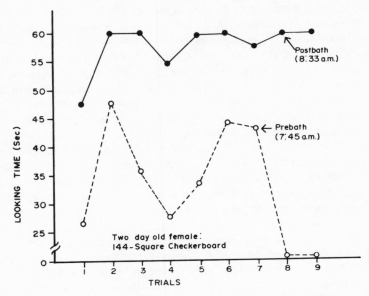

FIG. 6. Looking time of a two-day-old female infant in two state conditions.

parity; and (5) the factor of infant state poses a difficult problem in investigating neonatal visual attention.

D. Problems for Research, Possibilities for Assessment

Previous research on infant habituation, focusing either on tests of theory (e.g., Sokolov's neuronal model, discrepancy hypothesis) or on the study of parameters (e.g., length of intertrial interval) may be useful in the development of indices of infant functioning. Although this possibility is an intriguing one, a number of critical questions remain unanswered. For one, is the behavior displayed by an individual infant replicable? In effect, does the infant habituate at a comparable rate on two independent testings? In addition, are dishabituation functions similar on two testings? The test for recovery may be a useful vehicle for monitoring early discrimination capacities. However, since recovery may reflect state change it seems absolutely necessary both to monitor state and to answer the question of reliability of effect.

Figure 7 shows the looking time of an infant, at 51 and 75 hr after birth, to repeated exposure of a 4-square checkerboard pattern. At 51 hours the infant was judged to be awake, bright eyed, and showing some body movement. In addition, he had just been bathed. As Fig. 7 indicates, the infant met the decrement criterion on the eighth and ninth trials. Presentation of a 16-square target on trial 10 resulted in response recovery. Note that this habituation–recovery process is evident in the

total time he spent viewing the targets and in the number of times he looked away
or closed his eyes (the off-target behavior measure).

The infant was retested 24 hr later. His state was judged to be comparable to that
observed at the 51-hr observation. However, this time he was tested before he was
bathed. As Fig. 7 indicates, he reached the decrement criterion at the ninth and
tenth trials, matching fairly well his behavior 24 hr earlier. However, at this later
testing instead of introducing a novel target following decrement, the same target

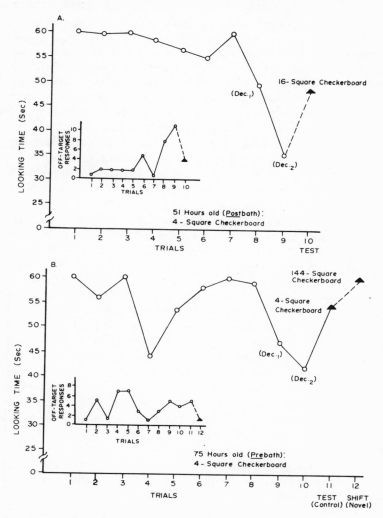

FIG. 7. Looking time (and frequency of off-target behavior) for a newborn observed at age 51 and 75
hr to exposure of the designated targets.

(a 4-square checkerboard) to which he had shown decrement was reintroduced. As Fig. 7 indicates, the infant showed a spontaneous recovery in looking time. (It is interesting to note that the spontaneous recovery effect is not reflected in the off-target behavior measure.) This infant, although requiring a comparable number of trials in reaching a decrement criterion on two independent testings, in one case (at 51 hr) displayed a fairly regular pattern of decrement and recovery; in the other (at 75 hr), he showed more variable behavior, possibly reflecting variation in state. It is evident that differentiating spontaneous variations in state from changes in visual attention due to experimenter manipulation poses serious problems for the investigator in this area.

Another question concerns the validity of the habituation measure. Assuming it is a reliable phenomenon for an individual infant, what precisely do different habituation rates and differential sensitivity to novelty allow us to infer about the infant's developmental status? Some evidence regarding this question has recently been reported by Marion Sigman and colleagues (1973). They found that "infants who performed well on a neurological exam [(developed by Dr. Parmelee)] tended to fixate the stimuli in the first few minutes and ceased to attend by the sixth trial [p. 464]." More research of this kind is needed in establishing how differences in early attentional behavior relate to external criterion measures of neurological and behavioral functioning.

A number of other studies have provided evidence of habituation as reflecting early cognitive functioning. For example, Lewis *et al.* (1967) reported relatively less rapid habituation to visual stimuli in a group of infants with Apgar ratings of 7, 8, or 9 in contrast to those having a perfect Apgar score of 10. An infant with anencephaly (a condition of relative decortication) has also been shown to fail to habituate to repetitive auditory stimulation (Brackbill, 1971). Similarly, the Russian investigators Polikanina and Probatova (1965) found that premature infants exposed to repetitive auditory stimulation showed slower "extinction" of the orienting response than did full-term infants. In addition, Eisenberg, Coursin, and Rupp (1966) have reported that speed of habituation to a repeated auditory tone varied systematically as a function of neurologic states. Two high-risk neonates (defined by premature status and low Apgar rating) showed no signs of habituation, whereas two infants judged to be "suspect" required almost twice the number of trials to reach the habituation criterion as did the normal neonates. Such evidence is intriguing in relation to possible development of assessment procedures using habituation indices.

Although the habituation measure is seemingly helpful in detecting differences among various groups of neonates, it is evident that its abilities as a predictor variable in relation to later cognitive functioning is far less probable. It may be that measures of habituation need to be combined with other indices of infant functioning in developing a developmental battery (or risk index). Integrating measures of infant attention and habituation with measures of infant sensitivity to contingencies in the environment (learning), infant state organization and caretaker–infant interaction, may significantly increase our abilities to predict developmental outcome at least on a short-term basis, and may provide an alternative to currently administered "baby tests."

In addition, monitoring infant capacity to regulate the intake of information in perceptual encounters with both inanimate objects and animate adults may provide useful data which could be incorporated into a risk index. In the next section, attention is focused on perceptual encounters of infants responding to and coping with imposed visual stimulation.

III. INFANT REGULATION OF VISUAL INFORMATION

In the course of investigations of habituation to visual stimuli in both infants in the first days of life and with older infants, different control mechanisms for regulating the intake of information have been observed. These various modes of input regulation may provide additional insight into the way young infants cope with environmental stimulation. In this section particular interest is focused on perceptual–motor behavior in the presence of repeatedly exposed inanimate visual arrays. Of interest is what infants do when confronted with a "familiar" stimulus and how infants react to novelty.

In general, upon initial exposure of a checkerboard pattern the newborn infant displays active visual scanning with little body movement. The eyes of the infant are wide open, and visual attention as measured by the time the eyes are on target approaches the entire duration of the exposure. With repeated presentations of the array, there is an increase in general motor activity, head turning, closing of eyes, looking away (Friedman et al., 1974), and hand–mouth activity. When the infant meets the habituation criterion, he may be fussing with eyes closed or turning his head and/or eyes away from the array. Two- and three-month-old infants show a greater degree of head control than newborns and seem to use head turning as their primary mode of target avoidance. Newborns, on the other hand, seem to use closing of eyes as their primary mode of input regulation. Fussing is observed with infants in both age groups with repeated target exposure. Introduction of a new stimulus following visual response decrement, in many cases, reinstates the original calm state and active and alert visual behavior observed in the initial trials of the procedure. In addition, in response to the new target, infants have been observed to show a widening of the eyes, direct intensive gaze, and active scanning (which in some cases seems to involve a suppression of a previous fussy, agitated state), furrowing of the brows, and suppression of yawning. Some older infants (2–3 months) have also been observed to display positive vocalizations with introduction of the novel target. By attending to the external event, the infant appears to be "controlling" internal reactions. Some infants after 30, 40, or 50 sec of active scanning of the novel target following fussy nonattentive behavior in the final habituation trials will begin fussing again as if they could no longer maintain control over their internal state. It seems to take considerable effort for the infant to try to maintain his attention to the novel event, as if he were constantly trying to keep the fussy state from overwhelming him. This is most apparent with the newborn infant, whose modes of input regulation may be limited as compared with the older infant. The latter seems to display a greater ability to control the intake of information by turning his head away from the array and then returning to the target, sometimes repeating this process a number of times.

In this regard, Brazelton *et al.* (1973), described the behavior of a 6-week-old infant visually presented with a small fuzzy monkey:

> [A] state of intense, wrapt attention built up gradually to a peak which was disrupted suddenly by the infant's turning away from the object, becoming active, flailing his extremities. He often cried out, breathed rapidly, looked around. . . . He often looked down or closed his eyes . . ., as if he were processing information about this object in the period of withdrawal [p. 14].

However, some infants show what has been called "obligatory attention" (Stechler & Latz, 1966), meaning that the infant is "stimulus bound" and seems unable to avoid the target. Such infants have been observed to show quite vehement fussing while still giving the observer the impression of trying to maintain visual contact with the stimulus. With most of these infants, termination of the session is required since the upset is so severe. Other infants, however, seem more capable of regulating intake by using such off-target behaviors as closing of eyes and turning away from the target. Lewis, Meyer, Kagan and Grossberg (1963) have also reported that "an infant [6 months old] might never take its eyes off a female or male face, yet might thrash about, the stimulus seeming to cause increased motoric excitement [pp. 6–7]."

Of particular interest in relation to situations in which presented visual stimuli are separated by intertrial intervals is the question of what the baby is doing between stimulus presentations. In many cases the infant seems literally to "take a break." He might look around, move around, or even yawn. These behaviors have been observed often enough in both newborns and older infants that they do not appear to be random events but seem to represent organized and relatively sophisticated modes of adapting to imposed visual stimulation.

Another mode of target regulation observed in both newborn infants (e.g., Friedman, 1972) and older infants (Bruno, 1974; Carpenter *et al.*, 1970) is the peripheral looking response. Here the infant's eyes are off target-center, sometimes at the outer edge of the stimulus. However, if some change is introduced into the visual field, the infant will almost immediately reorient to the center of the field. This process suggests that the infant is keeping the target in view but not giving it full attention. Such behavior seems to be a regulatory mechanism in that the infant avoids direct fixation of the stimulus while remaining in a vigilant and receptive state. An interesting sidelight to this behavior occurs when the infant is either in this peripheral viewing posture or clearly oriented off-target. In these cases, an attempt by the experimenter to reorient the baby's head may meet with great physical resistance. If the experimenter does finally manage to reorient the infant, the head usually snaps back into the peripheral or off-target position within seconds. The infant's determination to avoid contact with the stimulus appears strong.

Differential modes of responding to repetitious stimulation may reflect varying attempts to alter the stimulus environment. Some infants ranging in age from 4–12 weeks show what might be called "protest" behavior after exposure to a visual target. They fuss in short bursts with their eyes open and sometimes accompany this with a frowning facial expression. Mothers observing this behavior describe it as "asking for something to happen" or "crying out for a reaction" from the inanimate nonresponsive array. Similar behavior has also been observed with infants to nonresponsive three-dimensional facial arrays (Bruno, 1974; Carpenter et al., 1970). Carpenter et al. (1970) report that "there is frequently a controlled fussing at the target with eyes wide open and with a voice quality suggesting protest rather than distress . . . [p. 105]." Stechler and Carpenter (1967) have postulated that the young infant has two alternative ways of altering the stimulation he encounters. One mode, called "autoplastic", involves use of some of the regulatory mechanisms discussed above, such as looking away and closing of eyes. One limitation of the autoplastic modes however is ". . . that they do not in reality alter the environment but rather alter the perception of it" (Stechler & Carpenter, 1967, p. 185). Another mode, called "alloplastic", refers to altering the environment by way of social communication to a caretaker (e.g., crying). Both of these modes are used by young infants in response to encounters with perceptual input.

Bruner (1973) has used the term "buffering" to describe the infant's capacity to "protect (himself) from being victimized by his receptivity [p. 45]." This buffering process includes sleep and crying as well as the gaze-aversion behaviors being discussed here. Another form of buffering is nonnutritive sucking. The infant's use of a pacifier is a way of reducing arousal in the presence of an overstimulating environment. Bruner has found that nonnutritive sucking in the presence of visual stimulation tends to reduce the visual scanning activity of the infant. This is seen as a means of regulating the intake of visual information. The author has similarly noticed that some infants seem capable of tuning-out visual stimulation by "staring out in space" while still remaining oriented to the target. The infant, following active visual scanning of the target, and after many stimulus presentations, may display a blurry eyed stare. This behavior does not seem to indicate that the infant is asleep, since presentation of a new target reinstates the alert active scanning behavior. Rather it seems to be similar to Bruner's report of infants' responses to overstimulation, that of tuning out the stimulus.

In terms of early development, the evidence on information regulation suggests that, as early as the first few days of life, limited yet relatively effective modes of "tuning out" redundant input exist. Over the early weeks of life these regulatory modes may become more refined, giving the infant more active control over external input. Further research is needed in systematically studying these regulatory behaviors. Research in this area will provide valuable information on the nature of the infant's developing regulatory abilities in perceptual encounters with both animate and inanimate aspects of his environment.

What is the significance of the habituation process in regard to the environment in which the infant is developing? In the laboratory, the process of habituation is studies in a relatively structured situation in which the infant, usually seated in a standard infant seat, is repeatedly exposed to a visual stimulus, usually a two-dimensional pattern (e.g., a geometric form of checkerboard pattern). It is obvious that what is gained in experimental control over stimulus parameters and setting leaves much to be desired in comparability to situations in the infant's day to day environment. Infants are generally not exposed to triangles and checkerboards in their usual everyday encounters with the visual environment. Rather, much of the infant's visual input derives from his interactions with three-dimensional animate adults.

Stern (1973) relates the process of habituation to early interactive relations between mother and infant. He finds that "the presence of the infant's gaze . . . tends to hold mother's gaze on the infant. The mother then modulates the stimulus configuration of her facial and vocal performance, using as cues the infant's state of arousal and affect and the quality of his visual attention" ⌊p. 207⌋. The infant at this point may gaze away, returning after a short period to the "next round of mutual gaze." With repetition of these episodes a schema is being formed by both mother and infant of the facial–vocal–affective configuration displayed by each. One might expect therefore that habituation would occur with baby gradually losing interest in the stimulus complex of mother. However, Stern (1973) does not find this in his video-tape analyses of dyadic interaction. What seems to be happening is that mother is ". . . rapidly responding to any response decrement by recorrecting the stimulus level of her behavior [pp. 207–208]," comparable to introducing a novel visual array after habituation.

As Neeley (1973) has pointed out:

> Habituation behavior of infants may affect infant-caretaker interaction. . . . An infant who habituates quickly may receive a much wider variety of stimuli than an infant who habituates slowly. . . . On the other hand, an infant who habituates quickly may provide a source of frustration to the caretaker in her efforts to maintain his visual regard; this frustration may decrease or even extinguish her efforts toward interaction with the infant [pp. 59–60].

Studies by Stern (1971, 1973), Robson (1967), and Brazelton et al. (1973) have provided evidence that the visual behavior of the infant and caretaker involves a sensitive system which can lead to dysfunctional interactions when, for example, the visual approach behavior of one partner is responded to with withdrawal (i.e., looking away) by the other. An infant whose visual behavior presents inconsistent and erratic cues or signals for interaction may also trigger inappropriate caretaker responses, thus starting a cycle that could be dysfunctional in regard to later development.

In conclusion, basic research on the areas of visual attention and habituation may lead to development of early assessment techniques for detecting aberrant discrimination capacities and memory functioning. In addition, monitoring gaze-behavior to both inanimate and animate social stimuli may provide a sensitive indicator of differences among infants in regulating perceptual input.

ACKNOWLEDGMENTS

[1]Research reported in this paper was supported in part by a grant (HD-00983-10) to the Institute on Mental Retardation and Intellectual Development of the John F. Kennedy Center for Research on Education and Human Development and by a USPHS Research grant from NIMH to the author (MH-23196). Special thanks go to Peter Vietze, Peggy Parks Rogers, and Barbara Strain for their critical comments, Deborah Glick for editorial assistance, and Carl Rogers for statistical consultation.

REFERENCES

Bartoshuk, A. K. Human neonatal cardiac acceleration and dishabituation. *Perceptual and Motor Skills,* 1962, **15**, 15–27 (a)

Bartoshuk, A. K. Response decrement with repeated elicitation of human neonatal cardiac acceleration to sound. *Journal of Comparative and Physiological Psychology,* 1962, **55**, 9–13. (b)

Bell, R. Q. Some factors to be controlled in studies of the behavior of newborns. *Biologia Neonatorum,* 1963, **5**, 200–214.

Berg, W. K. Cardiac orienting responses of 6 and 16 week old infants. *Journal of Experimental Child Psychology,* 1974, **17**, 303–312.

Berg, W. K., Adkinson, C. D., & Strock, B. D. Duration and frequency of periods of alertness in neonates. *Developmental Psychology,* 1973, **9**, 434.

Berlyne, D. E. *Conflict, arousal, and curiosity.* New York: McGraw-Hill, 1960.

Boismier, J. D. A Markov analysis of behavioral arousal in the human newborn. Unpublished master's thesis, George Peabody College, 1970.

Bond, E. K. Perception of form by the human infant. *Psychological Bulletin,* 1972, **77**(4), 225–245.

Bottenberg, R. A., & Ward, J. H. Applied multiple linear regression. (Technical Documentary Report PRL-TDR-63-6, Personnel Research Laboratory, Aerospace Medical Division) Texas: Lackland Air Force Base, 1963.

Brackbill, Y. The role of the cortex in orienting: OR in an anencephalic human infant. *Developmental Psychology,* 1971, **5**, 195–201.

Brazelton, T. B., Koslowski, B., & Main, M. The origins of reciprocity: The early mother-infant interaction. In M. Lewis & L. Rosenblum (Eds.), *Origins of behavior.* New York: Wiley, 1973.

Bridger, W. K. Sensory habituation and discrimination in the human neonate. *American Journal of Psychiatry,* 1961, **117**, 991–996.

Bronson, G. Vision in infancy: Structure-function relationships. In R. J. Robinson (Ed.), *Brain and early behavior.* New York: Academic Press, 1969.

Bruner, J. S. Pacifier-produced visual buffering in human infants. *Developmental Psychobiology,* 1973, **6**, 45–51.

Bruno, L. A. Mother-stranger discrimination in six week old female infants. Unpublished master's thesis, Vanderbilt University, 1974.

Carpenter, G. C., Tecce, J. J., Stechler, G., & Friedman, S. Differential visual behavior to human and humanoid faces in early infancy. *Merrill-Palmer Quarterly*, 1970, **16**(1), 91–108.

Conel, J. L. *The postnatal development of the human cerebral cortex. I. Cortex of the newborn*, Cambridge, Mass.; Harvard University Press, 1939.

Dember, W. N., & Earl, R. W. Analysis of exploratory, manipulatory and curiosity behaviors. *Psychological Review*, 1957, **64**, 91–96.

Eastman, N. S., & Hellman, L. M. *Obstetrics*. (13th ed.) New York: Appleton-Century-Crofts, 1966.

Eisenberg, R. B., Coursin, D. B., & Rupp, N. R. Habituation to an acoustic pattern as an index of differences among human neonates. *Journal of Auditory Research*, 1966, **6**, 239–248.

Engen, T. & Lipsitt, L. P. Decrement and recovery of responses to olfactory stimuli in the human neonate. *Journal of Comparative and Physiological Psychology*, 1965, **59**(2), 312–316.

Fantz, R. L. Pattern vision in newborn infants. *Science*, 1963, **140**, 296–297.

Fenz, W. D., & McCabe, M. W. Habituation of the GSR to tones in retarded children and normal controls. Paper presented at the meeting of the Society for Research in Psychophysiology, Monterey, California, October, 1969.

Friedman, S. Detection of visual stimulus change by the human newborn: A habituation paradigm. Paper presented at the meeting of the Society for Research in Child Development, Minneapolis, April, 1971.

Friedman, S. Habituation and recovery of visual response in the alert human newborn. *Journal of Experimental Child Psychology*, 1972, **13**, 339–349.

Friedman, S., Bruno, L. B., & Vietze, P. Newborn habituation to visual stimuli: A sex difference in novelty detection. *Journal of Experimental Child Psychology*, 1974, in press.

Friedman, S., & Carpenter, G. C. Visual response decrement as a function of age of human newborn. *Child Development*, 1971, **42**, 1967-1973.

Friedman, S., Carpenter, G. C., & Nagy, A. N. Decrement and recovery of response to visual stimuli in the newborn human. *Proceedings of the 78th Annual Convention of the American Psychological Association*. 1970, **5**, 273–274 (a)

Friedman, S., Nagy, A. N., & Carpenter, G. C. Newborn attention: Differential response decrement to visual stimuli. *Journal of Experimental Child Psychology*, 1970, **10**, 44–51. (b)

Gemzell, C. A. Variations in plasma levels of 17-hydroxycorticosteroids in mother and infant following parturition. *Acta Endocrinologica*, 1954, **17**, 100–105.

Germana, J. Response characteristics and the orienting reflex. *Journal of Experimental Psychology*, 1968. **78**(4), 610–616.

Graham, F. K., & Clifton, R. K. Heart-rate change as a component of the orienting response. *Psychological Bulletin*, 1966, **65**, 305–320.

Gregg, C., Clifton, R., & Haith, M. Heart rate change as a function of visual stimulation in the newborn. Paper presented at the meeting of the Society for Research in Child Development, Philadelphia, March, 1973.

Hershenson, M. Visual discrimination in the human newborn. *Journal of Comparative and Physiological Psychology*, 1964, **58**(2), 270–276.

Hershenson, M., Munsinger, H., & Kessen, W. Preference for shapes of intermediate variability in the newborn human. *Science*, 1965, **147**, 630–631.

Jeffrey, W. E., & Cohen, L. B. Habituation in the human infant. In H. W. Reese (Ed.), *Advances in child development and behavior*. Vol. 6. New York: Academic Press, 1971.

Korner, A. F. Sex differences in newborns, with special reference to differences in the organization of oral behavior. *Journal of Child Psychology and Psychiatry*, 1973, **14**, 19–29.

Lewis, M. Individual differences in the measurement of early cognitive growth. In J. Hellmuth (Ed.), *Exceptional infant*. Vol. 2. *Studies in abnormalities*. New York: Bruner/Mazel, 1971.

Lewis, M., Bartels, B., Campbell, H., & Goldberg, S. Individual differences in attention: The relation between infants' condition at birth and attention distribution within the first year. *American Journal of Diseases of Children*, 1967, **113**, 461–465.

Lewis, M., Meyer, W. J., Kagan, J., & Grossberg, R. Attention to visual patterns in infants. Paper presented at the meeting of the American Psychological Association, Philadelphia, Pennsylvania, August, 1963.

Lipsitt, L. P. Learning in the first year of life. In L. P. Lipsitt & C. C. Spiker (Eds.), *Advances in child development and behavior,* Vol. 1. New York: Academic Press, 1963.

Mackworth, J. F. Vigilance, arousal and habituation. *Psychological Review,* 1968, **75,** 308–322.

Masland, R. L. The prevention of mental subnormality. In R. L. Masland, S. B. Sarason, & T. Gladwin (Eds.), *Mental subnormality.* New York: Basic Books, 1958.

McCall, R. B. Attention in the infant: Avenue to the study of cognitive development. In D. N. Walcher & D. L. Peters (Eds.), *Early childhood: The development of self-regulatory mechanisms.* New York: Academic Press, 1971.

McCall, R. B. Encoding and retrieval of perceptual memories after long-term familiarization and the infant's response to discrepancy. *Developmental Psychology,* 1973, **9,** 310–318.

Moffett, A. Stimulus complexity as a determinant of visual attention in infants. *Journal of Experimental Child Psychology,* 1969, **8**(1), 173–179.

Munsinger, H. Light detection and pattern recognition: Some comments on the growth of visual sensation and perception. In L. R. Goulet & P. B. Baltes (Eds.), *Life-span developmental psychology.* New York: Academic Press, 1970.

Neeley, C. A. Individual differences among neonates as stimuli for infant-caretaker interaction. Unpublished manuscript, George Peabody College, 1973.

Olley, J. G. Sex differences in human behavior in the first year of life. Unpublished manuscript, George Peabody College, 1971.

Pancratz, C. N., & Cohen, L. B. Recovery of habituation in infants. *Journal of Experimental Child Psychology,* 1970, **9,** 208–216.

Polikanina, R. I., & Probatova, L. E. On the problem of formation of the orienting reflex in premature born children. In L. G. Voronin (Ed.), *Orienting response and exploratory behavior,* Washington, D. C.: American Institute of Biological Science, 1965.

Pomerleau-Malcuit, A., & Clifton, R. K. Neonatal heart-rate response to tactile, auditory, and vestibular stimulation in different states. *Child Development,* 1973, **44,** 485–496.

Porges, S. W., Arnold, W. R., & Forbes, E. J. Heart rate variability: An index of attentional responsivity in human newborns. *Developmental Psychology,* 1973, **8,** 85–92.

Robson, K. S. The role of eye to eye contact in maternal infant attachment. *Journal of Child Psychology and Psychiatry,* 1967, **8,** 13–25.

Sackett, G. P. A neural mechanism underlying unlearned, critical period, and developmental aspects of visually controlled behavior. *Psychological Review,* 1963, **70**(1), 40–50.

Sameroff, A. J., Cashmore, T. F., & Dykes, A. C. Heart rate deceleration during visual fixation in human newborns. *Developmental Psychology,* 1973, **8,** 117–119.

Sigman, M., Kopp, C. B., Parmelee, A., & Jeffrey, W. Visual attention and neurological organization in neonates. *Child Development,* 1973, **44,** 461–466.

Stechler, G. Newborn attention as affected by medication during labor. *Science,* 1964, **144,** 315–317.

Stechler, G., & Carpenter, G. A viewpoint on early affective development. In J. Hellmuth (Ed.), *Exceptional infant.* Vol. 1. Seattle: Special Child Publications, 1967.

Stechler, G., & Latz, E. Some observations on attention and arousal in the human infant. *Journal of the American Academy of Child Psychiatry,* 1966, **5**(3), 517–525.

Stern, D. N. A micro-analysis of mother-infant interaction. *Journal of the American Academy of Child Psychiatry,* 1971, **10**(3), 501–517.

Stern, D. N. Mother and infant at play: The dyadic interaction involving facial, vocal and gaze behavior. In M. Lewis & L. Rosenblum (Eds.), *The origins of behavior.* New York: Wiley, 1973.

Thompson, R. F., & Spencer, W. A. Habituation: A model phenomenon for the study of neuronal substrates of behavior. *Psychological Review,* 1966, **73**(1), 16–43.

Walters, R. H., & Parke, R. D. The role of the distance receptors in the development of social responsiveness. In L. P. Lipsitt & C. C. Spiker (Eds.), *Advances in child development and behavior.* Vol. 2. New York: Academic Press, 1965.

18

PROCESS DEFECTS THAT MIGHT UNDERLIE ABERRANT LANGUAGE DEVELOPMENT

Earl C. Butterfield
George F. Cairns
University of Kansas

Students of language development have reached an important new consensus. It is that language depends upon and could not develop without prior cognitive and perceptual growth (Bloom, 1970, 1974; Bowerman, 1973; Brown, 1973; E. Clark, 1973; H. Clark, 1973; Lennenberg, 1971; MacNamara, 1972; Premack & Premack, 1974; Schlesinger, 1971, 1974; Sinclair-de Zwart, 1971, 1973; Slobin, 1973). Thus, Slobin (1973) argued that "the pacesetter in linguistic growth is the child's cognitive growth [p. 184]." MacNamara's (1972) premise is that "when infants begin to learn language, their thought is more developed than their language [p. 3]." Premack and Premack (1974) assert that language can be viewed as a map of existing perceptual and cognitive distinctions and that "if certain perceptual and conceptual abilities are not present, language cannot be acquired at all [p. 18]."

COGNITIVE AND PERCEPTUAL DATA MAY CONVERGE ON LINGUISTIC FINDINGS

This hypothesized dependency of language upon cognition might liberate the study of language development from one of its chief anchors, which is that poorly formed or grammatically incomplete utterances are open to multiple interpretations. Young and developmentally delayed children's speech, by virtue of its immaturity, is full of ambiguities. The younger or more delayed the child, the less complete and the more ambiguous his utterances. The student of language development has to resolve these ambiguities in order to draw conclusions about the nature of language development. As a consequence, his most basic data have been a complex mix of observation and interpretation. Acknowledging the primacy of perceptual and cognitive processes promises to unmix his data base by suggesting an objective alternative to such heavy reliance upon productive language. That alternative is the direct measurement of cognitive and perceptual processes. The hope is that the developmental psycholinguist will be able to employ assessments of cognitive and perceptual processes as independent checks on the validity of his interpretations of children's utterances, interpretations that he must make if he is to understand the development of linguistic competence.

There are as yet few empirical demonstrations of the utility of showing direct relationships between cognitive performance and linguistic performance. But there are enough instructive examples to give us hope that investigators of language development will soon be able to use variants of the invaluable technique of converging operations. Greenfield, Nelson, and Saltzman (1972) have shown that there are major changes between 11 and 36 months of age in the ways children nest cups that are graduated in size. Analyses of the nesting relations demonstrated by the children led the authors to conclude that the youngest children's strategy took the form of a simple sentence: subject–verb–object or, alternatively, actor–action–acted upon. The strategy of somewhat older children took the form of a compound sentence: subject–verb–object *and* subject–verb–object. The nesting strategy used by the oldest children took the form of a sentence containing a relative clause in which a single noun phrase served simultaneously as an object and a subject: subject–verb–(object, subject)–verb–object or, alternatively, actor–action–(acted upon, actor)–acted upon.

The critical observation in this experiment is that the developmental order of nesting strategies is the same as the developmental order of sentence production: simple sentences first, compound sentences second, and sentences with relative clauses third. This correlation allows Greenfield *et al.* (1972) to attribute greater significance to the developmental sequence of spoken sentence types than they could if they lacked the independent evidence that the cognitive strategies of children follow a similar progression. Thus, the convergence of cognitive and linguistic data can markedly strengthen the inferences of developmental psycholinguists. But, it is also true that the significance of these findings is tempered by the general difficulties of interpreting correlational evidence. Moreover, Greenfield *et al.* recognize that the delay between the emergence of nesting strategies and the emergence of spoken exemplars of the various sentence types poses difficulties. If there is a common underlying cognitive development that determines the manifest order of both nesting strategies and spoken sentences types, why should sentences manifest themselves so much later? Greenfield *et al.* (1972) say: "The precise developmental timing of different manifestations of the same capacity would depend upon relative amounts of experience in different domains, as well as upon the different information processing skills involved in the various manifestations of the single structure [p. 308]." By this view, one must not only analyze language and cognition, one must also work out the variables that determine when cognitive capacities are expressed in language.

Premack and Premack (1974) report data that show that it is possible to accelerate the expression in language of perceptual and cognitive capabilities already expressed in other behavior. They report that in 1965 Metz and Premack identified a group of institutionalized children who used imitative speech but showed no evidence of productive speech. Metz and Premack assessed these children's language comprehension by teaching them to point to the item (in a set of 4 objects, photos, or pictures) that corresponded to a word spoken by the experimenter. All of the children showed evidence of some receptive vocabulary. They correctly pointed to named objects, properties, and actions. Metz and Premack also taught the children to pick from an array of objects one they were told to take. With this procedure, they found that these institutionalized children showed no evidence of distinguishing morphological and grammatical forms. For example, none of the children distinguished between singular and plural forms of object names they had previously been shown to comprehend. Additional tests using simultaneous discrimination and match-to-sample procedures showed that the children could discriminate between single and multiple instances of a variety of objects. Thus, they did not lack the perceptual basis for using or comprehending the plural form. Moreover, when Metz and Premack trained one of these children on the plural, he "not only acquired it for the training material, but was able to transfer the distinction to non-training items [Premack & Premack, 1974, p. 18]."

The findings of Greenfield *et al.* and of Metz and Premack show that the development of apparently sufficient underlying conceptual and perceptual capabilities does not guarantee their immediate expression in language. But the success of Metz and Premack's training suggests that some linguistic forms need not have such delayed expression. Moreover, these latter findings show that language-delayed children who have underlying conceptual and perceptual abilities can be trained to use language forms that seem to depend upon the underlying abilities. What is required to teach language forms in the absence of apparently sufficient conceptual and perceptual behaviors? Is an underlying conceptual base necessary for the learning of language?

We know of no direct test of whether it is possible to teach a language form to children who do not manifest, in a nonlanguage test, the conceptual or perceptual skills that are apparently sufficient for that form. Premack and Premack (1974) report findings with the chimpanzee Sarah that seem to show the necessity of instructing her to make necessary perceptual equivalences before she could learn certain linguistic uses in Premack's plastic language. For example, Sarah had been taught to request fruit by writing sentences in Premack's plastic language. As rewards, she was given pieces of the fruit she requested. When tested to see whether she could match intact whole fruits with the fruit's name, which she had used in sentences, Sarah failed. To determine whether this was a linguistic failure, Premack and Premack employed a match-to-sample procedure in which pieces of fruit were to be matched with the whole fruit. Sarah failed this test, suggesting that her failure to match fruit names with whole fruits was a perceptual problem. Apparently she did not recognize which whole fruit any particular piece came from. That this was so seemed to be confirmed by the finding that, given only the opportunity to observe whole fruits being cut into pieces in preparation for experimental sessions, "Sarah learned the part-whole relations. She then passed both the non-linguistic and the linguistic version of the match-to-sample test [Premack & Premack, 1974, p. 41]."

The consensus we acknowledged at the outset, that a cognitive and perceptual foundation is necessary to language, does not rest primarily on experimental findings. It nevertheless has numerous bases. For example, the unanimous failure of efforts to create high-quality machine translations of one language into another stems from the inability to give machines either sufficient knowledge of the world or interpretative linguistic strategies. Understanding language thus seems to hinge crucially upon knowledge and cognitive devices. Analyses of the complexities and irregularities of the semantic, syntactic, and even the morphological rules of language suggest that an infant could never learn to use any language without referring to his nonlinguistic understanding of environmental regularities and speakers' meanings. There is also some evidence that deaf people, who have severely retarded speech development, nevertheless seem to reveal all the essentials of human thought.

In our view, the importance of this consensus is not diminished by the paucity of experimental data that it summarizes. We believe that its importance lies far less in its accuracy as a summary statement of existing findings than in the guidance it offers about how to collect additional data on language development, particularly that of very young infants and developmentally delayed children. We have already observed that this consensus highlights the possibility of measuring perceptual and conceptual behavior in order to provide converging validation for interpretations of linguistic behavior. We believe that programmatic use of this strategy would rapidly reduce to zero the importance of existing data on early language behavior, because it would yield more important data. This is true in part because the earliest productive language occurs so late after birth, and in part because there has been no very good suggestion about how to overcome this fact. The suggestion that follows from the consensus that language requires a base in cognition and perception is to look at the development of conceptual and perceptual behaviors that predate the emergence of productive language. The works of Greenfield *et al.* and of Metz and Premack show some ways to do this.

LINGUISTIC DATA CAN YIELD HYPOTHESES ABOUT COGNITIVE DEVELOPMENT

Another valuable service of the thesis that language depends on cognition and perception is to highlight the importance of our understanding of language as a source of hypotheses about cognitive and perceptual development. If language reflects perception and cognition, then linguistic analyses should yield useful hypotheses about perceptual and cognitive development. This possibility is exceptionally important, because one of the chief stumbling blocks to the study of cognitive development has been the lack of a coherent theoretical base to guide researchers.

We can cite only one well-worked-out example of the heuristic value of deriving predictions from our knowledge of language for the study of cognition and perception. It concerns the study of the development of speech perception which has stemmed from the motor theory of adults' speech (Liberman, 1970; Liberman, Cooper, Shankweiler, & Studdert-Kennedy, 1967; Studdert-Kennedy, Liberman, Harris, & Cooper, 1970). Eimas, Siqueland, Jusczyk, and Vigorito (1971) started the extension of the motor theory to the study of young infants, and Eimas (1974a, b) primarily, but others as well (Morse, 1974; Butterfield & Cairns, 1974; Trehub & Rabinovitch, 1972; Trehub, 1973) have pursued the implications of the adult work in the study of infants.

Studies of infants' speech perception build from the generalization that adults perceive speech differently than they do other auditory signals. The short-hand for this conclusion is that adults' speech perception is linguistically relevant. At least four observations support this conclusion. First, certain acoustic cues, for example, voice onset time, are used universally, that is, in the spoken forms of all languages. Second, some of the acoustic correlates of speech features, and specifically two of the few that can be generated synthetically by computers, are perceived categorically, unlike either auditory nonspeech or visual cues. Third, identical variations in certain synthetically generated acoustic cues are perceived differently when they are embedded in a speech context and when they are presented in isolation. Fourth, the electrical activity evoked by acoustic signals is localized in the left hemisphere of the brain if the signals are correlates of certain speech features, and it is not so localized if the cues are not correlates of those speech features. Dichotic listening experiments also support the notion of lateralized and localized speech perception.

Partly because some acoustic cues are used universally, partly because some speech stimuli evoke hemispherically localized brain potentials, and partly because of his inability to explain how people might learn to segment and discriminate speech stimuli, Eimas hypothesized that innate biological structures underlie perception in the speech mode. (The latter phrase is synonymous with linguistically relevant perception.) From this conclusion, he deduced the prediction that very young infants should also perceive speech linguistically.

This hypothesis might be tested by seeking infant analogues of the four phenomena that support the conclusion that adults perceive in a linguistically relevant manner, but this is impossible with respect to the observation that all spoken languages use similar sets of acoustic contrasts, because infants do not speak. Even if they did, the characteristics of their speech would not necessarily exactly mirror their perceptual capabilities. There are no comparably insuperable barriers to the search in infants for localized brain potentials in response to speech and nonspeech stimuli, and Molfese (1972) has recently reported that infants who average about five months of age show greater right hemisphere potentials for speech than for nonspeech auditory stimuli. Morse (1972) and Eimas (1974a) have both conducted experiments to determine whether infants discriminate isolated acoustic cues differently than they do the same ones in speech contexts. But, the hypothesis that infants perceive linguistically has been tested mainly by several experiments as to whether they perceive categorically.

For adults, categorical perception is established by showing that they do not discriminate between physically different synthetic stimuli to which they attach the same speech labels for example, /ga/, but they do discriminate highly accurately between no less physically similar stimuli to which they attach different speech labels. Adults are first asked to categorize a group of stimuli by listening and assigning labels to them. Despite the fact that the stimuli all differ on some acoustic cue, adults assign fewer labels than there are stimuli. Those to which they assign different labels are said to vary between categories. Adults are then asked to discriminate between pairs of stimuli that differ equally along the acoustic dimension: for some pairs, both members come from the same category, while for other pairs, the members come from different categories. If the within-category discriminations are made no better than chance and the between-category discriminations are made esentially perfectly, then perception of the underlying dimension is said to be categorical. The more within-category pairs that are not discriminated, and the more abrupt the increase in rate of successful discrimination around the category boundary, the more convincing the demonstration of categorical perception.

It has so far been impossible to secure categorical judgements from infants. Consequently, it has been impossible to make a completely adequate test of whether they perceive categorically, since this requires both categorization and discrimination functions. Eimas has overcome this limitation by assuming that infants would categorize synthetic stimuli precisely as adults do. This assumption allows him to infer categorical perception from infants' discrimination functions alone, if those functions are predicted by adults' categorizations of the stimuli.

Eimas has collected several sets of data that bear on the question of whether adults' categorical functions predict infants' discrimination functions. He has used the "high-amplitude suck" (HAS) procedure to compare differential responses to members of one within-category pair and one between-category pair along the voice–onset–time (VOT) dimension in several experiments with infants, and found evidence to suggest that the within-category pair was not discriminated while the between-category pair was, when the VOT boundary was the one used in spoken English. He has also found differences between pairs of stimuli that varied in place of articulation, that is, second formant transitions, when one pair came from within an adult category and one was composed of items from different adult categories.

Eimas (1974b) has concluded from his findings that infants perceive at least approximately categorically and therefore in a linguistically relevant fashion.

From the conclusion that both young infants and adults perceive particular synthetic stimuli in the same (linguistically relevant) fashion, Eimas reasoned that he could conduct experiments with adults to clarify the infants' perceptual processes. Accordingly, he executed a series of adult adaptation experiments from which he has inferred the existence of biologically determined linguistic feature detectors that are tuned to different portions of the various acoustic dimenstions that underlie speech cue perception. Other investigators have also explored various implications of Eimas's findings with different samples of infants (Butterfield & Cairns, 1974; Morse, 1972; Trehub, 1973; Trehub & Rabinovitch, 1972).

The foregoing work on infants' perception of speech illustrates that it can be heuristic to use our understanding of language to generate research about perceptual and cognitive development. We hope that more experiments will demonstrate this, and we take it that they will from the number of authors who are now deducing testable hypotheses about cognitive development from their understanding and analyses of language and its development. A paper by MacNamara (1972) illustrates this trend. From his thesis that an "infant uses meaning as a clue to language, rather than language as a clue to meaning," MacNamara offered speculations about the cognitive accomplishments that might underlie the child's learning of semantics, syntax, and phonology from the speech of people about him. For example, MacNamara points out that children first learn the names of objects, then the names for their variable states, and then the names of their more permanent attributes. From this, he suggests that children must very early distinguish from the rest of the physical environment objects like those to which people attach names, that later they must attend to varying states and activities, and only at a later age attend to the unvarying attributes of objects. Research like that of Bower (1966) offers some support for this hypothesized order.

Bower showed that as early as the second week of life, infants make defensive reactions to the illusion that an object is approaching them. Well prior to the time that it seems learning could account for these infants' knowledge that visual events might have tactual consequences, they reacted as if they would. That reaction, in turn, allows the inference that they perceive objects very early in life. By systematically varying the rate of movement and physical attributes of objects, and observing infants' visual tracking of the objects as they moved to and fro behind shields, Bower found evidence that children only gradually come to respond to changes in attributes that are normally invariant, while they respond very early to movement. This work was not designed to test MacNamara's theses, and trying to make it do that in every particular will not work. The point is that simple variants on Bower's procedures would allow an analytic series of experiments to test the notions that MacNamara has derived from his analysis of what must happen prior to language learning. MacNamara's speculations are not confined to the notions described above. Indeed, he has advanced rich series of expectations, and Bloom (1970), Bowerman (1973), Schlesinger (1971), and Sinclair-de Zwart (1973), among others, offer yet additional hypotheses that could guide intriguing developmental research into perception and cognition. Having performed such research with normal children, we would be in a position to ask whether defects in the normal cognitive and perceptual underpinnings of language could account for aberrant language development.

We are tempted, as researchers into mental retardation, to suppose that language deficits of the retarded are all secondary to defects of their cognitive or perceptual processes. We do think this hypothesis deserves full test. But the consensus that language builds on cognition and perception leaves room for the possibility of deficits in processes that are uniquely linguistic. Consider MacNamara's thesis that children rely in part upon their acquired knowledge of the meaning of words and syntax to infer the phonological rules of their language. He observes that phonological theory distinguishes between variations in speech sounds that convery differences in meaning and those that do not. The child's chore is thus to learn which variations to ignore and which to interpret. Regardless of the role of cognition in this process, the child will likely not solve the puzzle of his language if he does not attend to and discriminate amongst its spoken features. The distinction between a cognitive basis for language and language itself thus serves to highlight a useful division of experimental labor between examinations of cognition and perception of nonlinguistic events and examinations of more uniquely linguistic processes that might underlie speech and language defects.

PROCESSING SPEECH SIGNALS

In order to extract meaning from the speech stream, we must attend to it, segment it, and discriminate amongst its segments. It is possible that some language abnormalities stem from defects in these three apparently different processes. The study of the development of segmentation and discrimination has been severely constrained by our ignornace of the functional units of speech. Most developmental approaches to discrimination have been guided by the view that the functional segments of the speech signal are phonemes (e.g., Trehub, 1973; Morse, 1972; Eimas, 1974a; Butterfield & Cairns, 1974). Also, most students of the development of speech perception have adopted the view that phonemic discrimination can best be studied by examining infants' sensitivity to acoustic parameters that are sufficient for adults to categorize computer-generated stimuli into natural language phonetic classes (e.g., Eimas *et al.*, 1971; Morse, 1972). A few investigators have adopted the view that for infants, suprasegmental units, such as sentences, are the appropriate functional units of study. For these workers, changes in fundamental frequency contours or intensity patterns are pertinent discriminative stimuli (Kaplan & Kaplan, 1971).

Our view is that the specification of the functional units of speech and clarification of how their discrimination develops will not be accomplished until more direct methods for assessing infants' discrimination have been applied. No investigation of infants' speech discrimination has achieved a separation of the discriminative and reinforcing properties of the speech stimuli that they have examined. Consequently, it is not possible to clearly interpret behavioral changes from which investigators have wished to infer discrimination, and it is absolutely impossible to attach any meaning to a failure to observe a behavioral change in studies of infants' responses to speech stimuli. We have elaborated upon these difficulties and described potential solutions for them elsewhere (Butterfield & Cairns, 1974). Until more satisfactory procedures for the study of infants' discrimination have been applied, we see little point in trying to determine whether deficiencies in such discriminative capacities underlie aberrations in language development.

Attention to Speech

No such crucial limits of method attach themselves to studies of attention to speech, and two major lines of research show that speech has a potent effect on young infants' behavior. First, noncontingent speech changes infants' ongoing behavior (Condon & Sander, 1974; Simner, 1971; Webster, 1969). Second, contingent speech increases infants' response rates (Butterfield & Siperstein, 1972; Rheingold, Gewirtz, & Ross, 1959; Routh, 1969; Todd & Palmer, 1968).

Salience of noncontingent speech. Sinner (1971) presented newborn cries to some neonates and not to others. Those who received the noncontingent cry, cried more often and longer than those who did not. Condon and Sander (1974) performed frame-by-frame analyses of motion pictures of newborn infants to whom they presented recordings of running speech. They observed that the ongoing limb movements of the infants became synchronized with the presented speech. Speech has also been observed to change the ongoing behavior of older infants. Barrett-Goldfarb and Whitehurst (1973) found that one-year-olds decreased their rate of vocalizing when recordings of their parents' voices were presented. Moreover, one-year-olds showed preferences between their mother's and father's voices, as judged by the duration of their selections of which voice to listen to. The suppression of their own ongoing vocalizations was greater by the voice they preferred. Turnure (1971) found that the voice of an infant's mother produced motor quieting, even when it was distorted, as did the undistorted voice of a stranger. Moreover, 9-month-olds were quieted more than either 3- or 6-month-olds.

Webster (1969) performed a finer analysis of the suppressing effect of speech upon infants' vocalizations. He presented either vowel or consonant stimuli and observed infants' vocalic and consonantal productions. Vowels suppressed vocalic behavior, and consonants suppressed consonantal sounds. In summary, both neonates' and older infants' behavior is changed by noncontingent speech, and the character and degree of the suppression depends upon the age of the infant and upon the character of the speech presented to him.

Reinforcing properties of contingent speech. Butterfield and Siperstein (1972) showed that neonates would both increase and decrease their nonnutritive suck duration, depending upon which response would increase their access to singing voices. In the same laboratory, Butterfield and Cairns (1974) failed to increase neonates' rate of high-amplitude sucking (HAS) with contingent presentations of synthetic speech segments intended to sound like "ba" and "pa." Whether this is due to a lack of reinforcing properties of the synthetic stimuli or to problems with the HAS procedure remains to be determined (see Butterfield & Cairns, 1974, for an exposition of the methodological issues raised by the HAS procedure).

There have been many demonstrations that speech stimuli act as positive reinforcers for older infants. Todd and Palmer (1968), Haugan and McIntire (1972), Rheingold *et al.* (1959), and Weisberg (1963) demonstrated that the rate of infants' vocalizations increases when speech sounds are made contingent upon them. This was true despite the fact, cited above, that noncontingent speech decreases the vocalization rate of infants. Sheppard (1969) increased rates of both vocalization and leg kicking with contingent presentations of an infant's mother's voice and blinking lights.

Contingent and noncontingent procedures thus show that both neonates and older infants attend to speech. How does speech compare to other stimuli as an elicitor of infant attention?

Comparisons of speech and other noncontingent stimuli. Condon and Sander (1974) found that newborn infants synchronized their motor behavior with running samples of spoken English and spoken Chinese, but not with tapping or disconnected English consonant sounds. This suggests that newborns attend to some suprasegmental feature of speech. Simner's (1971) elegant experiments offer additional information about newborns' differential attention to speech signals. He found that white noise did not elicit crying as much as did another newborn's cry. This was true despite the fact that the moment-to-moment amplitude of the noise was very similar to that of the recorded cry. Thus, the newborns were apparently reacting to something other than the amplitude of the recorded cry. Simner found in another experiment that neither the cry of a 5½-month infant nor a synthetically-generated cry induced crying in newborn infants as much as the presentation of another newborn's cry. Thus, newborns seem to attend more to "speech" sounds that are similar to their own.

The only noncontingent comparison of speech stimuli with older infants was reported by Turnure (1971). She observed that both distorted and undistorted mothers' voices reduced the motor activity of children between three and nine months of age. The quieting effect was greater for the older infants, which Turnure interpreted as evidence of increased attention by older infants. Distortion had no observable effect.

Comparisons of speech and other contingent stimuli. Butterfield and Siperstein (1972) found that newborns would change their suck durations in order to increase their access to singing and its instrumental accompaniment. When the voices and instruments were presented separately, the voices produced as great an effect as the combined voices and instruments, whereas the instruments alone produced no differential behavior. When white noise was made contingent upon suck duration, infants responded so as to turn it off, rather than increase it as they did with the voices. Thus, these investigators showed three points on a neonatal reinforcement continuum: Singing voices are positively reinforcing; musical instruments are neutral; white noise is negatively reinforcing.

Haugan and McIntire (1972) attempted to compare the reinforcer effectiveness of speech, food, and tactile stimulation upon three- and six-month-old infants. For speech reinforcers, they employed adults' imitations of the infants' immediately preceding vocalizations. This form of reward was more effective than either food or tactile stimulation. As the authors point out the interpretation of this finding is complicated by the possibility that nonimitative speech might not have served as well. Moreover, there were greater delays in the delivery of food and tactile rewards, and there is no clear way to determine whether the deprivation schedules were the same for the three classes of stimuli.

Friedlander (1968, 1970) has examined the effects of redundancy and meaningfullness of speech samples on preference behavior of infants. His procedure allows the infant to choose between two programs of auditory stimulation, or by leaving a three-position switch in the neutral position to receive no stimulation. He has used this procedure to collect listening preference data from infants in their home environment. Although fine-grained analyses have not been performed on data gathered using this technique, several findings seem clear. First, Friedlander (1968) was able to demonstrate that infants 11–15 months of age would select a recording of the mother's voice with a bright inflection over the mother's voice with a flat inflection. Similarly, he demonstrated that an infant would choose a stranger's voice with bright inflection over his mother's voice with flat inflection. Also, a long message that repeated itself every 240 sec was progressively selected more over a 20-sec sample of the longer message. These results indicate that complex characteristics of the speech stream can control infants' behavior when they are about one year of age. Whether this is true for younger infants is unknown.

Attention of Aberrant Infants

To the best of our knowledge, there have been no adequate tests of whether infants with language impairments or those who are likely to develop aberrant language attend less or differently to speech than normal infants. We have attempted to make such comparisons in our newborn nursery, but we were unsuccessful. The birth rate in our hospital is less than 1500 infants per year, so that very few clearly aberrant children are available to us. Many of those who are at great risk for language problems, are also at risk for their lives. Consequently, we do not test them for fear of harming their chances of survival.

Friedlander, McCarthy, and Soforenko (1967) have used their listening preference techniques with four severely retarded infants whose developmental ages were less than one year. They secured usable data from two of these infants, but they did not employ speech stimuli with them. Both infants showed a strong preference for an ascending organ scale over a door chime, and they maintained this preferential behavior over long time spans and despite the fact that doing so required that they accurately track changes in the responses required to produce the two sounds. Thus, for older retarded infants at least, it would be possible to assess attention to speech.

IDENTIFYING PROCESSES THAT MIGHT UNDERLIE RETARDED LANGUAGE DEVELOPMENT

Mentally retarded people's language shows their retardation perhaps more clearly than any of their other behaviors. This may be seen even in intelligence tests, whose purest subscales, their vocabulary tests, are also their purest measures of language functioning. The question we would like to answer is what processes underlie their aberrant language development. That question cannot be answered yet, but the day when it may be seems to be coming.

We tried above to anticipate how and where the answers will be found. We emphasized what seems to us a key concept, which is that language depends upon cognitive and perceptual capabilities. The importance of this concept is first that it suggests places to look and ways to secure converging data for our observations of language development. The places are in the conceptual and perceptual abilities of children, particularly those who by virtue of their youth or their retardation have yet to develop many language forms. The second value of this concept is that it highlights the importance of linguistic observations as a source of hypotheses about cognitive and perceptual development. Few investigators of mental retardation have come to grips with the complexity of the deficits of their subject population, and we see not better cure for this than focusing on complex behavior like language and drawing testable hypotheses from our understanding of it. The third value of hypothesizing that cognition and perception underlie language is that it provides for a clear separation of experimental effort, while encouraging the investigator to keep in mind the fact that his work might ultimately fit into a larger, more complex scheme.

Perhaps the clearest message of our examination of the literature on the role of cognition and perception in language is that investigators have yet to take important advantage of the opportunities afforded by the fact that mentally retarded people develop language slowly. Many acknowledge that the study of retarded development can importantly clarify normal development, and we can think of no behavioral domain where this is more likely than in the study of language. Normal language development proceeds at such a rapid pace, and on so many fronts at once, that we undoubtedly miss many of its elements and their interactions when we study only normal children. It seems particularly lamentable, therefore, that so few experiments have examined the underlying determinants of the language of the mentally retarded.

ACKNOWLEDGMENTS

The preparation of this paper was supported by U.S.P.H.S. grants HD-02528 and HD-04756.

REFERENCES

Barrett-Goldfarb, M. S., & Whitehurst, J. Infant vocalizations as a function of parental voice selection. *Developmental Psychology, 1973, **8**, 273–276.*

Bloom, L. *Language development: Form and function in emerging grammars.* Cambridge, Mass.: MIT Press, 1970.

Bloom, L. Talking, understanding and thinking. In R. L. Schiefelbusch & L. L. Lloyd (Eds.), *Language perspectives: Acquisition, retardation, and intervention.* Baltimore: University Park Press, 1974, in press.

Bower, T. G. R. The visual world of infants. *Scientific American,* 1966, **215**, 80–92.

Bowerman, M. *Early syntactic development: A cross-linguistic study with special references to Finnish.* Cambridge, England: Cambridge University Press, 1973.

Brown, R. *A first language: The early stages.* Cambridge, Mass.: Harvard University Press, 1973.

Butterfield, E. C., & Cairns, G. F., Jr. Whether infants perceive linguistically is uncertain, and if they did, its practical importance would be equivocal. In R. L. Schiefelbush & L. L. Lloyd (Eds.), *Language perspectives: Acquisition, retardation, and intervention.* Baltimore: University Park Press, 1974, in press.

Butterfield, E. C., & Siperstein, G. N. Influence of contingent auditory stimulation upon non-nutritional suckle. In J. Bosma (Ed.), *Oral sensation and perception: The Mouth of the infant.* Springfield, Ill.: C. C Thomas, 1972.

Clark, E. V. What's in a word? On the child's acquisition of semantics in his first language. In T. E. Moore (Ed.), *Cognitive development and the acquisition of language.* New York: Academic Press, 1973.

Clark, H. H. Space, time, semantics, and the child. In T. E. Moore (Ed.), *Cognitive development and the acquisition of language.* New York: Academic Press, 1973.

Condon, W. S., & Sander, L. W. Neonate movement is synchronized with adult speech: Interactional participation and language acquisition. *Science,* 1974, **183**, 99–101.

Eimas, P. D. Speech perception in early infancy. In L. B. Cohen & P. Salapatek (Eds.), *Infant perception.* New York: Academic Press, 1974, in press.   (a)

Eimas, P. D. Linguistic processing of speech by young infants. In R. L. Schiefelbusch & L. L. Lloyd (Eds.), *Language perspectives: Acquisition, retardation, and intervention.* Baltimore: University Park Press, 1974, in press.   (b)

Eimas, P. D., Siqueland, E. R., Jusczyk, P., & Vigorito, J. Speech perception in infants. *Science,* 1971, **171**, 303–306.

Friedlander, B. Z. The effect of speaker identity, voice, infelction, vocabulary, and message redundancy on infants' selection of vocal reinforcement. *Journal of Experimental Child Psychology,* 1968, **6**, 443–459.

Friedlander, B. Z. Receptive language development in infancy: Issues and problems. *Merrill-Palmer Quarterly of Behavior and Development.* 1970, **16**, 7–51.

Friedlander, B. Z., McCarthy, J. J., & Soforenko, A. Z. Automated psychological evaluation with severely retarded institutionalized infants. *Amereican Journal of Mental Deficiency,* 1967, **71**, 909–919.

Greenfield, P., Nelson, K., & Saltzman, E. The development of rule-bound strategies for manipulating seriated cups: A parallel between action and grammar. *Cognitive Psychology,* 1972, **3**, 291–310.

Haugan, G. M., & McIntire, R. W. Comparisons of vocal imitation, tactile stimulation, and food as reinforcers for infant vocalizations. *Developmental Psychology,* 1972, **6**, 201–209.

Kaplan, E., & Kaplan, G. The prelinguistic child. In T. Elliot (Ed.), *Human development and cognitive processes*. New York: Holt, Rinehart and Winston, Inc., 1971.

Lenneberg, E. H. Of language, knowledge, apes, and brains. *Journal of Psycholinguistic Research*, 1971, **1**, 1–29.

Liberman, A. M. Some characteristics of perception in the speech mode. In D. A. Hamburg (Ed.), *Perception and its disorders, Proceedings of A.R.N.M.D.* Baltimore: Williams and Wilkins, 1970. Pp. 238–258.

Liberman, A. M., Cooper, F. S., Shankweiler, D., & Studdert-Kennedy, M. Perception of the speech code. *Psychological Review*, 1967, **74**, 431–461.

MacNamara, J. Cognitive basis of language learning in infants. *Psychological Review*, 1972, **79**, 1–13.

Molfese, D. L. Cerebral asymmetry in infants, children adults: Auditory evoked responses to speech and noise stimuli. Unpublished doctoral dissertation, The Pennsylvania State University, 1972.

Morse, P. A. The discrimination of speech and nonspeech stimuli in early infancy. *Journal of Experimental Child Psychology*, 1972, **14**, 477–492.

Morse, P. A. Infant speech perception: A preliminary model and review of literature. In R. L. Schiefelbusch & L. L. Lloyd (Eds.), *Language perspectives: Acquisition, retardation, and intervention*. Baltimore: University Park Press, 1974, in press.

Premack, D., & Premack, A. T. Teaching visual language to apes and language-deficient persons. In R. L. Schiefelbusch & L. L. Lloyd (Eds.), *Language perspectives: Acquisition, retardation, and intervention*. Baltimore: University Park Press, 1974, in press.

Rheingold, H. L., Gewirtz, J. L., & Ross, H. W. Social conditioning of vocalizations in the infant. *Journal of Comparative and Physiological Psychology*, 1959, **52**, 68–73.

Routh, K. Conditioning of vocal response differentiation in infants. *Developmental Psychology*, 1969, **1**, 219–226.

Schlesinger, I. M. Production of utterances and language acquisition. In D. I. Slobin (Ed.), *The ontogenesis of grammar*. New York: Academic Press, 1971.

Schlesinger, I. M. Relational concepts underlying language. In R. L. Schiefelbusch & L. L. Lloyd (Eds.), *Language Perspectives: Acquisition, retardation, and intervention*. Baltimore: University Park Press, 1974, in press.

Sheppard, W. C. Operant control of infant vocal and motor behavior. *Journal of Experimental Child Psychology*, 1969, **7**, 36–51.

Simner, M. L. Newborn's response to the cry of another infant. *Developmental Psychology*, 1971, **5**, 136–150.

Sinclair-de Zwart, H. Sensori-motor action patterns as a condition for the acquisition of syntax. In R. Huxley & E. Ingram (Eds.), *Language acquisition: Models and methods*. New York: Academic Press, 1971.

Sinclair-de Zwart, H. Some remarks on the Genevan point of view on learning with special reference to language learning. In L. L. Hinde & H. C. Hinde (Eds.), *Constraints on learning*. New York: Academic Press, 1973.

Slobin, D. I. Cognitive prerequisites for the development of grammar. In C. A. Ferguson & D. I. Slobin (Eds.), *Studies of child language development*. New York: Holt, Rinehart & Winston, 1973.

Studdert-Kennedy, M., Liberman, A.M., Harris, K.S., & Cooper, F. S. Motor theory of speech perception: A reply to Lane's critical review. *Psychological Review*, 1970, **77**, 234–249.

Todd, B. A., & Palmer, B. Social reinforcement of infant babbling. *Child Development*, 1968, **39**, 592–596.

Trehub, S. E. Infants' sensitivity to vowel and tonal contrasts. *Developmental Psychology*, 1973, **9**, 91–96.

Trehub, S. E., & Rabinovitch, M. S. Auditory-linguistic sensitivity in early infancy. *Developmental Psychology*, 1972, **6**, 74–77.

Turnure, C. Response to voice of mother and stranger by babies in the first year. *Developmental Psychology,* 1971, **4**, 182–190.

Webster, R. L. Selective suppression of infants vocal responses by classes of phonemic stimulation. *Developmental Psychology,* 1969, **1**, 410–414.

Weisberg, P. Social and nonsocial conditioning of infant vocalizations. *Child Development,* 1963, **34**, 377–388.

19
OVERVIEW AND SYNTHESIS

M. Ray Denny
Michigan State University

I am going to begin this overview with a little demonstration that takes only a couple of minutes and which requires your active participation. Note the upside-down L of Fig. 1. What I want you to do is trace this figure with a pencil when I say "go," with the drawing right in front of you. Your instructions are to start at the dot and do anything you want as long as you stay within the path. If I were to observe that you did *not* traverse the whole figure within a reasonable period of time, I'd say "go all the way." (1) O.K., start at the dot, do anything you want, GO! (2) Do it again, same instructions, start at dot and GO! (3) Again, same instructions, GO—and don't forget to go all the way. (4) Again, GO! (5) Once again, GO! (6) Again, start at the dot and GO!

O.K., one final time, with a new figure (Fig. 2), start at the dot, same instructions, GO! Now, did you first go the same way in the choice point of the T as you were forced to go in the inverted L.? Or, did you go the opposite way first?

The principal object of the demonstration was to familiarize you with the task—a paper-and-pencil version of the T-maze study that Dave Zeaman and Betty House ran with rats many years ago.

The purpose of introducing this task revolves about a sex difference that Leslie Cohen described in his paper on infant visual memory, as studied by habituation techniques. According to Cohen, male infants habituate more to visual stimuli than females, even though both regard the stimulus for the same length of time during its initial presentation. Seventeen years ago when I first presented this inverted L task to Michigan State University students, approximately 65% of the boys alternated, whereas only 35% of the girls alternated, regardless of which way the inverted L pointed. That is, if alternating is viewed as an example of habituation or getting bored with going only one direction, then one could argue from such data that adult males, like infant males, habituate more than their female counterparts. The trouble with this interpretation, according to data recently gathered at Northern Illinois and Michigan State universities is that in 1974 the women now

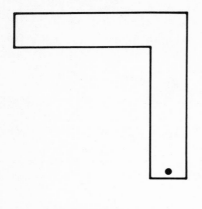

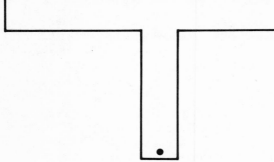

FIG. 1. Figure subjects drew in repeatedly.

FIG. 2. Figure used to test for alternation tendency.

tend to alternate like the men. A male chauvinist might infer that this generation-shift represents a sex role change that runs counter to the females' natural endowment, but I wouldn't stoop so low.

Since my main task is to attempt a synthesis of the material presented in this volume, I finally squeezed, to my own surprise, just about all of the papers into three categories:

I. What the future holds when early development is aberrant.

II. The implications of the use of pharmacological agents on mental retardation and other aspects of behavior.

III. The assessment of early behavior, especially in normal infants, as a predictor of later intelligent.

Let us turn to the first category. Here Isaacson told us that all brains are *not* the same. Therefore, the effects of specific damage to the brain are variable and probabalistic across individuals—a convincing point once it has been made. He also stressed that early damage, as long as it was beyond the very early period of prenatal development that precedes structural differentiation, was just as deleterious for subsequent behavior as later damage. In short, Isaacson claimed that there was no such thing as vicarious functioning—that "recovery" from brain injury could just as well involve structural changes (e.g., sprouting and aberrant fiber tracts) that were unfavorable as those favorable to behavior.

Such a view makes excellent sense for the facts of mental retardation—that developmental problems well before birth result in permanent retardation. But, since it took Bob Isaacson ten years of researching to arrive at this conclusion about vicarious functioning, I'm not so sure I'm ready to shed the notion after a few hours.

Many of the remaining papers in this category seemed to exploit an animal model. Denenberg, working with rats, ligated the main artery supplying blood to the uterine horns of the rat on day 18 or 19 of pregnancy. The surviving pups of ligated mothers weighed significantly less at birth, but the weight difference was not present at weaning or in adulthood. Between 66 and 88% of liveborn pups of ligated mothers survived until weaning, as compared with approximately 98% of sham-ligated pups. In adulthood the activity pattern of the ligated group on an open-field test differed significantly from that of the sham group: ligation made males less active and females more active.

Gil Meier explored the possibility of using primate colonies to study the effect of early mother–infant interactions on subsequent behavior of the infant. In a programmatic way, he was asking whether very early infant–parent interactions (the form or style they take) are critical to later development. Given there is contact and care, are other refinements in the interaction critical? What little evidence there is at the monkey level is only suggestive.

Gene Sackett also selected the monkey as a model, using computerized colony records of 12-years standing to study high risk neonates. For this group, the "epidemiological" approach revealed that male neonates had more low birth weights than females, more females lived past the neonatal period than males, and breeders under high stress are at high risk for delivering premature, stillborn, aborted, low-birth-weight, and short-surviving neonates. Sackett draws a parallel with the human situation, and in this connection it is interesting to point out that there are more male institutionalized retardates than female.

An apology is due Hicks and D'Amato. I was not able to read enough of their paper to respond to the abstract I saw. Essentially, they emphasized how adaptive rats can be when they suffer injury to the nervous system early in life.

Finally in this section on animal models, Gersh Berkson, referring to the study of blind infant monkeys, told us that there seems to be an evolutionary basis for caring for defective individuals. Of course, there was more; but there are also many more papers to cover.

The remaining papers dealing with the future of high-risk offspring focused on human neonates. Parmelee discussed the development of a cumulative risk score in the first nine months of life. Items included obstetric complications, visual attention, sleep polygraphs, exploratory behavior, etc. It is interesting to note that preliminary results indicated that visual attention items are one of the better correlated set of items with total cumulative risk score. As such, this correlation seems to represent a common thread running through the volume, as will be evident when the work on visual habituation is attended to. In brief, this work by Parmelee and associates seems promising and potentially helpful in the prediction of later development—especially for repeated predictions over short periods of time. Such predictability should also suggest appropriate interventions.

Two other attempts to differentiate normals from infants at risk included a paper by Kron in which this differentiation was based on sucking responses to various schedules of reinforcement and a paper by Thoman using 1-hr periods of observation of the sleep–wake states in the newborn to assess its organizational state or well being.

Category II on the effects of drugs on behavior included, at least by implication, attacks on customary medical practices with pregnant women. Yvonne Brackbill presented evidence that commonly used analgesics and anesthetics such as Demerol had an undesirable effect on the infant offspring's behavior. The behavioral measures used were standard infant scales or revisions thereof plus a measure of habituation of the orienting response (a jerking sort of startle response to an auditory stimulus that was set 5 dB above the threshold for the jerking response). Lack of habituation or failure to inhibit represents a departure from normal behavior.

Brackbill further reported that the behavioral effects were highly correlated with amount of medication or dosage and seemed to be relatively long lasting (present in 4-week-old infants). She also argued that vulnerability to the toxic effects of the drug was best assessed with more difficult response classes like inhibiting or eliciting a particular response rather than stable-state resting behavior or spontaneous responding.

Hutchings reported that the administration of an excess of vitamin A to rats during the early fetal period resulted in a reduced brain size and behavioral impairments in inhibiting responses and attending to relevant stimuli. Later administration via the pregnant rat during the midfetal period had very little deleterious effect, with the possible exception that fine motor coordination was disturbed. Such results point up the possibility that minimal brain dysfunction (MBD) in humans may result from maternal drug exposure.

The paper by Byron Campbell departed somewhat from the thrust of the other papers in this group. The focus was on the paradoxical effects of amphetamine on behavioral arousal in rats as a possible explanation of the calming effects of amphetamine on MBD children. Campbell found amphetamine produced a large increase in activity in 15-day-old rats when they are alone, but no increase when there is an anesthetized adult rat present (the paradoxical effect). If, on the other hand, the anesthetized animal is periodically moved, the 15-day-old given amphetamine *actively* regains or maintains contact with the anesthetized adult. At 20 days of age (and older) the paradoxical effect is gone; amphetamine simply increases random activity (the anesthetized animal is ignored).

Presumptively, the 2-year-old normal human child is like the 15-day-old rat with respect to developmental period and hyperexcitability. And an MBD child is presumably one who has not progressed beyond the two-year stage in terms of the dropping out of hyperexcitability. So, just as amphetamine increases the attachment of offspring to adult in the 15-day-old rat, it might be hypothesized that amphetamine does the same to the MBD child. That is, the child under amphetamine does what the teacher wants, cooperating to maintain effective contact and approval. Byron preferred not to be this explicit in his analysis, but I've taken the liberty (with his approval) of doing so.

According to Rodier and as previously suggested by Hutchings, the type of interference with development varies with time of insult. Rodier's work with mice specifically showed that chemically induced lesions on embryonic day 15 resulted in cell deficits in the cerebral cortex and hippocampus, while for day 19 there was no cell loss—just a smaller brain. This treatment on postnatal day 3 produced a cell loss only in the cerebellum. All animals showed behavioral abnormalities, varying with time of insult, and being most severe with earlier treatment.

Finally, Dick Butcher reported that teratogens like aspirin or excess vitamin A, administered to the dam, produce learning impairments without locomotor defects in the offspring, whereas those like OH urea produce both learning and locomotor defects and those like Diamox (acetazolamide) that do not affect the central nervous system produce only locomotor defects or forepaw abnormality.

The third category, dealing with the early assessment of infant behavior as a potential predictor of later intellectual development, included many interesting papers of which Claire Kopp's was no exception. Her preliminary data on fine motor behavior in 8-month-old infants could be interpreted to indicate that the infants with the more sophisticated response class or schema of manually examining an object may be destined for higher IQs than those who just looked at it.

The final set of papers that I am going to cover all deal with the habituation of looking behavior in human infants. The paper by Fagan set the stage for the other two by describing the technique and representative data. Given two visual targets to fixate, infants 2½ months or older spend more time fixating a novel or nonhabituated stimulus than a previously exposed target. Recognition memory of an exposed target increased with conceptional age and amount of original exposure and decreased with difficulty of discriminating between targets. Five- to six-month-old infants were capable of recognizing some targets to which they had been exposed days or even weeks in advance.

Individual differences among infants in recognition memory appear potentially important for the prediction of later intellectual functioning. When Down's syndrome and normal infants were compared on recognition memory tasks that were relatively easy, there was no significant difference between groups; when the task was more difficult (abstract patterns varying along a number of dimensions), however, the normal infants were clearly superior. Such a finding nicely illustrates the definitional view of intelligence that describes it as that aspect of behavior which interacts with difficulty or complexity. That is, the more difficult the task, the more important it is to be intelligent. This is a favorite definition of intelligence of mine, and I know that it is shared by Norm Ellis. Standard intelligence tests exploit this notion throughout, measuring difficulty in terms of performance at a certain age level and/or by varying the number of stimuli or responses in a test item. Both Brackbill and Kopp hint broadly at the same basic point about interaction with difficulty, making this notion a common thread in the volume.

Other aspects of Fagan's contribution also command attention. Some of the effects found with infants are quite reminiscent of retroactive and proactive interference effects found in adult human learning studies. For example, in infants a somewhat different stimulus that intervened between original test and delayed recognition test had an interfering effect on recognition of the target stimulus only if the intervening stimulus immediately followed the original test. This in turn reminds one of Revusky's interference hypothesis about why long CS–US intervals work in taste aversion conditioning of rats (the Garcia effect): the events in, say, the 1-hr CS–US interval are so unrelated to those events that bring about the conditioning of aversion that there is no interference.

Finally, in light of Underwood's law of forgetting, which says that we all forget at the same rate, most retardates included, as long as the responses were equally well learned to begin with, it would seem important to know whether the Down's syndrome infants and the normals were nicely matched on immediate recognition memory for hard designs (which could be done empirically by manipulating original study time before the delayed recognition tests were given). That is, was the deficit in the Down's syndrome infants a learning deficit or a memory deficit?

Leslie Cohen's paper, which we briefly referred to earlier, extends the work reported by Fagan by describing a technique in which the infant rather than the experimenter determines the duration of the exposure trial (fixation) and by introducing the plotting of "backward habituation curves." Just as Zeaman and House found very rapid learning using backward discrimination learning curves, Cohen found infants habituating in one trial with backward plotting—a method that describes how each individual performs. Cohen also reported that size was an important variable for getting attention and that complexity was important for holding it.

Continuing in the same vein, Friedman presented evidence indicating that habituation to visual stimuli can occur in some (possibly very select) infants in the first day of life and seems to be related to such factors as sex, age, state, and maternal parity. As already implied by others, individual differences in speed of habituation may be useful for early assessment of later development. Such measures seem to tap a type of inhibition deficit (slow habituating) that may characterize later retardation—a theme that also ran through papers by Brackbill, Hutchings, and Cohen.

20

COMMENTS:
THE STRATEGIES OF STUDYING
EARLY DEVELOPMENT
IN RELATION TO INTELLIGENCE

David Zeaman
University of Connecticut

An overview of so large and wondrously diverse a set of papers requires the abstraction of some general themes or assumptions underlying the set. One such assumption would appear to be that infancy is a particularly good or reasonable place to look for causes and correlates of mental retardation. This assumption is by no means obviously true. It would be more reasonable if the primary causal factor in retardation were exogenous rather than endogenous. The impression left by this large array of papers might be that retardation was chiefly caused by bad environments (both internal and external) in the year or two following conception, rather than by genetic factors operating at conception. Epidemiologists vary somewhat in their estimates, but the usual ball-park figures place the incidence of familial retardation at three times the frequency of nonfamilial or exogenous retardation.

No disparagement is intended for the study of exogenous factors in retardation. The papers in these symposia dealing with the developmental influences of teratogens, anoxia, radiation, CNS insults, obstetrical drugs, and nutritional deprivation are only to be commended. My point is simply that it is surprising that none of the researchers in this large group (which I suspect is not unrepresentative of the larger population of researchers in retardation) is studying genetic factors.

The preponderance of papers dealing with exogenous causes not unexpectedly makes use of animal subjects. Almost all of these study important factors that may cause aberrant development, but the behavioral meaures taken are seldom very cognitive. Activity level, reflexes, and exploratory behavior are the usual indices. Hutchings' paper was the exception. He used discriminative learning to measure deficit produced by vitamin A excess. It is easy enough to understand why the animal modelers would choose not to measure cognitive or complex processes in infant animals. It is hard enough to do this in adult animals, and many times harder in very young ones—a good argument for not using them.

A wonderment was generated in this overviewer: Why was no one doing animal research on genetic control of animal intelligence? Introductory texts still refer to Tryon's classic studies in this area, but the behavioral instrument he used, the maze, provides measures of learning that are confounded by affective, motivational, attentional, and retentional variables.

There have been advances in the study of animal discrimination learning and such theories as Sutherland and Mackintosh provide quantitative models of the discriminative learning process. These models, in conjunction with the currently rich literature on well-controlled experimental analyses of discriminative learning, provide theoretical parameters of such processes as learning and attention, which could be fine candidates for relation to genetic variables in animal breeding experiments. In short, it surprises me that no one appears to be following in Tryon's footsteps; no one uses the best available indices of animal intelligence to breed retarded and bright animals and discover what aspects of discriminative processes are heritable.

My comments thus far have dealt with those papers studying possible causes of retardation. A large subgroup of papers remains which attempts to find infant correlates of intelligence. These papers, for the most part, use human infants. Risk factors such as low birth weight and prematurity are related to behavioral indices of intelligence in infants. The new tool here is habituation, and the assumption is made that this process holds out the greatest hope for development of an infant intelligence test.

It is well known that existing scales of infant intelligence correlate negligibly with adult intelligence. The reason usually assigned is that these scales are comprised of items that measure physical rather than cognitive development of the infant. Habituation, however, has not been used in infant intelligence tests (primarily because much of the research in this area is new), and a major contribution of this volume to the area of mental retardation is the development of the idea that habituation may provide a basis for assessment of infant intelligence.

If overviewers are permitted some prognostications, I would like to go on record as predicting that attempts to use habituation to measure infant intelligence will fail. At best only the grossest degrees of mental deficit will be detectable using this measure. My judgment is based on these assumptions:

1. Intelligence has not matured sufficiently in infancy to permit reliable measurements of individual differences.

2. Habituation is not sufficiently cognitive or complex to be related to intelligence.

3. Measures of habituation are confounded by affective and motivational variables.

I would like to defend each of these three assumptions in turn.

1.   Intelligence, in the sense of Mental Age, grows with chronological age up to the age of 15 years in most individuals, including retardates. As a consequence of this maturational trend, the dispersion of individual differences in MA increases with CA. Theoretically, at the moment of conception the dispersion of individual differences would be zero. For adults the standard deviation of the population flattens out at approximately 16 IQ points. This growth in dispersion is empirically well established between the child and adult levels, but we have as yet no good data in infancy. If habituation measures were to provide these, they would have to be very good measures indeed to assess reliably such small individual differences. The usual Binet item carries a weight of 2 months of Mental Age. This would be a very gross unit at the infant level where individual differences must be small. To compensate for this we would need a large number of different habituation items arranged in a hierarchy of difficulty. This is precisely what Fagan has set out to do in his contribution. He has certainly gone further than anyone else in attempting to establish the feasibility of such a difficulty scale of habituation items. The question remains, however, whether enough items can be found to provide a sum reliable enough to measure the small individual differences in intelligence of infants. He has a tiny target and a crude instrument. Of course, the issue can only be resolved empirically. An advance has been made in that methods now exist for a test.

2. A number of writers, such as Jensen and Sheldon White, have drawn up scales of task complexity in attempts to relate these to developmental level. At the high end of these scales are such clearly cognitive functions as logical reasoning and grammatical language. At the intermediate levels of complexity are processes such as concept formation and discriminative learning. At the lowest levels are such functions as simple sensory–motor learning and classical conditioning.

At the lowest level of these scales, what is the relation to individual differences in human intelligence? The answer is that simple classical conditioning does not relate very well to intelligence. Literature surveys have shown the correlations of conditioning and intelligence to be low or nonexistent. In my laboratory we have found no relation of IQ to speed of simple classical conditioning of eye movements in a retarded population, although classical *discriminative* conditioning correlated with retarded IQ at the level of +.50.

In general, correlations of task performance and intelligence increase with task complexity. How complex a process is habituation? Where does it belong on the scale? Certainly down near the very bottom. Perhaps sensory adaptation or response fatigue may be less complex but there is no reason to rank it higher than simple classical conditioning, a poor correlate of intelligence. In summary, there are indirect inferential grounds for believing that habituation, although providing an index of behavioral plasticity, is not sufficiently complex or cognitive a process to relate well to intelligence.

3. Theoretical analyses of the habituation process are burgeoning and Cohen, in his paper, sets forth with admirable clarity the current state of this art. I will make use of his analyses to buttress my point that habituation measure are confounded by affective and motivational factors.

Theory, in this area, assumes that the habituation-dishabituation paradigm involves three subprocesses: (A) as the result of repeated stimulation there is formed some organismic record of this stimulation (a trace, image, schema, or engram); (B) when a different stimulus is then presented, the subject compares the new stimulus with the old one (or the trace of the old stimulus if only the new one is presented); and (C) a decision is then made to respond more strongly to the new stimulus than to the old one. In Cohen's experiments the infant prefers to *look* at the new (dishabituated) stimulus more than the old (habituated) stimulus. In other experiments, infants show their preferences for new stimuli by other responses, such as sucking, which instrumentally produce the dishabituated stimulus, or they show their attentional preferences by heart rate or EEG responses. In any case, the last theoretical subprocess in habituation is affective or motivational in nature. The subject demonstrates a preference for new over old stimuli. Although the first two subprocesses, the laying down of traces and the comparison of stimuli, may with a stretch be called cognitive, the last stage requires the infant to be curious, and although curiosity, too, may have some cognitive component it is also motivational in nature. This leads to difficulties in interpretation.

Curiosity is a fragile drive in that other drives can interfere with it; so too can training procedures. For example, the rat is highly curious. If forced to go to one side of a T-maze ten times in succession and then allowed to choose either side of an open T, it will choose the new side with virtual certainty. However, a shocked rat, or one that has been dropped or had his tail squeezed, will not alternate his choice. Worried rats prefer old stimuli over new. How about babies?

Normal and retarded children also have high curiosity. This has been shown in discriminative learning experiments with the following operations. The positive stimulus (alone) is presented to the child who responds to it and is rewarded. Next the child is presented with two stimuli, the old rewarded stimulus and a new stimulus. If the child is below 5 years of age, the choice of the new stimulus will be more likely. Children over 5 tend to prefer the old rewarded stimulus. The effect has been replicated in several published papers. The competition here is between the Law of Effect, which dictates choice of the old (rewarded) stimulus, and curiosity, which calls for choice of the shiny new stimulus.

Recent experiments in our laboratory have shown that retardates under 5 years of Mental Age can be trained to give up their curiosity. If they are never rewarded for choice of novel stimuli they gradually suppress their native preferences for novelty in return for M&Ms.

The implications of these findings for interpreting habituation data are direct. It is possible that individual differences in habituation may be related not to differences in trace formation or comparison but to individual differences in curiosity. These, in turn, may be the result of differences in either training history or in strengths of competing drives. Although it may be unlikely that very young infants would have differences in training histories, it may not be at all unlikely that a motivational enemy of curiosity—some infant equivalent of anxiety, irritability, or general gooseyness—may be the source of individual differences in habituation. This surmise is strongly suggested by the wide variability reported for infant preferences for novelty in habituation–dishabituation experiments. Some investigators, for example, Hunt, Greenberg, and others, have reported preferences for familiar stimuli in neonates, others such as Friedman report the opposite, and a number of other baby watchers get no preference for either old or new stimuli in infants below 2 months of age. Add to this the fact that there is some transition again from novelty to familiarity preference at age 5 years. It might be concluded that novelty preferences follow a funny function with age, not the smooth progression one expects for the maturation of intelligence. The unexplained sex differences in habituation are another case in point. If habituation reflects intelligence then the sexes start out life differently and end the same. Such fussiness in outcomes is easier to explain within the domains of affect, motivation, or preference than that of cognitive capacity.

Finally, the issue is again empirical. When the infant habituators manage to mount some controls for individual differences in novelty preference they will have a better case for inferring cognition from habituation. Meanwhile, I'm skeptical.

21

ABERRANT DEVELOPMENT IN INFANCY: OVERVIEW AND SYNTHESIS

Josephine V. Brown
Georgia State University
  and
*Department of Pediatrics,
Emory University School of Medicine*

The papers presented in this volume have been collected under the title "aberrant development in infancy." My first impression upon reading this title was that the volume would deal with factors that lead to the abnormal development of infants after birth, since the period of infancy is usually taken to last from birth until the beginnings of language development. However, after reading the papers, I became confused about the general topic under discussion. It might, therefore, be of value to attempt to define the topics we have actually dealt with here.

The contributors have addressed themselves to at least two components of the title: (1) the identification and prediction of aberrant infants at birth, and (2) the study of the development of infants who are either normal or aberrant at birth. I will comment on each of these topics.

Throughout the volume, the term "aberrant infant" is used synonymously with "at risk" for survival at birth, for impairment at birth, for prematurity, and for mental retardation. The use of such definitions poses the problem of identifying those newborns who are "at risk." The difficulty of such a task has been well illustrated by Parmelee *et al.* Gross abnormalities can be seen by the naked eye but slight deficits can often be detected only by careful behavioral testing. The most promising approaches to the latter seem to be those based on the measurement of the infant's recognition memory (Fagan), orienting reflex (Brackbill), fine motor behavior (Kopp), and cumulative risk (Parmelee *et al.*).

However, the problem is not just one of identifying aberrancy at birth but, more importantly, of identifying factors that lead to aberrancy at birth. Based on a study of 792 births to pigtail monkeys, Sackett and co-workers were able to identify maternal and paternal factors which were highly predictive of stillbirth, neonatal death, prematurity, mental retardation, and impairment. On the basis of this study it was concluded that "past performance in producing high risk conceptions is related to future risk," a conclusion that also holds true for humans (Parmelee).

The implication from these findings seems relatively simple: it is possible to prevent at least some aberrancy at birth by identifying and informing parents who are at risk of producing aberrant offspring. Issues concerned with the ethics of the prevention of aberrant births were not, but should have been, addressed. I often have the feeling that we, as psychologists who study the aberrant infant, have something at stake in keeping him "alive," a phenomenon not new in the history of childhood. For instance, the child made his first appearance on a tomb in the sixteenth century. "Curiously enough, his first appearance was not on his own tomb or that of his parents *but on that of his teacher*" (Ariès, 1962, p. 38; italics mine).

The second component of the title of this volume has to do, as you will recall, with development. However, one cannot talk about development independent of the organism. In fact, when I combine the condition of the organism at birth with his later development I arrive at four possible permutations: (1) the aberrant development of the normal infant; (2) the aberrant development of the aberrant infant; (3) the normal development of the normal infant; and (4) the normal development of the aberrant infant. It might be a useful exercise to see if and how the chapters of this book can be related to each of these topics.

Let us first look at the aberrant development of the normal infant. Thoman pointed out that normal infants at birth exhibit reliable individual differences in their behavioral states which are assumed to reflect basic neurophysiological differences and that organization of state behaviors develops in most cases in an orderly fashion. She has shown, furthermore, how the infant's state organization contributes to the pattern of mother–infant interaction. For instance, infants who are highly unpredictable in their behavior are difficult to respond to appropriately. Initial "normal" dyssynchrony between mother and infant then becomes easily magnified during development and can result in abnormal mother–infant interactions. A similar point was made by Meier in his presentation.

What about the aberrant development of the aberrant infant? Parmelee *et al.* pointed out that the outcome of aberrancy at birth is "strongly influenced by the socioeconomic circumstances of the children's environment and [that] that this influence is often stronger than that of earlier biological events." Not only do environments differentially affect the outcome of infants born "at risk," but the same environment affects males and females differently (Sackett *et al.*). For instance, the social behavior of male monkeys raised in adverse environments is considerably more damaged than that of female monkeys raised in similar environments. It is interesting to speculate whether such findings will also hold true for human infants. If so, it becomes critical to examine separately the development of abnormal male and female newborns as a function of the environment in which they grow up.

The third topic deals with the normal development of the normal infant. Most of the papers relevant to this topic dealt with the infant's capacity to process *visual* information (Cohen, Fagan, and Friedman). This concentration on the visual system results from the fact that the infant's vision is one of the few relatively well-organized behavioral systems at birth and one that reflects the maturity and integrity (Fagan) of the underlying central nervous system. It is questionable, however, to what extent findings based on these studies can be generalized to all normal infants. The most important problem I see is one related to sampling. Most researchers of infant vision have adopted the practice of excluding from their studies those infants who do not keep their eyes open for a specified length of time. Studies in my laboratory have shown that infants that keep their eyes open longer are also better able to fixate and follow. This phenomenon is so striking that we even coined the phrase: "the baby who looks more sees more " (Brown, Bakeman, Fredrickson, Hepler, Morgan, & Snyder, 1974). It seems, therefore, highly likely that infants are not excluded randomly from vision studies and that the visual capabilities of infants as reported in the literature hold only for infants whose visual system is relatively advanced.

A second problem with infant studies is that infancy researchers frequently draw conclusions from studies that use research paradigms whose rationale is often little understood. Butterfield and Cairns made a good case for questioning even *replicable* findings of infants' linguistic capabilities by showing, for instance, that similar results can be generated randomly by a computer. It is essential, therefore, to examine closely the paradigms that underlie research results when we assert the existence of certain phenomena.

A third problem is the extent to which we can generalize from the normal to the aberrant infant. I believe that we are able to do so only if we understand more about the underlying processes used by the infant to deal with environmental input. The two chapters most relevant to this point were the ones presented by Leslie Cohen and Evelyn Thoman. Cohen showed us that infant attention is "not a simple response [but] is a complex of behaviors involving at least two identifiable processes: an attention-getting process . . . and an attention-holding process." Thoman pointed out how the organization of the infant's biological states is related to his capacity to deal with stimulus input. A close examination of underlying processes seems to me the most promising avenue to a better understanding of the crucial differences between normal and aberrant infants.

It is essential that we understand more about the nature of the aberrant child in order to talk about the fourth topic, the normal development of the aberrant child. Probably the best criterion of the normal development of such children is one of adequate socialization. An adequate social environment can do much to ameliorate risk factors at birth. In Parmelee's study, for instance, 22 infants were classified high risk at birth, whereas only 11 of those infants were classified as high risk at 9 months of age. Parmelee stresses the importance of the early environment of the infant in compensating for some of the deficits at birth. By early environment, he means the parents and presumably the early socialization process. According to Parmelee "some parents appear intuitively able to provide an optimal environment for an infant with mild neurological deviances allowing him to compensate.'' This finding with human infants is strengthened by results from research reported by Berkson on the social responses to blind monkeys. He found that totally blind or partially blind monkeys developed a relatively normal interaction with the environment when the monkey troop was willing to compensate for the animals' deficit.

The key to the normal development of the aberrant infant then seems to be the quality of the very early mother–infant interaction. As Meier points out, styles of mother–infant interaction are established right after birth. However, to date, very little is known about these earliest interactions. We know the effects of some gross variables but we need to know more about infant and adult behaviors that need to be encouraged or discouraged.

The aberrant infant needs all the help it can get in order to compensate for his deficits, so that normal social responses will develop. At the present stage of our knowledge the most efficient way to provide this help to the infant is through the establishment of harmonious mother–infant interactions. The problem then becomes one of getting mothers tied in with their individual infants right after birth. Several studies have shown that mothers are particularly sensitive to their infants following birth (Barnett, Leiderman, Grobstein, & Klaus, 1970; Faranoff, Kennell, & Klaus, 1972; Klaus *et al.*, 1970, 1972; Leifer *et al.*, 1972; Seashore *et al.*, 1973), and that the frequency with which mothers visit their premature infants is a very good predictor of the quality of their later interaction (Faranoff *et al.*, 1972). Unfortunately, modern society does much to keep mothers and infants apart during this critical time. Mothers are given drugs during delivery, and as a result they and their infants are depressed following birth (Brackbill) and a physical separation is imposed by keeping infants in nurseries. These practices are especially pronounced when the child is born "at risk." The negative effects of these practices are compounded by the "mourning" reaction that the mother of the high risk infant often experiences. In fear and in anticipation of the death of her child she refuses to have contact with it (Kennell & Klaus, 1971). This is not a new phenomenon:

> As late as the seventeenth century, in *Le Caquet de L'accouchée,* we have a neighbour, standing at the bedside of a woman who has just given birth, the mother of five 'little brats,' and calming her fears with these words: 'Before they are old enough to bother you, you will have lost half of them, or perhaps all of them.' . . . People could not allow themselves to become too attached to something that was regarded as a probable loss [Ariès, 1962, p. 38].

These factors taken together can lead to an extreme breakdown in the mother–infant interaction. At Grady Memorial Hospital, for instance, 34%of the abused and battered children during 1973 had been born prematurely, and 85% of these were severely abused *prior to 15 months of age*.

Given that the aberrant infant's "survival" often depends on the quality of the care given to it by its mother, the questions that should be asked are: How can we get the mother tied to her infant and how can we get her to respond appropriately to the individual characteristics of that infant? In my work with infants in the high-risk nursery, I have concentrated on working out infant stimulation programs that are designed specifically to bring out the "human" qualities in the infant, that is, I try to make the infant more socially responsive. Once the infant becomes more active—responds to visual and auditory stimuli by fixating and quieting, responds to being held by relaxing, and smiles occasionally—I bring the mother in to work through prescribed exercises with the infant which allow her to observe these social responses on the part of the infant. The effects of such an approach on both the infant and the mother are often quick and dramatic. In one case, a mother who initially had to be brought in by the police to see her child, visited her child regularly after one week and was allowed to take the child home after three weeks. The success that I am having with these *individual* cases, however, brings with it its own problems. I know that in the long run, I and others will learn more through the systematic study of parameters that are most important in this process of early socialization, yet I find myself caught in an ethical bind and under pressure from the neonatologists to provide services that are relevant to patient care. It is then that I and others need to rely on those researchers who are willing to do the painstaking work involved in developing animal models (Berkson, Campbell, Denenberg, Sackett *et al.*) which might provide much needed information to the researcher interested in the development of the aberrant child.

REFERENCES

Aries, P. *Centuries of childhood: A social history of family life*. New York: Vintage Books, 1962.

Barrett, C. R., Leiderman, P. H., Grobstein, R., & Klaus, M. Neonatal separation: The maternal side of interactional deprivation. *Pediatrics*, 1970, **45**, 197–205.

Brown, J. V., Bakeman, R., Fredrickson, T., Hepler, R., Morgan, S. T., & Snyder, P. An ethological study of mother-infant interaction: An inner city sample. Symposium presented at the Southeastern meeting of the Society for Research in Child Development, Chapel Hill, N.C., February, 1974.

Faranoff, A. A., Kennell, J. H., & Klaus, M. H. Follow-up of low birth weight infants—the predictive value of maternal visiting patterns. *Pediatrics*, 1972, **49**, 287–290.

Kennell, J. H., & Klaus, M. H. Care of the mother of the high-risk infant. *Clinical Obstetrics and Gynecology*, 1971, **14**, 926–954.

Klaus, M. H., Jerauld, R., Kreger, N., McAlpine, W., Steffa, M., & Kennell, J. H. Maternal attachment, importance of the first post-partum days. *New England Journal of Medicine*, 1972, **286**, 460–463.

Klaus, M. H., Kennell, J. H., Plumb, N., & Zuehlke, S. Human maternal behavior at the first contact with her young. *Pediatrics*, 1970, **46**, 187–192.

Leifer, A. D., Leiderman, P. H., Barnett, C. R., & Williams, J. A. Effects of mother-infant separation on maternal attachment behavior. *Child Development*, 1972, **43**, 1203–1218.

Seashore, M. J., Leifer, A. D., Barnett, C. R., & Leiderman, P. H. The effects of the denial of early mother-infant interaction on maternal self-confidence. *Journal of Personality and Social Psychology*, 1973, **26**, 369–378.

22
CONFERENCE COMMENTS

Duane M. Rumbaugh
Georgia State University

In general, the progress of science is a reflection of long-term, systematic research programs. The steady accumulation of findings from a variety of programs tends to influence the conceptual thinking of scientists. The concepts that guide the thinking of the scientists are, in the final analysis, probably more valuable than are specific data. From time to time, there is a second way in which science progresses; that is when through following the more or less normal course of research a fortuitous, serendipitous breakthrough in ideas and/or methods occurs.

Through the course of the papers included in this volume, one is impressed primarily with the first above-described way in which science progresses —through the gradual accumulation of information and the modifications in concepts and thinking thereby obtained. There has been no real breakthrough suggested by any of the contributors to this volume; however, it is, of course, possible that breakthroughs in either thought or method might be just around the corner. That possibility notwithstanding, I believe that it is in order to advise researchers in this area that they should be, perhaps, more bold in the way in which they think about mental retardation, its parameters, and phenomena thereto related.

DEFINITION OF "ABERRANT" AND RESEARCH GOALS

Specific to the topic of this volume is the question, "What is the definition of the term *aberrant*?" There seems to be a lack of agreement as to what an appropriate, working definition of this term should be. On the one hand, it is clear that it can or could be defined in a strictly statistical sense. Any characteristic that falls a given number of standard deviations below the mean could be defined as aberrant; measurements that are a given distance above the mean might then be viewed as outstanding, complimentary, etc., anything but a handicap. The term aberrant can also be cast in an evolutionary/adaptive/survival context. In point of fact, Hicks

275

(Hicks & D'Amato) has done this in his paper, asserting that when the influence of an attribute runs contrary to survival, it is of an aberrant quality.

There is still at least one other way in which aberrant might be defined, and that is in terms of the social percept. Regardless of the distribution of the statistics and, perhaps, regardless of the evolutionary/adaptive/survival implications, it is conceivable that any attribute of an individual that is esthetically unpleasing or otherwise responded to prejudicially can be termed aberrant. In the latter instance it is clear that social learning and social norms can be the sole predicates as to whether or not something is termed aberrant.

Depending on the definition of the term aberrant, answers to the following questions will differ: What are the goals of research relating to aberrant attributes? Is it to minimize the frequency of aberrant attributes? Is it to enhance the survival prospects for those who have aberrant attributes? Is it to help integrate those with aberrant attributes into society, regardless of those attributes? Is it to help ensure that the individual is given every opportunity to achieve all of the competency of which he is capable, regardless of his aberrant attributes? Is it to define the conditions that ensure "normality" and minimize the impact of adjudged aberrant attributes? Is it all of these? Some of these? Or, are the goals far afield from these considerations?

NEED FOR THEORY

The definition of goals influences the development of theory, and in response to the papers published herein, I believe that research in this area can benefit from the development of a broad theoretical framework within which major questions can be orderly placed and unified. I propose that future contributors to this series give serious thought to the possibility of meeting beforehand and reviewing a proposed theoretical framework within which individuals might be encouraged to think and interpret their findings. Then, after the presentation of the contributions it is recommended that further time be spent reviewing the adequacy of the theoretical framework in light of the contributions presented.

I believe that these activities would help spawn over the course of years the development of a solid theoretical framework which will help unify research on mental retardation and on aberrant attributes and behaviors and serve to enhance the impact of the research on society. It is society, after all, that controls the purse strings, perhaps not specifically in a given year, but surely over the course of years. Society spends its money where it is convinced that it obtains the greatest return for its investment. To the degree that society becomes convinced that the support of research in mental retardation is of both immediate and long-term value, the dollars will be available.

Our society does not have to be convinced of the humaneness of caring for those who are mentally retarded or otherwise compromised by aberrant attributes. We should be able to build upon this expeditiously, capitalize upon it, if you will, through the careful definition of a theoretical framework within which a variety of research efforts can prosper.

None of this discussion is intended to restrict freedom of research and freedom of the investigator to select research questions of high interest to him. It is rather directed to the end of facilitating the orderly, scientific growth of thinking in the area of mental retardation and aberrant behavior. To the end that this is achieved, research efforts will be funded more adequately.

TEAM RESEARCH

Most researchers view themselves as highly individualistic, and indeed they are. Individualism has its merits, but it also has its limitations. We live in a day where the sophistication of research projects can be complemented through the pooling of expertise of scientists from various areas. To organize their expertise into a team effort can be highly problematic, but when it succeeds, it pays off ever so richly. Researchers in the field of mental retardation should attempt to reach out to colleagues in other disciplines and to incorporate them into cooperative research ventures. Not infrequently the prospects of funding are profoundly enhanced when this is done and done well.

DEVELOPMENTAL–COMPARATIVE FRAMEWORK

Another suggestion I want to offer is that there needs to be more attention paid to a comparative framework by those who address themselves to the phenomena of mental retardation. Within such a framework two questions present themselves; one has to do with the usefulness of animal models, and the second relates to the nature of the child. I believe that it remains an open question as to whether or not "animal models" can be used validly to attack problems in research on mental retardation. We must be very careful on this point. It might well be that it is far more problematic to find appropriate animal models for research in this area than in many areas of biomedical research, although even in biomedical research there are problems in the selection of appropriate animal models. That which is true for the animal model might or might not be true for the human. That risk notwithstanding, it is worthwhile to sharpen our thinking and research methods on the closest possible analogues of human behavior and development that can be found in animal forms.

On the basis of almost 15 years of research, I am convinced that the dimension of intelligence is one common to both human and nonhuman primates. Evolution of the brain has been one of the hallmarks of primate evolution and extant primates differ systematically in their brain development.

Comparative learning studies (Rumbaugh & Gill, 1973) have revealed a rather systematic relationship between brain development and the ability to transfer learning. Furthermore, results of recent research at Georgia State University

(Smith, 1973) have shown that there is a high and positive correlation between the scores that reflect the ability to transfer learning and the mental age values obtained by 4½-year-old children on a standardized test. Consequently, it seems reasonable to conclude that the measurements obtained at the nonhuman primate level do reflect to a significant degree the operations of cognitive processes which at the human level are said to determine expressions of intelligence. This being the case, it seems reasonable that emphasis should be given to the definition and use of animal models, particularly ones that are primates, to the end of better defining the maturational parameters of those processes germane to intelligence as expressed by the human.

The second question within the developmental–comparative framework is related to one's conception of the child. On the basis of the papers of this volume I was not clear as to how the participants viewed the child. Is it the case that we view the child as simply an immature adult? Or is it the case that we view the child as *in part* an immature adult but that due to his immaturity he is in many ways qualitatively different from an adult? We need to know more about the maturational staging of various psychological abilities and processes. This can only be accomplished through a more routine incorporation of age as a parameter in investigations of aberrant behavior and other phenomena related to mental retardation.

From the papers in this volume it is very clear that most investigators view the child as being highly vulnerable and sensitive. Those factors that have minimal, or functionally no, effect upon adult humans can have profound long-lived effects on the child. Consequently, it seems reasonable to conclude that probably all children are aberrant to some degree, or are at the very least in some significant way compromised in the development of their potential because of certain factors or conditions to which they have been exposed in the first few weeks, months, and years of life.

Work in this area is admittedly problematic, especially when we recognize that the effects of an experience/treatment in infancy might well be deferred in time, with the effects thereof being difficult to trace back to the original cause. Research on this point is anything but simple. Such research might be facilitated, however, by an attempt to categorize the kinds of variables that have deferred effects in time as opposed to those that have immediate effects, if any.

NEED FOR THE NURTURANCE OF RESEARCH METHODS

It helps all of us, from time to time, to be reminded of the fact that the meaningfulness of our data is directly related to the adequacy of the methods we designed and employed in our studies. And as our scientific understanding is very contingent upon the validity of the data, it behooves us to consider ever so carefully the adequacy of the methods we employ in the collection of these data. The practical implications of conclusions drawn from mental retardation research are frequently so profound, so great, that we would be well-advised to insist routinely upon the replication of findings and the demonstration of these findings through the use of a variety of methods prior to committing ourselves to particular conclusions. Only adequately conducted studies should be allowed to influence our thinking. It is *not* the case that a large body of data from a number of inadequate studies can provide a reasonable basis for drawing firm conclusions. Inadequate studies are what they are—inadequate—and the data and thoughts obtained from them should be carefully filtered out. Replications of important findings should be pursued vigorously.

It is clear that research on mental retardation and aberrant attributes is highly complex. However, as the welfare of man and society ultimately rests upon the potential of human children, it behooves researchers and theoreticians in the field of mental retardation to consider ways in which they can make their needs and voices heard, to the end of ensuring more adequate funding for the research necessary to understand the complexity of the myriad problems defined in this volume.

REFERENCES

Rumbaugh, D. M., & Gill, T. V. The learning skills of great apes. *Journal of Human Evolution*, 1973, **2**, 171–179.

Smith, S. B. Transfer index testing in children. Unpublished master's thesis, Georgia State University, 1973.

AUTHOR INDEX*

A

Adkinson, C. D., 223
Akert, K., 9
Akiyama, Y., 124
Altman, J., 111, 169, 175
Altmann, S. A., 90
Anders, T., 124, 126, 137
Andrioli, J., 169
Apgar, V., 114
Aries, P., 270, 272
Arnold, W. R., 229
Aserinsky, E., 123
Ashton, R., 123, 124
Austin, G. M., 3
Austin, L. L., 30, 44

B

Baer, P. M., 100
Bakeman, R., 271
Bakhtina, L. K., 182
Baisden, R., 4
Baltes, P. B., 154
Baron, D. H., 38
Barrett-Goldfarb, M. S., 249
Barnett, C. R., 98, 272
Bartels, B., 218, 232
Bartoshuk, A. K., 221, 222
Baruk, H., 150, 154
Bayer, S. A., 111
Beach, F. A., 29, 175, 181
Beckwith, L., 119
Bell, N. J., 92
Bell, R. Q., 96, 225
Bell, R. W., 92
Berendes, H., 95, 114, 116
Berg, W. K., 223, 229
Bergner, L., 60

Berkson, G., 49, 50
Berlyne, D. E., 217
Bernal, J. F., 98
Bernardis, L. L., 9
Bielauskas, L., 9
Bielert, C. F., 94
Bierman, J. M., 114, 116
Björklund, A., 4
Bland, B. H., 9
Blomquist, A. J., 9, 11
Bloom, L., 241, 247
Bobbitt, R. A., 93, 94
Boismier, J. D., 96, 223
Bond, E. K., 217, 219
Bonsall, R. W., 94
Bottenberg, R. A., 226
Bower, T. G. R., 247
Bowerman, M., 241, 247
Bowes, W. A., 60
Bowes, W. A., Jr., 95
Bowlby, J., 96
Brackbill, Y., 60, 95, 97, 232
Brainard, P. P., 149
Braine, M. D. S., 60, 114, 157
Brazelton, T. B., 60, 95, 140, 217, 219, 234, 236
Bridger, W. H., 110
Bridger, W. K., 225
Brink, J. J., 12
Bromwich, R., 117
Bronson, G., 228
Brown, R., 241, 271
Bruner, J. S., 149, 150, 152, 154, 235
Bruner, R. L., 111, 162
Bruno, L. A., 234
Bruno, L. B., 217, 235
Brutkowski, S., 15
Buck, C., 113

*Text citations only are given in this index. Reference pages are not given.

281